THE DESIGN AND USE OF SIMULATION GAMES IN EDUCATION

MODELING AND SIMULATIONS FOR LEARNING AND INSTRUCTION
Volume 2

Series Editors
J. Michael Spector
Learning Systems Institute, Florida State University, Tallahassee, USA
Norbert M. Seel
University of Freiburg, Germany and Florida State University, Tallahassee, USA
Konrad Morgan
Human Computer Interaction, University of Bergen, Norway

Scope

Models and simulations have become part and parcel of advanced learning environments, performance technologies and knowledge management systems. This book series will address the nature and types of models and simulations from multiple perspectives and in a variety of contexts in order to provide a foundation for their effective integration into teaching and learning. While much has been written about models and simulations, little has been written about the underlying instructional design principles and the varieties of ways for effective use of models and simulations in learning and instruction. This book series will provide a practical guide for designing and using models and simulations to support learning and to enhance performance and it will provide a comprehensive framework for conducting research on educational uses of models and simulations.

A unifying thread of this series is a view of models and simulations as learning and instructional objects. Conceptual and mathematical models and their uses will be described. Examples of different types of simulations, including discrete event and continuous process simulations, will be elaborated in various contexts. A rationale and methodology for the design of interactive models and simulations will be presented, along with a variety of uses ranging from assessment tools to simulation games. The key role of models and simulations in knowledge construction and representation will be described, and a rationale and strategy for their integration into knowledge management and performance support systems will provided.

Audience

The primary audience for this book series will be educators, developers and researchers involved in the design, implementation, use and evaluation of models and simulations to support learning and instruction. Instructors and students in educational technology, instructional research and technology-based learning will benefit from this series.

The Design and Use of Simulation Computer Games in Education

Edited by

Brett E. Shelton and David A. Wiley
Utah State University, Logan, USA

A C.I.P. record for this book is available from the Library of Congress.

ISBN 978-90-8790-155-4 (paperback)
ISBN 978-90-8790-156-1 (hardback)

Published by: Sense Publishers,
P.O. Box 21858, 3001 AW Rotterdam, The Netherlands
http://www.sensepublishers.com

Printed on acid-free paper

For Zane, David Enoch, Megumi, Noelle, and Johnny, our new little generation of gamers.

CONTENTS

BRETT E. SHELTON AND DAVID A. WILEY

INTRODUCTION

Pulling together a book is a time-consuming and difficult task, akin to herding cats that believe they have academic freedom. And in the process of following up on authors, checking references, and reformatting chapters to meet arbitrary formatting guidelines, each book editor eventually asks him or herself: why am I doing this?

For us, there are a number of answers to this question.

Our primary goal for the book is to help us figure out where we're heading in terms of the philosophies and practices of the design and use of computer games for supporting learning. We hope the book will be a useful resource for people working in a variety of disciplines, including game design, instructional design, simulation and training, and educational technology. It is possible that it only makes its mark as a measuring stick of how far we've come in the field of educational games, or a testament to the naivety of our current understanding.

As a sort of truth in advertising statement, we should say that neither of us are what might be called "educational game advocates." We believe our understanding of teaching and learning is sophisticated enough to admit that there is no "best" teaching method or technology that spans all domains, age groups, and cultures. Obviously, we feel that a number of strategic opportunities exist for educational games to have a positive impact on learning (or else we wouldn't have edited this book!), and some of these situations are discussed in these chapters. Still, the question remains as to what degree our collective efforts should be aimed at creating and researching "best approaches" to educational game design. What design principles really transcend context? Perhaps we should adopt a view of pure contextuality, simply creating designs and games that work for specific situations within specific domains, and not concerning ourselves with the development of context-free recipes that anyone can use in any situation. A desire to explore this question is another reason for the book.

A third reason for working on the book was to explore an interesting tension we felt at the Games, Learning, and Society conference in 2006. The tension is between "educational games people" who are working to blend game design with traditional instructional design, and "educational games people" who are working to blend game design with more of a learning sciences approach. We are particularly pleased with the manner in which this tension plays out within the book.

B. E. Shelton, D. A. Wiley (eds.), Educational Design & Use of Computer Simulation Games, 1–2.
© 2007 Sense Publishers. All rights reserved.

And finally, to be honest, this book was a chance for us to make time to work together and learn from each other on a specific project. The individual rewards in this category have at least equaled the more academic rewards we've described above.

The book is divided into two major sections: the first deals with the *design* of simulation computer games in education, the second focuses more on their *use* in specific educational contexts. Of course, most of the chapters have implications, if not downright direct relationships, to the other section. In fussing over the best way for the reader to experience these chapters, we eventually chose this kind of organization, but we just as adamantly support the idea that each chapter can be considered on its own--each making its own specific contribution standing by itself. Many introductory sections of books include an overview of the book's chapters and attempt to explain the logic of structure of the book. In a departure from tradition, we have chosen to place this content *in situ* between chapters, so that the reader does not have to continually refer to the front matter to understand why chapters are grouped together as they are or sequenced as they are. This information is available at the point of need, and we hope this will provide a better flow and overall experience for the reader.

We are looking forward to the open sharing of the material within this volume on the Internet and revel in the freedom for each author to distribute his or her work represented within these pages. We miss the planned contribution of Bill Winn, friend and mentor, whose work within this book would have certainly benefited all of us in many, many ways. Finally, we thank the contributors who offered to us the fruits of their hard labor and the patience to see this process through to completion.

May 1, 2007

SECTION ONE: DESIGN

In taking an empirical approach to the study of games and education – one of research and grounded theory, rather than advocacy – this section describes generally the instructional approach to the design and use of simulation computer games. Depending on the "school of thought," the approaches seem to vary: is the proper perspective to take what we know and practice with traditional instructional design and combine that with game design? Or are there other approaches, separated from traditional instructional design, that may be more effective?

GAMES IN EDUCATION: THE EPISTEMIC ARGUMENT

The first section provides and overview of games and how they are useful in teaching real-world concepts to students. Shaffer takes us into the world of history in his discussion of epistemic issues; what is taught and learned about history through game play, and how we might leverage epistemology within a gaming environment. Subsequent chapters describe how game designs achieve or fall short of the lofty expectations now being set by the educational community for using games in formal learning environments.

DAVID SHAFFER

IN PRAISE OF EPISTEMOLOGY[1]

The recent interest in video and computer games as educational tools follows a
tradition of looking at new technologies for educational purposes—a tradition that
suggests that new technologies will not live up to their potential for learning. It is
true, of course, that computers have been in existence for over half a century, and
have been used in classrooms for more nearly three decades, and that in that time
there has been no wholesale transformation of education as we know it (Cuban,
1986, 2001). But I will argue here that this is because education itself has been
conceived in the wrong way..

In this chapter I make the case that central to any discussion of games and
education is the concept of epistemology. *Epistemology* is, of course, the study of
what it means to know something, and here I suggest that games matter because
they provide an opportunity to learn in ways that are more authentic than current
school practices—but only if we consider how games change what it means to
know something—and thus what is worth learning and how we teach it. That is, we
can only understand the impact of games in and for education if we first reconsider
the epistemology (or epistemologies) of the digital age.

To do this I provide an example of one educational game, The Debating Game, that
does not rely on computer technologies—although one that could be easily adapted
to take advantages of a range of new media. I use The Debating Game to look at
some of the fundamental questions about educational games today through the lens
of epistemology. I ask: What defines a game? Why do games matter in educational
settings? And what does this suggest about the nature of schooling in the digital
age?

My argument will be that education has to be reconceptualized in a way that
moves beyond the traditional organization of schools. Schools as we know them
developed in a particular place and time to meet a specific set of social and
economic needs. But times have changed, and the way we need to think about
education has changed too. The academic disciplines of history, English, math, and
science are not the only way to divide the world of things worth knowing, the
forty-minute blocks of time in which they are currently taught using lecture and
recitation are not the only way to learn, and standardized tests of facts and basic
skills are not the only way to decide who has learned what they were supposed to
learn—and, in fact, these traditional school practices may not even be a particularly
appropriate way to organize education in the digital age.

---

[1] This chapter is adapted from Shaffer (2007), which makes a more extended argument for the
importance of epistemology in the design and analysis of educational games.

B. E. Shelton, D. A. Wiley (eds.), Educational Design & Use of Computer Simulation Games, 7–27

The argument has already been made that change is coming: that young people increasingly need skills in innovation to find good jobs and lead fulfilling lives, and that the economic vitality of our country depends in the long run on their ability to do so (Friedman, 2005; Shaffer, 2007; Shaffer & Gee, 2005; Shaffer, Squire, Halverson, & Gee, 2005). Autor, Katz, & Kearney (2006), for example, have shown that computers have already changed the skills that individuals need for economic success. The job market increasingly values non-routine work that requires complex thinking and pays high wages. So we need to think about how to prepare young people for life in the digital age that requires different skills—and different ways of thinking—than traditional schools were designed to teach.

In this chapter, I suggest that games are one important tool in addressing the challenge of thinking differently about education—but only if we think about thinking itself—about epistemology—in new ways. And I begin by discussing one such game in some detail....

THE DEBATING GAME

It was the beginning of the spring semester when a group of eighth graders filed into their school auditorium. On stage were two tables with two chairs each. On one table was a sign that said "Pro." The other table was labeled "Con." There was a podium and microphone in the center of the stage. The teacher was sitting at a table on the side of the stage with a second microphone.

Four students took their places behind the two tables at the center of the stage—Charles and Samantha at the Pro table, Adam and Louisa at Con.[2] The rest of the class sat in the front rows of the auditorium.

"Judges, Debaters, and honored guests," began the teacher. "Welcome to the Annual Foreign Policy Debate. Our topic for today"—and here the teacher raised his voice—"*Resolved*: That the United States went to war with Spain for selfish reasons."

Solemn-faced, he continued: "Arguing in favor of the resolution will be Charles Lewis and Samantha Bell; arguing against the resolution will be Adam Markowitz and Louisa Medina.

"In our debate today, each speaker will have four minutes for opening statements. Speakers will alternate from each team, beginning with those supporting the resolution. There will be a five minute intermission, then each speaker will have 2 minutes for rebuttal and concluding remarks. Judges will have five minutes to prepare their decision."

By this time the students on stage were sitting very still. Even though they had seen their peers go through this ritual earlier in the school year, they were clearly nervous. The large auditorium was quiet, except for the teacher's voice over the loudspeakers.

---

2 All of the names of students and others described have been changed. No demographic information (age, gender, ethnicity, socioeconomic status, and so forth) should be read into or from any of the pseudonyms.

"As moderator, I will act as timekeeper," he continued. "I will use the following signals:

"This signal," he said, holding up one finger, "will indicate that a speaker has one minute remaining.

"This signal," he said, moving his hand in a circle, "will indicate that a speaker has thirty seconds remaining.

"This signal," he said, waving his hand across his neck, "will indicate that a speaker has five seconds remaining.

"At the end of a speaker's allotted time, the moderator will turn off the microphone at the podium.

"Debaters, good luck. We will hear first from the side supporting the resolution."

Debaters and judges

I remember the speech well, because by the time this particular debate took place, I had given it nearly thirty times in my teaching career. The speech was designed to give a sense of gravity to the occasion for these eighth grade history students: to make the debaters and the judges take their job seriously. It was part of a game that these students were playing, called *The Debating Game*.

In this section of the chapter, I am going to describe *The Debating Game* briefly because understanding how and why it is a game is an important part of understanding how computer and video games can change our educational system A week before the debate, the Pro and Con teams had each received a detailed sheet of "Advice to Debaters." The advice described the format of the debate, and the criteria for victory: that the burden of proof in the debate is with the side arguing for the resolution. The advice in this packet of material was *substantive*— "This debate centers on two key ideas: what makes actions in history 'selfish,' and information about the Spanish American War"—but also *strategic*, suggesting how debaters might fashion their arguments to win the debate:

> As for the meaning of "selfish," you are on your own coming up with a definition that works for you in the debate. Remember, though, in a debate you need not argue for what you believe in. Whatever argument will win is the argument you should use.

The judges similarly received a sheet of instructions for playing their role, which included specific information about the criteria they should use for judging the debate: quality of the presentation, use of evidence, clarity of argument, and skill at rebutting the opposing team's positions. They were told explicitly that they were not supposed to judge based on their own beliefs, but rather on the strength of the arguments presented by each side:

> The criteria for victory in a debate—the criteria on which you should make your decision—is not which team is *right*, but rather, which team, makes a better argument.... Debate is more like a court case than a class discussion. You should judge not on the *truth* of a debater's position, but on her

presentation, use of evidence and sources of information, the clarity of her argument, and her skill at refuting points made by the opposing team.

The judges had to prepare a short paragraph justifying their decision immediately after the debate, and then a full report explaining their decision in detail. These reports were presented to the debaters, and thus had to be explicit, constructive, and sensitive.

This was not an easy game, in other words, and playing it meant following detailed instructions about how to be a debater and what it means to judge a debate fairly.

Is this *fun*?

With this brief description of *The Debating Game*, let's ask a fundamental question: What makes this a *game* and not just a clever classroom assignment to help students learn about the Spanish-American War? Aren't games fun, and about things that kids already care about? Isn't school about work, and about doing things that you *have* to do rather than that you *want* to do? And by that criteria isn't this schoolwork and not a game?

Well, actually, *The Debating Game was* fun. Students enjoyed playing, and not just because it was an excuse to avoid their regular history class for a day. This was a kind of fun that Papert (1980) characterized as *hard fun*: the kind of fun you have when you work on something difficult, something that you care about, and finally master it.

It wasn't that that these students cared about the Spanish American War more than any other eighth graders. What these players cared about as debaters was winning and losing, and the pride that goes with playing any game well in school and thus in the public eye. As judges, students cared because their opinions mattered. They were deciding who won and lost the debate, and their written assignment was not merely an exercise to be graded and forgotten; it was going to be read by their peers as an evaluation of their performance in the debate.

While *The Debating Game* was fun, however, that isn't why it was a game, because fun is not the defining characteristic of a game. On some superficial level we play games because we enjoy the experience overall. But quite often much of the time we spend on a game isn't about having fun. Suits (1967), for example, offers a definition of games that does not focus primarily on pleasure, as does Gee (2003) more recently (although both emphasize the goal-directedness of games that for reasons I discuss in the text below may not be central to the notion of a game). Vygotsky (1978) characterizes play in terms of rules and explicitly rejects the notion that play is centrally about enjoyment.

In *The Debating Game* debaters and judges do a lot of hard work preparing for the debate and preparing their responses to it, just as much of being on a football team is doing drills and calisthenics and weight training and running laps—things that, despite the coaches' protestations to the contrary, aren't much fun for most players. Players of video games spend a lot of time repeating very basic maneuvers to be able to progress to the next level. Recently, for example, I was talking online with a colleague while he was playing *World of Warcraft*. When I realized he was playing I apologized for interrupting and he replied: "It's ok. I'm just running some boring errands in the game." Johnson (2005) similarly describes in detail the frustrations and difficulties of playing many modern games—including some of the most popular games on the market.

If *fun* is not one of the defining characteristics of a game, however, winning and losing aren't either. Many traditional games are a competition: most sports, for example; chess, checkers and most board games; card games; and many children's games like Duck Duck Goose, Tag, or Hide-and-Seek. You can even win or lose when there is no competition at all, as in some forms of solitaire. But many games don't have winners and losers. In *The Debating Game* the debaters win or lose, but the judges don't. Similarly, winning isn't the goal in a game like *World of Warcraft*. You can become more powerful, but even the most powerful player in the game at any point in time isn't the *winner*. Bartle's (1990; 1996) framework suggests that there are at least four different types of players of multiplayer online fantasy games: players who like to succeed at tasks within the game world, players who like to find out as much as they can about the virtual world of the game, players who like socializing with others in the game, and players who like to gain power over other players. Although the details of Bartle's formulation has been questioned and expanded upon by other researchers (see, e.g., Steinkuehler, 2005), the basic point remains: different kinds of players enjoys different things about a game, and (particularly for the socializers and explorers) the game ends when you decide to stop playing,[3] not when you have "won" the game.[4] Different players can have different *end states* (Gee, 2003) for the same game—different ways to decide when they are done playing. For obvious reasons, games that let players find end states that are personally and socially meaningful are both more engaging and better for learning about things that matter in the world.

In a game like *Dungeons and Dragons*—the inspiration for many modern computer games—players take on a character and customize it. Once the character is brought to life, players take on the role of their character within the rules of the game. Fighters can do things wizards can't, and vice versa. Players can be good or evil, can accumulate wealth, become more skillful, or die in their adventures. The outcome is determined by a combination of a player's choices, the decisions of other players, and rolls of various combinations of dice within an elaborate system of rules. But in the end, no player can do everything. Becoming a master of one aspect of the game necessarily means not becoming good at another. As in life,

---

[3] A game (necessarily) ends when players decide to stop playing. However, that does not necessarily imply that "fun" is what keeps them playing. Motivations (for play and other activities) are both more complex and more holistic, in the sense described above: games need not be locally fun, to be motivating overall.

[4] Players in World of Warcraft do hold competitions, of course, including ladder tournaments in which players are ranked over time against each other. For an example see http://www.battle.net/war3/tournaments/season3.shtml.

there is no absolute state of victory. "Winning" is about playing the game well—not necessarily scoring more points than another player, accumulating the most treasure, or achieving some other pre-determined end state of the game. It is true, of course, that *Dungeons and Dragons* can be played as a competition, as can life itself. But for most players the game is about what one does rather than whether one wins.

Roles and rules

What makes a game a game, then, is neither "fun" or "winning and losing," nor even the idea that games are "safe," since games can have serious consequences: injuries in football, losses in gambling games, and so on—a point made eloquently by Geertz (1973) in his discussion of Balinese cockfighting.

Rather what makes a game a game is that it has some particular set of *rules* that a player has to follow. In a game, players are assigned particular *roles*—whether "white" and "black" in chess or "dwarf fighter" in *Dungeons and Dragons* or "It" in Tag—and playing a role means following some set of rules for behavior. In making this claim I am borrowing from Vygotsky (1978), who argued that "there is no such thing as play without rules" (p. 94). What Vygotsky meant is that in all play—even in what seems like open-ended play among very young children—a game creates some imaginary situation that has some implicit or explicit set of norms that determine what players can and cannot do.

By this definition, of course, any system of social activity can be viewed as a game—a position consistent with Goffman (1963; 1967; 1974; 1981), who analyzed social interaction in terms of games, Wittgenstein (1963), who viewed all language as a game, and Donald (2001), who describes careers as extended role playing games. Some game scholars argue for a more specific definition of a "game," but for every additional criteria, there are exceptions (Juul, 2003). Others have attempted to construct typologies of games, but all include some form of roles and the rules that constrain action within those roles (Lindley, 2005).

If you watch young children play, it often seems that more of the game is about deciding the roles and rules than about acting them out. One child will begin by saying: "Let's play we're orphans." To which another will reply: "No, not orphans, but our parents have gone away and we have to take care of ourselves and our four cats all by ourselves." And then the first child again: "And one of our cats will be sick and I'll be an animal-doctor and you can be a food-cooker." And so on, spending more time *setting up* an imaginary world they can inhabit than they do actually playing in the world they created.

The rules in these game worlds are, of course, the children's understanding of how orphans, pet owners, animal-doctors, and food-cookers behave in the world. To make this point, Vygotsky (1978) described two girls who are actually sisters and who also "play" at being sisters. It is a situation I know well from playing various versions of "family" with my daughters. My oldest child will say: "Let's play family. I'll be the older sister, and she can be the younger sister, and you can be the daddy." We're supposed to "play", in other words, the actual situation in our real family by explicitly acting by the rules that govern the roles of sisters and father. They are supposed to be especially nice to each other (unless they are being step-sisters, in which case they are supposed to be especially mean), and I'm supposed to play either a transgressive father ("Let's have ice cream for dinner!") or an ideal one ("Let's clean up the house and then as a special treat go to the circus!").

Lest we think playing family in a game of this sort is just child's play, consider that this is essentially what the best-selling computer game of all time, *The Sims*, is all about. The game's promotional materials tout the fact that players can "build relationships with other Sims and watch them blossom... or crumble. Hang with friends, throw parties, meet the love of your Sim's life, or just live the single life." Games like these are fun, but their value is in letting players live in worlds that they are curious about, or afraid of, or want desperately to be able to try out. As Vygotsky (1978) explains, all games are "the realization in play form of tendencies that can not be immediately gratified" (p. 94). In games, players do explicitly, openly, and socially what they will later do tacitly, privately, and personally. They are running simulations of worlds they want to learn about in order to understand the rules, roles, and consequences of those worlds. They are learning to think by examining alternatives in play, and from those experiences they are learning what it might mean to be social outcasts ("It"), war leaders ("white" or "black"), professionals ("firefighter" or "food-cooker"), members of a family ("father" or "sister"), and a host of other real and imagined characters in the world.[5]

It may seem odd to describe board games like Chess as worlds that players can explore by taking on particular roles.[6] But consider Dreyfus & Dreyfus' (1986) account of chess experts:

> Chess grandmasters, engrossed in a game, can lose entirely the awareness that they are manipulating pieces on a board and see themselves rather as involved participants in a world of opportunities, threats, strengths, weaknesses, hopes, and fears. When playing rapidly, they sidestep dangers in the same automatic way that a teenager, himself an expert, might avoid missiles in a familiar video game" (p. 30).

---

[5] Bruner (1976)argued that play provides an occasion to examine alternatives, although his work focused on physical rather than social situations. For more on play and its developmental role (see also Garvey, 1990; Lillard, 1993; Sutton-Smith, 1979; Sylva, Bruner, & Genova, 1976).

[6] Of course, many instructional simulations that are not particularly enjoyable offer rules and explorable worlds—and some even have defined roles for users to follow. Which is only to reemphasize that "fun" is not a defining characteristic of a game.

REFERENCES AND REBUTTALS

What makes *The Debating Game* a game, then, is that the students step into the roles of debaters and judges, and play by the rules that define those roles: they subordinate their own beliefs to the rules of evidence in a debate, focusing on who presented a better argument rather than who was right; they write an account of the debate not for the teacher but as feedback to their peers. They are, of course, not *actually* deciding on the merits of the Spanish-American War as historians, nor are they *actually* grading their peers. But they are acting as if they are doing so. Just as *Dungeons and Dragons* players are not actually *becoming* elves and wizards, but are acting according to the rules they (and the game's creators) think that elves and wizards live by.

Like *Dungeons and Dragons*, *The Debating Game* is a fantasy role playing game—let's call it *References and Rebuttals*—in which players take on the roles of debaters and judges to inhabit an imagined world in which they are making judgments about the morality of historical actors and about the skill of their own peers.

To see how such a game contrasts with traditional schooling, let's look at a section of an eighth grade history text that describes the Spanish American War (Wallbank, Schrier, Maier-Weaver, & Gutierrez, 1977). Notice how often the passage uses the passive voice—there are few historical actors here, only vague historical forces. Motives are ascribed not to individuals but to large groups of people. The war is not actually started by anyone in particular; it just starts. Thus:

> **The Spanish American War broke out.** During the late 19th Century, Cuba and Puerto Rico were swept by revolutions. These two countries were all that remained of Spain's New World empire. Both islands now wanted their own independence. Americans supported this desire and grew angry that the Cuban and Puerto Rican rebels were treated so harshly by the Spanish. These American feelings were backed up by other facts: (1) Americans had invested some $50 million in Cuba, (2) Cuba was the largest supplier of American sugar, (3) Cuba was strategically important because it controlled the entrance to the Gulf of Mexico.... When the American battleship *Maine* was mysteriously sunk in Havana Harbor... the United States declared war and defeated Spain in less than five months. As a result of the Spanish-American War, the United States took over Puerto Rico as well as the Philippine Islands in the Pacific.

The review questions from the text ask: "What were three reasons that the United States entered the Spanish American War?" and "As a result of the Spanish American War, America annexed: a. Mexico, b. the Philippines, c. Spain."

For example, ask them why

Let's compare that description of the war to how one player in *The Debating Game* looked at these events. I'm going to give a somewhat extended account here of one

Judge's Report because the contrast in content and style is quite striking between what was written by a team of professional historians and educators as a text book and this report produced by an eighth grader as part of a game. Notice particularly the completeness of this description and the way that the judge is not only writing about how the debaters used evidence to make their case, she is also using evidence herself:

Overall Presentation

Pro Side

The Pro side had a great overall presentation. Both speakers could have spoken slower and clearer because it was sort of hard to understand them and they were never short of time.... They sounded convincing by saying things like, "The first casualty lists did nothing to diminish the patriotic fever of a nation aware it was on the high road to international eminence. In fact, coming just after the news of victory at Manila, they spurred enlistments and stirred the hearts of even the most conservative of citizens." (*The Spanish American War* by Allen Keller.) This and other pieces of information made their argument sound convincing.

Con Side

Both speakers did a wonderful job on their overall presentation. They both spoke well but it would have been better if they both spoke a little bit louder. The argument was very convincing; they used quotations and statistics. For example they said that 216 people died when the Maine sunk.

Quality of the Argument

Pro Side

Their argument was very well stated. They made it clear by saying the three main reasons for the United States to fight in the war: to gain wealth, land expansion, and power. Most of their argument made sense but it was not convincing how exactly the Maine sank and how the people who were on it died. They made their point clear that the United States went to war with Spain for selfish reasons.

Con Side

Their argument also was very good. Their main argument was that the United States didn't want to become an imperialistic power and they made their point clear by saying that the United States wanted to help Cuba and not take over Cuba. They stated that historian Frank Freidal said, "That Cubans were not strong enough to win but not weak enough to surrender." This was a good statement because it is saying that the Cubans needed help and that is what the United States planned to do.

Use of Sources

Pro Side

They used very nice evidence. They both used many quotes, for example, one of them said, "It is the duty of the United States to demand, and the Government of the United States does hereby demand, that the Government of Spain at once relinquish its authority and government in the island of Cuba and withdraw its land and navel forces from Cuba and Cuban waters." (President McKinley sent a letter to Spain)....

Con Side

They also used great evidence. It was helpful that they showed the Judges their sources by laying the books in front of them. They used dates as well as quotes.... They might have not wanted to use as many quotes as they did because they could have just translated the quote into their own words because half of their debate was quotes. They said that the United States knew how it felt to be owned and that was a good piece of information.

Let's make a few observations about what this judge wrote. First, she was describing a debate in which players covered the essential elements of the war as reported by the text, including "the three main reasons for the United States to fight in the war: to gain wealth, land expansion, and power." But the debaters also clearly went far beyond the text, using primary source documents and secondary interpretations by historians to make their arguments. (As it turns out, this is even more impressive because the debaters had to prepare for the game *before* the class had read anything about the war in question.) Second, this judge was describing a debate in which the players were using evidence to argue for a particular interpretation of historical events, ascribing motives to historical actors to explain historical circumstances. They were arguing over whether we can call a nation's actions selfish, and about whether that definition applies to the United States in its decision to declare war on Spain in 1898. Third, this judge's report itself was clearly organized to discuss the criteria by which she was asked to judge the debate. This judge was not talking about her opinion, or about which side was "right" or "wrong." She was evaluating competing interpretations of historical events based on the strength of the arguments presented. Fourth, this judge used specific evidence from the debate itself to make her points, giving concrete examples and using those examples to explain her analysis of the debaters' arguments.

Finally, keep in mind that these were eighth graders who might otherwise have been expected only to be able to identify three reasons given in their text for the start of the war, and to know that as a result of the war, the United States annexed the Philippines.

Oh, that's from Fast! Forget it!

The reason *The Debating Game* matters here is that it illustrates how we can build a bridge from learning in the world to learning in games. The rules of the imaginary world of this particular game do a better job of representing what it means to think like an historian than the traditional text-lecture-and-recitation of many history classes. When we read the report of this Judge in the game—and read through the report to see how the Debaters were making their arguments—we can see that these players of *The Debating Game* were thinking more like real historians than like students trained to answer multiple choice questions about historical facts from a text book.

Wineburg (1991) studied the differences between history as traditionally taught in school and as practiced by historians. He gathered a set of documents about the "shot heard 'round the world" on the Lexington Green that started the American Revolutionary War: primary and secondary source texts as well as paintings made at different times of the scene of the battle. He gave this set of historical source material to eight historians and eight high school students and looked at how they used the documents to "try to understand what happened at Lexington Green on the morning of April 19, 1775" (p. 75).

The differences were striking. The students read the texts "from top to bottom, from the first word in the upper-lefthand corner to the last word in the bottom-righthand corner." They saw the documents as "vehicles for conveying information." They thought of bias as a binary attribute: either a text is biased or it isn't, either it is, as one student explained, "just reporting the facts" (what another student described as giving "straight information") or it is a biased account and thus not to be trusted.

For the historians, the documents were not vehicles for reporting facts in this sense. They were accounts written by distinct people at specific points in time, each with a particular perspective. The historians saw a key part of their task as interpreting these documents in relation to one another. They saw the texts "not as bits of information to be gathered but as social exchanges to be understood." For the historians, the question was never, "Is this source biased?" but rather, *"How does a source's bias influence the quality of its report?"* (Quotations from pp. 83-4.)

Wineburg compared how a student and a historian dealt with an excerpt taken from Howard Fast's 1961 period novel *April Morning*, which tells a fictionalized story of the battle on Lexington Green. On reading the document, both recognized it was a novel and said that they could not rely on the details from that source. Several minutes later, however, the student seemed to have incorporated information from Fast into his understanding of the battle scene. The historian, in

17

contrast, came upon a claim in a later document that the colonists formed ranks in "regular order." He remembered seeing the claim earlier and went searching through the documents. When he found it was from the novel, he laughed: "Oh, that's from Fast! Forget it!" As Wineburg explained:

A detail is first remembered, but the historian cannot remember its source. This recognition sends the historian searching for the sources of this detail, and, when reunited with its author, the detail is rejected. The reason is that the historian knows that there are no free-floating details, only details tied to witnesses... (p. 84). Contrast this with the student, who knew that information from a novel was suspect, but used it anyway a few moments later having forgotten the original source.

Wineburg concluded that what distinguished the high school students from the historians was not the number of facts that they knew about the American Revolution. Instead, the difference was in their understanding of what it means to think historically. For the students, history is what is written in the textbook, where "facts" are presented free of bias. For the historians, on the other hand, historical inquiry is a system for determining the validity of historical claims based on corroboration of sources in conversation with one another rather than an appeal to a unitary source of truth—a way of knowing based on using specific evidence to support claims rather than trying to establish a set of facts that exist without bias. As Wineburg said:

> It is doubtful that teaching these students more facts about the American Revolution would help them do better on this task when they remain ignorant of the basic heuristics [guidelines] used to create historical interpretations, when they cannot distinguish among different types of historical evidence, and when they look to a textbook for the "answer" to historical questions— even when that textbook contradicts primary sources from both sides (p. 84).

Epistemology

Wineberg argued that in learning history, these students did not, in fact, learn to think like historians. No amount of learning to appeal to an all-knowing textbook will teach students to understand historical texts in context with one another and with the period in which they are written. No amount of correctly-remembered facts will prepare students to sift through the historical record of newspaper articles, partisan reports, contemporary documents, and later historical accounts and from this tangled web of information construct and defend a historical interpretation (Collingwood & Knox, 1946; Doel & Sèoderqvist, 2006; Morris-Suzuki, 2005; Wineburg, 2001). In other words, the epistemology of most high school history classes does not match the epistemology of historical inquiry.

Epistemology, in this sense, is what Perkins (1992) has described as "knowledge and know-how concerning justification and explanation" (p. 85). In analyzing his results, for example, Wineburg refers to Schwab's (1978) concept of *syntactic knowledge*, which he describes as "knowledge of how to establish warrant and determine validity of competing truth claims in a discipline" (p. 84). Epistemology is a particular way of thinking about or justifying actions, of structuring valid claims. It tells you the rules you are supposed to use in deciding whether something is true, and epistemology in this sense is domain specific: mathematicians make different kinds of arguments than historians do. Buehl & Alexander (2005), for example, studied the domain specificity of epistemological beliefs from a psychological perspective: whether and how students have different understandings of the nature of justification and explanation in different disciplines. Donald (2002) has looked at the differences in the epistemological organization of fields of study at the collegiate level. In both cases, different disciplines and practices are characterized by different structures of argument and different criteria for verification of claims.

This may seem like an obvious point, but the differences between ways of thinking within subjects are often left out in discussions of thinking. Piaget's cognitive stages exist *across* domains: developmental stages that are the foundation of thinking in any subject, in any context (Gardner, 1982). Piaget's stages are compatible with the idea that different subjects have different ways of thinking: discipline-specific ways of thinking could have features in common for children of different ages. However, emphasizing the distinctiveness of different epistemologies is important because that is how academic subjects are organized—indeed, it is the very reason we have different disciplines in the first place. As Wineburg suggests, "the disciplines that lend us school subjects possess distinctive logics and modes of inquiry" (p. 73).

Epistemology is also important here because it shows why Wineburg's results are such a fundamental criticism of history instruction in schools. In his study, high school history students and historians had different epistemologies. They used different criteria for deciding that a statement is true or a claim is valid. For Wineburg's students, true facts were presented in a non-biased text. For his historians, truth depended on one's ability to support a historical interpretation with evidence from multiple sources. These high school history students and professional historians had different ways of justifying their actions—and thus were actually studying different disciplines.

Which brings us back to *The Debating Game*. To make a valid point in the game, a Debater has to advance a specific historical interpretation. The Debaters have to make interpretations about what happened in the Spanish American War, and why events unfolded as they did. The validity of those claims are evaluated by the Judges based on the clarity of the argument presented, and on the Debaters' use of historical evidence from primary and secondary sources. Although the Debaters are explicitly trying to win the debate, the terms by which they do so are a closer match to the epistemology of Wineberg's historians than to the multiple choice questions of their textbook. Similarly, the Judges themselves are put in a position of advancing an interpretation which they have to defend using specific evidence. Although the Judges are making interpretations about (and using evidence from) the debate itself rather than the war, the epistemology is similar: what matters is presenting an interpretation and defending it with specific evidence rather than appealing to authority to establish the legitimacy of a claim.

Of course, *The Debating Game*, by itself, can not take credit for creating the epistemology of professional historians. It was part of a curriculum that systematically reinforced the message that history was about trying to understand what had happened in the past by sorting through evidence and evaluating arguments based on that evidence. But by giving players roles whose rules of behavior emphasized the importance of competing interpretations of events supported by specific evidence, the game helped develop a more authentic view of history for the students who played it.

In this sense, then, epistemology is at the heart of what school is about. The intellectual and historical justification for the traditional disciplines—mathematics, science, history, language arts, and so on—are that these are the ways of thinking that are fundamental in anything that students will do when they finish school.

The idea of fundamental disciplines of knowledge goes back to the ancient Greeks, who divided knowledge about the world into the *quadrivium* of arithmetic, music, geometry, and astronomy and the *trivium* of rhetoric, grammar, and logic. If the details have changed (logic, arithmetic, and geometry now go together in the mathematics curriculum for example), the idea that some ways of understanding the world are basic to all the things we do remains the same.

The liberal arts curriculum of our schools, with classes in the basic disciplines of mathematics, science, history or social studies, English, art, and foreign languages is based on the idea that each of these disciplines represents a fundamental way of thinking: knowledge and skills that students need no matter what they will do in life. But what the example here and Wineburg's work suggests is that school classes are not doing such a good job of teaching kids these fundamental ways of knowing.

And the reason it doesn't is because that isn't what school classes were designed to do.

WHAT'S IN A GAME?

The Debating Game is a particular kind of game: a role-playing game in which the roles players take on require them to think and act in ways that matter in the world. To play *The Debating Game*, you have to accept a particular epistemology: a particular way of deciding when something or someone is right, of justifying what you do, of explaining and arguing for a particular point of view, course of action, or decision. In this sense, *The Debating Game* is an example of what I have described elsewhere as an *epistemic* game: a game that requires you to think in a particular way about the world (Shaffer, 2005, 2007).

Knees and toes

By this definition, of course, *School* is an epistemic game. The players take on particular roles: most are Students, a smaller number are Teachers, and still fewer are Administrators. There are clear rules—whether implicit or explicit—about how to play these roles, and the role of Student in particular carries certain expectations about how you have to think to succeed in the game.

The modern game of *School* as we know it was invented during the Industrial Revolution, at about the same time as the modern game of *Baseball*, in fact. And some of the same historical forces—urbanization, industrialization, immigration and migration—formalized and spread both games across the United States. It is in this period—in the middle and late 1800s—that most of what we think of as the structure of *School* was developed: the so-called "egg crate" school, with identical isolated classrooms, each with individual desks for individual students; age-graded classrooms filled with similarly-aged students; the nine month school year and 5 day school week; the 45 minute school period; and the Carnegie unit, or standardized class of 130 hours of instruction in a single subject.

In developing this basic framework—the *grammar of schooling* (Tyack & Tobin, 1994)—school leaders in the 1800s deliberately used the factory as a model for the orderly delivery of instruction. Just as theologians in the Enlightenment described God as a divine watchmaker and cognitive scientists today write about the mind as a computer, so factories in the late 1800s were a dominant model for explaining and organizing activity.[7] While superintendent of schools in St. Louis, William Harris wrote:

> The first requisite of the school is *Order*: each pupil must be taught first and foremost to conform his behavior to a general standard... to the time of the train, to the starting of work in the manufactory.... The pupil must have his lessons ready at the appointed time, must rise at the tap of the bell, move to the line, return; in short, go through all the evolutions with equal precision (Tyack, 1974, p. 43).

Students were asked to literally "toe the line," standing motionless and erect with their knees together and their toes against the edge of a board on the floor. After all, as one enthusiastic teacher asked: "How can you learn anything with your knees and toes out of order?" (Tyack, 1974, pp. 55-6). But if the factory model was embraced with enthusiasm, it was also a matter of necessity. As one critic wrote in the 1860s: "To manage successfully a hundred children, or even half that number, the teacher must reduce them as nearly as possible to a unit" (Tyack, 1974, p. 54).

The game of school

The rules of the game of *School* are well documented (see, e.g., Fried, 2005; Tripp, 1993). The grammar of schooling creates a *hidden curriculum*: the set of lessons that students take away from school about how they should act in the world, and about what it means to think and to learn (Jackson, 1968). The hidden curriculum

---

[7] For more on the way in which technology is used as a metaphor for social, natural, and psychological phenomena see (Tichi, 1987).

is what makes math class and history class and science class all seem so similar, even though the subjects are so different. The hidden curriculum is what makes the textbook's multiple choice questions about the Spanish American War seem so familiar—because we've all seen questions just like these before. Because the hidden curriculum pervades our schools, wherever and whenever we went to school we played more or less the same game.

When *School* was invented, though, this curriculum was anything but hidden. Quite the contrary, in fact. *School* was deliberately, explicitly, openly designed to impose a new urban discipline as a means to avert social strife in rapidly-expanding industrial cities. As Tyack suggests, it was a means to industrialize humanity. And that matters because the hidden curriculum of *School* is still very much with us. We tend to think of *School* as we know it as something necessary and inevitable. But it is not. It is just one particular game, invented in a particular time and place to achieve certain goals.

Not surprisingly, the epistemology of *School* is the epistemology of the industrial revolution—of creating wealth through mass-production of standardized goods. *School* is a game about thinking like a factory worker. It is a game with an epistemology of right and wrong answers. It is a game in which Students are supposed to follow instructions, whether or not they make sense in the moment. Truth is whatever the teacher says is the right answer, and actions are justified based on appeal to authority. *School* is a game in which what it means to know something is to be able to answer specific kinds of questions on specific kinds of tests. As Zoch (2004) and Fried (2005) suggest, contemporary schooling is characterized by passivity, epistemological uniformity, and rigidity.

Now, not every school or every classroom is like this, of course, and the hidden curriculum of school is about more than what happens in the classroom. There are sports teams and playgrounds and a host of other interactions that Students have in the game of *School* that shape what they learn about the world from playing. But in the era of No Child Left Behind, which links school funding to how well students perform on high-stakes standardized tests, it would be hard for a public school student to conclude at the end of the day that learning in any subject means more than learning how to identify the answer that someone else has already determined is right.

Better games

In other words, our sons and daughters go to school in factories. They are not working on a shop floor operating heavy machinery, but from the building to the curriculum to the schedule for the day, almost everything about *School* was designed—deliberately designed—in and for life in industrial America.

The problem is that industrial schools don't particularly encourage innovative thinking. We live in an era where global competition is sending overseas any job that relies on standardized skills and knowledge. When information can travel overseas with the click of a mouse, and barriers to trade in goods and services have been lowered to create a global economy, work flows to where it can be done for less money. As Brown and Duguid (2002) explain, the jobs in high-wage economies will be in "areas where making sense, interpreting, and understanding are both problematic and highly valued—areas where, above, all, meaning and knowledge are at a premium" (p. 95). Davenport similarly suggests: "It's not clear exactly what workers in the United States, Western Europe, and Japan are going to do for a living in the future... but it is clear that if these economies are to prosper, the jobs of many of the workers must be particularly knowledge-intensive" (p. 22). Already today nearly a third of the jobs in the workforce in the United States require complex thinking skills, and barely a quarter of all workers are up to the challenge.[8] In a post-industrial world we need to build better educational games than industrial *School*.

Better educational games don't necessarily require new technology. *The Debating Game* helps players to think about issues the way historians do: to understand complex situations and develop and defend their own point of view on controversial issues. But whether or not new technologies are *required* to build better educational games, it is clear that we need to ask: Can we use computers to build games in which players learn to think creatively—games in which young people can learn the epistemologies of innovation they need to succeed in a digital age of global competition?

The answer appears to be that we can.

Consider, for example, *Civilization*, a well-known and widely-played strategy game that lets players build an empire throughout human history. Players choose a civilization to lead, and beginning with a stone-age settlement make strategic decisions to invest in technological development or trade, to use diplomacy or cultural exchange, religious conversion, or open warfare to help their civilization grow and thrive. The game is based on a historically-accurate model of advances in technology, religion, and the arts, and Squire's (2004; in press) studies of the game suggest that as players master the game system, they can begin to ask and play out historical experiments. While "experiments" are not the usual activity of historians, simulations are a growing part of other social sciences. Many world history textbooks, particularly at the middle school level, tell a story about Western progress. In contrast, Civilization gives players an opportunity to think in terms of a materialist-determinist approach to history (Diamond, 2005). In this view of history, geographical location, ease of trade, and access to raw materials create structural conditions that shape historical developments. In this sense, the game Civilization is a particularly rich context for thinking about one particular epistemology of historical inquiry.

But games only work in this way when we recognize that we need to think carefully not just about what kinds of things players do in a game, but about what

---

[8] The statistics come from Davenport (2005). Although specific numbers in both categories depend on exactly what is counted as knowledge work and complex thinking skills, even conservative estimates show there is already a gap between the jobs available in the economy and skilled workers to fill them. Evidence that computer technologies are responsible for the high skill demands of the modern workforce can be found in Autor et al. (2003).

justifies those actions. How do you know in the game when you have made a good decision or a bad one? What kind of evidence is available to base your decision on, and how are you supposed to evaluate that evidence? What makes something "true" in the sense that you can use it to guide your choices in the game?

These are, of course, very different issues than the questions asked by some about games. These are not questions about whether games can make learning more "fun" or more "motivating." These are not questions about whether and how games can teach traditional content better than traditional instructional methods.

Rather, as I have argued elsewhere (Shaffer, 2005, 2007), thinking about games from the perspective of their epistemologies opens up a new and important way of thinking about education itself. To prepare for life in a world of global competition that values innovation rather than standardization, young people need to learn to think like innovators. Innovative professionals in the real world have ways of thinking and working that are just as coherent—and just as fundamental—as any of the disciplines. The work of creative professionals is organized around what I call *epistemic frames*: collections of skills, knowledge, identities, values, and epistemology that professionals use to think in innovative ways. Innovators learn these epistemic frames through professional training that is very different from traditional academic classrooms because innovative thinking means more than just knowing the right answers on a test. It also means having real world skills, high standards and professional values, and a particular way of thinking about problems and justifying solutions.

Thinking in these terms lets us build *epistemic games*: games that recreate the process of how people in the real world learn to think like creative professionals. With these games, young people don't have to wait to begin their education for innovation until college, or graduate school, or their entry into the work force. In these games, learning to think like professionals prepares players for innovative thinking from an early age.

This approach to games and education opens up a number of big questions: What role can (and should) such games play in how we educate children for life in a high-tech, global, digital, post-industrial world? Should these be part of the curriculum of school? Should they be played at home—or on portable game players—like commercial video games? What should games for learning look like, and—more important—what kind of learning happens when children play them?

These are important questions that are only beginning to be addressed. The answers thus far are promising, as my own work (Shaffer, 2005, 2007), and the work of others represented in this volume show. My point here as been to suggest that these questions are made both more fruitful and more urgent when we look at the new possibilities games provide for education through a very old lens: the lens of epistemology and the question of how people think about problems that matter in the world.

REFERENCES

Autor, D. H., Katz, L. F., & Kearney, M. S. (2006). *The polarization of the U.S. labor market.* Retrieved April 1, 2006, from http://post.economics.harvard.edu/faculty/katz/papers/akk-polarization-nber-txt.pdf

Autor, D. H., Levy, F., & Murname, R. J. (2003). The Skill content of recent technological change: An empirical exploration. *Quarterly Journal of Economics, 118*(4).

Bartle, R. A. (1990). Who plays MUAs? *Comms Plus!,* 18-19.

Bartle, R. A. (1996). Hearts, clubs, diamonds, spades: Players who suit MUDs. *Journal of MUD Research, 1*(1).

Brown, J. S., & Duguid, P. (2002). *The social life of information.* Boston: Harvard Business School Press.

Bruner, J. S. (1976). Nature and uses of immaturity. In J. S. Bruner, A. Jolly & K. Sylva (Eds.), *Play, its role in development and evolution.* New York: Basic Books.

Buehl, M. M., & Alexander, P. A. (2005). Motivation and preformance differences in students' domain-specific epistemological belief profiles. *American Educational Research Journal, 42*(4), 697-726.

Collingwood, R. G., & Knox, T. M. (1946). *The idea of history.* Oxford,: Clarendon press.

Cuban, L. (1986). *Teachers and machines: The classroom use of technology since 1920.* New York: Teachers College Press.

Cuban, L. (2001). *Oversold and underused : Computers in the classroom.* Cambridge, Mass.: Harvard University Press.

Davenport, T. H. (2005). *Thinking for a living : How to get better performance and results from knowledge workers.* Boston, Mass.: Harvard Business School Press.

Diamond, J. M. (2005). *Guns, germs, and steel : The fates of human societies.* New York: Norton.

Doel, R. E., & Sèoderqvist, T. (2006). *The historiography of science, technology and medicine : Writing recent history.* London ; New York: Routledge.

Donald, J. G. (2002). *Learning to think : Disciplinary perspectives* (1st ed.). San Francisco: Jossey-Bass.

Donald, M. (2001). *A mind so rare: The evolution of human consciousness.* New York: W.W. Norton and Company.

Dreyfus, H. L., & Dreyfus, S. E. (1986). *Mind over machine : The power of human intuition and expertise in the era of the computer.* New York: Free Press.

Fried, R. L. (2005). *The game of school : Why we all play it, how it hurts kids, and what it will take to change it* (1st ed.). San Francisco, CA: Jossey-Bass.

Friedman, T. (2005). *The world is flat: A brief history of the twenty-first century.* New York: Farrar, Straus and Giroux.

Gardner, H. (1982). *Art, mind, and brain: A cognitive approach to creativity.* New York: Basic Books.

Garvey, C. (1990). *Play.* Cambridge, Mass.: Harvard University Press.

Gee, J. P. (2003). *What video games have to teach us about learning and literacy.* New York: Palgrave Macmillan.

Geertz, C. (1973). Deep play: Notes on the Balinese cockfight. In *The Interpretation of Cultures: Selected Essays* (pp. 3-30). New York: Basic Books.

Goffman, E. (1963). *Behavior in public places; notes on the social organization of gatherings.* [New York]: Free Press of Glencoe.

Goffman, E. (1967). *Interaction ritual; essays on face-to-face behaviour* ([1st] ed.). Garden City, N.Y.,: Anchor Books.

Goffman, E. (1974). *Frame analysis : An essay on the organization of experience.* New York: Harper & Row.

Goffman, E. (1981). *Forms of talk.* Philadelphia, PA: University of Philadelphia Press.

Jackson, P. W. (1968). *Life in classrooms.* New York,: Holt.

Johnson, S. (2005). *Everything bad is good for you: How today's popular culture is actually making us smarter.* New York: Riverhead Books.

Juul, J. (2003). The game, the player, the world: Looking for a heart of gameness. In M. Copier & J. Raessens (Eds.), *Level up: Digital games research conference Proceedings* (pp. 30-45). Utrecht: Utrecht University.

Lillard, A. S. (1993). Pretend play skills and the child's theory of mind. *Child Development, 64*, 348-371.

Lindley, C. A. (2005). The semiotics of time structure in ludic space as a foundation for analysis and design. *Game Studies, 5*(1).

Morris-Suzuki, T. (2005). *The past within us : Media, memory, history.* London ; New York: Verso.

Papert, S. (1980). *Mindstorms: Children, computers, and powerful ideas.* New York: Basic Books.

Perkins, D. (1992). *Smart schools.* New York: Free Press.

Schwab, J. J. (1978). Education and the structure of the disciplines. In I. Westbury & N. J. Wilkof (Eds.), *Science, curriculum, and liberal education* (pp. 229-272). Chicago: University of Chicago Press.

Shaffer, D. W. (2005). Epistemic Games. *Innovate, 1*(6), http://www.innovateonline.info/index.php?view=article&id=79.

Shaffer, D. W. (2007). *How Computer games help children learn.* New York: Palgrave.

Shaffer, D. W., & Gee, J. P. (2005). *Before every child is left behind: How epistemic games can solve the coming crisis in education* (WCER Working Paper No. 2005-7): University of Wisconsin-Madison, Wisconsin Center for Education Research.

Shaffer, D. W., Squire, K. D., Halverson, R., & Gee, J. P. (2005). Video games and the future of learning. *Phi Delta Kappan, 87*(2), 104-111.

Squire, K. D. (2004). Sid Meier's civilization III. *Simulations and Gaming, 35*(1).

Squire, K. D. (in press). Civilization III as a world history sandbox. In M. Bittanti (Ed.), *Civilization and its discontents. Virtual history. Real fantasies.* Ludilogica Press: Milan, Italy.

Steinkuehler, C. A. (2005). *Cognition & learning in massively multiplayer online games: A critical approach.* Unpublished Doctoral Dissertation, University of Wisconsin.

Suits, B. (1967). What is a game? *Philosophy of Science, 34.*

Sutton-Smith, B. (Ed.). (1979). *Play and learning.* New York: Gardner Press.

Sylva, K., Bruner, J. S., & Genova, P. (1976). The role of play in the problem-solving of children 3-5 years old. In J. S. Bruner, A. Jolly & K. Sylva (Eds.), *Play, its role in development and evolution.* New York: Basic Books.

Tichi, C. (1987). *Shifting gears : Technology, literature, culture in modernist America.* Chapel Hill: University of North Carolina Press.

Tripp, R. L. (1993). *The game of school : Observations of a long-haul teacher.* Reston, Va.: Extended Vision Press.

Tyack, D. (1974). *The one best system: A history of American urban education.* Cambridge: Harvard Univ Press.

Tyack, D., & Tobin, W. (1994). The grammar of schooling: Why has it been so hard to change? *American Educational Research Journal, 31*(3), 453-479.

Vygotsky, L. S. (1978). *Mind in society.* Cambridge, MA: Harvard University Press.

Wallbank, T. W., Schrier, A., Maier-Weaver, D., & Gutierrez, P. (1977). *History and life : The world and its people.* Glenview, Ill.: Scott, Foresman.

Wineburg, S. S. (1991). Historical problem solving: A study of the cognitive processes used in the evaluation of documantary and pictorial evidence. *Journal of Educational Psychology, 83*(1), 73-87.

Wineburg, S. S. (2001). *Historical thinking and other unnatural acts : charting the future of teaching the past.* Philadelphia: Temple University Press.

Wittgenstein, L. (1963). *Philosophical investigations* (English text reprint ed.). Oxford: Blackwell.
Zoch, P. A. (2004). *Doomed to fail : The built-in defects of American education.* Chicago: I. R. Dee.

David Shaffer
Educational Psychology, Curriculum and Instruction, and the Academic Advanced
Distributed Learning Co-Laboratory
University of Wisconsin-Madison

TRADITIONAL, HISTORICAL, AND CONVERSATIONS BETWEEN BRIDGING APPROACHES

Melding game design into instructional tools would seem a natural progression from traditional instructional design approaches to game design. After all, these techniques have achieved a substantial measure of success in the development of computer-based instruction at a variety of levels. From this perspective, the first chapter provides a discussion of the history of game design and use within instruction, and explores ideas of where the next realms of "meaningful discovery" will come within gaming and education.

Then, the subsequent chapter describes a traditional approach to the design of educational games, the history and substance of such an approach, and argues ultimately for methods for combining the positive aspects of game motivation with those of existing design. This chapter eavesdrops on a conversation about related insights, questions, and opinions from the standpoint of instructional designers and commercial game developers. In experiencing these perspectives, one can appreciate the rich history of designing for learning and the new possibilities that exist for creating meaningful (and fun) experiences.

RICHARD VAN ECK

SIX IDEAS IN SEARCH OF A DISCIPLINE

Okay, so there are really far more than six ideas in what we are now calling the field of digital game-based learning (DGBL), but with apologies to playwright Luigi Pirandello (1925), I made it six so the title would work. The title of his original play, *Six Characters in Search of an Author*, revolved around six characters in a play that had not yet been written. As an egregious example of placing the cart before the horse, this play also captures the essence of where I see the field of DGBL right now--more a collection of coherent but loosely organized ideas in search of a discipline. In this chapter, I propose to discuss ten critical tasks that can help define the field of DGBL, but of course this list is not exhaustive and many may disagree with the relative importance of each. Although this list reflects the ideas that seem most relevant to me, my purpose in outlining these ideas is to start, rather than end, a conversation.

In my opinion, DGBL is at a crossroads, and the choices we make right now will determine whether we become a field or fade away as just another "flavor of the day" in education and instructional technology. When we first began discussing DGBL in the late 80s, we were dismissed as, at best, educators who wanted to make learning "fun," and, at worst, contributors to the slow decline of standards, hard work, and the traditional school. Proponents of DGBL intuited that games could be effective tools for learning since much of what went on during gameplay required mental effort and focus. This was not enough to generate a persuasive argument, however, for two reasons.

First, these intuitions did not rise to the level of theory, which precluded even the design of research to study DGBL. To be sure, we had a rich history of research on play theory, and even on the use of games (e.g., board games, card games, math tournaments, and role playing) in limited domains (e.g., business, mathematics, and history). Digital computer games appeared to be different from earlier kinds of games, though, and inspired dreams of deeper learning and greater roles in learning environments because of their ability to engage learners in constant iterative cycles of thought, action, feedback without any human intervention. Games seemed a natural extension of our hopes and dreams for computer-based learning and individualized instruction, which many thought would revolutionize education.

Secondly, and perhaps most importantly, members of the educational establishment, at the urging of a traditional-minded citizenry, co-opted the argument: "school is not about fun, it's about learning." It didn't matter that DGBL

B. E. Shelton, D. A. Wiley (eds.), Educational Design & Use of Computer Simulation Games,31–60

proponents wanted the debate to be about learning theory, because what nearly everyone else focused on were the issues of fun and motivation (synonymous terms for many, but distinct concepts to educational researchers who see motivation more in terms of self-efficacy, goal setting, persistence, and perseverance). If we wanted a debate at all, we had to address these issues up front. So, those interested in taking games seriously as learning tools spent the better part of the next 25 years being just as vociferous in our contention that the impetus for using games as educational tools was about effective learning principles, NOT really about fun.

To back this up, in the 1980s and 1990s we conducted research on DGBL based on existing and newly developed theories such as situated cognition and learning (e.g., Brown, Collins, and Duguid, 1989), anchored instruction (e.g., Bransford, Sherwood, Hasselbring, Kinzer, & Williams, & the CTGV 1990; 1991; 1992a; 1992b; 1992c; 1993), and play theory (e.g., Rieber, 1996; Sutton-Smith, 1997; Crawford, 1982). We began to study how commercial games could be designed for educational use (e.g., *Jasper Woodbury*, CTGV, 1997) or built by students as programming and problem-solving activities (e.g., Yasmin Kafai, 1995). This research, as a whole, showed that the structure of digital games often reflects these powerful theories of learning which have themselves been validated with a variety of media, settings and learners during the latter half of the 20th century. In the meantime, games continued to become more sophisticated and more popular, and game players became older (!) and more a part of the educational systems we proposed to change.

All of this has come to a head in the last 6 years, resulting in a growing acceptance of games as effective learning tools. While we still hear the same arguments about play vs. work, for the most part the debate about *whether* games can play a part in learning is over. The question at the center of debate now is *how* games can play a part in learning. This is a question, however, that we are ill-equipped to answer. While we have begun to make the shift from proselytising to theories, models, and prescriptions. DGBL as a field is still in its infancy. We began to build a canon of scholarship and collected wisdom in the 90s through the contributions of books like Gredler's *Designing and Evaluation Games and Simulations* (1994), articles like Reiber's "Seriously Considering Play," and Malone and Lepper's theory of intrinsic motivation (1987).

This canon was expanded through contributions by Prensky (2001) and Aldrich (2004) at the turn of the new century, giving voice to arguments about the changing nature of learners in school and industry, and practical applications of games as learning and training tools. In the last 3 years, we've seen an explosion of articles and texts on games and learning, with journals that would not publish anything on games and learning now devoting entire issues to the topic, and books like James Gee's ground-breaking book *What Video Games Have to Teach Us about Learning and Literacy* (2003), which many view as the first scholarly text in DGBL in its struggle to become a field.

THREE CHALLENGES FACING DGBL

In spite of all this progress and acceptance of DGBL, we are in danger once again of having the debate co-opted. We do not yet have the theoretical and research base we need to establish guidelines for practice, and, while we have everyone's attention now, we do not yet know what to say. The longer that goes on, the more likely it is that the debate about how and why games can play a part in learning will move forward without us. The only argument we seem to have been successful in communicating to parents, teachers, and administrators is that we think games can be useful in learning: not how or why. This is not sufficient to guide practice. And yet, guidance for practice is precisely what DGBL will be asked to provide in the next 5 years.

While we have a promising base of research to draw on, previous studies fail to rise to the level of coherent theories and models of DGBL, which represents the first of what I see as three significant challenges facing DGBL. Why is it important to establish theories and models for DGBL? Because with validated theories and models we are more likely to establish effective practical guidelines for DGBL, which is the second challenge facing DGBL. Such guidelines, in turn, will allow us to establish a more coherent body of high-quality DGBL examples, which I see as the third challenge facing DGBL. This latter challenge is important for two reasons. First, this gives us the best chance to show early successes, which will keep momentum and interest going. Second, good examples are needed to help us further refine and validate our theories and models, and to generate new models and theories. This cycle (formulating and validating theories and models, developing guidelines for practice, and studying the resultant practice) represents the basic process that occurs in all established fields of scholarship, and is why DGBL is not currently a field, but rather a collection of ideas. Figure 1 presents an illustration of the research cycle needed in DGBL.

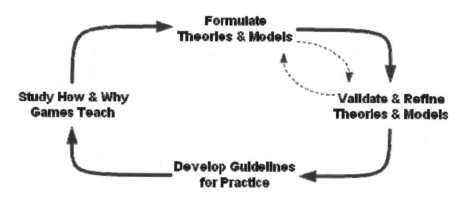

Figure 1. Research cycle for establishing DGBL as a discipline.

I mentioned earlier that there were ten tasks that I believe are necessary for DGBL to become a field, in fact, these ten tasks are a means of addressing the three significant challenges I've just outlined:

Challenge One: Generating & Validating DGBL Theories & Models
1. Develop new interdisciplinary models
2. Develop and evaluate tools for game analysis
3. Blend taxonomies of games and learning

Challenge Two: Generating Guidelines for Practice
4. Study games and problem-solving
5. Study "twitch" games and visual processing in professional practice
6. Reexamine and refine studies of sex differences in games
7. Study cultural differences in gameplay & design

Challenge Three: Generating a Body of high-quality DGBL
8. Extend research and design with artificial intelligence as a field and in games
9. Develop new discourse models for distributed learning & cognition
10. Develop authoring tools for content integration in intelligent learning games (ILGs)

As I've described above, these challenges are interdependent, and the success we have in meeting each successive challenge will be predicated on the success we have in meeting its predecessor, which makes it somewhat difficult to be precise about the later challenges. Obviously, if guidelines for practice must arise from theories and models of DGBL, which are themselves informed by practice, we can only talk about these challenges in an abstract fashion. Given the importance and complexity of the first challenge, the space limitations in this chapter, and that I have addressed challenges 2 and 3 in more detail elsewhere (Van Eck, 2006c; Van Eck, 2006a), I will devote the majority of the balance of this chapter to challenge one.

CHALLENGE ONE: GENERATING & VALIDATING DGBL THEORIES & MODELS

First and foremost, we *must* resist the temptation to define this field from within any single domain or community. There is a natural tendency to approach any new field from within the community in which we are most expert. This is not a bad thing, in that in doing so we bring to bear powerful theories and models that have stood the test of time in other disciplines, and this has important benefits to our field. However, *before* we take that approach, we must *also* be cognizant of the ways in which other disciplines and communities approach the same topic. One reason for this, of course, is to avoid reinventing the wheel--if someone has managed to define or validate a principle or concept already, it is a poor use of our time to do the same.

It is also important to recognize that efficiency, while desirable, is not even the most significant reason to be aware of other disciplines. The real sea changes in DGBL are likely to occur precisely at the intersection of multiple fields, disciplines, and communities and because of the synergy of ideas that can occur when multiple perspectives come to bear on a single issue. When we attempt to reconcile the similarities and differences between similar ideas in different disciplines (e.g., narrative theory from English and narrative psychology from cognitive psychology), we generate a dynamic interplay of ideas that quickly leads us to new theories (e.g., narrative in DGBL) that could not exist otherwise. What's more, these new theories then often have a generative effect, leading us back to still other related concepts in different disciplines (e.g., discourse theory in English and psychology and communication, and artificial intelligence and intelligent tutoring systems in cognitive psychology).

By looking to multiple fields throughout our scholarship, we are forced to consider already existing knowledge and ideas from a novice perspective, which allows for new insights not always possible by existing researchers within that discipline. There is value in reading with a fresh eye, not the least of which is that when theory does appear to be sufficient within one domain, we may find it in other domains and adapt it instead of creating new, un-informed theories within our own disciplines.

The problem is that we are not seeking out or recognizing those points of synergy between and amongst the different communities involved in DGBL (e.g., psychology, linguistics, English, education, communication, instructional design, and game development). The debate in the press, at conferences, and on ListServs like Serious Games is lively, passionate, and highly productive. The temptation, however, when ideas clash is to retreat into our own disciplines and generate what we see as "the answer" to the issues we discuss. That's OK, as long as we continue to share those ideas after we generate them and hold them up for scrutiny from multiple perspectives. This is why our texts MUST include texts as seemingly different as Raph Koster's *A Theory of Fun for Game Design* (2005), James Gee's *What Video Games Have to Teach Us About Learning and Literacy* (2003), Noah Wardrip-Fruin and Pat Harrigan's edited book *First Person: New Media as Story, Performance, and Game* (2004), Chris Crawford's *The Art of Computer Game Design* (1982), and Marc Prensky's *Digital Game-Based Learning* (2001).[1] Such disparate approaches are critical to understanding how and why games work, which is our first critical task in this process.

---

[1] And this is only one half of the debate! The other half arises from the generation and sharing of DGBL examples. Theories and models of DGBL cannot arise solely by means of philosophical debate and empirical studies; they must also be informed by a body of practice (e.g., lots of games). Likewise, we are not likely to develop great DGBL examples from the application of theory alone. Like most disciplines, DGBL is both an art and a science, and neither can privileged at the expense of the other. However, we have so LITTLE theory at this point that our attempts at practice (and to provide guidance to others) will meet with limited success without immediate attention to the scientific side of DGBL.

How Games Work

As I mentioned earlier, this is a more important question right now than the still more popular question of DO games work. We cannot begin to ask this question until we have some idea of why we think they may work under different circumstances. We all have our own ideas about how and why games work and therefore our own ideas of how to design or implement DGBL within a given domain and environment. It follows that not all of these ideas will turn out to be accurate. Therefore, not all of the designs and implementations thus generated will result in the desired evidence that games teach anything. At the end of the day, then, we would only be able to say that some games work for some people some of the time, but we couldn't say which games, which people, or which times. That's hardly the basis of a new field of study.

The good news is that many of us have already begun to lay out our theories of how and why games work. What actually remains to be done, however, is to synthesize these interdisciplinary theories into coherent models of DGBL. My purpose in this section will not be to definitively state how games work--there are many excellent texts and articles out there that attempt to answer that question. I have my own ideas about DGBL which I do not purport to be any more accurate or complete than anyone else's. I have outlined some of these ideas in other texts, in particular my chapter in *Games and Simulations in Online Learning: Research and Development Frameworks*, edited by David Gibson, Clark Aldrich, and Marc Prensky in which I discuss four principles of learning that immersive adventure and adventure hybrid games embody (Van Eck, 2006a):

- **Principle 1:** Games Employ Play Theory, Cycles of Learning, & Engagement
- **Principle 2:** Games Employ Problem-Based Learning
- **Principle 3:** Games Embody Situated Cognition & Learning
- **Principle 4:** Games Encourage Question-Asking Through Cognitive Disequilibrium and Scaffolding

These principles do not apply to all games, and my purpose in generating them was not to outline how games work in general, but to talk about how we might build intelligent learning games by drawing from multiple fields of research. This, in fact, is what I will close this chapter with, as it encompasses the last three of the ten areas I described earlier. The next section will describe some of the theories from which these principles arose. My hope is to illustrate the explanatory power of a multidisciplinary approach to DGBL, and how the synergy it generates can thus lead to new theories and models in this emerging discipline.

Cognitive Benefits of Games. There is a documented increase in average scores on intelligence tests across all cultures that use these tests. The increase was discovered by James Flynn, a political scientist from New Zealand, and was dubbed the Flynn Effect. The increase varies according to study and population, but overall it appears to equate to a three-point increase every ten years (e.g., Colom, Lluis-Font, & Andres-Pueyo, 2005). The increase tends to be in the lower half of the distributions of these tests, which has led to speculation that these increases were due to nutritional factors (e.g., Colom et al., 2005) but evidence exists for these increases even in countries during times where general nutrition declined (Wikipedia, 2006). Others speculated that the increases were the result of increased access to and time spent in education settings because the tests in part measure educational factors and content (e.g., Jensen, 1989), but tests such as the Raven Progressive Matrices (Raven, 1938) which are heavily weighted measures of general intelligence, or "g", that measure abstract, nonverbal reasoning using visual patterns, are among those that show the greatest increase (Johnson, 2005). Among the alternative explanations for this effect is the increase in leisure time across many cultures and the concomitant exposure to increasingly cognitively complex mass entertainment such as video games. Given recent evidence (e.g., Green & Bavalier, 2003) that video games improve visual processing of a variety of information, this hypothesis seems plausible (the Raven Progressive Matrices are heavily dependent on interpreting abstract visual patterns).

Whether one chooses to accept this hypothesis or not, it nevertheless raises some very interesting questions about games and cognition. What might the "cognitive complexity" of games look like, and how can it be explained by existing theory and research?

Play Theory. Play theory says that play is the most effective instructional technique regardless of domain. This conclusion is based largely on the observation that we learn more in the first years of life than we do in any other corresponding time in our lives (Lepper & Chabay, 1985). Only mammals and birds engage in play, indicating that the role of play in fostering higher learning is critical (Crawford, 1982). Rieber (1996) says research in "anthropology, psychology, and education indicates that play is an important mediator for learning and socialization throughout life" (p. 44) and that "Having children play games to learn is simply asking them to do what comes naturally. . . . However, playing a game successfully can require extensive critical thinking and problem-solving skills" (p. 52).

The problem, according to play theory, is that at some point in our development, play is replaced by work, which may account for poor motivation in schools today. In Kindergarten, the dominant mode of learning is play, and we accept that. As one progesses through higher grades, however, play is gradually decreased. By the time an individual enters the workforce, we see play as leisure rather than learning. "Work is respectable, play is not" (Rieber, 1996, p. 43), and so our school and work lives are dominated by work instead of play. Far from being opposites, however, play and work can be synonymous when work is its own reward (Rieber).

Play itself is complex, just as games and learning are complex processes. But complexity itself is not enough explanation; what is it about play and its attendant complexity that makes it so effective as an instructional strategy? Part of this answer can be derived from examining the interaction inherent in play activities. Play requires interaction--it is not possible to be passive during play. To be sure, play in its most free-form sense (e.g., kids in a backyard) appears to be unconstrained, but closer examination reveals that even such open-ended play is in fact guided by rules and goals, just as games are. These rules may change frequently during play, but they demand and constrain actions on the part of each player; anyone who does not "play by the rules" will suffer consequences (in the game, socially, or both).

The constant cycle of action and reaction that occurs in play also sheds light on the complexity and effectiveness of play. The turns we take in board games, at bat, or on offense and defense are a constant cycle of interaction. Likewise, when we roll dice, twirl spinners, perform an action, and respond the actions of those around us, we are actively participating and engaged in the activity in physical and/or mental ways. Each of our actions, in turn, results in some form of feedback, often contiguous to the action, whether social (from players) or informational (from the game materials and rules). This constant cycle of action, feedback, and reaction according to the constraints of the rules is in large part what drives the learning and engagement that occurs during games.

Flow. Mihalyi Csikszentmihalyi describes an internal state called flow, which he argues is the optimal learning state (1990). In flow, learners (or game players) are immersed to the extent that they lose track of time and the outside world. Connections between and among concepts are made rapidly, physical and mental efforts are perfectly synchronized, and every action flows one from the other in a seamless experience in which one's attention is completely absorbed.[2] Games (at least successful ones) promote flow. Flow and engagement, if not one and the same thing, are certainly highly related constructs within game experience. Players who rank games as "good" often report flow-like conditions (e.g., Lazzaro, 2004). This may be one reason that games are so effective at teaching.

Games Keep Players in the "Zone". Another theory, proposed by Vygotsky (1962, 1978), called the Zone of Proximal Development (ZPD) has some explanatory value for games and learning. This theory, loosely speaking, holds that there are three categories of tasks in learning. Those tasks that learners can accomplish autonomously, without any assistance, those that they cannot accomplish no matter how much assistance they are given (whether for developmental reasons, a lack of prerequisite skills, etc.), and those that are within their reach when provided minimal support (which he called scaffolding) by another. This last category of tasks define the ZPD, and represent the ideal state of learning. It may already have occurred to you that this "zone" may also be related to flow, in that flow during learning is most likely to occur within the ZPD. To promote maximum learning, learners should be in the ZPD for as much of the learning as is possible, and the scaffolding should be the minimum support necessary for the learner to make progress, and require the maximum cognitive effort on the part of the learner. When this happens, learning is encoded more effectively, connected to existing knowledge structures in more ways and more efficiently, and as a result is retained better.

---

[2] It should be noted that flow is not the same thing as "fun," although it MAY be the same thing as what Nicole Lazzaro (2004) calls "hard fun," nor are flow activities easy or even entirely pleasurable. Note that rock climbers exert a great deal of effort during climbs and may even injure themselves (pulled muscles, strained fingers, raw fingertips and scrapes, etc.), yet many report experiencing flow.

Consider now how games and game players interact. Raph Koster (2005) writes in his book of his observations of his children as they played tic-tac-toe. They enjoyed this game and played it frequently until suddenly, almost overnight, they stopped and never went back to it. They had mastered the game and realized it was a non-winnable game at that point. He also observed this in his own game play, as well as the opposite reaction in which a game he contemplated playing would result in a repeated cycle of failure. The games we engage in retain sufficient challenge for us that we cannot automatically solve them, yet not so much that they are beyond our reach. Challenge must be optimized for the learner in order for the game to be intrinsically motivating, for the learner to be in the ZPD, and for the learner to experience flow.

It is important to note that we are supported (scaffolded) within the game through several factors. First, games often have a tutorial mode or initial mission which, while ostensibly part of the fantasy world of the game, are in actually designed to bring all players up to a common set of prerequisite knowledge and skills. We can generally not proceed until we have demonstrated each of these skills, and with each error, the game provides scaffolding and support. For instance, in the war game *Medal of Honor: Allied Assault*, we begin in a boot camp where we master navigation (turning, moving, crouching, climbing, jumping) weapon and tool use, etc. In each case, we are given instructions and told to demonstrate the skills. If we wait too long, we are reminded and prompted (to hit the tab key to see our objectives or last instructions, for instance). Another example is in Star Wars: Knights of the Old Republic, which begins with a narrative movie that leads up to our character awakening to the calls of a friend who is there to help us get off the ship which is under attack. In reality, this is a training mission for interacting with the game, and he provides guidance if and as needed until we have mastered the progressively more complex skills and escaped. Once these missions are completed, we move on to the "real" game.

Secondly, games have levels of difficulty, with each level requiring more and more knowledge. Often, this entails combining previous skills (akin to assembling rules to solve novel problems) as well as new knowledge. As we master each level, we are promoted on to increasingly complex levels (leveling up). Novices then take a long time with early levels, while more skilled players move through initial levels quickly, but both eventually reach a level of appropriate challenge.

Thirdly, games often have difficulty settings, allowing the player to self-select the challenge level (e.g., easy, medium, difficult). Each selection requires more or less of the player as a result, allowing expert players to up the difficulty so that the early levels are more challenging, and the novice player to make it easier to complete these levels. What is interesting is that players will choose harder settings to challenge themselves--a factor not often seen when school children are working on traditional homework assignments!

Finally, games provide extensive and pervasive feedback in situated ways (pressing on a locked door produces an "oomph," and "It's locked! I'll have to find a key somewhere"). This constant scaffolding is buttressed by hint books, hints on the game website, cheats and walkthroughs generated by other game players which together provide enough resources for the player to self-regulate their progress and select just enough information at just the right time to continue to make progress.[3]

Accommodation, Assimilation, & Cognitive Disequilibrium. Piaget held, among other things, that knowledge was generated through individuals working with new information in a process of assimilation or accommodation. Assimilation occurs when we encounter new facts that are compatible with our existing schemas and mental models and we are able to fit that information into existing "slots". For example, when a child encounters granite for the first time and correctly identifies it as a "rock" because it shares characteristics with her mental model of rocks (hard, irregular in shape, etc.). Accommodation occurs when the internal representations of knowledge must be altered to accommodate the new information. For example, when a child sees a bear and mis-identifies it as a kind of dog because her model for dog is insufficiently constructed (e.g., anything with 4 legs and fur is a dog) and her parents warn her to run rather than pet it, she must accommodate the information by revising her model for dog AND generating another for bear. Assimilation is the easiest process, and accommodation the hardest. In reality, assimilation and accommodation co-occur regularly, which together accounts for many misconceptions (because we assimilate when really we should accommodate).

Piaget believed that the key accommodation was a process called cognitive disequilibrium. Cognitive disequilibrium occurs most often when assimilation fails[4] and we are confronted (either implicitly in the environment when we attempt to pet the bear and it attacks us, or explicitly through feedback and instruction, as when our parents yell for us to run away), by contradictory information. Put another way, when we think we know what something is and find that it is in fact something else, we are in a state of cognitive disequilibrium.

Games promote accommodation by generating cognitive disequilibrium. In fact, these two theories (ZPD and cognitive disequilibrium) go a long way toward explaining what makes a game engaging. If the challenge is too low, cognitive disequilibrium is never triggered. If challenge is too high, cognitive disequilibrium can never be resolved. Games engage by constantly presenting the player with challenges that are within their ability to solve, but which require significant effort to do so (enough that support is often required and provided within and without the game).

Problem Solving & Question Asking. But cognitive disequilibrium is only the starting point; resolving cognitive disequilibrium is where the learning actually takes place, and is another area in which games excel. What happens when cognitive disequilibrium is triggered is that the player automatically enters into a problem-solving mode in which hypotheses are formulated, tested, and revised

---

[3] If you would like to see this principle in action, come up behind a player in the middle of solving a game obstacle and give them the answer from a cheat sheet. I suggest you then move very quickly to avoid injury!

[4] It can also occur when accommodation fails, in that we mis-categorize something we observe as new information requiring modification of an existing model or requiring its own model, when in fact it is an unfamiliar instance of something that we already have a sufficient mental model of.

until accommodation (or assimilation) occurs. Games reward this kind of problem-solving; the very kind we hope to promote in scientific inquiry for instance. They are particularly successful at this in part because they are closed systems within which the player *knows* there is a solution, unlike in the real world when effort may be put forth forever with no resolution. This in turn promotes persistence, perseverance, and motivation, which in turn promote self-efficacy and autonomy.

This cycle of problem-solving is keyed by yet another theory of learning that games promote. Question asking (a part of the larger field of discourse) has been shown be critical to the learning process (Graesser and Person, 1994), which is critical to the learning process. Unfortunately, question-asking is rarely done (Otero & Graesser, 2001). Students generally ask 6-8 questions per hour (Graesser et al., 1999), for example, most of which are shallow (e.g., Graesser and Person, 1994). Research not only shows that question-asking is key to comprehension, problem solving, reasoning, and other cognitive activities, it also shows that students who are trained to ask good questions become better learners (Otero & Graesser, 2001).

Questions are also related to the concepts of self-regulation and metacognition in learning. Good learners constantly make predictions and ask themselves questions. Question asking itself is a way of activating and examining existing schemas which is key to effective encoding of new information. Questions help emphasize, refine, and build the relationships between and among concepts and ideas. Cognitive disequilibrium and concomitant problem-solving in games results in frequent question formulation and answering (assuming the player continues to interact with the game rather than quit).

Moving Beyond the Distinctions

These theories, and the many others that are discussed in DGBL, illustrate that DGBL is not so much a new way of learning so much as it is a very efficient way of embodying some of the most effective learning theories known to the learning sciences. There is a term in counseling called occupational psychosis, which refers to the tendency for us to view the world through the glass of our occupations. Thus, policemen tend to ascribe base motives to actions because this is what they see most of their professional lives. We have got to resist this kind of psychosis, to move beyond the distinctions created by our professions and to recognize that while there appear to be hard lines between disciplines and between the concepts and instantiations of theory within games, games are effective because they blur these lines rather than emphasize them. We tend to view learning as a discrete set of stages because doing so allows us to attend to those stages during the design process. However, when we then *preserve* those distinctions within the instruction, we make it nearly impossible to implement the kinds of learning that games do naturally. Assessment and practice are seamlessly integrated with knowledge acquisition within the game. One never learns something without demonstrating it if not immediately, then nearly so. One never demonstrates something without immediate feedback. One does not flounder within a game for long without getting (or seeking) scaffolding to allow them to move on. This type of assessment is radically different from our conceptual view of assessment within schools, which may help explain why our schools are failing in so many respects; we've replaced the natural modes of learning and assessment (play, situated practice, etc.) with artificial ones that strip all context from knowledge.

Just as the events of learning are seamless in games, so are many of the distinctions we make about the theoretical perspectives we take about DGBL. Games, instructional design, cognitive psychology, communication, etc. are all part of the same process when it comes to DGBL, and we have to stop making the distinction between games and learning that have characterized much of the debates between our professions as we struggle to become a discipline. In the next section, I will discuss some of the things that I think instructional design has to offer DGBL now.

Contributions of Instructional Design

I mentioned earlier that we must be cognizant of research and theories from multiple fields; one of the best ways to do that is to read what those in other fields have to say about DGBL and its related precepts from within those fields. It follows, then, that we must also write about DGBL from within our professions so that others can read and incorporate our ideas. There are three reasons why I think that instructional design can contribute meaningfully to the field of DGBL.

First, instructional design is itself and interdisciplinary field, having its origins in psychology, education, and communication. Essentially a systems view of designing learning and now human performance technology, it has evolved slowly over time as the intersection of these three fields. Many of the texts in our classes come from researchers and scholars in these fields as well, although we do not make those distinctions per se, and much of our research is published in journals within these and other fields (computer science, learning sciences, etc). So when we think about DGBL from an instructional design point of view, we are in some ways thinking about it from the perspective of all of these fields.

Second, instructional design takes a systems view of designing effective learning and performance solutions to human learning and performance problems in any setting, any domain, with any learner. This systems approach to analyzing, designing, developing, implementing, and evaluating instructional or performance solutions is particularly well-suited, in my opinion, to looking at DGBL. It forces one to consider the wide range of environmental, social, political, and individual learner characteristics in developing or implementing DGBL.

Third, the field of instructional design has its roots in the audio/visual instruction movement in the first half of the last century, which became the larger movement of media studies in general. Because of this, and because of the problems we've seen in technology integration during the last 30 years, instructional design is as often as not referred to as instructional design and *technology*. This latter term reflects both our origins and our adoption and participation in technology integration. We are used to examining, from a systems perspective, the strengths and weaknesses of a medium and aligning instructional outcomes with affordances of the medium. What follows, then, are some of the specific contributions of ID(T) to the emerging discipline of DGBL.

Not All Games Are Alike. There is a tendency to speak of all games as a single instructional medium. To be sure, this is accurate when speaking of the field as a whole, as we do when speaking of all books as "literature" and all movies as "cinema". But just as doing so collapses important boundaries in cinema, for example, (few would argue that the *Battleship Potemkin* is the same kind of movie as *Bill and Ted's Excellent Adventure*!) lumping all games together collapses critical differences in the function and role of different games. And it is not just a matter of genres, as the film examples above might seem to indicate; what film studies do is examine all of the critical features (cinematography, acting, direction, script, etc.) that make films unique. So while it sometimes makes sense to talk of games as a medium, and while it also makes sense to talk about different game genres (adventure, strategy, role-playing, etc.), it is also important to talk about the critical features and attributes of different kinds of games for supporting different kinds of experiences and interactions, which in turn has implications for instructional uses of games.[5]

Part of this can be addressed by differentiating the field by the use of terms like DGBL, which implies only computer or console games, but this does not go far enough, as computer games refers only to the medium of expression, and not the game itself. Card games, *Jeopardy*-style games, action games, and adventure games can all be digital in form, yet each will have it's own characteristics that make it more or less suited to different instructional uses. It follows, then, that depending on what kinds of skills one wants to foster in DGBL practice, different forms and styles of games will be required. This kind of analysis is one of the things instructional design has established models, heuristics, and procedures for doing.

In 1965, Robert Gagné (one of the founders of ID) published *Conditions of Learning*, in which he proposed five types (varieties) of learning: motor skills, attitudes, cognitive strategies, verbal information, and intellectual skills. Intellectual skills are further refined into five other categories, presented here in order of complexity from most to least: problem-solving, rules, defined concepts, concrete concepts, and discriminations (presented in order of complexity from most to least). Each of these varieties of learning require different types of instructional events and strategies. While this may seem to be common sense today, prior to this book all instruction was approached the same way, using the same activities and strategies for all types of learning (many still do!). By looking at the varieties of games and the varieties of learning at the same time, we can begin to see that there is a potential to developed blended game and learning taxonomies (e.g., see Van Eck, 2006a).

---

[5] I do not mean to imply that we should privilege the one over the other. As Raph Koster (2005) discusses, studying games as an art form is critical to advancing our understanding of games. However, the 'genrefication' of games is frequently done and masks critical features of games that must also be studied. My point here is to bring these distinctions to light so that they are also part of the process.

Another of Gagné's contributions to instructional design is in his Nine Events of Instruction (Gagné, 1965). Gagné examined the psychology literature on models of learning and both studied the educational literature on instruction and observed the best practices of teachers in the classroom. From these activities, he derived a series of internal events necessary for information processing, and a series of external events in instructional delivery that, when aligned with those internal events, produced the most effective teaching.

It is important to recognize that these events are not a new model for designing or delivering instruction as much as they are an instantiation of what the best learning and instructional practices have been since humans began the practice of instruction (formal and informal). Many people mis-characterize instructional design as a strictly linear, prescriptive process, with these principles serving as templates rather than models and heuristics. In fact, ID codifies those things that ALL effective instruction does, whether designed by an instructional designer or not. The purpose of these principles and models is to allow us to think about them while designing and developing instruction, NOT to apply each concept or element one after the other with no thought to creativity, engagement, etc. These are core principles of effective instruction, not templates for creating instruction. To represent them as the latter is to mistake the forest for the trees.

Gaining attention need not be the result of asking for attention (although that IS one way to do it). Another might be to walk up to the front of the room and throw money into the garbage can (a friend of mine did this prior to a speech on coin collecting). Both serve to gain attention, but one is more dramatic and effective than the other, and ALSO serves to set the stage for the second event (informing of the objective, which in this case is learning about money in a new way). The teacher in the movie *Dead Poets Society* tore pages out of books and threw them around the room as a way of gaining attention. The point is, there are many subtle ways to employ each of these events, sometimes at the same time, and sometimes repeated in different order (imagine only gaining attention once during an instructional activity that encompasses reading some text just after returning from lunch, and you'll see why some of these events need to be revisited many times!).Games are a perfect illustration of this point; few would argue that games use a linear, lock-step approach to teaching what it is they teach. Table 4 illustrates both the nine events and examples of the actual way they are employed in effective instruction such as commercial video games.

Table 4. Oil & Water, or Peaches and Cream?

Nine Events	Examples of Nine Events from Games
Gain Attention	Motion, cut scenes, noise, music, character speech, health meters, attacks, death
Inform of Objective	Documentation for the game, introductory movies, cut scenes, character speech, obstacles that limit movement or interaction
Recall Prior Knowledge	Environmental cues (e.g., in Laura Croft: Tomb Raider, ledges that look like those trained on in the earlier tutorial), obstacles (search for solutions involves recalling solutions and events from earlier in the game)
Present Instruction	All of the above (characters, environment, objects, puzzles and obstacles, conversation) arranged according to goals of game
Provide Guidance	Cut scenes, non-player character (NPC) or player character (PC) speech, hint books, cheats and walkthroughs, friends, partial solutions to puzzles (pressing on the wall makes it rumble, but it does not open). Also, much comes from the learner themselves as they process what has occurred in the game, but the arrangement of the actors and objects in the environment and the structure of the story itself also provide implicit guidance
Provide Practice	Players cannot progress through the game without demonstrating what they know or think they know—all knowledge is demonstrated within the confines of the game narrative and structure.
Provide Feedback	Character speech, sounds, motion, etc., Player gets past the obstacle or achieves the goal, or does not. Every action has immediate feedback, even if that feedback is that nothing happens.
Assess Performance	Movement through the game IS assessment. Nothing is learned that is not also demonstrated.
Enhance Retention & Transfer	Things learned early in games are brought back in different, often more complex forms later. Players know that what they learn will be relevant in the short and long term.

Developing Tools for Design and Evaluation

The two examples from the field of ID described above have direct bearing on both the theory and practice in DGBL, and show how our models can lead to heuristic tools for both research and practice, for analysis and evaluation. Without these models, theories, and practical guidelines, we cannot hope to answer the big questions that will face us in the next 5 years. The point is not to arrive at a set of prescriptive tools that will allow us to "connect the dots" and build great DGBL. Rather, we need these tools so that we can help scaffold the practice of generating DGBL in terms of critical attributes and characteristics. For instance, an heuristic for game strategies and learning outcomes does preclude the development of creative games that incorporate the art and creativity that characterize commercial game development today, but it WOULD help avoid the use of strategies that support verbal information (e.g., stating a rule) rather than problem-solving (demonstrating rules to generate solutions to problems).

We need, for example, to develop operational definitions of theories and models within games. What are the critical features of engagement, cognitive disequilibrium, and models of problem solving in games? I have argued that engagement may be a function of cognitive disequilibrium in games; how do we validate and measure these constructs? Can we develop tools and methods to support or even automate this process during design of new games or analysis of existing games? Can we create tools that are aware of these features and distinctions in ways that will facilitate communication with LMSs for instance? What are the implications for game design?

These are questions that can only be answered AFTER we have developed models and theories of DGBL, built the analysis and evaluation tools we need to study them within games, and conducted the research we need to validate and refine our models and theories.

As an example of how these theories and models may guide development and implementation of DGBL:

- **IF** we know the extent to which content is situated in games (situated cognition and learning), **THEN** we can make and test predictions about engagement and efficacy
- **IF** we understand how challenge and support are structured in games (ZPD & Intrinsic motivation) **THEN** we can predict and test if and how learners will stay in the ZPD, be engaged, etc.
- **IF** we know how often games generate cognitive disequilibrium (Piaget) **THEN** we can make predictions about whether those games will promote problem solving
- **IF** we know how content & prior knowledge are aligned (assimilation/accommodation & instructional design) **THEN** we can implement and test different support and strategies (scaffolding) for accommodation and assimilation
- **IF** we know how learning and game taxonomies align, **THEN** we can develop and test DGBL that should address appropriate learning levels

This is the kind of focused, theoretically driven base we need to develop in order to generate guidelines for DGBL, which is the focus of the second challenge facing DGBL.

CHALLENGE TWO: GENERATING GUIDELINES FOR PRACTICE IN DGBL

Part of this second challenge is a continuation of the first challenge, in that the models and theories we propose should be used to design studies to validate those same models and theories, and to refine and extend them where and when necessary. Likewise, we cannot develop guidelines for practice without conducting research on the effects of various principles and constructs like cognitive disequilibrium on learning, and on the interaction among these principles and game and learning taxonomies. In this sense, practice and research must proceed at the same time and in such a way that they constantly inform each other. The results of this process must then also inform our theories and models of DGBL as outlined in challenge one. In addition, questions regarding cultural, age, gender, and other individual differences in game preference, interaction, and learning will need to be vigorously pursued if we are to develop practical guidelines for where, when, how, and with whom DGBL is appropriate.

Studies of Games and Cognition

We should conduct studies of games and cognition, with engagement, cognitive disequilibrium, scaffolding, endogenous fantasy, game taxonomy, and challenge as independent variables, and learning taxonomy, motivation, and attitude as dependent variables. We should vary cognitive disequilibrium and endogenous fantasy and measure the effect on engagement and problem-solving, for instance, and should follow up with studies to measure the interactions of these independent variables. We should develop DGBL that is designed to address individual learning taxonomic levels and measure their effectiveness for learning and compare them to other forms of instruction. Does DGBL promote deeper learning, faster learning, and promote transfer? Under what conditions, and with whom? We MUST have studies to point to for each of these questions (even if they are too few to be anything but preliminary evidence). We need to be able to at lest point to one study for each of these questions to say "here is how we believe DGBL works in this regard, so work with this while we continue to refine and extend our knowledge." A focused research agenda could generate such studies for these questions in a year or two, but not if we are all working individually in a haphazard fashion.

We need to conduct longitudinal studies of games and cognition. One-shot, short term studies with small n's are valuable and necessary, but they are not sufficient to answer some of these questions. We know that problem-solving and transfer, two of the hottest areas in the learning sciences right now and two that many of us believe games can promote, cannot be taught directly as sets of rules or principles, but instead require multiple exposures in multiple domains over long periods of time if they are not to remain context-bound (e.g., Black & Schell, 1995; Bransford, Franks, Vye, & Sherwood, 1989; Bransford, Sherwood, Vye, & Rieser, 1986; Brown, Collins, & Duguid, 1989; Gagné, Wager, Goals, & Keller, 2005; Perkins & Salomon, 1989). Would playing certain kinds of games (e.g., adventure/strategy games) for a school year be enough to increase problem-solving? For how many hours per week? Could this be done outside of normal class time? Only longitudinal studies can answer these kinds of questions. Likewise, for the less labor intensive forms of DGBL (games at the lower learning taxonomic levels) it should be possible to conduct studies with large enough ns to warrant more confident conclusions, and in fact SOME researchers should have it in their power to conduct such large scale studies for even higher order cognitive skills. Carrie Heeter and Brian Winn (in press) have recently completed a study of a game they developed to teach about evolution, in which 292 students participated online, for instance.

We should also study action games to see what kinds of practical applications there are for games in different professions. Kirkpatrick's four levels of evaluation (1994) lists the highest levels as transfer (level 3) and results (level 4). Just as with most learning taxonomies and instruction, typical evaluation rarely reaches these highest levels. This is also true of many of the studies we do generate; we have little evidence for the generalizability (transfer) of results to real world settings, and little ability to state the strength of the effects (results). For example, one of the most compelling and rigorous studies of games in the last 5 years was conducted by Shawn Green and Daphne Bavalier at the University of Rochester (2003).

This study showed that video game players had better visual processing skills (they could keep track of more objects at a time, could track moving objects better, were more accurate in their counting of objects, and had faster reaction times throughout) than non-video game players. What made their study so much more compelling, however, was that they then trained non-video game players on an action video game for ten hours (one hour per day) over two weeks, and found nearly identical performance among these players, thus indicating both a causal link for action games and visual processing, and that these were skills that could be improved rather than abilities that explain why some people play games and others do not.

Yet even this study falls short of the kind of research we need to support DGBL. What people are going to want to know for implementation is where, when, and with whom these things will make a difference. We need to extend these studies and build on each other's research to find the answer to these questions. For example, we have just completed a study of air traffic control tower students and video game play at the University of North Dakota's John D. Odegard School or Aerospace Sciences that builds upon the findings of the Green and Bavalier study. It occurred to us that if 10 hours of video game play could improve people's ability to count and track stationary and moving objects, and to do so faster than otherwise possible, air traffic control tower operators might benefit in meaningful (applied) ways both in tower and radar operations.

It also occurred to us that if what appeared to be more abilities than skills could actually be improved this dramatically, other "stable" abilities like the cognitive style of field-dependence field-independence (visual processing of figures) might be similarly impacted, so we included the Group Embedded Figures Test (GEFT, Witkin, Oltman, Raskin, and Karp, 1971), which has been shown to be related to a variety of academic performance measures, as a dependent variable. The results of this study are not available at this writing, but have practical implications for the training of aviation students and perhaps for all students. We need to conduct studies of the effect of different games and game strategies on different performance outcomes, but we also need to take the next step and determine what difference in the real world (professional and educational) these outcomes will make.

Studies of Individual Differences in DGBL

One of the biggest challenges facing instructional design right now is that the increased global presence of companies and the trend toward outsourcing and online training requires that we be able to develop training for multiple cultures within a single company. The best we have been able to do is to develop "cultural value-free" training that is then "localized" by instructional designers living and working within the different cultures the training is to be delivered.[6] This is because we don't really KNOW what those cultural differences might be, having not made such studies a priority despite repeated calls by many to do so over the last 10 years.

This issue will be critical to DGBL as well, for three reasons. First, and most obviously, education and learning are global endeavors now, and the increase in online learning alone is enough to justify studies of cultural differences in game preference, interaction, and learning. Second, our classes and training rooms are comprised of people from multiple cultures[7], so if we are to implement DGBL anywhere, we will have to consider these cultural differences. Third, just as game players are likely to differ in game play and preference, so are game *researchers and practitioners* likely to differ in the games they create, implement, and study. Some of the most interesting findings and approaches are likely to come from different countries as a result, just as multiple disciplines generate powerful synergies in DGBL research. I was an invited speaker in the U.K. Open University (July, 2006), and during one recent conversation on definitions of games, a student posted the link to Jesper Juul's keynote defining games (2003) a version of which also appears in the Waldrip and Fruin (2004) text. During this same conversation, someone mentioned an "eLearning" course provided at the Pädagogiche Hochschule Zürich, Switzerland (a university for applied sciences in teaching) that was called 'gender for beginners & eLearning'. The idea was for participants to take on different identities and roles within an online environment. While not a game, the implications for research in DGBL are obvious, yet I would never had come across it if not for cross-cultural communication, and the idea itself may have been partly a product of the cultural views of gender and technology.

A good place to begin these studies, it seems to me, is to examine the sales of different games in different countries. Are the same games popular? Where do popularity of games diverge by country? What games are popular? Once we find this information, we could conduct analyses of these individual games to see what the features and characteristics are, compare that to the literature on cultural differences in general, and begin to formulate (and validate) models and theories for cultural differences in DGBL. It is the individual features of game play that are most critical in this regard rather than the larger question of "what kinds of games do [people from country x] prefer?"

---

[6] Actually, there is no such thing a culturally value-free training, as we are learning, any more than there are "neutral" observers in ethnographic research.
[7] And by the way, "culture" and "country" are non-equivalent terms.

The need for the study of individual differences in DGBL is not just limited to culture, either. Age and gender are two other potential sources of individual differences in game play and preference. In particular, I believe we need to re-examine sex differences in game and strategy preference. Much of the research in this area is out of date, and while people are re-examining these questions (e.g., Heeter, 2003; Van Eck et al., 2006d, and the upcoming *Beyond Barbie and Mortal Kombat* edited by Jasmin Kafai, Carrie Heeter, Jill Denner, and Jen Sun), much of what can be found today repeats what has become conventional wisdom regarding girls and games. Yet if digital natives are different, then aren't more girls now digital natives than were so in the 90s when much of the research on girls and games was conducted? How much of what was true then is true now? There is some evidence that at least some things have changed.

For example, we conducted a year-long study of DGBL both in terms of game play and game design with 5th and 6th grade students. For half a year, they came in and played a different computer game for one hour each week (games were chosen to equalize exposure to the full range of game types). For the second half of the year, they designed their own games. They worked in groups of 5 (all boy, all girls, 3 boy/2 girl, and 3 girl/2 boy), and we collected data on the games they preferred and on their attitudes toward technology, math, and science. Conventional wisdom led us to believe that girls would do best in the all-girl groups, that girls would in general not like games or would prefer "girl" games (e.g., *Rockett's New School*), and that girls and boys would think technology was not equally appropriate for boys and girls.

Interestingly, the first thing we found was the most girls (and boys) believe technology was appropriate for both sexes, which immediately contradicted one expectation. Further, we found that girls attitudes remained unchanged in this regard, whether they were in all girl groups, boy majority groups, or boy minority groups, thus negating a second expectation based on conventional wisdom and prior research. Boys in the girl majority group, however, came to believe technology was less appropriate for girls than they had initially! Both boys and girls, incidentally, came to believe that science, math, and technology were both not as related or difficult as they had at the start of the study, indicating that game play and game design can improve attitude toward technology. Finally, while we found that there *were* sex differences in game preference (girls did and boys did not like *Rockett's New School*, and boys did and girls did not like *Battlezone*), boys and girls liked adventure games equally, even to the point that boys liked *Nancy Drew* (after they had stopped groaning and started actually playing it!).

And even in the games they both reported liking, the *way* they chose to play those games differed dramatically. With the game *Sim Safari,* for instance, which both boys and girls rated highly, girls focused on building houses with plumbing, Jacuzzis, etc., validating Maslow's hierarchy of needs in terms of shelter and safety. Boys, in turn, built swamps and immediately overpopulated them with alligators and jaguars!

This latter aspect highlights an important aspect of these studies. We should look not just to game genre preference, but to differences in game*play* and feature or strategy preference within games, as this is likely to be most informative for individual differences in DGBL as a whole. Finally, we must examine differences in all aspects of DGBL, including styles of problem solving, differences in the roles or features engagement and cognitive disequilibrium, support and scaffolding, etc. If we don't do this, we have little hope of meeting challenge three.

CHALLENGE THREE: GENERATING A BODY OF HIGH-QUALITY DGBL

Clearly, the long-term success of DGBL will rely on implementation that is guided by validated interdisciplinary models and theories, the research that springs from them. Our practice is also likely to be most successful if we use the outputs of the first two challenges to develop DGBL practices within a framework of the learning sciences. In particular, I believe instructional design has a lot to offer, whether we are talking about integrating commercial games into the curriculum, developing instructional games from the ground up, or having students develop games.

Much of how I believe instructional design can contribute to this process can be found in earlier work (integrating commercial games: Van Eck, 2006c; designing learning games: Van Eck & Dempsey, 2002; Van Eck, 2006a). Just as theory has to guide our analysis, evaluation, and research with games, so must it guide our implementation of games in learning environments for instructional purposes. It is important to make a distinction here between instructional uses of games, and the use of games to promote non-specific skills and abilities. Some of our early research will undoubtedly point the way toward the use of games to promote certain non-domain specific abilities. Put another way, we will find that games promote implicit or enabling skills that in turn support the development of expertise in specific domains of practice.

So while games have the ability to promote all varieties of learning, some learning will be accomplished as general training (e.g., improving reaction times, visual processing, dexterity, attitude toward content) and others will be the result of specific instructional designs within different content areas (e.g., using *Civilization* to teach problem-solving and concepts in history, developing games to teach problem-solving, transfer, rules, and concepts in mathematics, or using jeopardy style games to teach verbal information).

As I alluded to at the beginning of this section, there are three ways to implement DGBL in school and corporate settings. We can have learners design and develop games, we can integrate commercial games into the curriculum, or we can build games to teach from the ground up. Each of these approaches has its strengths and weaknesses, and each has its place in the practice of DGBL. Having learners design games is of primary use in educational settings, and is largely non-instructional as I have defined earlier, so I will not spend much time on this approach except to say that we should continue both the practice and the study of this approach to DGBL.

The other two approaches, integrating commercial games into the curriculum and building instructional games, have a far shorter history and one characterized by much more inconsistent success. As a result of this, and because they are both designed to directly address domain-specific instructional content, instructional design can play a critical role in guiding our practice in both approaches. I have described this process for both approaches elsewhere in far more detail than is possible or necessary here (Van Eck, 2006a; Van Eck, 2006c). Instead, I will briefly describe these approaches and discuss the particular advantages and challenges of each in establishing a rich body of practice in DGBL.

Integrating Commercial Off-the-Shelf (COTS) DGBL

COTS DGBL has been shown to be effective (e.g., McFarlane, Sparrowhawk, & Heald, 2002), which is one of the reasons that the NESTA FutureLab & Entertainment Arts game company have partnered to study the use of games in classrooms in the U.K. (2005). It is, in my opinion, among the most practical approaches for quickly building a body of practice in DGBL, for two reasons. First, the costs of developing games preclude this use by most educators; commercial games are much more practical to use from an economic standpoint. Certainly, the open-source game engines like *Neverwinter Nights* and other inexpensive engines and game development platforms are beginning to change this, but cost is not the only issue. The learning curve and development time required for building games are prohibitive for widespread adoption and implementation by teachers, and while this too is changing, there is a limited number of people who will avail themselves of this approach for the next few years, which in turn constrains the number of games (and thus DGBL examples) available to us. To be sure, COTS DGBL is not an effortless process, and teachers need instructional support initially as they learn how games work, how they can be tied to curriculum goals, standards, and objectives, and how to design instructional and assessment activities around them, but the essential skills sets are within their reach in ways that is not true for other forms of DGBL.

So why does it matter how many people are involved in this, and why should we care how many educators we can get involved? We need to show game development companies and textbook publishers that there is widespread use and interest for games in the classroom. Until we show there is an economic base for games in learning environments, we will have limited success in convincing both industries to pursue the development of serious games. While we may argue until we are blue in the face that the failure of the edutainment industry in the 80s was caused in equal parts by bad business models and marketing, and by poor integration (if that word can even be used) of content within games, but the fact remains that a lot of people lost a lot of money in edutainment, and they are understandable gun-shy about anything that even smells like education. We have to build a critical mass of DGBL practice in the classroom to encourage a re-investment in the process. Game developers are the engines for this development, and textbook publishers will be the vehicle for aligning games with content (with the help of instructional design).

To effectively support this kind of DGBL, we must do three things. First, we need to build collections of examples of DGBL organized in databases that are searchable by standards, grade level, game, etc. There are a limited number of early adopters who will build lesson plans around games. There are more who, if given examples and ways to search for examples appropriate to their needs, will then implement DGBL. There is a third group who, upon seeing respected peers within their institutions implementing COTS DGBL successfully, will seek out support from these people to find out how to do the same thing. As these second two groups become comfortable implementing previously designed COTS DGBL, many will consider developing their own examples, which can in turn serve as examples to others. Such databases will expand the reach of COTS DGBL beyond the innovators and early adopters.

Integrating commercial off-the-shelf involves re-purposing and integrating commercial games within a given class, lesson, unit, or curriculum. There are several challenges to doing this effectively which are not immediately apparent to many at first glance. Instructional design takes a systems view of instruction, including the environment, learner, content, resources, strategies, and technology. This systems approach is manifested in instructional design models, all of which share the same essential characteristics despite being designed for different purposes and philosophies. These characteristics are Analysis (of the learner, content, outcomes, environment, etc.), Design (of the instruction, including objectives, assessment, strategies, media), Development (of the instruction, based on the design specifications), Implementation, and Evaluation. This process is often called ADDIE (add-ee) for short. While the ADDIE process is not specifically designed to support the re-purposing of media (like games), the principles are useful in developing curriculum that makes use of games as an instructional medium or strategy. I have outlined the process needed to integrate (COTS) games into the curriculum elsewhere (Van Eck, 2006c) and in much more detail than space permits here. Suffice it to say that while COTS DGBL requires effort and resources to do well, instructional design provides a useful set of tools and processes to support this process, which is well within the capabilities of teachers working within the constraints of the existing curriculum and school system.

Building Games from the Ground Up

The second way of establishing a body of DGBL is to build games to teach different subjects. The advent of several new game development tools and engines, the decreasing learning curve for these tools, and the increasing skills of those interested in building learning games have all converged to make this a much more viable option than even 3 years ago. There is also a growing interest among individual game developers, if not companies, in Serious Games, and I suspect that we will see a significant increase in the number of learning games available. Once again, the design of these games must be guided by both the science of learning and the theories, models, and tools I have described earlier in the discussion about challenge one. These games will also benefit from the use of instructional design models and principles, in that ID will safeguard the still significant investment of time and effort it takes to build serious games.

There are hundreds of researchers and game developers who are working on building these Serious Games, and the body of DGBL created is both advancing the field through practice and providing good examples for study. One particular way of building DGBL[8] that holds a great deal of potential lies in what I call intelligent learning games (Van Eck, 2006a). This approach relies on interdisciplinary theory and tools from, among others, artificial intelligence, narrative psychology, pedagogical agents, authoring tools, and discourse studies. ILGs are a concrete example of the synergy and efficiencies that exist by taking an interdisciplinary approach to DGBL: validated tools and models, a rich base of research studies to draw from, and a convergence of several compatible approaches to generate powerful learning tools in a short period of time. ILGs are what account for three of the 10 areas for research I postulated at the beginning of this chapter, artificial intelligence, new models of discourse & distributed learning, and authoring tools & EPSSs for content integration, and they will all be addressed within the context of building ILGs.

Integrating Content in Games without Killing the Game.
This has been one of the most significant challenges we have faced in designing serious games, and it still dominates most of our professional and personal discussions in this regard. Traditional approaches have been more about *combining* games and content rather than *integrating* them. Yet we know that a strength of games is that content is seamlessly integrated within the game, with progress toward achieving the learning objectives being continually assessed as learners are required to demonstrate mastery. We know that putting a "book" in a game to deliver large amounts of text-based instruction is NOT integration, yet such are the approaches that have characterized our early attempts at building educational games. We need to find ways to make the content a part of the game world.

If we look at many immersive adventure, strategy, and role-playing games today, we find that it is typical to interact with several characters (either NPCs, non-player characters controlled by the game AI, or PCs, player characters controlled by other game players). There exists in psychology and instructional design a growing body of research on what are called pedagogical agents. Pedagogical agents are animated characters (real or fantastic) akin to NPCs. The computer-based instruction they are embedded in controls what they say and how they say it.

It is not much of a stretch to see how agents could be used in ILGs, then. They have the potential to become characters in game, adopting roles that are consistent with games (e.g., co-investigator, mentor, police experts, military commanders at

---

[8] And I want to emphasize, this is only one way of doing so. It is, however, a way that leverages a great deal of research and theory from multiple fields over the last 30 years, which is something I have been arguing for as a means of advancing DGBL as a discipline.

command central, a team member like in the Mayo clinic model of healthcare, or simply a colleague or peer who has relevant content expertise.

PAs may offer potential for the integration of content in games, but they do little in the way of providing guidance. By combining them with another learning technology from cognitive psychology and AI called intelligent tutoring systems (ITS), we get not only a way of integrating content in games, but of structuring that content for effective learning. ITSs work by engaging the learner in a tutoring conversation to elicit from the learner as much as possible as they solve a problem within a given domain. The ITS, many of which now incorporate agents, uses a variety of sophisticated technologies (natural language generation, latent semantic analysis, speech act classification, algorithms to determine matches to expected responses and selection of suitable responses for those that are unexpected). It is possible, then, that they could be used to structure and deliver content through PAs as part of game environments as well, and in fact many researchers have called for the blending of ITSs with other technologies such as AI, agents, & games (Laird & van Lent, 1999), ITSs and immersive environments (Ravenscroft & Matheson, 2002; Regian, Shebilske, & Monk, 1992; Rickel, 2001; Shute & Psotka, 1996).

These ITSs have been shown, over the course of the last 30 years, to be nearly as effective as human tutors (Corbett et al., 1999) in many domains (Graesser et al., 1999; Anderson, Boyle, & Reiser, 1995; Schofield and Evans-Rhodes, 1989; Gertner & VanLehn, 2000; VanLehn, 1996; Stevens & Collins, 1977). Part of their success lies in the power of discourse, and the role in particular of questions, hints, and prompts.

Hints and prompts, of course, are used as scaffolding to keep the learner in the ZPD, which we have seen is one of the principles inherent in game design, so the potential for integrating ITSs with the game world exists. And in fact, games often make overt use of questions and hints, such as when a list of possible questions is presented when talking to an NPC, or when the game provides time reminders or even verbal communications from NPCs to keep the learner on track.

So pedagogical agents, ITSs, and discourse theory (all theories and learning technologies from multiple disciplines) can be synthesized to guide the development of DGBL. Obviously, this is a much more complex process than the brevity of this description implies. I describe this process in much more detail elsewhere (Van Eck, 2006a).

SUMMARY

I set out to discuss ten areas that are critical to study in order to help establish DGBL as a discipline. Those ten areas are derived from what I see as three challenges facing DGBL in the next five years:

Challenge One: Generating & Validating DGBL Theories & Models
1. Develop new interdisciplinary models
2. Develop and evaluate tools for game analysis
3. Blend taxonomies of games and learning

Challenge Two: Generating Guidelines for Practice
4. Study games and problem-solving
5. Study "twitch" games and visual processing in professional practice
6. Reexamine and refine studies of sex differences in games
7. Study cultural differences in gameplay & design

Challenge Three: Generating a Body of high-quality DGBL
8. Extend research and design with artificial intelligence as a field and in games
9. Develop new discourse models for distributed learning & cognition
10. Develop authoring tools for content integration in intelligent learning games (ILGs)

By now I hope it is clear that each of these challenges relies, in the long-term, on our having met the preceding challenges. Obviously, we cannot literally wait until each is completely achieved. Be we must be aware of the interrelated nature of each challenge, and we must address the most pressing questions which I have attempted to outline here. If we can begin to answer these questions for ourselves and for those who will soon need the answers (even if they do not ask the questions), we will make the transition to a field and discipline. We have a window of opportunity here, and the need for real educational reform may never have been stronger, but that window will not stay open forever.

REFERENCES

Aldrich, C. (2004). *Simulations and the future of learning: An innovative (and perhaps revolutionary) approach to e-learning*. San Francisco: Pfeiffer.

Anderson, J. R., Boyle, C. B., & Reiser, B. J. (1985). Intelligent tutoring systems. *Science, 228*, 456-462.

Black, R. S., & Schell, J. W. (1995, December). Learning within a situated cognition framework: Implications for adult learning. Paper presented at the annual meeting of the American Vocational Association, Denver, CO. (ERIC Document Reproduction Service No. ED 389 939)

Bransford, J. D., Franks, J. J., Vye, N. J., & Sherwood, R. D. (1989). New approaches to instruction: Because wisdom can't be told. In S. Vosniadou & A. Ortany (Eds.), *Similarity and analogical reasoning* (pp. 470-497). New York: Cambridge University Press.

Bransford, J. D., Sherwood, R. D., Hasselbring, T. S., Kinzer, C. K., & Williams, S. M. (1990). Anchored instruction: Why we need it and how technology can help. In D. Nix & R. Spiro (Eds.), *Cognition, education, multimedia: Exploring ideas in high technology* (pp. 115-141). Hillsdale, NJ: Erlbaum.

Bransford, J., Sherwood, R., Vye, N., & Rieser, J. (1986). Teaching thinking and problem solving. *American Psychologist, 41*(10), 1078-1089.

Brown, J. S., Collins, A., & Duguid, P. (1989). Situated cognition and the culture of learning. *Educational Researcher, 18*, 32-42.

Cognition and Technology Group at Vanderbilt. (1990). Anchored instruction and its relationship to situated cognition. *Educational Researcher, 10*(6), 2-10.

Cognition and Technology Group at Vanderbilt. (1991). Technology and the design of generative learning environments. *Educational Technology, 31*(5), 34-40.

Cognition and Technology Group at Vanderbilt. (1992a). An anchored instruction approach to cognitive skill acquisition and intelligent tutoring. In J. W. Regian and V. J. Shute (Eds.), *Cognitive approaches to automated instruction* (pp. 135-170). Hillsdale, NJ: Erlbaum.

Cognition and Technology Group at Vanderbilt. (1992b). The Jasper experiment: An exploration of issues in learning and instructional design. *Educational Technology Research and Development, 40*(1), 65-80.

Cognition and Technology Group at Vanderbilt. (1992c). The Jasper series as an example of anchored instruction: Theory, program description, and assessment data. *Educational Psychologist, 27*(3), 291-315.

Cognition and Technology Group at Vanderbilt. (1993). Anchored instruction and situated cognition revisited. *Educational Technology, 33*(3), 52-70.

Cognition and Technology Group at Vanderbilt. (1996). Multimedia environments for enhancing learning in mathematics. In S. Vosniadou, E. De Corte, R. Glaser, & H. Mandl (Eds.), *International perspectives on the design of technology-supported learning environments* (pp. 285-305). Mahwah, NJ: Erlbaum.

Cognition and Technology Group at Vanderbilt. (1997). *The Jasper Project: Lessons in curriculum, instruction, assessment, & professional development*. Mahwah, NJ: Erlbaum.

Colom, R., Lluis-Font, J.M., and Andrés-Pueyo, A. (2005). The generational intelligence gains are caused by decreasing variance in the lower half of the distribution: Supporting evidence for the nutrition hypothesis. *Intelligence 33*, pp. 83-91.

Crawford, C. (1982). *The art of computer game design*. Out-of-print book retrieved November 12, 2006, from the World Wide Web: http://www.vancouver.wsu.edu/fac/peabody/game-book/Coverpage.html.

Csikszentmihalyi, M. (1990). *Flow: The psychology of optimum experience*. New York: Harper Perennial.

Gagné, R. M. (1965). *Conditions of Learning*. New York: Holt, Rinehart and Winston.

Gagne, R. M., Wager, W. W., Golas, K. C., and Keller, J. M. (2005). *Principles of instructional design*. 5th ed. Belmont, CA: Wadsworth/Thomson Learning.

Gee, J. P. (2003). *What video games have to teach us about learning and literacy*. New York: Palgrave MacMillan.

Gertner, A. & VanLehn, K.(2000) Andes: A coached problem solving environment for physics. In G. Gauthier, C. Frasson & K. VanLehn (Eds), *Intelligent tutoring systems: 5th international conference*. Berlin: Springer.

Graesser, A. C., & Person, N. K. (1994). Question asking during tutoring. *American Educational Research Journal, 31*, 104-137.

Graesser, A. C., Wiemer-Hastings, K., Wiemer-Hastings, P., Kreuz, R. & Tutoring Research Group. (1999). AutoTutor: A simulation of a human tutor. *Journal of Cognitive Systems Research, 1*, 35-51.

Gredler, M. (1994). *Designing and evaluating games and simulations: A process approach*. Houston, TX: Gulf Publishing.

Green, C. S., and Bavelier, D. (2003) Action video game modifies visual selective attention. *Nature, 423*, 534-537.

Heeter, C. (2003). Girls as designers. Unpublished study funded by the NSF to examine the role of gender in game design.

Heeter, C., and Winn, B. (in press). Designing gender-enhanced games for classroom learning in Yasmin Kafai, Carrie Heeter, Jill Denner, and Jen Sun (Eds.) *Beyond Barbie and Mortal Kombat: New perspectives on gender and computer games*, Boston, MA: MIT.

Jensen, A. R. (1989). Rising IQ without increasing g? [A review of The Milwaukee Project: Preventing mental retardation in children at risk]. *Development Review, 9*, 234-258.

Johnson, S. (May, 2005). Dome improvement. *Wired*, 13.05.

Juul, J. (2003). The game, the player, the world: Looking for a heart of gameness. In Marinka Copier and Joost Raessens (eds) *Level up: Digital games research conference proceedings*, Utrecht: Utrecht University, 30-45. □ http://www.jesperjuul.net/text/gameplayerworld/

Kafai, Y. B. (1995) *Minds in play: Computer game design as a context for children's learning*. Hillsdale, NJ: Lawrence Erlbaum Associates.

Kafai, Y. B., Heeter, C., Denner, J., Sun, J. (in press). *Beyond Barbie and Mortal Kombat*. Boston, MA: MIT.

Kirkpatrick, D.L. (1994). *Evaluating training programs: The four levels*. San Francisco, CA: Berrett-Koehler.

Koster, R. (2005). *A theory of fun for game design*. Scottsdale, AZ: Paraglyph.

Laird, J. E., & van Lent, M. (2000). Human-level AI's killer application: Interactive computer games. *AAAI/IAAI*, pp. 1171-1178.

Lazzaro, N. (2004). Why we play games: Four keys to more emotion without story. Online article retrieved from the World Wide Web on July 15, 2006, from http://www.xeo design.com/xeodesign_whyweplaygames.pdf.

Lepper, M. R., & Chabay, R. W. (1985). Intrinsic motivation and instruction: Conflicting views on the role of motivational processes in computer-based education. *Educational Psychologist, 20*(4), 217-230.

Malone, T. W., & Lepper, M. R. (1987). Making learning fun: A taxonomy of intrinsic motivations for learning. In R. E. Snow & M. J. Farr (Eds.), *Aptitude, learning and instruction: III. Conative and affective process analyses* (pp. 223-253). Hillsdale, NJ: Lawrence Erlbaum.

McFarlane, A., Sparrowhawk, A., & Heald, Y. (2002). Report on the educational use of games: An exploration by TEEM of the contribution which games can make to the education process. Retrieved July 15, 2006 from http://www.teem.org.uk/publications/teem_gamesined_full.pdf.

NESTA Futurelab, (2006). *Close to 60% of UK teachers want computer games in the classroom*. Retrieved July 13, 2006, from http://www.nestafuturelab.org/about_us/press_releases/pr11.htm.

Otero, J., & Graesser, A.C. (2001). PREG: Elements of a model of question asking. *Cognition & Instruction 19*, 143-17.

Perkins, D. N., & Salomon, G. (1989). Are cognitive skills context-bound? *Educational Researcher,* 18(1), 16-25.

Pirandello, L. (1925). *Six characters in search of an author.* Rome, Italy: Newton Compton.

Prensky, M. (2001). *Digital game-based learning.* New York: McGraw-Hill.

Raven, J.C., (1938). *The raven progressive matrice*s. Scotland: JC Raven, Ltd.

Ravenscroft, A., & Matheson, M. P. (2002). Developing and evaluating dialogue games for collaborative e-learning. *Journal of Computer Assisted Learning 18*(1), pp. 93-101.

Regian, J. W., Shebilske, W. L., & Monk, J. M. (1992). Virtual reality: An instructional medium for visual-spatial tasks. *Journal of Communication, 42*(4), 136-149.

Rickel, J. (2001). Intelligent virtual agents for education and training: Opportunities and challenges. Paper presented at the *IVA 2001,* Berlin.

Rieber, L. P. (1996). Seriously considering play: Designing interactive learning environments based on the blending of microworlds, simulations, and games. *Educational Technology Research and Development, 44*(2), 43-58.

Schofield, J. W. & Evans-Rhodes, D. (1989). Artificial intelligence in the classroom. In D. Bierman, J. Greuker, & J. Sandberg (Eds.), *Artificial intelligence and education: Synthesis and reflection* (pp. 238-243). Springfield, VA: IOS.

Shute, V. J., & Psotka, J. (1996). Intelligent tutoring systems: Past, Present and Future. In D. Jonassen (Ed.), *Handbook of Research on Educational Communications and Technology.* Scholastic Publications.

Squire, K.D. (in press). Design research for game-based learning. *Educational Technology.*

Stevens, A. & Collins, A. (1977). The goal structure of a Socratic tutor. In *Proceedings of the National ACM Conference.* New York: ACM.

Sutton Smith, B. (1997). *The ambiguity of play.* Cambridge, MA. Harvard University Press.

Van Eck, R. (September, 2006a). Building intelligent learning games. In David Gibson, Clark Aldrich, & Marc Prensky (eds) *Games and simulations in online learning research & development frameworks.* Hershey, PA: Idea Group.

Van Eck, R. (2006b). The effect of contextual pedagogical advisement and competition on middle-school students' attitude toward mathematics and mathematics instruction using a computer-based simulation game. *Journal of Computers in Mathematics and Science Teaching, 25*(2), 165-195.

Van Eck, R. (2006c). Digital game-based learning: It's not just the digital natives who are restless.... Invited cover story for *Educause Review, 41*(2).

Van Eck, R., & The AIM Lab at the University of Memphis (February/March, 2006d). Using games to promote girls' positive attitudes toward technology. *Innovate Journal, 2*(3).

Van Eck, R., & Dempsey, J. (2002). The effect of competition and contextualized advisement on the transfer of mathematics skills in a computer-based instructional simulation game. *Educational Technology Research and Development, 50*(3).

VanLehn, K. 1996. Conceptual and metalearning during coached problem solving. In *Proceedings of the Third Intelligent Tutoring Systems Conference,* eds. C. Frasson, G. Gauthier, and A. Lesgold, 29-47. Berlin: Springer-Verlag.

Vygotsky, L. S. (1962). *Thought and language.* Cambridge, MA: The M. I. T. Press.

Vygotsky, L. S. (1978). *Mind in society: The development of higher psychological processes.* (M. Cole, V. John-Steiner, S. Scribner, & E. Souberman, Eds.). Cambridge, MA: Harvard University Press.

Wardrip-Fruin, N., & Harrigan, P. (2004). *First person: New media as story, performance, game.* Cambridge: MIT.

Wikipedia, 2006. Flynn effect. Online entry retrieved from the World Wide Web on July 15, 2006, at http://en.wikipedia.org/wiki/Flynn_effect#_note-0.

Wiktin, H.A., Oltman, P.K., Raskin, E., & Karp, S. A. (1971). *Group embedded figures test manual.* Palo Alto, CA: Consulting Psychologists Press.

Richard N. Van Eck
Instructional Design & Technology
University of North Dakota

JAMIE KIRKLEY, SONNY KIRKLEY AND JERRY HENEGHAN

BUILDING BRIDGES BETWEEN SERIOUS GAME DESIGN AND INSTRUCTIONAL DESIGN

A Blueprint for Now and the Future

Creating serious games that touch people's imaginations may act as a catalyst for a much-needed renaissance in learning. Most commercial games focus on fun, and educational games focus on learning – combining the two so that neither fun nor learning is sacrificed is challenging. While serious games alone will not solve all of the challenges in education and training, they will greatly contribute to our ability to design learning environments that are contextualized, engaging, and motivational.

Serious game is a term used to describe the use of video games for purposes other than entertainment. The term has been used in various contexts for decades (Abt, 1968), but its recent popular incarnation began in 2002 with an initiative at the Woodrow Wilson International Center for Scholars which led to the Serious Games Initiative, Serious Games Summit and serious game tracks at existing conferences. Serious games covers a broad spectrum of uses such as education and training, healthcare, advertising and promotion of social change. Serious games operate at the nexus of where gaming and computer graphics technology meet with instructional design and the needs of modeling and simulation.

As serious games have emerged as an innovative approach to learning and training, we, the authors of this chapter have worked together to analyze and reflect on key issues and questions of how to build productive bridges between game design and instructional design, two fields that must come together for the industry to mature. As part of this, we offer an examination of the challenges as well as design principles, models, and teaming structures for serious game design teams. Our primary goal for this chapter is to help the field move past broad generalizations stating that instructional designers suck the fun out of games and game designers suck the learning out of games. Instead, we want to begin a conversation on how people with distinct areas of expertise can work together to develop productive relationships that result in innovative serious game designs that will inspire and engage players of all ages.

B. E. Shelton, D. A. Wiley (eds.), Educational Design & Use of Computer Simulation Games, 61–83.

In writing this chapter, we held a series of conversations between designers at our two companies (Information in Place Inc. and Virtual Heroes Inc.) and colleagues[1] as well as recorded conversations between the authors. The participants in the dialogue and the chapter authors are an:

- Instructional designer and researcher, Jamie Kirkley
- Instructional game designer, user interface designer, and researcher, Sonny Kirkley
- Entertainment and serious game developer, Jerry Heneghan

The goal of this chapter is to share a professional dialog around some of the core issues we see being discussed at conferences, on listservs, and in articles related to serious games. We have intermixed dialog from our conversations with elaborations of the themes from the literature as a way to begin addressing these issues. While we definitely do not have all the answers, we have found the discussion to be extremely helpful for creating a common ground as well as exploring critical issues in serious games.

THE DESIGN OF SERIOUS GAMES: WHERE ARE WE NOW?

Jerry: The area of serious games is an evolving and nascent market. It has evolved out of traditional modeling and simulation as well as interactive multimedia and instruction. It's the conversion of training and education with entertainment. Most early work has been done by small firms or lone academics in the wilderness or by researchers who are working on government grants. As this market evolves, what we are starting to see are pure Serious Games companies who want to revolutionize learning, training, and education in terms of being an offshoot of traditional interactive multimedia or modeling and simulation.

Sonny: We have a lot to learn from these early pioneers. For instance, the edutainment market has left much to be desired with regard to meaningful and engaged learning and has given us lessons on how *not* to develop serious games We can also learn from what has and has not worked in e-learning. While many e-learning courses are little more than online books or reference materials with little authenticity, engagement or collaboration, there are some good models. So we have to look at these lessons

[1] *We wish to thank Bob Appelman, Len Annetta, and Virtual Heroes and Information in Place designers.*

learned from both past work to use games for education as well as other media in order to better understand how to best design learning environments for meeting our goals. Also, serious games are usually part of a larger learning environment in which other technologies and instructional approaches are being used. We are just learning how to blend all of this together to create meaningful learning experiences.

The defense sector has been the largest investor in serious games in recent years and has gained much attention for games such as the high profile America's Army and Full Spectrum Warrior. However, a large variety of games have been developed across a range of industries and for a variety of purposes. Use of serious games falls in three general categories:

- Using entertainment video games for non-entertainment purposed without modification such as *Civilization* in school classrooms or *Steel Beasts* for military training;
- Modifying entertainment games for non-entertainment uses such as a medical training mod of Unreal Engine3® called *HumanSim™* and *GNN Visualization*, which is a mod of the Valve Source game engine for forest data visualization.
- Developing entirely new games for non-entertainment purposes such as *Making History*, a World War II history game or the United Nations/ISDR *Stop Disasters* for teaching principles of disaster preparedness.

The credibility of serious games has grown steadily over the past decade from the work of scholars such as Henry Jenkins at MIT and James Paul Gee at University of Wisconsin, as well as through reports advocating the use of games such as Federation of American Scientists' Summit on Educational Games Report (2006), the New Media Consortium, and EDUCAUSE's 2006 Horizon Report (2006).
In a review of research on the use of educational video games by Egenfeldt-Nielsen (2005), three generations of educational games were identified: edutainment, commercial entertainment titles, and research-based educational video games. Edutainment titles often have a strong educational component but have tended not to be motivating, to based on a behaviorist approach and to emphasize changing behaviors through repeated actions. Commercial entertainment titles offer a variety of ways to learn and difficulty is varied but they are not explicitly designed with educational goals in mind so often fall short of meeting goals. The third generation focuses on research-based educational games that take into account the context of the use of the game, facilitating learning through collaboration, construction of knowledge, and changing the roles of teachers and students. However, they often lack the budget and technology to compete with entertainment games. Each generation offers insights into how to best design and deploy video games for meeting learning goals.

DEFINING TERMS AND COMMON UNDERSTANDINGS

Jamie: One thing we have is this baggage with definitions and common understandings. The first issue is perhaps understanding the difference between educational games and serious games. If you think of serious games, you think sexy, sophisticated, and powerhouse gaming capabilities. If you think educational games, people do not get nearly as excited. A lot of them have been developed, but a lot of them have not been designed well. The field of serious games has evolved, and no one ever calls them educational games. What can Serious Games bring to the table that educational games have not?

Jerry: My challenge for everyone is to stop comparing this to the edutainment of yesteryear and traditional e-learning and think in terms of how you elevate best practices from the medium of interactive technology and interactive entertainment in inspiring and educational young people to learn, to be adaptive socially, to communicate effectively, to learn about cultural moirés and different societies. But it does not necessarily have to be boring or dumb.

Jamie: So one hot topic is what is the definition of and what is the difference between a simulation and game. Can you talk about this and tell me how it impacts design or understanding of design principles?

Jerry: Games have rules, goals and objectives, stories or representations, conflict, composition, opposition, challenge, competition, interactivity and immersion, and there are outcomes and feedback. Players will react to the feedback whether they are exploring and developing and adjusting hypotheses. Games are a medium just like film. To try to shoehorn things into a rigid set of criteria is foolishness, just enough to just try to convince you there are more possibilities out there. How do players play games? They probe the environment, they reflect on reaction and form hypotheses, they re-probe the environment based on their hypotheses, and they accept or reject hypotheses and reformulate ideas. And they begin again.

Sonny: I guess my personal bias is that I don't care what the definitions are—I don't care what makes a game or doesn't make a game? I want to have the toolbox of capabilities. I want to inspire and teach kids and adults, whether I am designing a hazardous materials game or a middle school science game. This is why I am at the table doing this. I'm not as concerned about the definitions as some people are. I'm more concerned about what I need to put in the mix in order to meet my goals.

64

Sometimes this may be a specific type of simulation or a fantasy game...As an industry, do we need to clearly define what a game is and what it's not? Do we need to say that these five or so points are all we are going to deal with? How do we start talking about this in a way that makes sense?

Jerry: I agree -- we don't think we need to get wrapped around the axle of rigid guidelines. I think there are certainly things everyone will agree on. If you look at the America's Army Adaptive Thinking and Leadership application, which is a virtual sandbox, it also fits within the rules of a game. People are probing the environment, they are forming hypotheses, they are suffering defeats, and they are victorious in achieving their mission objectives. They are using an immersive experience to enable them to learn, and they are learning in a fairly safe environment. Some of the learning comes internally, some of it comes from awareness of what other people are doing, and some of it comes from assessment and feedback from others in terms of their examining your performance. [For more information on ATL see Raybourn, Deagle, Mendini, & Heneghan, 2005.]

As the dialogue above illustrates, designers don't tend to care how something is classified, they concern about what tools or features can be used to meet stated goals. it is important to have clearly defined definitions when conducting research on the effectiveness of games for learning as compared to other approaches such as simulation (Fletcher & Tobias, 2006). Also, these clearly defined definitions enable researchers and designers to examine prior research on an approach such as simulations (e.g., Andrews & Bell, 2000; Blaiwes & Regan, 1986; O'Neil & Robertson, 1992) and glean relevant information for their work.

Fletcher and Tobias (2006) presented a table to help distinguish between the world of computer simulations and the type of simulations that might be called computer games. Their emphasis and interest was on games as an emerging form of instructional simulation. While there are no standard, precise, widely accepted distinctions between games and simulations in the industry. Some of the distinctions in Table 1 key on the differences in emphasis.

Table 1. Some differences between computer simulation and computer games.

Simulations	Games
Emphasize reality over entertainment	*Emphasize entertainment over reality*
Concern with scenarios and tasks	*Concern with storylines and quests*
Emphasis on task completion	*Emphasis on competition*
May not be interactive	*Necessarily interactive*
Not all simulations are games	*All games are simulations*

"IT'S ABOUT THE DESIGN, STUPID."[2]

Sonny: We all risk being *stupid* if we forget the *design* as this is a central driving factor of creating serious games. Perhaps this is the most obvious place where game designers and instructional designers can begin to build common processes and understandings. No matter what type of job title or the type of expertise, the goal is to create a design that is effective...though what effective means might vary among different members of the team. While this may involve similar as well as distinctively different processes across disciplines, the focus is on using proven design principles, processes, and models. But how do we operationalize the areas of game design and instructional design around a core set of design principles, models, teaming strategies, and other common goals?

Jamie: When I first met and worked with the Virtual Heroes game designers, I frankly found that I (as an instructional designer) found more similarities than differences between instructional design and development and game design and development processes. I think anytime you develop a product, you use some similar processes. In looking at Virtual Heroes' game treatment documents, I saw how they were similar to design documents that we use. When these fields talk at each other, they often miss the similarities. By building on those similarities, we can bring different areas together and build on what people do best. If we can begin to develop and use some common language and processes, we can begin to build more effective design and development models.

Jerry: Yes, I agree. What we need to do is to communicate with each other. Those who will be really successful when the serious game market explodes, in a good way in terms of funding, are those who can put together hybrid teams who work well together and who bring something unique to the table.

Games are inherently learning environments, its what people learn that determines if its an entertainment game or a serious game. As Gee (2003) points out, what is learned from a game is a function of the design of the game. This is also the belief held by instructional designers. In fact, Duffy and Kirkley (2004) have stated that it is the design of the instruction rather than the technology that impacts learning. Therefore, it follows that clearly defining the game's educational goals by the learning objectives it supports is important. In fact, Gee (2003) identified 36 learning principles or outcomes that can result from playing video games. This richness of learning principles illustrates the strong power of games for training. However, it is critical that we remember that assessments and evaluations must be conducted in order to determine if learning and transfer occurred, and steps must be taken to examine what aspects of the serious game supported learning effectiveness and transfer.

DESIGNING SERIOUS GAMES FOR LEARNING

Jamie: So how do we design games to support learning while maintaining the engagement and fun? How do we enable players to understand how their actions and decisions have impacted the current situation -- and still keep it fun? And how do you support instructors and teachers so they are an integral part of the learning process?

Jerry: If you're going to use games for learning, you need to create training support packages or instructor guides for ways to facilitate the learning. Instructors shouldn't be intimidated by the games. We've created an Adaptive Thinking and Leadership platform for the Army where the instructor is still the master in the classroom in terms of providing feedback, creating situations, throwing curveballs at the students, and modifying situations. One of the goals for ATL is to develop ways to help the instructor manage the workload so he or she can be effective and can adapt and change things on the fly as needed.

Studies by the Kaiser Family Foundation have found that nearly half of all children under age 6 have used a computer, and 30 percent have played video games. On average, 8 to 18-year-olds spend just under 50 minutes daily playing video games, adding up to 25 hours per month. In fact, many of today's teenagers live by the cult of computer games. Online gaming remains an entire subculture with its own meeting places, characters, and environments" (Jayakanthan, 2002, p.98). Even people whose lives had remained untouched by computers have been drawn into the computer arena through the lure of games.

Video games have long been viewed as strictly entertainment. However, recent developments of video games have emerged to support their role in learning and shaping our behaviors. Steven Johnson, author of the book *Everything Bad is Good For You: How Today's Popular Culture is Actually Making Us Smarter*, states that video games present sophisticated situations in which players must analyze patterns, develop goals, and make decisions about actions. This presents cognitive challenges where we must develop systems and lateral approaches to thinking.

James Gee (2003) and Steinkuehler (2005) provide perhaps the most compelling reason to adopt video games – to improve critical thinking and literacy. Players must take on new identities, solve problems through trial and error, and gain expertise or specific types of literacies to be successful in a game. A player learns to think critically while at the same time gaining embodied knowledge through interacting with the environment. Gee (2003, p.48) states that "video games situate meaning in a multimodal space through embodied experiences to solve problems and reflect on the intricacies of the design of imagined worlds and the design of both real and imagined social relationships in the modern world." This locus of ownership of both the process of constructing and sharing knowledge, and of knowledge itself, is shifting. Learners are not only willing to participate in the construction of knowledge; they are starting to expect it (NMC, 2005). Following are some ways that video games can support engagement and exploration, interaction and community, as well as complex systems.

Virtual environments encourage students to explore beyond the boundaries of given material, thus stimulating proactive and exploratory nature that enables and facilitates the student to become a self-reliant learner (Taradi, 2005). Video games in particular are designed around the principle of self-reliance. They have to teach someone how to play by using training modules and embedded scaffolding (e.g., screen says press B to start over). Players learn by trial and error rather than reading a manual. Dede (2004) states that virtual environments motivate learning by providing challenging, curiosity, beauty, fantasy, fun, and social recognition. Video games immerse players in a virtual environment where learning can occur because they are engaged. Rieber (1998) has argued that digital games engage players in productive play. He defines productive play as learning that occurs by building microworlds, manipulating simulations, and playing games. This has shown to help improve motivation and the self-regulation of learning.

The multidisciplinary nature of games lends itself to whole-curriculum programs, where knowledge is applied across many subjects. It can be difficult to isolate a single skill or discipline in a game, and the interrelation of content can itself be very instructive (New Media Consortium [NMC], 2005). Because games allow for rich interaction, the lines between collaboration and competition begin to blur. It is often the competitive nature of humans that is the motivator for people to learn and excel (Yu, 2000). (Although competition is inherently between two or more beings, one can also compete with themselves to better their previous efforts.)

With all of these affordances, games offer powerful tools for learning and assessing performance and knowledge. However, it comes down to not only how the game is designed but how it is designed into the learning environment. Effectively designed learning environments are driven by theories (what we believe) of how people learn and effective use of training methodologies that support those theories. For instance, Kirkley, Kirkley, Myers, Tomblin, Borland et al (2006) developed the problem based embedded training (PBET) approach for designing instruction to support the development of competencies as well as expertise. This theory driven methodology was developed to support the blending together of existing and new approaches such as serious games. By using a well-defined theory and methodology, we increase the likelihood that our instructional materials will be effective and that how they are used together will promote better learning and transfer. Too often in serious games, organizations develop a wonderful game but no work is put into supporting how that game will be used in the learning environment. In one our current projects, we are adapting PBET, now called Mission Based Training (MBT), to develop not just a hazmat game but entire modules that use multiple types of games throughout the course to support various kinds of learning outcomes. For instance we are using 3D immersive first person games, drill-and practice games for learning core concept running on cell phones, and simulation-games for learning core behaviors and communication skills using Flash games in a Web browser. The learning theory underlying MBT helps ensure the students and instructors are provided a coherent and integrated training package and that the games are used as intended in the classroom.

A major problem is that many game designers worry that adhering to a theoretical and methodological framework may inhibit their creativity and design. However, their design will reflect their own conscious or unconscious beliefs (i.e., theories) about how people can learn best in their game. What we propose is that by using research-based instructional theories and methodologies will ensure a higher likelihood of success than an ill-defined personal opinion. Unfortunately many people's models of learning are what they experiences in schools, rows of desks in a classroom with the teacher up front dispensing information. This scares game designers away from "education" because they perceive formal education as sometimes boring and certainly not like a game. In fact, good instruction is almost always like a good game–learners engaged and driving instruction, a rich and authentic context in which to engage with content and so on.

DEFINING AND BALANCING GAME DESIGN AND INSTRUCTIONAL DESIGN

Sonny: Some have suggested that part of this conflict in the field between the instructional design side and the game design side may be an economic issue where people are vying for contracts and funding. Where would you put your money or place your bet on who would make the best serious games, those that are entertaining, engaging, and instructionally sound? Will it be the game companies or instructional design firms?

Jerry: You've hit on the problem. The problem right now is that they are mutually exclusive things, and the dialogue is not happening. People are talking at each other and not talking to each other. Academics are talking at game developers, game developers are talking at academics, and military and simulation people are somewhere in the middle. There are few successful instances of people being able to pull integrated teams together.

Sonny: I agree. But the point I was trying to get at is, if you have these existing organizations or capability sets, who is driving the process to make serious games? If you are trying to figure out how to make a good instructional game or instructional simulation or interactive media, can you start with existing organizations? If so, is it better to start with a game firm or instructional design firm and try to build in the capabilities? Or do we have to start with a brand new type of organization? Who will be successful?

Jamie: So how does instructional design and game design fit together ?

Jerry: For me, instructional design is a discipline, a process, a body of knowledge, and years of expertise on how to put things together that traditional game development companies do not have. But if you look at Serious Games, you are looking at something that's immersive, it's fun, it's entertaining, and we're putting that together. Whether it's 2D, side-scrolling, something on a Nintendo DS or a fully immersive 3D experience, games and interactive technology constitute a medium. It's a medium like film, like graphic novels or comic books.

Sonny: I don't think it matters which one you start with. What is important is that we make use of what each field brings to the table in terms of things we value (e.g., collaboration), processes, and tools and find effective ways as a team to integrate them. It may also be that to a degree, the best mix may depend on the type of serious game and the audience. A disaster response game might be heavier on the instructional design side while a leisure time educational game might focus more on enjoyment and thus the team may focus much more on fun game play. Of course, if we go too far in either direction we lose the value of collaborating across disciplines.

Serious game-based learning environments are complex from a design and development point of view, and most instructional designers have no background in how to design these or even how to appropriately utilize them. Additionally, game designers have little or no expertise in learning and instruction. Thus, there is a gap between the areas of serious game design and instructional design that must be addressed in order to effectively design and utilize these learning environments.

Game production companies have often relied on traditional software engineering methods such as the waterfall model when designing and developing games (see Table 2 from Kirkley, Tomblin, & Kirkley, 2005). With this process, each step is completed before the next one is started. The advantage of the waterfall model is control of the time, schedule, and compartmentalization of project roles. However, this approach does not allow for iterative development, prototyping, or user testing and revision without considerable loss of time, effort, and product costs. The process becomes even more problematic when key revisions are needed (and they often are). For example, changes to one aspect of the game can have drastic effects on other aspects. A simple change in storyline can impact core components of programming, graphic design, instructional design, and interaction design within a game. Therefore, a systemic but flexible approach must be applied as it is impossible to predict all the possible changes and issues that will arise before the development begins or ends.

Besides the overall step-wise nature of the process, other challenging factors exist as well. No longer do we have game environments that are as simple as Pac Man. One designer (or even one type of designer) cannot effectively create the complex games that exist today. This requires that designers of all types (e.g., instructional, game, interface, interaction and process) work together. In fact, due to the increasing complexity of game designs, (Morrison, 2000) states that cooperative design is encouraged amongst stakeholders through all stages. In fact, input from all is necessary for design document to be understood and be of use to all stakeholders.

Deeply enriched learning environments and interactions exist in today's games that require exhaustive design that is extremely iterative in nature. Additionally, the prevalence of user input and usability require iterative approaches. Design documents are usually used to define product goals, design features, and development specifications. However, with the complexity of games as well as the increasing complexity of games themselves as well as design processes, these documents tend to become large, unwieldy, and difficult to use. Designers, programmers, and artists need to participate in the creation and adaptation of the design and rapid prototyping process.

Table 2. Key Elements of ISD and Game Development Processes

Instructional Systems Development ADDIE SAT Model http://www-tradoc.army.mil/tpubs/ regs/r350-70/350_70_exe_sum. htm#ES-3	*Game Development Waterfall Phases http://www.gamedev.net/columns /gameengineerin /gup/default.asp*
Analysis • Needs Analysis • Audience Analysis • Mission Analysis • Task Analysis • Job Analysis	Phase One • Game Conception • Target Audience • Platform • Time Frame • Game Features
Design • Training Requirements • Design Media • Design Individual training Courses • Produce student performance measures Formative Evaluation	Phase Two • Character & Story Designs • User Experience • Storyboards • Art & Story Bibles • Technical Specifications
Development • Write Lesson plans • Produce training media • Acquire Training resources • Train Instructor • Prepare Facilities • Formative evaluation	Phase Two • Construction • Quality Check • Play Testing • Alpha Testing • Beta Testing
Implementation • Distribute the training material	• Gold Release
Summative Evaluation • Test for instructional quality • Needs assessments	• Post Mortem

Within the design process, there are also many complex variables and roles at play, and communication can easily break down. This results in confusion about the product goals, outcomes, and project roles. Thus, there is a huge need to manage the design complexity of game design and development and to use new processes of rapid prototyping so as to produce games that are effective training tools.

Instructional designers experience similar challenges with their own design and development processes. The traditional ADDIE model, which stands for analysis, design, development, implementation, and evaluation, is often implemented in a lock step process where various phases of design and development are completed before the next one is started. This typical approach has a reputation of being too slow and impractical for real world issues, especially when used in a rigid linear fashion as with an inexperienced designer.

WHO DRIVES THE PROCESS?

Sonny: We've been to a lot of conferences, and everyone has been talking at a surface level about how to balance game design and instructional design. But what does it mean at an operational level? How do you make these trade-offs? What is it that you actually do? I think these are the kinds of questions we need to answer.

Jamie: There is a real need for fresh air in the space in regard to this question. I'm tired of the generalizations I hear about the different types of designers being pitted against one another as if there is no common goal. Let's talk about creating ways to work together.

Jerry: There is definitely room for disruptive thinking. With regard to Serious Games, the real magic occurs when you can take best practices and thoughtful ideas and create composite teams that have instructional designers, writers, game designers, academics, subject matter experts, and creative people who can bring it all together. What people need to focus on is how to become part of a team (even a virtual team) so that they can change how people think or how to change the human condition. Those who are interested in Serious Games, those who are committed to shipping a product that really helps people – those people will be successful by participating in multi-dimensional teams. That's the whole package.

There have been repeated calls at conferences and in the literature for the involvement of instructional designers in the design and development of serious games (Fletcher & Tobias, 2006; O'Neil, Wainess, and Baker, 2005). However

Prensky (2001) notes that the opposite may be true and this his experience and the experience of other game designers has been the addition of an instructional designer often results in stale, boring, educational games, and he points towards the criticisms of the instructional design process within the field itself (Gordon & Zemke, 2000). However, we would like to point out that few instructional game designers are trained in game design, just as few game designers have training in instructional design. Rather than attaching personality types to specific fields, we recommend that two fields come together to develop common processes and methodologies that can result in more effective game design. This is critical for serious games that require demonstrated learning objectives to be met.

New types of instructional designers and game designers are needed—ones who understand learning and gaming focused on complex problem solving, decision-making skills, development of expertise, and situational aspects of learning and cognition. The strengths of instructional designers are that they have the ability to conceptualize and design the learning environment in which the game is being used, to translate game goals into instructional goals, and to help develop models that link the critical aspects of the art and science of instructional design. For example, a serious game designed to facilitate development of decision making skills within a domain will need to rely heavily on game designers to translate the scenarios, environmental cues, and other contextual factors that support authenticity and relevancy for learners. Thus, an instructional and game designer could learn much from each other about how to systematically design a learning environment that is situated in real-life types of events that the learner would encounter.

In turn, new types of game design strategies are needed that expand into understanding how to interpret the learning goals and evaluative markers of educational games into serious game play and fun. The strengths of game designers are that they are experts at creating game play design and interactivity that are fun, visually appealing, and that engage learners for hours on end.

Instead of disparaging an entire profession, perhaps a better approach is to break down what each discipline brings to the design table and compare that to the needs of a serious game design project. In numerous private conversations and conference group discussions, we have heard people on both sides staunchly take the stand that the instructional designer or game designer *must control the process* and decisions. In one meeting, a team of serious game designers said they bring in the instructional designers, let them talk about what they want and then once they are gone go about developing the real design the way they think it should be. They clearly were placing low value on the instructional designers that had historically worked with. We have also spoken with instructional designers at large corporations who want a game developed and who have funds to hire game companies, but they have reservations about game designers being able to design a game where more serious learning objectives can be met with rigor.

While our focus is on the tensions between instructional designers and game designers, the role of subject matter experts is also problematic. In many cases, they have neither instructional design or game design experience and therefore can pose a problem for all aspects of the design. In reporting on the making of Re-Mission, Dave Warhol and Tim Ryan (2006) discussed the difficulties of working with cancer experts to balance fun game play with accurate science. We have also found this in our own work as subject matter experts often lack expertise in learning and gaming, so they may have either an ideal outcome or a real lack of trust with the outcome, and this can greatly impact the successful design of a game.

DESIGN STUDIO OF THE FUTURE

Taking this in account the design studio or design team of the future will need to adapt tools and techniques that help composite teams work effectively together. Over the past few decades, spiral design approaches and user-centered design models have been implemented that enable designers to engage in iterative design . From an instructional design perspective, this requires using innovative development processes such as rapid prototyping (Tripp & Bichelemeyer, 1990) and participatory design (Schuler & Namioka, 1993) to meet the needs of supporting learners in achieving complex performance goals. These approaches are being adapted from both instructional design and software design fields so they should feel familiar to most designers. As we adapt these for serious game design, we need an integrated process that supports both instructional and game design in the design of fun, engaging, and effective games for training. To address this need, Kirkley, Tomblin & Kirkley (2005) developed the Serious Game Instructional Systems Design (SG-ISD) model (Figure 1). This model blends together elements from the ADDIE, Waterfall, iterative design, rapid prototyping and other models to provide a high-level composite process in which designers of all types, as well as experts and production staff, work together in a collaborative and iterative manner. This model was integrated into a prototype serious game authoring tool design developed by the Information In Place Inc. team (Kirkley, Kirkley, Myers, Tomblin, Borland, Pendleton, Borders & Singer (under review).

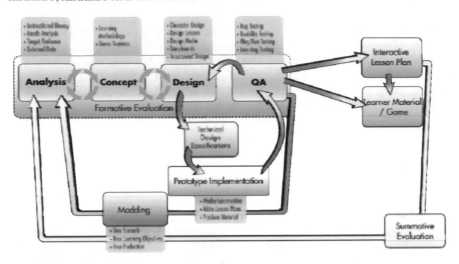

Figure 1. The Serious Game Instructional Systems Design Model

SERIOUS GAMES SUCCESS STORIES

Jamie: Given what's occurring now, we need to look at the success stories in serious games and consider how to capitalize on innovative designs, approaches, and processes. So what are the real success stories in the Serious Games area where a good balance between instructional design and game design have been achieved?

Jerry: The first thing that comes to mind is the game Food Force put out by the United Nations. It has been successful in terms of numbers of downloads and numbers of people who have participated in the experience. They have been able to have fun and understand the unique challenges of that organization and how they do their business. There are also companies who have had success like Breakaway Games with A Force More Powerful, which has been critically acclaimed.

Sonny: I think two of the most successful serious games has been the Adaptive Thinking and Leadership (ATL) project Virtual Heroes built using America's Army and HopeLab's Re-Mission Game. ATL built in assessment tools, promotes communication in a multiplayer environment, the instructor has powerful tools to manipulate the scenario, it's designed to fit within a class time limit and it has a wonderful debriefing (after action review) capability. Reflection is key in these environments. Re-Mission, a game designed for teenagers with cancer, did a good job balancing the science and medicine of cancer treatment with patient fun and engagement. They also evaluated outcomes of the game to definitively document positive impact on behaviors and attitudes, which is something the serious game field needs more of in order to not only improve design but to gain increased acceptance in the marketplace.

Jerry: While anyone can get a video recorder, not everyone can be a Steven Spielberg. Those people who want to make industrial training films or documentaries or other kinds of genres can decide what they are good at or team with people who can help them. But interactive technology is a medium that's fairly new. We've had only 20 years in terms of electronic games, and there are many opportunities. Those who will be successful are the ones who will push the boundaries, push the limits, and do things not ever done before. That's why Will Wright is so successful. The things like the Sims or Spore, while not necessarily the most sophisticated technically, provides an immersive experience that people enjoy, learn with, and build communities. This is where we need to come together.

NEXT GENERATION SERIOUS GAMES: WHAT'S NEXT?

Sonny: So what's next on the horizon for serious games?

Jerry: I think the interactive game industry is stagnant—specifically I mean the interactive entertainment industry—it's $35 billion a year globally and $7.5 billion a year in the U.S. I've talked to several prominent game developers, and there is an acknowledgement and awareness that there is a stagnant nature out there where people are locked into specific genres like action, adventure, MMOGs, role-playing, and first person shooter. Once again, the people who can think outside the box, create something original, and provide an experience that people will enjoy – and who have the sheer persistence to find funding and partnerships to make it happen—those are the people who will be successful. Someone was recently likening the game industry to the television industry where there are certain publishers who spend all the money and they are only comfortable with certain formulas and genres. So people will get bored, and if people get bored, they will move onto other things.

Jamie: Do you think this is similar to the Indie films explosion where directors have left the Hollywood formulas and controlling aspects of formulas to create uniquely different movies...?

Jerry: Yes. As a parent and serious game developer, the thing I am most excited about is using games to teach STEM education. By STEM, I mean science, technology, engineering, math...and even applied and liberal arts. How do you reach that wired generation who are digital natives? We need to take advantage of that. Also, the interdisciplinary needs and workforce development can be supported by game technology. When you can inspire and educate people, that's really powerful.

A newly emerging area of interest for learning is complex systems. Thinking reflectively about complex systems is a crucial skill for the modern world where workplaces, communities, government, global institutions, and the environment are all complex systems (Gee, 2003). Complex systems such as communications, economics, and ecologies are important not only because they impact real life but because they need to be understood by an informed citizenship in order to be part of a participatory democracy. Because of the growing importance and interrelatedness of global systems, Sabelli (2006) recommends that we reorganize the school curriculum around these complex scientific issues instead of traditional disciplines. Computer-based modeling and experimentation play a critical role in examining complex systems. For example, the ability to manipulate and visualize data facilitates examining complex systems issues. Because of this, Sabelli recommends using computers as part of the educational approach. Video games, in particular, present useful and imaginative ways to examine complex systems and their interacting relationships in an engaging and interactive experience (NMC, 2005). In their report titled Federation of American Scientists (2006) recently called video games the next great discovery, as they offer a way to captivate students so much that they will spend hours learning on their own time.

Sonny: Jerry, I've heard you use the term first person explorer. This is an interesting term in light of talking about new genres. Can you explain what a first person explorer is, and how does it differ from what's been out there before? Can you also explain how we can take existing genres and create something new, especially that are more in line with using serious games in education?

Jerry: The concept of first person exploration was, I believe, first coined at Virtual Heroes. It came out of some pretty lengthy discussions we had about how to make a non-violent game for an organization like NASA or someone interested in space exploration where part of the fun of the game was scientific authenticity that was based on coolness points and not on blowing something up. In a first person explorer, the challenge is man vs. nature or man vs. machine, not man vs. man. For those of us who have been around for a while, we go back to Wolfenstein and Doom and early Quake. We've come to the conclusion that the dumbest way to interact with an environment is to give someone a big gun and crosshairs so they can just blast the environment. While we get a certain amount of satisfaction out of interacting with an environment this way, this is very much a knuckle-dragging, preliminary kind of experience. There are so many other levels of creativity and collaboration that we have not explored. My message is to let's stop talking about it, and let's make something. Or let's create a team, or be part of a team that will make something that is worthwhile. Let's inspire people in the healthcare profession, let's make in-service people more proficient in their mission-critical job skills, or let's inspire people to want to go into STEM-related career fields. That's very exciting. [First Person Explorer was first described in Virtual Heroes, 2006.]

Jamie: A lot of these games are aimed at children, tweens or older. How do you get them to want to play these first person exploration games? I've examined three teenagers playing Ghost Recon over a week's time. I had a lot of different games they could choose from, but both they and different groups of their friends chose Ghost Recon and Star Wars. These games have quite a bit of violence. They spent several five to ten hour stretches playing those games with just a few five-minute breaks. I recorded a transcript of some of their game play sessions, and I was amazed in the analysis of this at how much of their conversation was focused on serious problem solving, collaborating as a team, and doing strategic and critical thinking. I want to see students just as engaged in a math-science game for five hours as they were in this Ghost Recon game. How do we get them to want to do the first person exploration game?

Jerry: Along the lines of the metaphor of a space exploration game, we need to find what will be fun beyond where most young people are just used to blasting each other, let's make it man versus nature or technology. We've thought of challenges based on real science parameters where you use your head and understand how the science works, whether its physics, astrophysics or geology. The fun can be team efficiency or comparative team performance. You have a mission that is a timed event, and you can time yourself like an obstacle course based on other people as you navigate your way through a complex, interactive environment where there are challenges along the way. This is similar to the challenges found in games like Survivor. This would be rolled into a platform for scientific collaboration, research, and rapid prototyping using advanced games technology. First person exploration is not limited to space exploration, but it also could be used to explore the ancient Pyramids of Giza or the rainforest. Right now, the Discovery Store has a lot of DVDs and videos, but there is not much interactive where you can interact with animals or plant life in the environment. Perhaps people have not been encouraged to do that because the publishers do not think it's not commercially viable. We do think it's viable, and we think there is a world of opportunity there. As a field, we need to figure out the secret sauce to create those products so we can get some real innovation in learning.

CONCLUSION

In this chapter, we have hit on a lot of issues that game designers, instructional designers. SMEs, and those funding and developing serious games are thinking about – how to balance fun and engagement with learning, how to build effective design teams that use each other's strengths, how to create common models and processes, and how to develop innovate games that will revolutionize learning, not only the outcomes but how we define and understand it. In fact, one of the strengths of technology is that it keeps us from getting too comfortable in our seats. As new technologies emerge, so do new forms of communicating, collaborating, and creating. This calls for constantly rethinking our approach to design and development, especially as we are challenged to deal with new design concepts and capabilities (e.g. what can your game engine do), different types of designs (e.g., how will your learner experience and process virtual environment), and how game design and instructional design can come together to create learning environments that are increasingly authentic, engaging, and that help people to see the world from a different perspective, even if for a short period of time. In order for our field of serious games to emerge into a viable industry, we need to learn to value each other and how to move together towards the end goal we all want to see, positive impact on the people who play our games and look to us to teach and inspire them in meaningful ways.

REFERENCES

Abt, C. (1968). Games for learning. In S. S. Boocock & E. O. Schild (Eds.), *Simulation games in learning*. London: Sage Publications.

Andrews, D.H., & Bell, H.H. *(2000)*. Simulation based training. In S. Tobias, & J.D. Fletcher. (Eds.) *Training and retraining: A handbook for business, industry, government, and the military (pp. 357-384)*. New York: Macmillan Gale Group.

Appelman, R. (2005). Experiential modes: A common ground for serious game designers. *International Journal of Continuing Engineering Education and Life-long Learning, 15* (3-6), 240-251. Accessed online November 10, 2007 http://www.indiana.edu/~drbob/EM/IJCEELL 15_3-6_ Paper 09.doc

Appelman, R. & Wilson, J. (2005). Games and simulations for training: From group activities to virtual reality. In J. Pershing (Ed), *Handbook of human performance technology*. San Francisco, CA: Pfeiffer.

Blaiwes, A. S., & Regan, J. J. (1986). Training devices: Concepts and progress. In J. A. Ellis (Ed.) *Military contributions to instructional techology* (pp. 83-170) New York, NY: Praeger Publishers.

Bransford, J. D., Brown, A. L., & Cocking, R. R. (Eds.). (2000). *How people learn: Brain, mind, experience and school*. Washington, DC: National Academy Press.

Duffy, T. M. and Kirkley, *J. R. (2004)*. Learner-centered theory and practice in distance education: Cases from higher education. *Mahwah, NJ: Lawrence Erlbaum Associates*.

Egenfeldt-Nielsen, S. (2005). *Beyond edutainment: Exploring the educational potential of computer games*. Doctoral Dissertation. Accessed online November 1, 2006 http://www.seriousgames.dk/downloads/egenfeldt.pdf

Falstein, N. (2004). Natural Funativity. *Gamasutra*. November 10, 2004.

Fletcher, J.D. & Tobias, S. (2006). What research has to say (thus far) about designing computer games for learning. Paper presented at the American Educational Research Association, Chicago, IL.

Federation of American Scientists. (2006). Summit on educational games: Harnessing the power of video games for learning. Washington, DC: Federation of American Scientists.

Gee, J. P. (2003). *What video games have to teach us about learning*. New York: Palgrave.

Jayakanthan, R. (2002). Application of computer games in the field of education. *The Electronic Library, 20*(2), 98-102.

Jonassen, D. H. (2004). Learning to solve problems. An instructional design guide. San Francisco, CA: Pfeiffer.

Kirkley, S. E., Kirkley, J. R., Myers, T. E., Tomblin, S. T., Borland, S. C., Pendleton, W. R., Borders, C., and Singer, M. (Under review). *Problem based embedded training (PBET): A constructivist instructional methodology and authoring tool to support competency-based training for ground soldier system*. [Contractor's report currently under review for ARI Technical Publication.]

Kirkley, S. E., Tomblin, S., & Kirkley, J. (2005). Instructional design authoring support for the development of serious games and mixed reality training. In *Proceedings of the Interservice/Industry Training, Simulation and Education Conference* (I/ITSEC). Arlington, VA: National Defense Industrial Association.

Kirrimuir, J. (2002). Video gaming, education, and digital learning. *D-Libe Magazine*, 8.

New Media Consortium. (2005). *The Horizon Report* (No. ISBN 0-9765087-0-2). Stanford, CA.

O'Neil, H. F., & Robertson, M. M. (1992) Simulations: Occupationally oriented. In M.C. Alkin (Ed.) *Encyclopedia of educational research* (Sixth Edition) (pp 1216-1222). New York, NY: Macmillan.

Prensky, M. (2001). *Digital game-based learning*. New York: McGraw-Hill.

Raybourn, E.M., Deagle, E., Mendini, K., & Heneghan, J. (2005). Adaptive thinking & leadership simulation game training for special forces officers. I/ITSEC 2005 Proceedings, Interservice/Industry Training, Simulation and Education Conference Proceedings, November 28-December 1, Orlando, Florida, USA.

Sabelli, N. (2006). Complexity, technology, science, and education. *Journal of Learning Sciences, 15*(1), 5 - 9.

Schuler, D., and Namioka, A. (Eds.). (1993). *Participatory design: Principles and practices*. Hillsdale, NJ: Erlbaum.

Shaffer, D. W. (2006). *How computer games help children learn*. New York: Palgrave Macmillan.

Taradi, S. K., Taradi, M., Radic, K., & Pokrajac, N. (2005). Blending problem-based learning with Web technology positively impacts student learning outcomes in acid-base physiology. *Journal of Advanced Physiological Education, 29*, 35-39.

Tripp, S., and Bichelmeyer, B. (1990). Rapid prototyping: An alternative instructional design strategy. *Educational Technology Research and Development, 38*(1), 31 - 44.

van den Bosch, K. & Riemersma, J. B. J. (2004). Reflections on scenario-based training in tactical command. In S. Shiett, L. Elliott, E. Salas, & M. Coovert (Eds.), *Scaled worlds: Development, validation and applications* (pp. 1 - 21). Burlington, VT: Ashgate Publishing.

Virtual Heroes (2005). *America's army AAR systems*. Virtual Heroes Game Design Documentation. Unpublished manuscript.

Virtual Heroes. (2006). *First person exploration*. Virtual Heroes Game Design Documentation. Unpublished manuscript.

Warhol, D., & Ryan, T. (2006). *The making of re-mission: A case study of the integration of entertainment software and games for health*. Presentation at the Games for Health Conference. Accessed online November 10, 2006 http://www.gamesforhealth.org/presentations/the-making-of-re-ission.ppt

Jamie Kirkley, Ph.D.
Information in Place Inc.
Indiana University

Sonny Kirkley, Ph.D.,
Information in Place Inc.
School of Informatics, Indiana University

Jerry Heneghan
Virtual Heroes Inc.

EXPLORING ALTERNATE APPROACHES TO SIMULATION COMPUTER GAME DESIGN

As with any "traditional" approach to designing instruction, there are cases when one method seems to work better under particular circumstances or when another method works better for a particular population of learners. So then we can wonder, is putting our effort into combining traditional instructional methods for game design even the best use of our time? Or are there other approaches that might offer additional flexibility for localizing instruction for a particular population, for specific content, through a given genre? The following chapters offer some thoughts on how different perspectives for designing instructional games might be attained through alternative means.

The first chapter in this section highlights a model-layer approach, proven successful in simulation design, for a case of museum instruction. The next chapter advocates design based on aligning in-game activity to instructional goals in an effort to build games that help students achieve "standards" while maintaining the motivational, engaging properties of commercially successful games. The third chapter in this section offers evidence for the value of activity-based reflection during the design process in order to keep track of modifications to instructional objectives as the game evolves. Each of these chapters offers a slight departure from what is espoused in the previous sections as they try to shed light on differing approaches to game design.

ANDREW S. GIBBONS AND STEFAN SOMMER

LAYERED DESIGN IN AN INSTRUCTIONAL SIMULATION[1]

ABSTRACT

This chapter reports the design of an instructional simulation for use as a museum display that incorporates elements of game design theory, narrative theory, and instructional theory within a layered design framework. The purpose is to show how multiple theories from distinct fields converge to influence a single design and to show how design elements arising from different theories work together to produce artifacts capable of operating outside narrow views of the theory's traditional venue and metaphor. The chapter will show how the structures supplied by the different theories combined to provide a "discipline" (Schön, 1987) for the design and how theory-related design language terms that begin as abstractions are integrated and given specific dimension during design.

INTRODUCTION

The worlds of instructional designers and game designers overlap more today than in the past due to the enormous financial success of the game market and the visible effect of games on user engagement. Similarly, the practice of design itself is receiving more attention, providing new insights into design techniques that contribute to more sophisticated learning experiences. The boundaries of instructional design, communication design, and game design are becoming less distinct as a new field of environment and experience design emerges.

PURPOSE

This chapter reports the design of an instructional simulation for use as a museum display that incorporates elements of game design theory, narrative theory, and instructional theory within a layered design framework. The purpose is to show how multiple theories from distinct fields converged to influence a single design and to show how design elements arising from different theories worked together to produce artifacts capable of operating outside narrow views of the

---
[1] The work reported in this chapter was supported in part by National Science Foundation Grant #ESI-9804614. Bill Mitchell, the primary on-site instructional designer for this grant contributed significantly to the designs described.

theory's traditional venue and metaphor. This chapter shows how the structures supplied by different theories combine to provide a "discipline" (Schön, 1987) for a specific design and how theory-related design language terms that begin as abstractions can be integrated and given specific dimension during design. In particular, this will be an account of how considering the layered nature of the design allowed the designers to "weave" together elements with diverse theoretical connections into a single, coherent experience design.

DESIGN PROBLEM AND CRITERIA

The design problem in this case consisted of the need for a multimedia product that was mobile, computer-based, interactive, and kiosk-housed for use in public venues, such as museums, classrooms, shopping malls, zoos, nature centers, public events, libraries, and community centers. The theme of the display was "Treasuring Our Natural Heritage". The display was one part of a comprehensive outreach program targeting 7th to 12th grade youth with interactive traveling exhibits, science kits, and professional-quality video documentaries for public broadcast. The message portrayed by the media products concerned the economy of nature, drawing a parallel between the economic functions carried out by individuals and groups within a human community and the interdependent services provided by all living things in the larger natural world. This metaphor described *occupations* of plants and animals through which *goods* and *services* are exchanged within living habitats for mutual benefit.

The goal of the project was wide distribution of this message through the several media forms mentioned, with emphasis on interactive media easily integrated into teacher plans involving activity and engagement on the part of the learner. Therefore, for the design of the interactive mobile display, conveyance of message, length of engagement, and enjoyment were the priority design criteria. Our goal became to exceed the average museum display engagement time, which is generally understood to be two minutes or less (Bell et al, 1993; Nourbakhsh et al, 2005; Spencer & Angelotti, 2004).

We wanted to solve this design problem in a particular way. Copying prior designs was less desirable to us than rationalizing our designs according to design theories. Even if it meant the final product would end up looking like prior designs on the surface, we wanted to test a particular approach to design that focused the designer's attention to underlying architectural structures that we hoped would lead to a more rationalized but complex design.

This does not imply that our goal was complexity. But without appropriate thought tools for designing (of which we feel the layered view of design described later is an example) designs in any field reach a ceiling that limits the exploration of new design variations and ultimately confines the designer to copying old design patterns. For example, the limited conceptions of the early western European musical tradition (c. 900 C. E.) were only expanded as it was perceived that there were many unexplored dimensions of musical organization. As the dimensions of counterpoint, rhythm, and repetitive transformational structures were disentangled and then explored, musical designs became both more complex and more interesting and varied—not as a goal, but as a by-product of exploration.

We realized that exploring the dimensions of an instructional design in greater detail would cause us to draw on multiple different types of theory, integrating constructs from many sources into particular areas of the design. To achieve this, we appealed to a framework of design layer theory, which is described next.

DESIGN FRAMEWORK OF LAYERS

We wanted to frame our design using a theory most recently described by Gibbons and Rogers (2007) that views instructional designs in terms of semi-independent layers that represent key functions considered common to all instructional artifacts. Functional layers themselves decompose into functional subdivisions that constitute sub-layers, and each layer is associated with a number of design languages appropriate to the expression of design solutions for that layer. A designer expresses a design solution for a particular artifact using design language terms appropriate to the functions carried out within each layer.

The layered concept of design layering originated in fields other than instructional design. Schön (1987) describes architectural design in terms of *domains* which represent sub-problems solved to arrive at a complete design. Each domain focuses on decisions related to a set of functions or qualities of the completed design, and each possesses a unique design vocabulary appropriate to solving problems within the domain. Table 1 contains a sampling of Schön's domains. Typical vocabulary terms associated with each domain are shown in the left column. Most terms can be traced to their origin in published theories of building design ("geometry of parallels"), to common usage ("warehouse", "beach cottage"), or to personally held design abstractions ("carry the gallery through and look down here"), which are equivalent to personally-held design theory terms.

Brand (1994) also describes building designs in layered terms, using the term *layer* in place of Schön's *domain*. Brand's layers include a structure layer (typified by descriptions of *beams, foundations*, and *pillars*); a skin layer (described in terms of *sidings, walls*, and *surface materials*); and other layers, each associated with its own set of terms representing problem solving structures for that layer.

High-level instructional design layers described by Gibbons and Rogers include:

- A control layer within which controls are devised by which a learner can express choices regarding content, strategy, viewpoint, and session control to the instructional source
- A representation layer within which messages from the instructional source are given symbolic sensory form so that they can be experienced by the learner
- A message layer capable of interpreting strategic plans and mapping them onto symbolic resources
- A strategy layer capable of forming and executing strategic plans and guiding instructional message formation

- A media-logic layer capable of executing symbolic resources and managing control operations in proper synchrony
- A data management layer that provides for recording, analysis, reporting, and use of data from interactions
- A content layer that provides subject-matter or knowledge structures to be operated upon by the other functions

Table 1. Schön's domains of an architectural design (excerpted from Schön, 1987).

Domain	Definition	Typical vocabulary terms
Siting	Features, elements, relations of the building site	"Land contour", "slope", "hill", "gully"
Organization of space	Kinds of space and relation of spaces to one another	"A general pass-through", "inside/outside", "layout"
Form	1. Shape of building or component	"Hard-edged block"
	2. Geometry	"A geometry of parallels"
	3. Markings of an organization of space	"Marks a level of difference from here to here"
	4. Experienced felt-path of movement through a building	"Carry the gallery through and look down into here, which is nice"
Structure/technology	Structures, technologies, and processes used in building	"A construction module for these classrooms"
Building character	Kind of building, as sign of style or mode of building	"Warehouse", "hangar", "beach cottage" …
Building elements	Buildings or components of buildings	"Gym", "kindergarten", "ramp", "wall", "roof", "steps"

Design layers and their associated design languages provide a way for the designer to merge constructs from a variety of theories into a design, since many design languages originate in the expression of a theory (Gibbons & Rogers, 2007).

DESIGN DESCRIPTION

A description of one of the software products from the "Treasuring Our Natural Heritage" project will provide an example of the contributions of different layers to a simulation design and the manner in which different theories are employed to solve the design problems presented at each layer. This description will use a narrative style so that later discussions of the layer contributions to the overall design may be more understandable.

The product called *Habitat Hike* was designed to introduce the biological concept of a food web. Within a food web animals and plants supply services to each other by capturing, storing, and transferring energy from the sun (as Primary Producers, Consumers, and Predators), or by breaking biological material back down into reusable nutrients (as Decomposers). Plants and animals do this within the local economy formed by an ecological community of species within a particular habitat—a set of living conditions favorable to particular set of species that live in a complex relationship. Each organism fills one of the four roles within its habitat. Different living conditions are found in different habitats, and each habitat supports life for its unique collection of plants and animals. *Habitat Hike* simulates a hike through seven different habitats encountered on a hike up Mount Borah (12,662 feet in elevation, located in the Challis National Forest in Idaho).

The simulation introduces learners to the unique plants and animals of each habitat, at the same time making them aware of an abstract biological relationship that exists among the animals and plants of every habitat. The hike up Mount Borah begins with a video introduction whose through-the-eyes view indicates that the learner-as-hiker is just arriving at the first habitat with a task to perform (Figure 1).

Figure 1. Video introduction makes it appear as if the learner was just arriving at the first stopping point on the trail up Mount Borah.

This first habitat is Chilly Slough—a wetland habitat. The learner's task is to identify four species of animal and plant within the habitat that have an interdependent relationship with each other: each fills a specific role, either as a Primary Producer, a Consumer, a Predator, or a Decomposer. Figure 2 shows the interface used by the learner to select one organism for each of these roles. Multiple sets of animals can be chosen into the roles, so there are multiple right and wrong combinations of four. A correct set of choices might include "duckweed-coot-mink-aquatic bacteria"; another set might include "cattails-muskrat-mink-aquatic bacteria".

The video portion of this display consists of a 360-degree panorama (complete sphere) of the slough environment. Animals and plants that can be selected from this environment are given emphasis with a halo outline. Four boxes arranged horizontally at the bottom of the display hold the learner's correct responses as they are made. The prompt in the second box in Figure 2 indicates that a Primary Producer is the first expected selection. Arrows connecting the boxes show relationships through which energy and nutrients flow, though it is not expected that the learner will recognize this relationship at first. Rather, the generic food web story told in these four boxes unfolds as the learner makes responses that are either correct or incorrect within each of the seven habitats on the hike.

Only certain responses are acceptable: ones that reflect the actual role relationships of the animals within the habitat. A learner cannot be assumed to possess this knowledge prior to the interaction, so how can they be expected to respond correctly? For this, the design relies on (a) the persistent curiosity of the learner, (b) exploratory behavior at the interface, and (c) information available in different locations in the interface that scaffolds the learner to correct answers.

Multiple sources of helpful information are available at the user interface. A red-naped sapsucker pictured at the upper right on the display is a help-accessing control (and a mascot). The bird's graphical head moves up and down in a way characteristic of the bird's normal head movements to attract learner attention and provoke curiosity and exploration. This roll-over control gives task directions to the user ("locate and click on a primary producer") along with a definition of "primary producer" to help the learner's search through the graphic environment. This game-like interaction resembles a puzzle in which individual pieces may be tested for fit. Failures are accompanied by corrective messages that actually provide more useful information than a correct answer.

Figure 2. This interface asks the learner to enter one organism into each of four habitat roles: Primary Producer, Consumer, Predator, and Decomposer. These roles exist in all habitats, and the learner fills them for each of the seven habitats encountered on the hike up Mount Borah.

By choosing a "food web" icon located directly above the response boxes and to the right, the learner can obtain a complete schematic of the interrelationships of all of the highlighted organisms within the current habitat. Figure 3 shows one kind of food web information obtained by selecting this icon. It displays the network of energy and nutrient sharing within the current habitat among organisms, according to organism roles (as Primary Producers, Consumers, etc.).

91

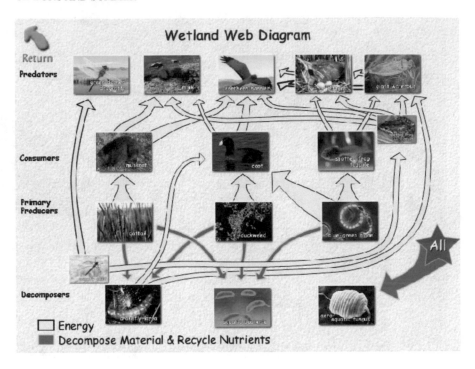

Figure 3. The display of food web relationships in the Chilly Slough habitat according to organism role (e.g., Primary Producer, Consumer, etc.).

As the learner moves the mouse over any of the pictures in this network, the picture expands, suggesting more possible interactions. If the mouse is clicked with the cursor over an organism, the display in Figure 4 appears, showing the food web relationships from the point of view of one organism. Figure 4 shows the information for the Muskrat: which organisms it eats, what eats the Muskrat, and what decomposes it. This information is available for each animal in the habitat. This interaction was deliberately designed to have a "playful" feel. The graphical interaction is spry, and there is much inherent interest in just watching the dynamic changes of this useful information source as the mouse rolls over and selects different graphical elements.

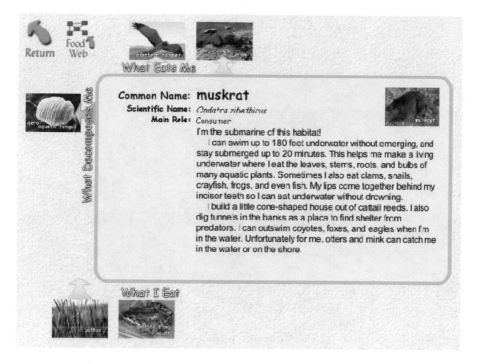

Figure 4. The display of food web relationships pertaining to one organism in Chilly Slough (in this case, the Muskrat).

When a correct choice of Primary Producer is made from the environment display, the picture of the organism appears in the Primary Producer box, as shown in Figure 5 and the user is rewarded with a positive, up-beat chirp from the sapsucker mascot. The next role box in the sequence (the Consumer box) shows a message asking for a Consumer to be selected. In this case an acceptable organism selection is one that eats cattails, since cattails have been fixed now as the Primary Producer.

Figure 5. "Cattails" has been correctly selected as a Primary Producer in Chilly Slough (one of the three possible Primary Producers at the Slough). The next task of the learner is to identify a Consumer. In this case, the corrective message shows that the learner has mistakenly selected a dragonfly as a consumer of cattails.

Feedback (post-response) messages appear following both correct and incorrect responses. These messages are normally somewhat lengthy because they contain information intended to allow the learner to see the information and reasoning that can be used while making future selections. In many cases, as shown in Figure 6, they suggest role connections between organisms, even when those relationships are not needed to make the present selection. This is so that inter-organism role relations will be in the foreground of the learner's attending. Continuation messages are concrete and use verbal imagery and drama to increase the memorability and interest value of the information.

Figure 6. A continuation message obtained by selecting "more info" from a post-response message. In this case, the response was an incorrect one.

Learners continue to respond until all four role boxes are filled with a selection of four acceptable organisms. When this happens, a video clip walks the learner visually from the current habitat up the mountain to the next habitat while telling them an auditory story to orient them to the next habitat. Within that habitat the learner finds a new set of organisms but an identical task—to fill the four role boxes appropriately. Figure 7 shows the environment for the "streamside" habitat. When all of the habitats have been challenged successfully, the learner is shown a video sequence of the last section of the hike—all the way up to the mountain peak (Figure 8).

Figure 7. The streamside habitat, an example of another one of the seven total habitats in Habitat Hike.

Figure 8. The final destination of the hike through seven habitats: Borah Peak.

This extended description of the interface and interaction designs is not intended to depict an ideal. Most designers will find something they feel could be improved. However, it does provide sufficient substance for a discussion of the underlying features of the design, which is the next subject.

DESIGN FEATURES, LAYERS, AND DOMAIN THEORIES

From the beginning of the design process the most important goal was to increase the length of the average learner's engagement within an environment in which there was no obligation to participate. As we have noted, in such situations the average length of engagement is in the range of two minutes or less (e.g. Nourbakhsh et al., 2005; Spencer & Angelotti, 2004). This placed the most importance on features of the design that could (a) attract users, (b) retain user interest for a longer interaction, and (c) convey the message of how food webs work through a rich diversity of units with repeated conceptual structure. Two operational principles were chosen to pursue the goals of initial attraction and longer engagement: (a) a game-like interaction, and (b) a story structure. The

97

game-like interaction had many arguments to recommend it: the natural playfulness of the target population, the popularity of games among the age group, and the likelihood that a more interesting interaction could be sustained in a game-like context. The strongest argument, however, turned out to be the nature of the subject-matter itself, which was essentially a single story told and re-told in the patterns of relationship among the organisms in different habitats.

That story structure consists of a Primary Producer fixing energy and nutrients which then pass on to a Consumer and a Predator in turn, only to be used up or broken back down into nutrients by Decomposers. Early on, the possibility of simply telling the story at the interface was considered, but it became apparent that the real learning goal was not just to know of these relationships but for the learner to be able to "see" them, uncoached, wherever they might be observed in the future, and that there would be an increased likelihood that the learner would actually use the pattern to understand observed ecological relationships. The goal was that the learner would learn to "tell" the story, not just recognize it. We recognized that this learning would require multiple opportunities to act out the "telling" before it became a familiar, fluent process. Accordingly, we set an additional operational principle which could be termed *repeated practice activity*. This operational principle would involve the learner in the repeated telling of the same general story in multiple detailed versions, until an abstract form of the story had been internalized, without the general story itself being made explicit in the form of a traditional instructional presentation.

These initial commitments implied that our design efforts would be selected from the multiple instructional theories that correspond with the operational principles: theories connected with: (a) the design of game-like interactions, (b) the instructional use of narratives, and (c) the design of repeated practice trials. These were accepted as high-level "disciplines" (Schön, 1987), or bounding constraints, within which the remainder of the design would be created. According to Stokes (2006), these would be the *constraints* on the design that would be expected to lead to a *creative* solution. From these three areas of theory, we needed to choose or combine theories that applied to our purposes.

It is important to note that making these initial design commitments placed constraints on later design decisions in two ways: (a) it eliminated certain design possibilities (such as extended didactical presentations) from further consideration, and (b) it constrained the designers to include certain kinds of elements in the design (such as response-and-feedback conversational patterns) in a way that replaced some of the information-delivery functions that otherwise would be carried out by the didactics.

The game design theory we used was most closely aligned with the one described by Salen and Zimmerman (2004), which describes game design principles in terms of the multiple aspects of a game—its rules, its play quality, and its social qualities. We coupled this theory of game-like interactions with a theory of *intentional learning* (Bereiter & Scardamalia, 1993) and a theory of *situated learning* (Lave & Wenger, 1991) both of which recommend that the tasks learners engage in during instruction should be as similar as possible to tasks that require the use of the knowledge in everyday settings.

We used a theory of learning from narrative forms like that of Graesser et al. (2002) and Schank (1990, 2002). Both describe factors for the encoding of information in a form that resembles normal experience easily recalled for use in future reasoning. To fit these theories to our purpose of having the learner "tell" the story, we used Schank's principle of learning following expectation failure (Schank et al., 1994) which relies on a self-motivated and self-directed process of explaining following expectation failure that takes the form of mistakes during performance.

As we have already mentioned, the commitment to these theories had several effects on the design: (a) it incorporated certain types of structure (such as task performance environments, narrative structures, and feedback following incorrect responses) into the design as building blocks, and (b) it eliminated certain other types of structure (such as extended expository presentations) from the design, and (c) it anticipated later design decisions and limited their scope in light of the decisions already made. Making these commitments did not supply theoretical guidance to complete the design. Several bounded synthetic theories (for making representations, for creating control sets, etc.) had to be applied to complete the details of the functions for different layers.

How did our commitment to these theories correspond with our assumption of the layered nature of the design? We found that these decisions had provided the main structures in the content and strategy layers. Our commitment to the story as a form for the subject-matter constituted a decision at the content layer. Our commitment to having the learner "tell" the story repeatedly as a means of instituting it as part of the learner's normal cognitive practice constituted a decision at the strategy layer, as did using Schank's method of expectation failure. The commitment to a game-like interaction constituted a third commitment at the strategy layer. The concept of layers helped us keep these initial priorities in order as the design process advanced.

Having made these commitments, many design decisions remained. Each of the remaining decisions also resided within the layered design structure:

- We designed a set of controls (control layer) that corresponded with the meaningful actions of the learner during story-telling within the game-like environment.
- We had to design a set of message structures (message layer) capable of carrying out the conversational acts of the larger strategy.
- We had to design a set of symbolic representations (representation layer) of the environment, the controls, and the display of the messages.
- We had to define the role that recorded data would play in governing the future course of possible interactions (data management layer).

Could the order of layer-related decisions have been different? We believed it could have been. For example, the problem could have been presented to us with priority on speed of message delivery, minimizing cost, or maximizing speed-of-development, in which case decisions related to the message or representation structures would have been placed in a priority position, making them the constraining factors for the rest of the design.

DETAILED DESIGN WITHIN SUBSEQUENT LAYERS

These primary commitments created a framework within which the detailing of the design could proceed. This detailing consisted of (a) further structuring, (b) assigning specific dimensions to structures, and (c) assigning properties to structures. All of these required the use of layer-related design constructs and theories.

The design process within each layer was similar to the process of a building designer creating a window design (a new design *structure*) within an existing wall (the design *context*). Given the selection of the abstract structure (window)—many questions of dimension and property remain: How tall? How wide? What shape? How paned? How framed? How placed in the wall (elevation from floor and ceiling)? How fit to the wall (sunken or flush)? What type of glass? How mounted?

Similar kinds of structuring, dimensioning, and property-setting questions existed within each layer after the general framework of decisions at the content and strategy layers had been set. Each subsequent decision had the same effect as the initial decisions: curtailing of some lines of design and inclusion by constraint of other lines. For example, the decision to create the spherical-view visual environment entailed integrating the controls for the visual software seamlessly with controls for organism selection, interface navigation, and session management. The decision to use the producer-consumer-predator-decomposer narrative structure required the visual representation of the narrative in abstract form (at the bottom of the display), suggested the need for the food web display-and-querying mechanism, and placed constraints on the kinds of and distribution of plants and animals in each habitat. The commitment to multiple practice opportunities led to the need for the response-and-feedback conversational unit, which in turn led to the need for a common and consistent message structure for the feedback message elements.

RESULTS

The *Treasuring Our Natural Heritage* project provided one of the earliest opportunities to apply layered design concept deliberately to an instructional simulation. The finished *Habitat Hike* was implemented with thousands of learners in Idaho public schools and over 100,000 learners in libraries and other community contexts. Data gathered during use indicated that the length of the average engagement was over eight minutes, more than four times the target criterion. We do not attribute this surprising result to the use of layers in the design. However, we feel that this success in motivating the learner and the relative ease with which the design was evolved justifies drawing some conclusions about the value of layers to the designer.

First, the design itself was completed in a very short period of time. Though the production of message content, media resources, and programming took a normal amount of time, the design itself was surprisingly economical and easy to produce. This was unexpected, considering that the design team included non-designers and was made up of people from different specialty areas (design, subject-matter, computer programming) who had not worked together before. The foreshortening of the design period was possible because the maximum attention could be given to the decisions most central to the project's design goals. This in turn was made possible by the clear identification of the hierarchy of design goals provided by the designer's understanding of layers. It is not unusual in a team composition of this type for minor design issues to take attention away from major structuring questions, resulting in much longer design periods. This was not a problem in the design of *Habitat Hike*.

Second, the layer architecture did not itself have to be the focus of the design effort. Though layers were referred to by designers talking with designers, the conversation between the designers and the subject-matter expert could be in terms of the content and messages with which the expert felt most comfortable. Often in other projects, the mechanisms of the designer intrude into the subject-matter expert's world, forcing them to adopt the terminology and processes of the designer. This is true, for example, in projects where much time is spent in task analysis or the writing of instructional objectives. Discussions during the design of *Habitat Hike* focused on the nature of the learner's experience and learning outcomes, and only the designers had to be concerned with "the [designer] behind the curtain".

Third, the architecture of layers helped the designers to focus the application of multiple instructional design theories. They allowed the designers to identify and present a range of options for the key structures of the design and clarify which issues were of primary and secondary importance. In this way, each part of the design problem received attention in proportion to its importance, and it was easy to trace decisions to theory and identify which ones could change and which had to remain constant to protect the theoretical integrity of the design.

CONCLUSION

The layered design framework was beneficial in the design of this simulation because it gave the designers a language for talking about the design and a similar language for talking with other team members about characteristics of the design without asserting the designer's view of the world unnecessarily. The framework of layers facilitated focusing multiple instructional design theories on parts of the design to which they were most critical, and it demonstrated to the designers that the design process could be shortened and the design made more interesting, even for newly-formed teams.

REFERENCES

Bell, B., Bareiss, R. & Beckwith, R. (1993). Sickle cell counselor: A prototype goal-based scenario for instruction in a museum environment. *Journal of the Learning Sciences, 3*(4), 347-386.

Bereiter, C. & Scardamalia, M. (1993). *Surpassing ourselves: An inquiry into the nature and implications of expertise.* Chicago, IL: Open Court Publishing Company.

Brand, S. (1994). *How buildings learn: What happens after they're built.* New York: Penguin Books.

Gibbons, A. S. & Rogers, P. C. (2007). The architecture of instructional theory. In C. M. Reigeluth and A. Carr-Chellman (Eds.), *Instructional-design models and theories, Vol. III.* Mahwah, NJ: Lawrence Erlbaum Associates.

Greasser, A. C., Olde, B. & Klettke, B. (2002). How does the mind construct and represent stories? In M. Green, J. Strange, and T. Brock (Eds.), *Narrative impact: Social and cognitive foundations.* Mahwah, NJ: Lawrence Erlbaum Associates.

Lave, J., & Wenger, E. (1991). *Situated learning: Legitimate peripheral practice.* Cambridge, UK: Cambridge University Press.

Nourbakhsh, I., Hamner, E., Dunlavey, B., Bernstein, D. & Crowley, K. (2005). Educational results of the personal exploration rover museum exhibit. In *Proceedings of the 2005 IEEE International Conference on Robotics and Automation,* Barcelona, Spain, April 2005, pp. 4278-4283.

Salen, K. & Zimmerman, E. (2004). *Rules of play: Game design fundamentals.* Cambridge, MA: MIT Press.

Schank, R. C. (1990). *Tell me a story.* Evanston, IL: Northwestern University Press.

Schank, R. C. & Berman, T. R. (2002). The pervasive role of stories in knowledge and action. In M. Green, J. Strange, and T. Brock (Eds.), *Narrative impact: Social and cognitive foundations.* Mahwah, NJ: Lawrence Erlbaum Associates.

Schank, R. C., Kass, A. & Riesbeck, C. K. (1994). *Inside case-based explanation.* Hillsdale, NJ: Lawrence Erlbaum Associates.

Schön, D. A. (1987). *Educating the reflective practitioner.* San Francisco, CA: Jossey-Bass Publishers.

Stokes, P. D. (2006). *Creativity from constraints: The psychology of breakthrough.* New York, NY: Springer Publishing Company.

Spencer, D. & Angelotti, V. (2004). It's a nano world: Findings from a summative study. Unpublished report, Cornell University Nanobiotechnology Center. Retrieved March 6, 2007 from http://www.informalscience.org/.

Andrew S. Gibbons
Department of Instructional Psychology and Technology
Brigham Young University

Stefan Sommer
Department of Biological Sciences
Northern Arizona University

BRETT E. SHELTON

DESIGNING EDUCATIONAL GAMES FOR ACTIVITY-GOAL ALIGNMENT

A perspective on how to improve current practices

INTRODUCTION

ALICE was beginning to get very tired of sitting by her sister on the bank and of having nothing to do: once or twice she had peeped into the book her sister was reading, but it had no pictures or conversations in it, "and what is the use of a book," thought Alice, "without pictures or conversations?"

What indeed, can we expect from our newest trend in education, implementing moving pictures and conversations with instruction through simulation games? Lewis Carroll's familiar narratives *Alice's Adventures in Wonderland* and *Alice Through the Looking Glass* provide helpful imagery for many of the queries, explorations and assumptions we currently make about this latest Wonderland of academia. So what are the goals for the designers and researchers of educational games, or perhaps more importantly, what *should* be the goals?

Perhaps not a goal in itself, a tenet of educational technology research is to develop and study new ways of utilizing technology to support effective instruction. Recently, using computer-based simulations and games in a variety of educational contexts has come to the forefront of this research agenda. Although there are several positions taken by game design researchers and instructional design researchers, most share a common focus: combining theoretical perspectives to design and develop technology-based tools for use in a variety of settings. These approaches have followed a number of models and have been supported through a number of scientific-based philosophies in education:

- constructionist building of knowledge (Barab, Hay, Barnett, & Keating, 2000; Moshell & Hughes, 1995)
- constructivist activity (Dede, 1995; Jonassen, Peck, & Wilson, 1999; Roschelle, Pea, Hoadley, Gordin, & Means, 2000)
- problem based learning (Barrows, 1986, 1996, 2002; Soloway et al., 2001)
- project based activity (Blumenfeld, Fishman, Krajcik, & Marx, 2000; Fishman, Marx, Blumenfeld, & Krajcik, 2004)

B. E. Shelton, D. A. Wiley (eds.), Educational Design & Use of Computer Simulation Games, 103–130.

- artifact-based, inscriptions and distribution of knowledge (Gordin & Pea, 1995; Roschelle, 1992; Suchman, 2000)

In recent work, various technology researchers have used these approaches within their own definition of computer simulations and games, considering educational games as having intended learning outcomes that combine autonomous and interactive elements in a contrived environment (Davison & Gordon, 1978; Hertel & Millis, 2002; Jones, 1987). The action and interplay within the environment represents complex situations or phenomena and a level of social, distributed knowledge (deJong & vanJoolingen, 1998; Windschitl, 2000). Other researchers have argued that this definition is an improvement over prior definitions, that fail to consider the potential and nature of social interplay between participants, the intended audience of the instruction, and the instructional objectives of the exercise (Shelton & Wiley, 2006b).

The emerging theoretical approaches and the simulations and games derived from them show promise for helping educational technologists reach their goals of efficient, effective, appealing instruction for complex material (Shelton, 2003; Squire, Barnett, Grant, & Higginbotham, 2004; Winn, 2002; Winn & Windschitl, 2002). However, the field has yet to address how these resources are being designed and built to accommodate and be used advantageously by persons with varying abilities. I have received emails from teachers from around the world asking how to implement an educational game developed for use in their classrooms. One teacher from Pennsylvania asked how to use the game with "remedial readers" in her class of junior college students. Another instructor from Jakarta asked how he could use a game in his class of physically challenged students. Unfortunately, I did not have an informed answer for either of these questions. In this chapter I will argue that current approaches to using educational simulations and games are incomplete and have yet to bare the educational results of their potential. Further, very little attention has been given to a design consideration that should help map motivation to the instructional goals of educational simulations and games, while the potential exists to exploit the nature of these tools to address students with specific learning needs.

Therefore, by the end of this chapter, the need to clarify a basic approach directed at *devising, designing, and developing educational simulations and games for persons with varying abilities* should be made. Rather than viewing educational simulations and games as decontextualized artifacts existing independently of learners' interactions with them, appropriate strategies will allow the research to develop in ways that allow the resources to mediate the way both the designers and the users of the technology come to understand conceptual material. This learning process exists in contexts that include both formal and informal learning environments, addresses issues of universal design and usability, and integrates typologies of simulation game approaches that target specific cognitive challenges.[1]

WHY TO WE NEED NEW FRAMEWORKS?

"Curiouser and curiouser!" cried Alice

While instructors of multiple scientific disciplines are embracing educational computer games through a variety of philosophies and technologies, no rigorous frameworks for their design and use exist. In this section, I will explain current approaches to using educational games to facilitate learning, and contrast the assumptions of these approaches with current research. I will then characterize the design and development framework I believe is necessary for supporting the learning community more effectively.

Current approaches to designing and using educational games

Educational researchers and lay persons alike tend to believe the use of educational games can change the way students learn. But like other instructional media, educational games are only tools that enhance learning when designed and implemented in accordance with principles of effective instruction. Two approaches to designing and using educational games in the context of these principles currently dominate the published literature and conference presentations. Some researchers advocate an approach rooted in game design theory, emphasizing the educational importance of motivating and engaging learners (Zimmerman & Fortugno, 2006). Others advocate approaches rooted in instructional design, creating meaningful activities that are somehow driven by and assessed through traditional means (VanEck, 2006). Yet many scholars, myself included, believe the most appropriate approach lies at the intersection of traditional game theory and instructional design theory.

Undoubtedly, the people interested in games research who work in different disciplines have vastly different perspectives on what is important in making these games instructionally effective. It is a Mad Hatter's tea party of researchers with just as many opinions. But even within this huge diversity of interests, few if any researchers have worked to bring the benefits of these approaches to underserved groups. Many students are not afforded the same opportunities to use instructional

---

[1] For the remainder of this chapter, I will use the term "educational games" when describing the spectrum of computer-based tools that include instructional simulations with game-like elements and educational games with simulation-like qualities. I recognize the many differences in how genres of computer-based simulations and games can address different aspects of learning, and can be dissimilar in a number of other respects. However, I will use the term "educational games" in the effort to be inclusive of most types and to maintain clarity and brevity throughout my arguments.

games due to their physical or cognitive disabilities, and the limitations of the educational tools themselves. Even more glaring, a balance between building motivational, engaging games has not converged with the kinds of promising learning outcomes desired by most educators who use games in their teaching. So, what are the important research questions, and what is it that we as educational technologists can do to address these challenges? I believe we should begin by adopting a position of skepticism instead of being educational games advocates. Too many assumptions remain about what games do and to what advantages we can use them. Cuban (1986) highlighted the utter disappointments of the realized potential of each new technology and how its use would *change the face of education, how it's practiced, and how students will learn* since 1920, and thus far we should add educational games to the list. The assumptions are many, and are indicative of how games:

- Can help people teach. Most evidence has been contrary to this notion thus far, in that instructors have little time to prepare lessons around the use of games for classroom use, or are not gamers themselves, or do not have enough instructional support, or cannot align them with state and national standards (Kirriemuir, 2002, 2003; Kirriemuir & McFarlane, 2003; Shaffer, Squire, Halverson, & Gee, 2004).

- Can help people learn about complex relationships and phenomena. The evidence exists to support this notion within contextualized pockets and in situ experimental situations, but has yet to be implemented across multiple contexts or at any reasonably large scale (Barab, Hay, Barnett, & Squire, 2001; Hayes, 2002).

A sound philosophy of research-into-practice includes many of the questions that echo those of Squire (2002), when he advocated a learning sciences approach to studying educational games, looking to the kinds of activity that go on within and between individuals and the artifacts they use to develop understandings of complex material. We still know little about how these understandings translate to the "real world" and if and when they are applicable. We know little about the impact of these games and how they can align with more formal learning environments. The development of hybrid theories and approaches to learning-type games are necessary to advance the field. The creation and study of games based on these hybrid theories is crucial. Therefore, the continual questioning of the existing assumptions is important to better understand if and how instructional games can and should be used within formal and informal educational environments.

Parallel to the issues of using computer games effectively in traditional school-based environments is an issue with the design and development cycle for building educational games for students with learning disabilities, even while preliminary evidence suggests that some of these tools have the potential for effectively addressing specific impairments. Diggs (Diggs, 1997) offers a case that shows how computer technology, including educational games, helped a fourth grade student with learning disabilities and behavioral disorders begin to succeed academically and to interact with his peers. Other researchers discuss the benefits of educational games for cognitive impairments, including the increased motivation of learners and the ability to customize the tools for specific types of challenges (Blum & Yocom, 1996; Shiah, Mastropieri, Scruggs, & Fulk, 1994). Additional research has suggested that these types of activities help students with learning disabilities in areas of writing, memory tasks, geography and the application of problem-solving skills (Conderman & Tompkins, 1995; Okolo, 1992; Welch, 1995). While most studies indicate the potential of these tools, not all of the evidence is in agreement. Christensen and Gerber (1990) indicate that a non-game-like approach was more effective for cognitively impaired students for a drill-and-practice exercise, perhaps due to the distractions and load of the non-instructive elements of the activity. These studies exemplify the potential of educational games for students with learning disabilities with a special eye toward the proper design and implementation.

ELEMENTS OF EFFECTIVE INSTRUCTIONAL GAMES

"A cat may look at a king," said Alice. "I've read that in some book, but I don't remember where."
"Tut, tut, child!" said the Duchess. "Everything's got a moral, if only you can find it." And she squeezed herself up closer to Alice's side as she spoke.

Disparities between educational games approaches and current research on learning

When discussing the use of educational computer games in formal learning environments, it is helpful to distinguish between three types of games. The first, which might be termed "entertainment games," includes computer games designed for entertainment purposes that are "repurposed" in the context of lessons. For example, *SimCity 3000* and *Age of Empires*, commercially available games, are used as tools in the classroom to teach students to understand complex, dynamic models (e.g., community planning and geographic placement of services) and to improve thinking skills (BECTA, 2001). The games' entertainment value has been used to motivate students to participate in the learning activity, and the game activity has been repurposed into a lesson. One downside of this approach is that much of the substantial "learning" that is reported is secondary or unintentional (Kirriemuir & McFarlane, 2003). Secondary or unintentional learning occurs when

107

a player learns concepts or skills not associated with the goals of the activity. Examples of unintentional learning are acquiring social skills from participating in the game environment, learning how to better use the controls of the game, or gaining an understanding of what abilities the arch nemesis has. To clarify, it is not that unintentional learning cannot be beneficial, it is more that within a structured learning environment in which specific learning goals are intended, unintentional learning is not very helpful. And from a designer's perspective, it is not useful.

The second type, which might be termed "reward games," includes games explicitly designed for education that rely on "reward" systems to motivate students in the learning activity. The reward systems are not associated with learning activity, but rather act as a means to an end so that the player is rewarded for "correct" behaviors. These games often come in the form of basic skill practice such as a typing tutor in which the reward system may become the focus of the game or a distraction from the learning activity. An example in this category is drill-for-skill games like many of those in the *Jumpstart* series. The success of these games is limited to reinforcing recognition and response times through practicing repetitive procedures. One downside of this approach is that "reward" systems may not have enough motivational power to help learners reach complex instructional or reflective goals. Other arguments suggest that "rewards" games are more effective for less complex kinds of cognitive practices, or that excessive rewards may lead to activity that actually detracts from the learning objectives, which is common to the third type of game.

The third type, which might be termed "distraction games," includes those that are specifically designed for learning but contain overwhelming levels of game-like attributes that ultimately distract the players from the learning objectives (Kirriemuir, 2003). For example, *Supercharged!* is an educational game designed to teach students about electromagnetic fields. Squire et al. (2004) found that some students struggled to achieve a deep understanding of the activity's non game-like components. Some students felt more compelled to "win" the game, rather than the activity associated with "winning." Therefore, attempting new strategies or playing the complementary levels to learn about electromagnetic fields was less interesting. Research suggesting why this third category of games has failed to reach its expected potential also suggests what might be done to develop games that lead to effective learning. Shelton (2005a) suggested the potential of using computer games for instruction may be observed by understanding the problems associated with their design. Working to align game activities with instructional goals may help balance the motivations for playing the game. Findings from this research suggest that the problems with some games may not be found in the idea of gaming but how the games are structured or aligned with their learning objectives.

Toward a new theoretical framework

In prior work with partial funding from the state of Utah, I have attempted to describe both ontological and functional aspects of educational games. This work continues based on identified elements of learner-player motivation--the first three based on modified video game motivation elements (Lepper & Chabay, 1985; Malone, 1980; Malone & Lepper, 1987; Shelton & Wiley, 2006b) and the final on social interaction analysis (Steinkuehler, 2003; Steinkuehler & Chmiel, 2006):

- *challenge* – the gamer is provided a goal, and activities (neither too complex nor too simple) are required to make progress within a situation or environment
- *proclivity* – an environment that holds a personal interest, drawing an individual toward the subject matter in a way that sustains interest
- *uncertainty* – imagining a number of possible outcomes to an activity, and the desire to want to reach an attainable stopping point which requires a measure of persistence
- *social interaction* – peer collaboration is an effective way for a child with low ability in learning, paired with a child of high ability, to lead to cognitive benefits for both children (Fawcett & Garton, 2005)

Aldrich's six criteria for what counts as an educational simulation (2004a; 2004b), based on the *Virtual Leader* simulation and surrounding project, are divided into two categories that describe the delivery elements of the simulation and the type of content within the simulation. His delivery criteria are simulation, game and pedagogy; his content criteria are systems, cyclical and linear. However, some have argued that his described delivery elements fail to adequately emphasize the role of intelligent participants within the simulation. Further, his criteria of pedagogy does not provide an emphasis on the issues that surround learning, including the way information is represented, and aspects of cognitive load.[2]

Based on a working perspective of what an effective educational simulation does, I define an effective educational simulation as: *with the intention of helping learners achieve desired outcomes, an instructional simulation combines autonomous and interactive elements in a contrived environment that represents complex concepts or phenomena of the real world*. Outcome measures and advantages include the ability for the student to learn at their own pace, the student is able to retain and apply what they learned, and the educational game is accessible to multiple learning styles. Using the criteria from Aldrich as a starting point for defining the elements of effective instructional simulations, I emphasize the pedagogy and engagement factors within the simulation scenario of what makes for *essential criteria*:

- Addresses a learning issue
  - o Complex – requiring a level of depth beyond what one sees in simple "walk-through instruction"

---

[2] With Aldrich's content types, I assume they only specify a computer-based environment that also provides simulation-like features of repeatability, scalability, and cost-effectiveness. However, I am unsure if this assumption is warranted.

- o Intentional – directed instruction aimed at identified problems, but may be exploratory in nature
- Contains learning objectives or goals
  - o Explicit or implicit, depending on how they fit within the flow of the scenario
- Includes participants with constraints (rules)
  - o Not observers, requires a level of interaction
  - o Includes an environment with constraints (rules)
- Contrived for other-world experiences, and/or
  - o Mimics real-world processes, sequences, etc.
- Operates by a facilitating mechanism – includes required hardware, software, and non-computer based resources
- Requires activity
  - o Interactive (contains feedback, adaptation, choice)
  - o Autonomous (embedded information)
- Based on non-random outcomes
  - o Sequences of events produce a predictable outcome, ultimately tied to learning goals
  - o Events within a scenario may have random qualities
- Repeatable (different choices may produce different outcomes)

In addition to the essential criteria listed above, I recommend keeping other design criteria in mind as well in order to take full-advantage of what educational games may offer:

- Scalable
  - o Internal – the simulation may be expanded to include multiple players
  - o External – the platform may be developed to include multiple scenarios based on similar instructional objectives
- Contains representations not possible / affordable to experience in the "real world"
- Cost-effective

These definitions and criteria have assisted in forming a grounded basis for analyzing educational simulation games in a variety of settings. Through this experience, research such as that contained in this volume may continue an effort for the merging of philosophies and approaches from industry training, game design theory and instructional design theory to help inform the designers and developers of technology and games-related. Using these definitions and criteria, researchers may choose to turn a special eye toward how these tools are used by persons with varying abilities as they mediate their understanding of complex concepts and phenomena. This emerging broad base of educational games research, such as that within this volume by Nelson et al., Squire et al., Barab et al. and Steinhuehler, positions the field well to carry out the proposed activities.

I believe that a more rigorous understanding of the ways in which learners actually use educational games, that is, a more rigorous understanding of the ways that educational simulations and games mediate educational activities, will provide significant value to science, mathematics and technology education for persons with differing abilities. This increase in understanding will serve to launch a very productive course of educational technology research. In the next section, I provide an example of students using educational games for problem solving activities.

ACTIVITY-GOAL ALIGNMENT THEORY

Once more she found herself in the long hall, and close to the little glass table. "Now, I'll manage better this time," she said to herself, and began by taking the little golden key, and unlocking the door that led into the garden. Then she went to work nibbling at the mushroom (she had kept a piece of it in her pocket) till she was about a foot high: then she walked down the little passage: and then--she found herself at last in the beautiful garden, among the bright flower-beds and the cool fountains.

Alice eventually learns that in Wonderland, the keys she finds fit the doors she is supposed to enter, and eating just the right amount of mushroom will make her the proper size to move forward. In fact, she is learning from her environment what the important things are to attend to. So is what we learn from studying those who play games truly beneficial, worthwhile, and valid? Shaffer et al. (2004) write that games are changing the way we learn by giving players the opportunity to participate in different game-created worlds and to learn by doing. Education researchers suggest the use of computer games may help transform the way students think about their world (Holland, Jenkins, & Squire, 2003; Steinkuehler, 2003). The bulk of the evidence suggests that computer simulation games can be used to increase student motivation, teach problem solving strategies, and help students understand the meaning of context (Gunter, 1998; Hayes, 2002). I generalize that educational games may provide learning benefits if the beneficial potential games offer can be organized into the game itself, and into the social activity surrounding the game. What we learn from playing educational games is truly beneficial only when they are designed according to valid principles of effective instruction. We need frameworks to understand what these principles are.

River City, developed at Harvard by Dede, Ketelhut, and Nelson (2004), represents players as an avatar in a virtual world with the purpose of finding out what is causing a disease in a local town. When beginning the game, the players may choose the name of their avatar as well as their character. The creators of the game designed a particular character after Ellen Swallow, the first woman to graduate from MIT with a chemistry degree, with the intent of increasing motivation for female players. While these game-like characteristics were added to enhance the experience of the player and create high levels of motivation, they also have the potential to distract from the learning activity in the same way "reward" system games do. Both *Supercharged!* and *River City* are examples of computer games designed for learning that have enjoyed some success for learning outcomes. However, the motivation attributes of each of these games were not necessarily designed to be balanced with the instructional activities, and some disconnect was reported with how students approached their designed learning activities and their motivation for playing.

This idea of aligning game activities with learning goals is meant to improve educational game design so that learning experiences for the players will be considered engaging from the perspective of the learner and successful from the perspective of the instructor. It addresses the problem with the first category of educational computer games by designing the games specifically with instructional objectives in mind and creating games whose primary purpose is for learning (Shelton 2005b). Designing for activity-goal alignment ensures that a correct balance of game-like attributes are included for motivation, but that the activities within the game are meaningful, and therefore exist as more than just a means to an end. The game includes motivation-inducing attributes of challenge, proclivity, and uncertainty, yet directs them toward the learning goals, thus differentiating them from games within the second and third categories mentioned previously (Shelton and Wiley 2006b). Gibbons and Fairweather (2000) offer similar advice when designing for instructional simulations in waves. It is important to look for alignment of activities with instructional goals, and that the design of the environment and model structure match the "action" of instructional goals. The design should ensure that problem solving in the environment offers the correct types of practice with desired instructional support. If designing and developing in a series of iterations consistent with activity-goal alignment is achieved, we theorize that the instructional game that results will be highly motivating and be useful for learning. In essence, the learning will be fun.

In short, although there is a body of evidence to build on, there is still a great deal of work to be done in designing theoretical frameworks for the design and utilization of educational games. For the present discussion, existing approaches must be re-examined in light of current research in teaching, design and learning, to take into account the difficulties with current approaches described above, and be grounded in accounts of actual use. The unit of analysis can be neither the player-learner nor the educational game itself, but must instead be the "person-acting-with-mediational-means" (Wertsch, 1991), or more specifically, the learner-problem-solving-using-games-as-tools.

IMPLEMENTING ACTIVITY-GOAL ALIGNMENT

"I quite agree with you," said the Duchess; "and the moral of that is--Be what you would seem to be--or if you'd like it put more simply--Never imagine yourself not to be otherwise than what it might appear to others that what you were or might have

been was not otherwise than what you had been would have appeared to them to be otherwise."

"I think I should understand that better," Alice said very politely, "if I had it written down: but I can't quite follow it as you say it."

To this point I have asserted that communities of learners who use simulations and games exist and the practices of these communities have made an impact within educational research. In this section I present a brief example of an interaction from such a learner, comment on the example in terms of the obstacles described above, and compare the case to current educational games approaches. In this way, I endeavour to explain more clearly the potential impact of designing educational games through activity-goal alignment.

Interactive fiction: an appropriate medium for alignment

Games can exist within virtual worlds or environments that can give the player a feeling of presence with high levels of engagement (McMahan, 2003). Games have been utilized to address different types of learning as well as a variety of subject matter ranging from history to engineering and mathematics (Squire et al 2004, Shaffer et al, 2004). The interactive nature of games lends itself readily to a supporting role in teaching. One exciting possibility is the use of games in experiencing a classic text in a new media form. Interactive fiction (IF) is a new media form that provides players the opportunity to experience text in a way that provides a blend of entertainment and education.

Generally, IF is a game format that tells a narrative or story by offering a text-based description of a series of locations, non-player characters and rich description. The player interacts with the narrative through a computer program that parses the text responses of the player and advances the game accordingly. The player is a character within the story and the story progresses as a consequence of the actions of the player. Traditional IF games have come in the form of "text adventures" such as the *Zork* trilogy and *Hitchhiker's Guide to the Galaxy* in the early 1980s, but there remains a faithful subculture of writers and programmers of IF to this day. In the majority of IF games there are numerous puzzle-solving scenarios that help the player advance within the narrative. Consequently, IF requires that the player gives more attention to thought than to action. (Granade, 2005) IF also creates an explorable world that is experienced through text (Short, 2005). The nature of IF and its potential to experience traditional text in new ways make it a suitable candidate for learning experiences using classic works of fiction. Montford offers the opinion that one clear match between IF and classic texts is the idea of "text-in and text-out." The interface of IF in its text-based form offers a basic level of symmetry, consistent with experiencing text in its native paper-and-ink format (Deshrill, 2004, Montfort, 2003).

Additionally, IF can provide successful learning experiences with classic texts by reinforcing and augmenting the instructional aims of a standard English classroom. Reading comprehension and fluency, poetic devices, literary analysis, character motivation, and examination of narrative and plot structure can all be explored. IF can offer the benefit of maintaining the original published form of the text. It may not be necessary to edit, condense, or otherwise alter the original text. Along with traditional learning goals, we feel that it is possible to experience further learning outcomes that may be unintended but nonetheless beneficial to the player. These outcomes include problem solving, spatial reasoning, and increased confidence. IF is portable as well as scalable so that it may be incorporated into classroom activity, group-work, or as a stand-alone product for an individual. Ladd (2006) has written that using IF to teach computer science has resulted in positive outcomes by teaching programming fundamentals combined with creating a project that is both motivating and difficult. We suggest that instructional technologists, armed with activity-goal alignment theory as their guiding tenet will be able to incorporate IF with classic text instruction for English.

Case example: Voices of Spoon River

The following excerpt is taken from the *Voices of Spoon River* project within the Creative Learning Environments Laboratory at Utah State University (http://cle.usu.edu/CLE_IF_VOSR.html). Students of a 9th grade English class studied early 20th century American poetry through the use of an educational game. Secondary learning goals include aspects problem solving. Highlighted here is an example analysis of two students interacting with an educational game. Portions of the interaction have been removed in order to preserve space. A screen capture of the interface is pictured in Figure 1.

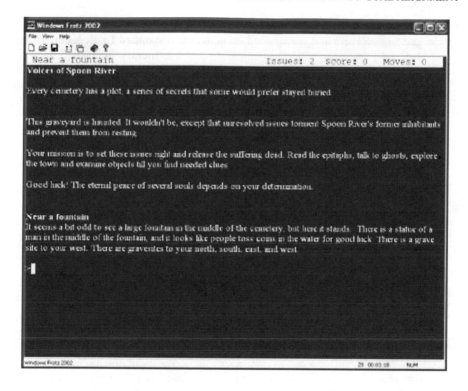

Figure 1. Voices of Spoon River interface.

In these examples we see a modified form of the problem solving process described by Nelson (1999).

- Learners negotiate a common understanding of the problem through a series of questions and restatements,
- learners' problem solving are implied, as each learner considers the problem and responds with further clarifications, thoughts, or ideas through their actions,
- learners gather information from a variety of sources, including non-player characters (NPCs), "help" directives, other players and initial documentation,
- a solution is attempted, and further questions are raised, beginning the problem-solving cycle anew.

I led the research team in studying how students' problem solving goals aligned with their game activity to help us determine whether or not they achieved the designed learning outcome. In this case, we first examined the "Judge Somers issue" as outlined in Table 1 below. We identified expected outcomes as designed by the game developers and unexpected outcomes as performed by students.

Table 1. Examples of learning goals, game-based activity and the activity outcome

Game-based activity	Learning goal activity	Activity outcome
Find Somers as a NPC. Put a headstone recognizing him in the cemetery, where he currently has an unmarked grave.	Problem solving Recognizing and acting upon symbolic references	Expected: Students found a tombstone and used a wheelbarrow to haul and dump it on an empty spot to mark the Judge's plot.
Solve poetry puzzle in order to get clues and solve issue for Somers	Reading comprehension: understanding literary terms and character analysis	Unexpected: One student tried pushing the wheelbarrow up some stairs because she thought the Judge was located there.

By reviewing the game transcripts, we could see what each student did during game play. Judge Somers is buried in an unmarked grave. To resolve his issue, players need to find a tombstone and take it to his unmarked grave. In the course of the game, players will encounter the judge in a photography studio where he appears to stop them from going up some stairs until they first resolve his issue. After the judge gives the instructions, he disappears. Because of this experience, Maria, a student player, thought that the judge's ghost was upstairs. From her game transcript, we recognize that she tried multiple times to push the wheelbarrow with the tombstone in it up the stairs. In her interview she was asked why she did this, to which she replied, "I didn't know where the tombstone was supposed to go. I thought that it had to go to the ghost but it didn't; it had to go to the empty spot." She left the wheelbarrow there for a while and explored other regions of the game. After finding the empty spot in the graveyard, she made the connection that this was the place for the tombstone. She then went directly to the wheelbarrow and pushed it to the unmarked grave and resolved the judge's issue.

Even though Maria performed an unexpected outcome, she was able to finally resolve the issue. However, another student did perform what the designers expected for this issue. Melissa was able to find the clues and solve the problems that lead her to ultimately resolve Judge Somers'. In her interview, Melissa talked about how the activities of the game helped her understand what items needed to be used and what action was required to resolve the issue. She talked about how walking around the town of Spoon River helped her make connections between items and the actions that needed to be performed to resolve the issue. "I would go through and I would first read an epitaph and something wouldn't make sense, but then I would go through the game and I would find an object and think, 'Oh, that is what it's for,' and then it would come together and then I would understand it."

116

Both of these students demonstrated a functioning example of the problem solving process by aligning their game play actions with the instructional goals of the exercise (Nelson, 1999; Shelton, 2005a). Because Maria had not yet performed all game activity needed to find necessary information, she had come to the incorrect conclusion of taking the tombstone to the ghost of Judge Somers and not the empty gravesite. However, Melissa had performed all of the necessary game activities and achieved the correct solution. Although their methods were different, they both demonstrated that game activity lead to fulfilling learning objectives, specifically, resolving the "problem" of Judge Somers.

Paras and Bizzocchi (2005) discuss the importance of reflective activity as also aligned with game play, and thus within the course of achieving instructional goals:

> In educational game design it is important to ensure that learning takes places within the realm of play, even if learning is only made possible through reflection. To do so, reflection must appear to the learner as one of the many in-game goals that drive the game-play.

There exists some evidence suggested by the transcripts of in-game reflection of character motivations and connections with one another, in fact, the genre itself allowed for such reflection due to its nature of having to wait for player input for narrative progression (Scoresby, Duncan & Shelton, 2006). It may very well be the case that the game genre itself dictates the effectiveness of activity-goal alignment during game play, a point recently discussed by Dickey (2006) and worth further exploration for subsequent study.

Discussion of the sample case and current educational games approaches

We address the question of aligning the structure of the games with the learning objectives by examining the challenges faced by learning technologists. Researchers who have studied the integration of computer games designed as part of an instructional exercise have reported their success and limitations. Further studies continue to investigate new ways of implementing computer games as teaching tools in both formal and informal learning environments (Gee, 2003; Shaffer et al., 2004). Designers of educational games must address issues concerning the format of game play and how to avoid attributes that may distract from the learning activities. So what are the primary design issues instructional technologists face when beginning their design? Brown and Duguid (2000) suggest that learning about something is limited to gaining information, whereas learning to become something requires both information and experience. For example, learning about being a doctor and learning to become a doctor are two very different things. When designing games, instructional technologists should try to design instructional tools that help the learner to become something. Being an active participant in one's learning in an educational game is assisted by aligning the game's activities with the intended instructional goals.

Aligning game activities with learning goals is meant to improve educational game design so that learning experiences will be considered engaging from the learner's perspective and successful from the instructor's perspective. It addresses the problem with the first category of educational games by designing specifically with instructional objectives in mind and creating games whose primary purpose is learning (Shelton, 2005b). Designing for activity-goal alignment ensures that a correct balance of game-like attributes are included for motivation, but that the activities within the game are meaningful, and therefore exist as more than just a means to an end. The game in this example case includes motivation-inducing attributes of challenge, proclivity, and uncertainty, yet directs them toward the learning goals, thus differentiating them from games within the second and third categories mentioned previously. It is important to look for alignment of activities within instructional goals, and to match the "action" of instructional goals with the design of the environment and model structure. The design should ensure that problem solving in the environment offers appropriate types of practice with desired instructional support. If designing and developing in a series of iterations consistent with activity-goal alignment is achieved, I theorize that the resulting educational game will be highly motivating and useful for learning. In essence, the learning will be more like "fun" even if it is not the same as the kinds of activity associated with most commercially successful games.

The sample case includes a small number of learners, yet scalability (in terms of simulation-game-bandwidth) is not an issue. Learners are provided with meaningful learning support "anytime anywhere" within the games, yet most cases are rich with human-to-human interaction. Educational games are successfully embedded in meaningful learning contexts, but the design, development and use of them is done *by* humans *for* other humans. It is because that play within these scenarios is naturally occurring and exists in environments of social interaction that the resulting activity can be deemed as significant.

ROLE OF PRESENCE AND FLOW

SHE took her off the table as she spoke, and shook her backwards and forwards with all her might. The Red Queen made no resistance whatever: only her face grew very small, and her eyes got large and green: and still, as Alice went on shaking her, she kept on growing shorter--and fatter--and softer--and rounder-- and—and it really was a kitten after all.

Perspective certainly counted for something when Alice awoke from her experience in Wonderland. In the same vein, the kinds of learning experiences through virtual interfaces in simulation game environments impact their design and use. In *Voices of Spoon River*, we chose an interface of text-based input and output to help reflect the kinds of literacy objectives we were trying to achieve, matching those of state and national standards. Subsequently, we built *VOSR 3D*, a 3D version of the same game but whose interface could be set to either first-person or third person perspective (see Figure 2). The textual components of both the original

Voices of Spoon River and *VOSR 3D* were consistent in terms of object use and description, and therefore the game play was consistently aligned in both versions with the primary learning objectives. Yet the games would appear to be very different in how the player interacted with the environment in each version. By changing the learner's perspective of the game, we undoubtedly altered the way the learner came to understand the information as gleaned from the virtual environment. The issues of flow, presence and immersion continue to effect the way games are experienced, even when keeping the design philosophy of activity-goal alignment intact.

Figure 2. Screenshots of VOSR 3D *in third-person perspective (above) and first-person perspective (below).*

Researchers have consistently referred to the link between presence, the sense of "being there" in an environment, and positive learning outcomes despite the variations among the learning activities that take place in virtual environments and the different kinds of virtual reality interfaces (Azuma, 1997; Hedley, Billinghurst, Postner, May, & Kato, 2002; Winn & Windschitl, 2002). Researchers generally acknowledge that immersion, the extent to which the computer system delivers a surrounding environment, is a vital element in contributing to the sense of presence and therefore may also be linked to positive learning outcomes. Yet, Slater (1999) warned that researchers and educators should not assume presence is positively correlated to task performance. Research is needed to explore the nature of immersive technology and presence with regard to their roles in learning activities. The notion of flow, or the state of being cognitively engrossed by an activity, is also linked with positive learning outcomes and is often confounded with issues of presence within the research literature (Csikszentmihalyi, 1988; Witmer & Singer, 1998). In order to explore the nature of presence and flow in immersive systems, it is necessary to find how different viewing perspectives impact them given the wide range of technology that is available and in use.

Since the application of artificial or computer-generated environments as learning contexts, researchers have questioned the effects of presence and immersion in learning activities (Hedley et al., 2002; Sheridan, 1992; Winn, 2002). Some early results indicated a "link" between presence and student learning, with correlations between positive learning outcomes and students' self-reports of degrees of presence (Witmer & Singer, 1998). High levels of presence may involve the focusing on a task within the virtual environment, or contrarily, high levels of presence may involve the perception of being enveloped, thus being acutely aware of the perceived environment regardless of task. Understanding the nature of presence in virtual environments has been further compounded by a number of studies that are based on the assumption that the positive correlation between presence and learning is a given, regardless of the type of virtual environment or the type of administration of the learning activity (Fjeld, Schar, Signorello, & Krueger, 2002; Winn, Windschitl, Fruland, & Lee, 2002; Woods & Billinghurst, 2003).

For a more consistent focus of conversation around these points, the characterization of immersion should be agreed upon as the extent to which the computer system delivers a surrounding environment, one that blocks sensations from the real world, accommodates many sensory modalities, and has rich representational capability (Slater, 1999; Slater & Wilbur, 1997). By changing viewing perspectives of the game play activity within desktop environments from 1st person, 3rd person, and "none" perspectives (text-based) we are changing the relative "immersiveness" of the system. The sense of presence is defined as the feeling of being in an environment even if one is not physically there. The feeling of presence is also congruent with the environment and the situation within that environment (Robillard, Bouchard, Fournier, & Renaud, 2003). When someone is focused on the situation they become aware of what is in their environment. Being able to focus and recognizing the artifacts within the environment help add to the sense of presence (Fontaine, 1992). The measurements of flow are involvement, concentration, loss of sense of time, loss or lack of self-consciousness, and a feeling of superiority. These measures of flow all lead to an intrinsically rewarding experience (Csikszentmihalyi, 1988). To reach a substantive state of flow, a person's skills have to be adequate to deal with the challenges of the situation (Hargadon, 2001; Slater, 2003). If the skill level is too low, a person will not reach this state of flow due to frustration of not performing at a desired skill level. Some researchers have said that presence and emotion are not connected. Others have said that emotions are how we experience our environment and that emotions may play a role both as a way of determining and a cause of the feeling of presence (Baños et al., 2003). The emotional nature of the experience is a factor that needs to be investigated with the intention of establishing relationships to both presence and flow.

Studies such as those begun by Taylor (2002) are needed to determine the cognitive effects that immersion, presence and flow have on a learning activity with a specific gaming viewing perspective. The results will be useful in formulating further inquiry into the design of effective learning tools using virtual 3D environments. By developing and using a consistent set of terms, researchers will be provided with a more useful means to communicate results across research venues and within scientific literature. Future studies of learning with artificial and gaming environments may be more likely to be based on a shared vocabulary with consistent meanings to communicate (a) what cognitively is happening with students as they interact with virtual/real objects and environments and (b) what aspects of mixed-reality and virtual interfaces afford different uses among learners. Based in part on those results, additional phases of research can help to substantiate the claims of presence and flow for new educational games.

Therefore, two vital research questions are:

- How does the viewing perspective of the player impact his/her feeling of presence and flow? By considering current frameworks for researching the relationships between immersion, presence, flow and learning and applying these frameworks to a more broadly defined set of virtual environments (Bystrom, Barfield, & Hendrix, 1999), the objective is to refine and inform future research with improved terminology.
- What, if any, are the links between learning strategies, presence, and flow in a designed learning exercise using computer games with different viewing perspectives?

To address these questions, investigations are needed to determine what role viewing perspective plays within immersive environments for game players to reach a substantive level of presence or flow. This work has begun (see Scoresby & Shelton 2007) using a qualitative analysis of responses to interview questions and an analysis of students' videotaped activities to help identify relationships between cognitive states and the learners' interactions with virtual objects. Ultimately, the findings of this and other needed research in this area will help to clear the confusion in the field by clarifying the roles of presence and flow within learning activities, and provide a consistent vocabulary across future research with regard to various gaming environments.

THE FUTURE FOR ACTIVITY-GOAL ALIGNMENT, RESEARCH AND PRACTICE

Alice asks The Cheshire Cat: "Would you tell me, please, which way I ought to go from here?"
The Cat responds, "That depends a good deal on where you want to get to."
Alice replies, "I don't much care where so long as I get somewhere."
"Oh, you're sure to do that," says the Cat, "if you only walk long enough."

In a move toward extending existing efforts that are emerging from computer games studies, I see three areas of research outcomes needed from the proposed ideas within this chapter: the development of design and utilization frameworks, the application of those frameworks, and the development of new resources using activity-goal alignment.

Development of educational games design and utilization frameworks and techniques.

The first product of ongoing research should be a group of theoretical frameworks and strategies for designing and creating educationally effective simulations and games that are accessible to all individuals. Research should help determine the effectiveness of the games across all populations of students in accordance with activity-goal alignment to further assess the success of their use in meeting educational standards. This research should build upon previous work in educational simulation design approaches and in teaching theory and design of educational games.

Application of the frameworks.

Second, in parallel to framework development, game development is needed with application of the frameworks to substantiate guidelines for the accessible design of educational simulations and games. These guidelines will parallel the effort of accessibility principles currently in effect and will be grounded in practices identified and studied through the framework development portion of ongoing research. The effort should include tracking the progress in the design and development of established simulations already in-use to refine recommendations and standards for instructional computer game accessibility for commercial and non-commercial development.

Development of new and existing resources for creating educational games.

Many of the existing resources identified in the application of frameworks should be used as projects to re-work with the created compliance activity-goal alignment guidelines. A number of projects are eligible for remixing through this work, including those within the NSDL repository and those available from OpenCourseware initiatives such as MIT OCW. As new projects surface, development is needed to create resources for building instructional computer simulation games that address learning issues within formal education environments and are aligned with state and national standards. The effort is to offer appropriate versions of the games that are accessible to a vast range of students who would not normally be able to engage with them.

SUMMARY

Last year, I received a phone call from a group of high school educators and administrators from the "four corners" region of Utah. They were addressing issues and resources related to the NSF Star Schools grant application with the hope of achieving a technological infrastructure for their rural and underprivileged population of students. "We have a question," they said. "A criteria in the Star Schools RFP states that our proposal must have a plan to implement 'simulations and games' within our curriculum. How do we do that? What should we do?" Like the emails from teachers mentioned in the Introduction who asked me how to implement educational games within their classrooms, I did not have an informed answer to many of their questions. With the ideas and agenda proposed within the pages of this and other chapters of this volume, we as technologists, game designers, and educators have the opportunity to address more of these challenges and provide more of the answers. There may be many ways to discover some of the answers. The approach I argue is for instructors and game designers alike to develop and understand their instructional objectives before they begin game design, and then make sure to align their game activities with those objectives. Perhaps this requires a new view on the old "objectives-plus-aligned-curricular-materials" view of classic instructional design.

At the beginning of this chapter I asserted that the main interest in computer-based simulations and games was in their ability to facilitate flexible delivery of complex information while maintaining high levels of motivation. I argued that despite the existence of a variety of approaches to designing worthwhile educational games, a number of them have not met educational expectations and that new frameworks were needed for their design and use. This gap in effective approaches is extremely evident in the case of persons with varying abilities, whose population of students suffers from a lack of empirical attention in this field. However, the process of designing games by aligning the game play activity with the instructional objectives is a promising beginning. It is through the presentation of the educational game case of learning problem solving skills, along with the presentation of evolving analytic techniques to study learning through student activity that I hope to have explained the merit of this design approach. I then presented an example of an educational game used to facilitate learning in a problem-solving context that was built with activity-goal alignment. I suggested that an approach of ethnographic study of the use and mediated understandings of simulation game tools was appropriate to study how students achieved positive learning outcomes, and the challenges of design were worth the benefits to students who played the game. The ethnographic studies are an appropriate and effective strand of research to help create guidelines for eventual compliance standards by Federal, State and local agencies. Re-working the guidelines into existing and new products, along with the presentation of these results to a wide audience through conferences and publications, provides a means to influence a wide audience. It is through this discussion I hope to have made explicit the kind of impact this kind of continuing research will have on the educational, instructional and technology design communities.

I believe that a more rigorous understanding of the ways educational games function in these existing, interaction-rich communities will provide the basis for instructional strategies with the potential to revolutionize learning for gamers. Following a more focused plan, the future of educational game research activity will work to implement recommendations into new and existing educational tools. Specifically, the research will shed significant light on the role of educational games in education, and will provide solid grounding to a long-term research agenda dedicated to understanding the effects and potential benefits of technology on learning.

REFERENCES

Aldrich, C. (2004a). *Simulations and the future of learning*. San Francisco, CA: Pfeiffer.
Aldrich, C. (2004b). *Six criteria of an educational simulation*. Retrieved November 15, 2004, from http://www.learningcircuits.org/NR/rdonlyres/F2ED000A-7A59-4108-A6CB-1BE4F4CC1CA5/4719/clark_e2.pdf
Azuma, R. T. (1997). A survey of augmented reality. *Presence, 6*(4), 355-385.
Baños, R. M., Botella, C., Alcañiz, M., Liaño, V., Guerrero, B., & Rey, B. (2003). Immersion and emotion: Their impact on the sense of presence. *Cyberpsychology & Behavior, 6*(5), 467-476.
Barab, S. A., Hay, K. E., Barnett, M., & Keating, T. (2000). Virtual Solar System project: Building understanding through model building. *Journal of Research in Science Teaching, 37*(7), 719-756.
Barab, S. A., Hay, K. E., Barnett, M., & Squire, K. (2001). Constructing virtual worlds: Tracing the historical development of learner practices. *Cognition and Instruction, 19*(1), 47-94.
Barrows, H. S. (1986). A taxonomy of problem-based learning methods. *Medical Education, 20*(6), 481-486.
Barrows, H. S. (1996). Problem-based learning in medicine and beyond: A brief overview. *New Directions for Teaching and Learning, 68*, 3-12.
Barrows, H. S. (2002). Is it truly possible to have such a thing as dPBL? *Distance Education, 23*(1), 119-122.

BECTA (British Education Communications and Technology Agency) (2001). *Computer games in education project*. Retrieved July 15, 2005, from http://www.becta.org.uk/research/research.cfm?section=1&id=2826

Blum, T., & Yocom, J. (1996). A fun alternative: Using instructional games to foster student learning. *Teaching Exceptional Children, 29*(2), 60-63.

Blumenfeld, P., Fishman, B., Krajcik, J., & Marx, R. W. (2000). Creating usable innovations in systemic reform: Scaling up technology-embedded project-based science in urban schools. *Educational Psychologist, 35*(3), 149-164.

Brown, J. S., & Duguid, P. (2000). Learning - In Theory and in Practice. In *The social life of information* (pp. 117-146). Cambridge, MA: Harvard Business School Press.

Bystrom, E. K., Barfield, W., & Hendrix, C. (1999). A conceptual model of the sense of presence in virtual environments. *PRESENCE: Teleoperators and Virtual Environments, 8*(2), 241-245.

Christensen, C. A., & Gerber, M. M. (1990). Effectiveness of computerized drill and practice games in teaching basic math facts. *Exceptionality, 1*(3), 149-165.

Conderman, G., & Tompkins, B. J. (1995). State the facts. *Teaching Exceptional Children, 27*(3), 57-58.

Csikszentmihalyi, M. (1988). The flow experience and human psychology. In M. Csikszentmihalyi & I. S. Csikszentmihalyi (Eds.), *Optimal Experience* (pp. 364-383). Cambridge, UK: Cambridge University Press.

Cuban, L. (1986). *Teachers and machines: The classroom use of technology since 1920*. New York: Teachers College Press.

Davison, A., & Gordon, P. (1978). *Games and simulations in action*. Great Britain: Woburn Press.

Dede, C. (1995). The evolution of constructivist learning environments: Immersion in distributed, virtual worlds. *Educational Technology, 35*(5), 46-52.

Dede, C., Ketelhut, D. J., & Nelson, B. C. (2004). *Design-baesd research on gender, class, race, and ethnicity in a multi-user virtual environment.* Paper presented at the American Educational Research Association (AERA).

deJong, T., & vanJoolingen, W. R. (1998). Scientific discovery learning with computer simulations of conceptual domains. *Review of Educational Research, 68*(2), 179-201.

Deshrill, M. (2004). *Interview with Nick Montfort.* Retrieved August 16, 2005, from http://www.eboredom.20m.com/features/interviews/montfort1.html

Dickey, M. D. (2006). Game design narrative for learning: Appropriating adventure game design narrative devices and techniques for the design of interactive learning environments. *Educational Technology Research & Development, 54*(3), 245-263.

Diggs, C. S. (1997). Technology: A key to unlocking at-risk students. *Learning and Leading with Technology, 25*(2), 38-40.

Fawcett, L. M., & Garton, A. F. (2005). The effect of peer collaboration on children's problem-solving ability. *British Journal of Educational Technology, 75*(2), 157-169.

Fishman, B., Marx, R. W., Blumenfeld, P., & Krajcik, J. (2004). Creating a framework for research on systemic technology innovations. *The Journal of the Learning Sciences, 13*(1), 43-76.

Fjeld, M., Schar, S. G., Signorello, D., & Krueger, H. (2002,). *Alternative tools for tangible interaction: A usability evaluation.* Paper presented at the IEEE and ACM International Symposium on Mixed and Augmented Reality (ISMAR), Darmstadt, Germany.

Fontaine, G. (1992). The experience of a sense of presence in intercultural and international encounters. *PRESENCE: Teleoperators and Virtual Environments, 1*(4), 482-490.

Gee, J. P. (2003). Semiotic domains: Is playing video games a "waste of time"? In *What Video Games Have to Teach Us about Learning and Literacy*. New York: Palgrave MacMillan.

Gibbons, A. S., & Fairweather, G. B. (1998). *Computer-based instruction: Design and development*. Englewood Cliffs, NJ: Educational Technology Publications.

Gordin, D. N., & Pea, R. D. (1995). Prospects for scientific visualization as an educational technology. *The Journal of the Learning Sciences, 4*(3), 249-279.

Granade, S. (2005). *Introducing Interactive Fiction*. Retrieved October 15, 2005, from http://brasslantern.org/beginners/introif.html

Gunter, B. (1998). Tapping into players' habits and preferences. In *The Effects of video games on children: The myth unmasked* (pp. 29-48). Sheffield, England: Sheffield Academic Press.

Hargadon, D. Y. (2001). The pleasures of immersion and engagement: Schemas, scripts and the fifth business. *Digital Creativity, 12*(3), 153-166.

Hayes, E. (2002). *Find out who you really are: Adult learning in virtual worlds.* Paper presented at the Adult Education Research Conference (AERC), North Carolina State University, Raleigh, NC.

Hedley, N. R., Billinghurst, M., Postner, L., May, R., & Kato, H. (2002). Explorations in the Use of Augmented Reality for Geographic Visualization. *PRESENCE: Teleoperators and virtual environments*.

Hertel, J. P., & Millis, B. J. (2002). *Using simulations to promote learning in higher education*. Sterling VA: Stylus Publishing.

Holland, W., Jenkins, H., & Squire, K. (2003). Chapter 1: Theory by design. In M. J. P. Wolf & B. Perron (Eds.), *The video game theory reader* (pp. 25-46). New York: Routledge.

Jonassen, D. H., Peck, K. L., & Wilson, B. G. (1999). Learning by reflecting: What have we learned? In *Learning with technology: A constructivist perspective* (pp. 217-231). Upper Saddle River, NJ: Merrill.

Jones, K. (1987). *Simulations: A handbook for teachers and trainers* (2 ed.). Great Britain: Kogan Page.

Kirriemuir, J. (2002). Video gaming, education and digital learning technologies. *D-Lib Magazine, 8*.

Kirriemuir, J. (2003). *The relevance of video games and gaming consoles to the higher and further education learning experience*. Retrieved July 15, 2005, from www.ceangal.com

Kirriemuir, J., & McFarlane, A. (2003). *Use of computer and video games in the classroom.* Paper presented at the Digital Games Research Association (DiGRA), Utrecht, Holland.

Ladd, B. C. (2006). The Curse of Monkey Island: Holding the attention of students weaned on computer games. *Journal of Computing Sciences in Colleges, 21*(6), 162-174.

Lepper, M. R., & Chabay, R. W. (1985). Intrinsic motivation and instruction: Conflicting views on the role of motivational processes in computer-based education. *Educational Psychologist, 20*(4), 417-430.

Malone, T. W. (1980). *What makes things fun to learn?* Unpublished Ph.D. Dissertation, Stanford University, Stanford, CA.

Malone, T. W., & Lepper, M. R. (1987). Making learning fun: A taxonomy of intrinsic motivations for learning. In R. E. Snow & M. J. Farr (Eds.), *Aptitude, learning and instruction Volume 3: Conative and affective process analysis*. Englewood Cliffs, NJ: Erlbaum.

Moshell, J. M., & Hughes, C. E. (1995). *The virtual academy: A simulated environment for constructionist learning* (No. JMM95.23): University of Central Florida.

McMahan, A. (2003). Immersion, engagement, and presence: A method for analyzing 3-D video games. In M. J. P. Wolf & B. Perron (Eds.), *The Video Game Theory Reader* (pp. 25-46). New York: Routledge.

Montfort, N. (2003). Toward a theory of interaction fiction. In E. Short (Ed.), *IF Theory* (3.5 ed.). St. Charles, IL: The Interactive Fiction Library.

Nelson, L. M. (1999). Collaborative problem solving. In C. M. Reigeluth (Ed.), *Instructional design theories and models: A new paradigm of instructional theory* (pp. 241-267). Hillsdale, NJ: Lawrence Erlbaum Associates.

Okolo, C. M. (1992). The effect of computer-assisted instruction format and initial attitude on arithmetic facts proficiency and continuing motivation of students with learning disabilities. *Exceptionality, 3*(4), 195-211.

Paras, B., & Bizzocchi, J. (2005). *Game, motivation, and effective learning: An integrated model for educational game design.* Paper presented at the Digital Games Research Association (DiGRA): Changing Views -- Worlds in Play, Vancouver, BC.

Robillard, G., Bouchard, S., Fournier, T., & Renaud, P. (2003). Anxiety and presence during VR immersion: A comparative study of the reactions of phobic and non-phobic participants in therapeutic virtual environments derived from computer games. *Cyberpsychology & Behavior, 6*(5), 467-476.

Roschelle, J. M. (1992). Learning by collaborating: Convergent conceptual change. *The Journal of the Learning Sciences, 2*(3), 235-276.

Roschelle, J. M., Pea, R. D., Hoadley, C. M., Gordin, D. N., & Means, B. M. (2000). Changing how and what children learn in school with computer-based technologies. *The Future of Children, 10*(2), 76-101.

Scoresby, J., Duncan, S. M., & Shelton, B. E. (2006). *Voices of Spoon River: Exploring early American poetry through computer gaming.* Paper presented at the Games, Learning & Society 2006, Madison, WI.

Scoresby, J. & Shelton, B. E. (2007). *Visual perspectives within educational computer games: Effects on presence and flow within virtual learning environments.* Paper presented at the American Educational Research Association (AERA) Conference, 2007, Chicago, IL.

Shaffer, D. W., Squire, K. R., Halverson, R., & Gee, J. (2004). *Video games and the future of learning.* Retrieved October 20, 2005, from http://www.academiccolab.org/resources/gappspaper1.pdf

Shelton, B. E. (2003). *How augmented reality helps students learn dynamic spatial relationships.* Unpublished Doctoral Dissertation, University of Washington, Seattle.

Shelton, B. E. (2005a). *Designing and creating interactive fiction for learning.* Paper presented at the New Media Consortium (NMC) Online Conference on Educational Gaming, Internet.

Shelton, B. E. (2005b). *Designing and developing instructional games: A project to align learning activity with instructional goals.* Retrieved October 25, 2005, from http://it.usu.edu/cle/CLE_alignment.htm

Shelton, B. E., & Wiley, D. (2006a). *How do I get in the game?: The papers, projects, and practices of teaching educational games* Presented at the Games, Learning & Society 2006, Madison, WI.

Shelton, B. E., & Wiley, D. (2006b). *Instructional designers take all the fun out of games: Rethinking elements of engagement for designing instructional games.* Paper presented at the American Educational Research Association (AERA) 2006, San Francisco.

Sheridan, T. B. (1992). Musings on telepresence and virtual presence. *PRESENCE: Teleoperators and Virtual Environments, 1*(1), 120-125.

Shiah, R.L., Mastropieri, M. A., Scruggs, T. E., & Fulk, B. J. M. (1994). The effects of computer-assisted instruction on the mathematical problem solving of students with learning disabilities. *Exceptionality, 5*(3), 131-161.

Short, E. (2005). *What's IF?* Retrieved October 15, 2005, from http://emshort.home. mindspring. com/whatsif.html

Slater, M. (1999). Measuring presence: A response to the Witmer and Singer questionnaire. *PRESENCE: Teleoperators and Virtual Environments, 8*(5), 560-566.

Slater, M. (2003). *A note on presence terminology*, from http://presence.cs.ucl.ac.uk/presenceconnect/articles/Jan2003/melslaterJan27200391557/melslaterJan27200391557.html.

Slater, M., & Wilbur, S. (1997). A framework for immersive virtual environments (FIVE): Speculations on the role of presence in virtual environments. *PRESENCE: Teleoperators and Virtual Environments, 6*(6), 603-616.

Soloway, E., Jackson, S. L., Klein, J., Quintana, C., Reed, J., Spitulnik, J., et al. (2001). *Learning theory in practice: Case studies of learner-centered design*: HI-CE, University of Michigan.

Squire, K. (2002). Cultural framing of computer/video games. *Game Studies, 2*(1).

Squire, K., Barnett, M., Grant, J. M., & Higginbotham, T. (2004). *Electromagnetism supercharged! Learning physics with digital simulation games.* Paper presented at the International Conference of the Learning Sciences 2004 (ICLS 04), Santa Monica, CA.

Steinkuehler, C. A. (2003). *Videogaming as participation in a discourse.* Paper presented at the Annual Conference of the American Association for Applied Linguistics, Arlington, VA.

Steinkuehler, C. A., & Chmiel, M. (2006). *Fostering scientific habits of mind in the context of online play.* Paper presented at the 7th International Conference of the Learning Sciences, Bloomington, IN.

Suchman, L. (2000). *Located accountabilities in technology production.* Retrieved June 27, 2001, from http://www.comp.lancs.ac.uk/sociology/soc039ls.html

Taylor, L. N. (2002). *Video games: Perspective, point-of-view, and immersion.* Unpublished Masters Thesis, University of Florida, Gainsville.

VanEck, R. (2006). *Where do we go from here? Ten critical areas to guide future research in digital games-based learning.* Paper presented at the Games, Learning & Society 2006, Madison, WI.

Welch, M. (1995). It's in the bag: An instructional game to promote positive student attitudes toward writing. *Teaching Exceptional Children, 27*(2), 63-65.

Wertsch, J. V. (1991). *Voices of the mind.* Cambridge, MA: Harvard University Press.

Windschitl, M. (2000). Supporting the development of science inquiry skills with special classes of software. *Educational Technology Research & Development, 48*(2), 81-95.

Winn, W. (2002). Learning in artificial environments: Embodiment, embeddedness and dynamic adaption. *Technology, Instruction, Cognition and Learning, 1*(1), 87-114.

Winn, W., & Windschitl, M. (2002). *Strategies used by university students to learn aspects of physical oceanography in a virtual environment.* Paper presented at the American Educational Research Association, New Orleans, LA.

Winn, W., Windschitl, M., Fruland, R., & Lee, Y. (2002). *When does immersion in a virtual environment help students construct understanding?* Paper presented at the Internactional Conference on the Learning Sciences (ICLS), Seattle, WA.

Witmer, B. G., & Singer, M. J. (1998). Measuring presence in virtual environments: A presence questionnaire. *Presence: Teleoperators and Virtual Environments, 7*, 225-240.

Woods, E., & Billinghurst, M. (2003). *Empirical study of museum learning with augmented reality.* Paper presented at the Australian New Technologies 2003, Sydney, Australia.

Zimmerman, E., & Fortugno, N. (2006). *Game design essentials.* Paper presented at the Games, Learning & Society 2006, Madison, WI.

Brett E. Shelton
Department of Instructional Technology
Utah State University

RYAN M. MOELLER, JASON L. COOTEY, & KEN S. MCALLISTER

"THE PERIPATOS COULD NOT HAVE LOOKED LIKE THAT," AND OTHER EDUCATIONAL OUTCOMES FROM STUDENT GAME DESIGN

INTRODUCTION

Several recent studies have sought to prove that computer games[1] teach players something, from basic literacies to advanced problem solving skills (Kirriemuir, 2002; Gee, 2003; Prensky, 2003; and McAllister 2005). In fact, the majority of literature on game design and education addresses how and what people learn by playing particular games. In this chapter, we offer evidence to support a hypothesis of computer game-oriented education: that computer game-based pedagogy can be significantly enhanced when students are allowed to design and build the games with faculty guidance.

Building on the work of psychologist J. Piaget, S. Papert (1980) draws a hypothesis similar to ours when he advocates the use of computer programming as an effective teaching tool: "The child programs the computer. And in teaching the computer how to think, children embark on an exploration about how they themselves think" (p. 19). Seif El-Nasr and Smith (2006) support this claim, citing the following learning objectives for a student game design project:

> **software development and design**, including team work, building critiques and reflections on others' work, project scheduling, project management, iterations and refinement, and prototyping;
> **programming concepts**, including threading and event-based programming, object-oriented programming, component-based development, and software patterns;
> **artistic concepts**, including lighting, architecture design, and character design; and
> **game concepts**, including game design, game mechanics, and balancing game aesthetics and game play. (p. 17)

As readers of this volume already know, computer games hold considerable pedagogical potential. Not only can they be used to teach software programming and design, teachers can use games to teach specific subject matter and research methods. For the authors of this chapter—all of whom teach and conduct research in the humanities—this subject matter can take several forms, including history, politics, and culture.

B. E. Shelton, D. A. Wiley (eds.), Educational Design & Use of Computer Simulation Games,131–154.

By using inexpensive commercial and open-source game engines and development tools, students can design and implement original content—stories, characters, environments, music, and so forth—into their own games without extensive extracurricular education.[2] Many such game engines exist and are available for experimentation and delivery on virtually all platforms, from most flavors of Windows and OS X, to UNIX, Linux, BEOS, FreeBSD, and PC-DOS. Additionally, there are several game development toolsets that make it possible to create games for deployment on the Web. Some games, such as *Half-Life 2* (Sierra Entertainment 2004) and *Unreal Tournament 2004* (Atari 2004), even include development tools on the game disk itself, making the creation of additional game levels both convenient and inexpensive. Game engines and toolkits are also available for nearly every type of game, from 1st person shooters and role playing games to puzzle and simulation games. A particular favorite of the authors of this chapter is the *Aurora Toolset*, which came bundled with the popular game *Neverwinter Nights* (Atari 2002). *Aurora* (see Figure 1) is a powerful application that is simple enough to use for middle-schoolers (the front-end is primarily point-click and drag-drop oriented), but complex enough for commercial quality game development: in its advanced mode, *Aurora* includes a comprehensive scripting language, the ability to support linked applications written in full-blown programming languages like C++, and the capacity to accept custom 3D objects created in high-end graphics and animation suites.

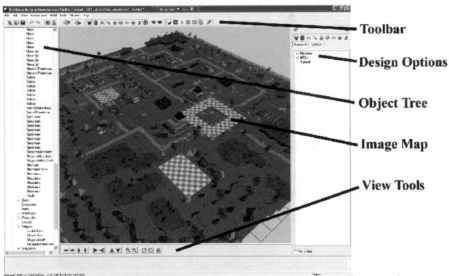

Figure 1. Aurora toolset with aerial view of Stageira tileset.[3]

Additionally, because *Aurora* is now several years old, it will run on most Windows-based student computers.[4] The authors of this chapter, at least, have found *Aurora* to be very effective for helping students see the connection between creativity, research, and the practical application of technical skills.

These anecdotal findings are supported by several research studies executed in the past two decades. In addition to Y.B. Kafai's influential work on game design and academic motivation among children (Kafai 1995; 1998), Puntambekar and Kolodner (2005) found that design activities are an effective way to help students learn the content of a course. In "Toward Implementing Distributed Scaffolding: Helping Students Learn Science from Design," Puntambekar and Kolodner show that student-centered game design provides "students with motivation for engaging in scientific inquiry and rich affordances for learning and applying science content" (p. 186). In particular, they identified seven subprocesses that need to be supported by teachers involved in design processes:

> (1) statement of [students'] understanding of the challenge, (2) generation of questions for exploration, (3) generation of a set of learning issues, (4) generation and articulation of initial ideas, (5) generation and articulation of a second and more refined set of solution ideas, (6) description of solutions, and (7) selection of criteria for evaluating solutions. Supporting these subprocesses would serve two purposes. It would help students keep records essential to making good design decisions and engaging well in designing and learning, and it would provide us with documentation of students' thinking, knowledge, and capabilities. (p. 191)

Although Puntambekar and Kolodner's study was conducted on middle school children, we propose that design work accesses the same high level thinking in

Figure 2. LGI members set up equipment for a game study night.

students at more advanced levels. We support these claims with evidence from a joint computer game design and development project undertaken by researchers in the Learning Games Initiative (LGI)—a multi-institutional, transdisciplinary research collective that studies, teaches with, and builds computer games—at Utah State University and the University of Arizona (see Figure 2).

Aristotle's Assassins (see Figures 3 and 4) is a computer game "mod" built with the *Aurora Toolset* that runs under the *Neverwinter Nights* game engine. Begun in

Figure 3. Screen capture from Aristotle's Assassins depicting custom Greek temple.

late 2004 by a group of researchers in the Learning Games Initiative, *Aristotle's Assassins* was initially designed to offer players a simulation of the ways in which Greek politics, philosophy, and musical developments were all interacting in the 4th century BCE. In its first year, a detailed design document was compiled by Learning Games Initiative researchers at the University of Arizona (LGI-UA); this document outlined the game's narrative, provided backgrounds on the game's major and minor characters, included historical summaries of significant real-life events that took place during the time in which the game's narrative unfolds, and included numerous pieces of concept art—character illustrations, environment sketches, and in-game musical motifs. These materials were all developed by the diverse LGI-UA team, which consisted of undergraduate and graduate students, university staff and faculty, and several community professionals. In its second year, the project was transferred to the LGI team at Utah State University (LGI-USU), which had acquired funding for the development process. In this chapter, we describe some of the design decisions that founded *Aristotle's Assassins* in its early stages, as well as the reasons why some of those decisions were eventually changed.

Figure 4. Screen capture from Aristotle's Assassins depicting custom army barrack.

To begin, we turn first to an overview of activity theory as a basis for our reflective accounts of the computer-mediated design process in building *Aristotle's Assassins*. The activity system discussed in this chapter falls chiefly between Puntambekar and Kolodner's design subprocesses 4 and 5 (2005; p. 191). We posit that project management (rather than "teaching" per se) becomes the primary focus for instructors who choose to teach with computer-mediated design processes. This is because, as we describe below, the onus of learning with game design comes at the moment when students articulate a refined concept (design) within the context of an activity system (typically a class project or learning objective).

WHY ACTIVITY THEORY?

Activity theory has its roots in the work of 20th century Russian psychologists Vygotsky, Luria, and Leont'ev who sought a new foundation for their research in Marxist philosophy (Sanders 2005). Among the foundational principles of activity theory is the "unit." Vygotsky (1962) suggests that both thought and word function as a single unit, functioning as a system, rather than as independent meaning-making operators. In fact, Leont'ev (1978) argues that the analysis of an activity— a set of actions undertaken to accomplish specific goals—consists of "bringing into psychology such units of analysis as carry in themselves psychological reflection in its inseparability from the moments that give rise to it and mediate it in human activity" (p. 7). There is no separation between the reflection—processing and interpreting—and the context in which activity generates the object of reflection. Put simply, the word is a reflection of thought. Units like word and thought are especially important when an analyst seeks to identify exactly what actions, people, and materials fit into the moment—or context—that gives rise to the object of reflection. One basic purpose of activity theory, then, is to understand how consciousness and activity work to both expand and constrain one another such that both individuals and communities are transformed.

Leont'ev's analysis of various childhood activities coheres well with Papert's work among students tasked with building software; in both cases there is an emphasis on context as an influential component of meaning making: "Like other builders," writes Papert, "children appropriate to their own use materials they find about them, most saliently the models and metaphors suggested by the surrounding culture" (p. 19). The same is true of the computer game development project at LGI-USU: the project team, game design, lab equipment, software, and the "modding" itself are all part of the context—"tools" and "actions" as activity theorists would say—that comprise the dense meaning-making web of this sustained "activity." This emphasis on connectionism is what makes activity theory uniquely applicable to better understanding educational planning, project management, and evaluation because it seeks to articulate actions with outcomes in a complex activity system by carefully studying six fundamental elements:

- activity: outcome-oriented actions toward a predetermined goal;
- object: the goal of the activity;
- subjects: the actors who perform the activity;
- artifacts: objects that mediate the activity;
- community: contextual influences like rules, roles, and users that influence the activity;
- outcome: the result of the activity.

By isolating elements of the activity system into discrete parts, project managers and teachers can better understand the complex meaning-making activities that students undertake with designing a content-based computer game.

While much of the work of early activity theorists focused on the behaviors and memory processes of children, in recent years activity theory has been usefully applied in the field of human-computer interaction to describe how users and computer systems work with and against each other. Nardi ("Activity theory;" 1996) has described this work as:

[offering] a set of perspectives on human activity and a set of concepts for describing that activity. This, it seems to me, is exactly what HCI research needs as we struggle to understand and describe "context," "situation," "practice." We have recognized that technology use is not a mechanical input-output relation between a person and a machine; a much richer depiction of the user's situation is needed for design and evaluation. (p. 4)

By drawing on the work of her earlier colleagues, Nardi updates activity theory and argues that it provides the rich depiction of users necessary for the effective design of better software and hardware interfaces. As humanities scholars approaching computer game design and project management, this contextualized, rich description appealed to us.

Because its focus is on the mediation of activity by communities, artifacts, and objects, activity theory predisposes scholarly inquiry to investigations of the specific effects of mediated activity on the outcome of a particular design. In other words, activity theory provides an explanation for shifts in outcome and design found within the culture or ecology of production. According to Kaptelinin (1996),

> Activity theory differentiates between processes at various levels. *Activities* are oriented to motives, that is, the objects that are impelling by themselves. Each motive is an object, material or ideal, that satisfies a need. *Actions* are the processes functionally subordinated to activities; they are directed at specific conscious goals. According to activity theory, the dissociation between objects that motivate human activity and the goals to which the activity are immediately directed is of fundamental signification. (p. 55)

Activity theory looks for contradictions or the cognitive dissonance created between the goals that human subjects set for a particular activity and the mediating objects of that activity. These mediating objects, to Nardi ("Studying context;" 1996), constitute much of the context surrounding a particular activity:

> Activity theory, then, proposes a very specific notion of context: the activity itself is the context. What takes place in an activity system composed of object, actions, and operation, *is* the context. Context is constituted through the enactment of an activity involving people and artifacts. Context is not an outer container or shell inside of which people behave in certain ways. People consciously and deliberately generate contexts (activities) in part through their own objects. (p. 38)

With the *Aristotle's Assassins* project, the contradictions, the dissonance among the activity's goals and mediating objects, and the shifts in our perceptions of the project's progress have been manifold. Studying them through the lens of activity theory has given us new insights into the possibilities of using game design and project management to teach students humanities content. The remainder of this chapter details the development of *Aristotle's Assassins'* context, and explores the ways in which we think that activity theory can provide a useful framework for understanding project management generally and educational game design, especially at that crucial moment between the generation of the idea (subprocess 4) and the refinement of that idea (subprocess 5) which is where, we argue, the most meaningful learning potential of the design process is located. We also suggest how activity theory can be useful planning tools for instructors wishing to have their own students develop engaging computer games that prove highly educational in both the playing and the building.

ARISTOTLE'S ASSASSINS: GAME DESIGN

Aristotle's Assassins is a PC computer game built on the *Neverwinter Nights* game engine. Designed primarily to teach players about the politics, philosophies, and music of ancient Greece, it uses both simulation and role playing as key elements of the gameplay. To date, a demonstration module of the game has been completed, as well as a promotional video. The demonstration module is a small portion of the complete game, yet despite its modest size it manages to include:

- the city environments of both Athens and Stageira, Aristotle's birthplace;
- a half-dozen immersive desert areas that feature a bandit camp, a sphinx, caves, and encounters with several mythological creatures;
- several hours of game play;
- ten richly interactive (i.e., conversational) non-player characters (NPCs);
- an array of side quests that permit players to interact with various aspects of every major location in the game, from conversations with Ancient Greek philosophers to learning how to fight with Greek weapons;
- a custom designed 3D Greek temple;
- several custom designed 3D Greek common buildings.

Community, subjects, and artifacts

As noted above, *Aristotle's Assassins* was initially designed by LGI-UA and built by a team at LGI-USU.[5] LGI-UA developed the concept, drafted the design document, created concept art and music, prototyped several game levels, and participated in numerous meetings to determine the strengths and weaknesses of various modding tools. Upon selection of the *Aurora Toolset*, LGI-UA set about identifying the primary features of *Aurora* that would likely be used in the prototyping stage and creating an online forum and file-sharing system on the LGI website (http://lgi.mesmernet.org). The project was then handed off to LGI-USU, which had the funding, the project management expertise, and the technical know-how necessary to overcome some of the long-term challenges in the development process. For instance, LGI-USU adapted the game concept to the limits of the game engine and the design tool, revised the design document to account for the ongoing achievements in development, and discovered innovative ways to reconceptualize the game given the necessary changes made to the various game levels.

The LGI-USU team consisted of one faculty member, a graduate student process documenter, and two undergraduates: one responsible for graphic design and the other for developing interactions and narrative content.

Object: Game description

Because it was built with the popular, fantasy role-playing game engine *Neverwinter Nights*, *Aristotle's Assassins* is more than an electronic textbook.

Rather, the game's players can develop their avatar while interacting with characters and environments drawn from the history of ancient Greece. *Aristotle's Assassins* experiments with the principles of stealth learning by emphasizing compelling puzzles, mysterious events, and historical settings and characters.[6]

The gist of the game goes like this: On the way to a command performance on the *Peripatos*, the player—who plays a young musician—discovers a plot to murder the famous philosopher Aristotle (see Figure 5).[7] By trying to prevent the murder, the musician accidentally turns Aristotle into stone and, in the process,

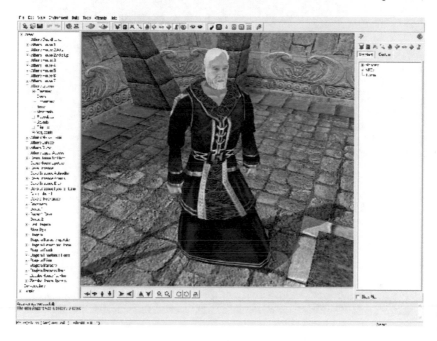

Figure 5. Character rendering of Aristotle from within the design tool for Aristotle's Assassins.

discovers that he has been an unwitting tool in a battle between two warring secret societies. The player—as the accidental assassin—must then avoid execution by uncovering the plot against Aristotle and determining how—and whether—to seek justice for its perpetrators. The player's journey involves the manipulation of two secret societies, each set upon supporting their own political objectives two years prior to Alexander the Great's death. The player uses the magical powers of music to straddle the opposing moral systems (see Figure 6) that are the basis of the game engine's mechanism for determining which in-game characters are hostile to the player and which are not. As the player works to pit the secret societies against one another, she or he must learn about and then side with one of the secret society's public political fronts. Developing relationships with the different political parties involves unique plotlines that support multiple endings and replayability. The climactic end of the game involves an animated representation of history up to the present day that depicts subsequent historical events had the player's actions actually taken place. Consequently, certain endings project what history might have been like had different political factions gained sway in 4th century Greece. Players will have experienced an immersive game that permits them to discover the significance and interconnectedness of Grecian political, philosophical, and musical developments.

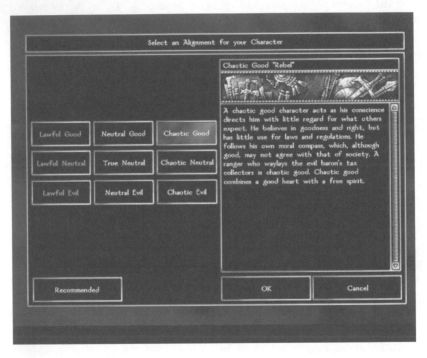

Figure 6. A depiction of possible character alignments within the game Neverwinter Nights and subsequently in Aristotle's Assasins.

Activity: Design and learning outcomes

To successfully design a Greek story that met both the expectations of players in an immersive, fantasy game and the educational goals of the design team, the LGI-USU team determined early in the project that *Aristotle's Assassins* would benefit from a clear technical development plan. The execution of such a design strategy took place in an activity system. In the case of LGI-USU, activity theory highlights areas in the activity system where reflection could improve the efficiency of both actions and the quality of produced objects; as B. A. Nardi ("Activity theory;" 1996) reminded us, a system that seeks to understand "the interpenetration of the individual, other people, and artifacts in everyday activity" (p. 8). However, activity theory is not just for static system analysis; rather, a careful system assessment details exactly how shifts in practice occur and whether those shifts are good for the system.

Our design plan included the following learning outcomes for players of *Aristotle's Assassins*:

- to gain a better understanding of the historical significance of the political turmoil surrounding the period in ancient Greece when Aristotle was becoming an influential teacher;
- to learn enough about ancient Greek culture to be able to make informed decisions about when to negotiate or persuade and when to fight;
- to learn about the role of philosophical and practical schooling in ancient Greece and how these institutions affected daily life and information gathering processes; and
- to learn about ancient Greek music and its relationship to contemporary politics and philosophy.

Concomitantly, the designers of *Aristotle's Assassins* needed to find creative, innovative ways to consciously build these learning objectives into the design of the game. For example, we dramatized the political turmoil surrounding a burgeoning democracy in ancient Greece by placing Aristotle in a complex relationship to King Philip (Alexander the Great's father and Aristotle's first major benefactor) and by creating secret factions that were more and less amenable to Philip's and Alexander's rule. We also included "persuade" options in more important character interactions and gave players the option to talk instead of fight: after Aristotle's assassination, the player character Mellifluous is framed for the murder and must argue his or her way out of a potentially lethal situation.

These choices affect gameplay by altering the circle of friends and enemies that a player's character can work with. Consequently, these relationships—or lack thereof—contribute in specific ways to the progress the player can make through the game's story by expanding and limiting what the player can find out about different events and by prohibiting or permitting the player to delegate particular time-saving or difficult tasks to various NPCs. Gender roles became one of the most interesting features of the game as we created both male- and female-oriented conversation trees for the NPCs; gamers playing as male musicians would have different conversations than gamers playing as females. Thus, one of the earliest learning moments in the game occurs when players realize that they are receiving highly biased information, and that this bias stems not only from gender but also from profession. In ancient Greece, a highly patriarchal society, musicianship was generally a female occupation. Thus, a virtuosic female musician might well be celebrated in some circles (due to excellence in the art of music) but shunned in others (because of her gender). A virtuosic male musician, on the other hand, might have been shunned by people supportive of the patriarchy (because he practiced an effeminate art), viewed suspiciously by those confused by the boy's decision to take up music as a profession, and respected by some for being counter-cultural. Through relatively simple dialogical turns of phrase, all of these implications can be readily and intriguingly suggested; the player is learning politics, music, and philosophy. For example, in one of our play testing scenarios, we had players choose opposite genders and play the game more or less simultaneously and side-by-side. The play testers ended up assisting each other at various points in the game because they were privileged to key information at different stages of the game.

In a static activity system, learning outcomes are the clear product of expected activities; however, fairly early in our design process, we noticed a shift in the LGI-USU activity system due to the research work of one of the undergraduate team members, Robert. His role was to write several new dialogues for the game and he needed to research ancient Greece in order to realize his role. While there was no surprise that he learned about Greek history, culture, and mythology, he surprised everyone when he made critical observations about how to design the 3D custom images of Aristotle's Peripatos and Lycium (places in the academy where Aristotle would teach). Robert made his critical observations in a design meeting in which the team was seeking to troubleshoot problems with the custom images. The team was discussing references to the Peripatos and Lycium in the design document; while there were no pictures, the document's description of gameplay amidst the structures was quite specific. However, Wilson—the undergraduate assigned to do the 3D custom modeling—was discussing discrepancies between what he found in scholarly books on Greek architecture and the design document. After Wilson had related his frustrations, some of his proposed solutions, and the limits posed by his graphic design software, Robert adamantly stated that the Peripatos could not have looked like the one the design document described. He proceeded to give a detailed argument based upon his readings in history, culture, and mythology. This revelation is what Puntambekar and Kolodner (2005) depict as the fifth subprocess of design: "[generating] and [articulating] a second and more refined set of solution ideas" (p. 191).

As we discussed this issue with the LGI-UA team that had drawn up the original design document, another discovery emerged: virtually everyone involved in the project had experienced similar epiphanies. One team member related the experience of listening to the sample background tunes composed by Bryan Pearce, our lead musician, and realizing that medieval European monastic chants—which are still part of Roman Catholic and Greek Orthodox monastic liturgies today—are built on the ancient Greek musical modes we'd begun to embed in the game. Another student noted that she'd never realized how similar ancient Greek and ancient Egyptian mythology was until she began researching the literary relationships between monsters, gods, and politicians. As *Aristotle's Assassins* has developed, there have been innumerable debates about how things looked, what knowledge would have been common and where, and even what kinds of soil and erosional characteristics existed during Aristotle's time. And because both LGI-UA and LGI-USU had deeply transdisciplinary collaborative resources to draw upon from the international LGI collective, these findings and experiences—although they pushed the boundaries of any team's knowledge set—were not difficult to come by. This quality of game design—that it is inherently creative, expansive, practical, and research oriented—has now become a touchstone for much of the Learning Games Initiative's development and outreach projects, from workshops at public libraries for local youth to after-school classes we lead at area high schools.

IDENTIFYING THE PARTS OF THE ACTIVITY SYSTEM

Robert's observation about the Peripatos may seem relatively insignificant and perhaps even to be expected in a complex collaborative project; however, from the perspective of activity theory, even the slightest cognitive ripple can significantly reconfigure a project's final outcome. Understanding the things people do requires individuals, communities, cultures of production, and artifacts to be mapped together as a system. The theory avoids the separation of human motive and activity so that consciousness is as much a part of the object as the subject whose activity makes the object. Mwanza (2001) outlines an eight-step model to identify the parts of an activity system: the activity, object of activity, subjects in this activity, influence of artifacts on the activity, rules mediating the activity, roles mediating the activity, the community in which the activity is conducted, and the outcome of the activity. While Mwanza's steps are adequate to identify interpenetration in LGI-USU before and after the team understood various shifts in the activity system, the shifts become more distinct if the steps clearly identify the "before" paradigm independent of the "after" paradigm. This might seem an odd distinction in a theory that seeks to avoid separating the parts from the whole; however, in the case of paradigm shifts, before and after simply separates the different ways LGI-USU understood the same activity system. To this end, Mwanza's eight steps will highlight LGI-USU's activity system before the paradigm shift and demonstrate how teaching students through design—at least from a project management perspective—must remain a flexible, yet organized process of development and reflection.

Identify the activity of interest

Put simply, the "activity" of this project was the implementation of informed design choices. In design meetings, LGI-USU met to report on progress made on design decisions from the previous week; in addition, the team met to discuss necessary changes, new assignments, and upcoming stages of development. While team members became increasingly specialized in their independent research and design activities, the design meeting was the place where implementation procedures were worked out. This activity involved multiple tools, chief among them the aim to insure that our ongoing research and development practices were always guided by the original educational objectives we'd set out for *Aristotle's Assassins*. The original design document guided the early stages of the project, for instance, and so many of our design choices simply came from this document. However, there were other informative tools beyond the design document that we came to rely on heavily later in the project, especially at critical design moments. It was at these times that team members identified innovative resources that may not have occurred to them had the development process continued as originally planned, prior to the shift in the activity system. At these moments, the team often looked outside the activity system for educational support, discovering for example:

- Scholarly books and articles on all aspects of Greek life, architecture, and culture;
- Period manuscripts in facsimile form that directly recounted quotidian life in and around the time of Aristotle;
- Technical manuals and tutorials on game design, graphics programs, and the game engine;
- Online community forums, especially for building tile sets within the game engine and for importing custom content into the game environment;
- Electronic resources on the WWW including travel guides, images depicting specific locations in Greece, wikis on Greece and ancient Greek culture, and instructions on how ancient Greek musical instruments were constructed and played.

The team members used these tools to complete research, stay aligned with educational objectives, and develop the game. Therefore, the combination of tools and individual efforts produced an educational Greek adventure replete with both role-playing and simulation mechanics. Consequent to the LGI-USU activity system, the team was able to design and implement the following additional educational objectives:

- Realizing differences in the roles and interactions between Greek men and women and different classes of citizens and non-citizens circa 325 BCE;
- Recognizing significant architectural features of ancient Greece, including columns and aqueducts;
- Understanding possible roles for agency among various religious and political factions;
- Recalling and learning classical mythology and philosophy;
- Considering the roles historical figures played within their specific historical contexts;
- Recognizing the significance of historical events on shaping one's particular place in time/space;
- Becoming familiar with Greek geography and landscape.

While these additional outcomes meant more work for the designers, in a sense the hardest part of this work—doing original research—had already been accomplished as a by-product of other development processes. Thus, in doing what was originally thought to be the important but relatively mundane work of building the game by trying to follow the previously determined construction guidelines in the design document, the builders discovered that they themselves were becoming subject matter experts on many aspects of ancient Greece and Greek life. By refining and implementing the initial design concept (see Puntambekar and Kolodner; 2005; p. 191), the LGI-USU team demonstrated significant investment in the entire project. This is the crucial moment in students' learning processes, where their ideas, concepts, and research influence the activity system itself. This influence is exerted not when executing the wishes of the original design team, but when faced with transforming the design into an actual product.

Identify the object of activity

The object of the activity was the creation of a fun but historically accurate and educational game that simulated certain characteristics of ancient Greece. The game had to be immersive: a combination of history, appearance, and sound that consistently challenged players to learn how to think and act like an ancient Grecian. The object of our design was the detailed Greek environment which players can enter and explore without uncovering references to either the real world but especially the native *Neverwinter Nights* game.

Identify the subjects in the activity

The subjects were members of the LGI-USU design team: Robert, Wilson, Jason, and Ryan. There were also student play-testers, an online peer community (the LGI Forum), and faculty reviewers. All three of these latter subjects provided varying levels of review. The LGI Forum (see Figure 7) is primarily constituted by researchers at both Utah State University and the University of Arizona. Both research sites have academic investment in the success of *Aristotle's Assassins* as a model of an educational game's potential. LGI's longstanding mission has been to study, teach with, and build computer games, both to understand games themselves more fully and to discover new teaching and research opportunities. As the project evolved, LGI-UA team members and LGI-USU team members interacted frequently, generating almost 90 posts in 22 distinct forum topics. As is typical in all LGI projects, professional position and academic rank have little bearing on who does what; the ideals of sweat equity, mutual teaching and learning, and collaboration rule.

Identify the influence of artifacts on the object

Activity theorists define an "artifact" as an object that mediates a particular activity. In the case of projects like ours where the object was the production of something more or less tangible, the object itself (*Aristotle's Assassins*) can become an artifact in future activities (e.g., playing the game, using the game in a classroom to teach certain principles, and so forth). In this way, the remaindered artifact becomes a representation of the activity system's object. LGI hopes that

145

Figure 7. Screen capture of the LGI Forum.[8]

those who play *Aristotle's Assassins* will learn about the history, mythology, culture, music, politics, and appearance of ancient Greece while they are immersed in the epic adventure of the game. Yet playability and narrative elements have placed certain constraints on the historical accuracy of some of the elements in the game. For example, we worried about the architectural and geographical accuracy of Aristotle's Peripatos, but were unrepentant about his completely fabricated assassination attempt early in the game.

In this way, *Aristotle's Assassins* is itself becoming a representational artifact of the project's activity system, representing the project's object in very specific ways (e.g., particular interpretations and depictions of historical accounts, translation issues, platform dependencies, interface aesthetics, etc.). As a result of this self-reflexive turn in the project—the turn that gave rise to this chapter—the object of the artifact has become an artifact itself, thus giving rise to a new activity system. Teachers and project managers who are attuned to the flexibility inherent in any activity system will help students understand where their influences as subjects affect larger systems.

Identify the rules mediating the activity

There were many explicit and implicit rules that governed this project. The explicit rules concerned lab and computer use, the parameters set out in the design document, and the constraints of our development tools. The lab where most of the actual gameplay was developed, for example, is on a university campus in a building separate from the English department (the home department for most of the developers). Therefore, standard building hours restricted the team's access to the lab. In addition, the lab was the location for at least one other research project, thus limiting the amount of access the LGI-USU team had to one computer. One consequence of both rules—building access and computer assignments—was that independent research outside the lab became standard as opposed to synchronous team collaboration more generally. The implications of these explicit activity rules was significant: actual game development—hands on building and testing on the computer—was slowed considerably while the depth of content research increased tremendously. This has had impacts on the development timeline, on the design document, and, consequently, on the object itself.

Implicit rules in the project included expectations among LGI members concerning collaborative practices, and about the level of input by off-site team members, as well as the characteristics of what makes games fun, what particular game styles look like, and so forth. Like explicit rules, these implicit rules have shaped the object of our activity in very specific ways. The considerable Role-Playing Game (RPG) experiences of several key developers have led to the creation of a new game—original graphics, original music, original dialogue and plot—that to our beta testers appeared quite standard, and in a few instances even cliché. On the one hand, we see the value of familiarity in projects with a human-computer interaction component; but on the other hand, this implicit rule set seems to have superseded the explicit rule we prescribed in the design document to create a game that was significantly different from most other RPGs, both in terms of educational content and setting. Implicit rules also co-determined other elements of the activity, particularly those that focused on personnel. For example, when a key designer accepted a job after graduation, he was unable to continue his involvement in the project, which thereafter changed direction slightly because his expertise was no longer available.

In terms of project management, these implicit and explicit rules function as constraints that must be accounted for in the activity system. In our case, the rules mediated the activity insofar as they pushed the LGI-USU design team into more independent, content-based research than we had originally intended. Project managers and teachers, then, should be aware of what effects explicit and implicit rules can have on the activity system.

Identify the role that mediates the activity

The following people had major roles in the activity once the project entered the development phase:

- Robert: dialogue writer;
- Wilson: 3D object creator and scripter;
- Jason: process documenter and designer;
- Ryan: project manager and faculty advisor.

During the first semester of work, however, these roles became more complex. Robert became the project's historical and cultural researcher. Wilson's role shifted into a custom software troubleshooter. Jason invested time into learning the design tool and the design tool's scripting functions. Each of these roles—as well as several roles that preceded the development stage—mediated the activity at different times. The historical researcher, for instance, at several points redirected the activities of other team members after discovering historical evidence that particular features of the initial design were flawed. The software troubleshooter on more than one occasion had the unenviable task of informing his team that the development could not proceed along projected lines because the available software and hardware resources were unable to meet the need. The toolset expert was sometimes able to create innovative solutions to obstacles that had stymied the project, putting the object onto a track that had previously been dismissed as impossible. And the faculty advisor was able to secure funding at several key points that allowed the activity to continue beyond the originally allotted time, and with resources the team had thought it would not be able to acquire. Furthermore, as project manager, the advisor set the agendas for weekly meetings, established project deadlines, and facilitated shifting roles and objects within the project. Thus, in complex collaborative activities, mediating roles may shift depending on current conditions and proximity to the object's conclusion, making rigid role statements somewhat counterproductive when learning is a part of the object of the activity system.

Identify the community in which the activity is conducted

The lab in which most of the development occurred—the Creative Learning Environments (CLE) lab—and its administrators comprised the primary community within which the LGI-USU team conducted their activity. The CLE lab is the product of Utah State University funding and is responsible for demonstrating research and the production of innovative educational game applications. While funding and administration do not pose constraints on the efficiency of lab research and productivity, there is a pressure to provide evidence of significant work. Therefore the project's artifacts and object assist (hopefully) in the justification of further funding; *Aristotle's Assassins* represents one potential research element of the CLE lab.

The Learning Games Initiative comprised a secondary community for the *Aristotle's Assassins* activity. Both the LGI-UA and the LGI-USU teams posted all their notes, test content, sample levels, and project reports on the LGI website for the perusal of other members. This shared research space lent a sense of accountability and historical record to the work of its disparate research partners.

As part of the LGI archive, these records and resources are freely available to other research teams engaged in different but perhaps aesthetically, pedagogically, or managerially related projects.

Identify the outcome

After some reflection, LGI-USU discerned the need to re-evaluate their activity system. While the team met its original design objective, the objective was not met by means of the activity system as originally defined at the beginning of the project. In fact, had the project proceeded without alterations, the team would not have reached the objective. For example, had we not felt some amount of constraint by the rules of the system—specifically access to the collaborative workspace—the individual content research may not have been as extensive. Had we not experienced shifting roles and left subjects more constrained by their discrete job descriptions, we never would have realized the potential for greater historical accuracy in our architectural models and geographical space.

The activity system thus required new descriptions. This is what Berkun (2005)—a long-time project manager for Microsoft—describes as a mid-term game in project development. He advocates for smaller shifts in the activity system (although, admittedly, he does not call it this) that can be more easily managed by project managers if properly documented and worked on in collaboration among team members (p. 285). One of the advantages of applying activity theory to a project as dynamic as this one is that it gives researchers specific points at which to focus their analyses in order to better understand how and why the activity mutated in the ways it did.

OBSERVATIONS AND LESSONS LEARNED

In this chapter, we have used Mwanza's eight steps (2001) to set up our activity system for reflection and for application to project management and understanding the complexity of student learning outcomes. Taken together as a unit, these steps suggest that there is a way to process or interpret the activity system such that the pedagogical benefits of game design become clear and precisely highlights the critical connections students make between computer game development and learning outcomes. For example, we originally intended that players of our game would learn about Greek culture and politics; however, we did not realize that by designing 3D models and in-game conversations, our student developers would also become such subject matter experts. In addition, Mwanza's steps showcase how useful activity theory is for the discussion of game development and project management. The following section details our post-project insights.

The critical connections between information, tools, and people constitute the activity

Even informed design choices are subject to transformation in the face of an activity's dynamic tools, rules, and roles. As a result, new connections among the element of any activity co-evolve with the design choices themselves. Rather than simply using information to accomplish a goal, a kind of designed dialectic materializes such that work done toward accomplishing a goal feeds back into the system and modifies the pathways leading toward that goal. This goal is also altered; thus, the object becomes the same thing only different, so to speak. Both Papert (1980) and Gee (2003) identify this type of high-level design as evidence of learning. Papert suggests that most forms of learning require concrete thinking, rather than formal thinking; yet the computer design that he advocates requires students to integrate *both* types of thinking and to constantly reassess the consequences of these connections in order to accomplish complex tasks. Similarly, Gee discusses the concept of "transfer"; that rare occasion when students can solve unfamiliar problems by transferring knowledge from other domains that have similar solution structures (p. 123). Thus, making critical connections during design meetings, for example, is a much more complex action than simply applying one rule-set or knowledge domain to a particular problem.

In contexts where the production paradigm is guided by a predetermined valuation of what constitutes expeditious, significant, or sufficient activity, the various tools, rules, and roles tend to be highly discrete and rigidly enforced. In such environments—for instance on factory floors, in rank-and-file military maneuvers, and specialized facilities for producing particular technologies—production schedules and outcomes can be predicted with considerable accuracy, though opportunities for innovation tend to be severely limited. In contrast, activities guided by production paradigms that are less predetermined offer considerable opportunities for discovery and learning, though the precise nature of this learning is difficult to predict.

Under such conditions, we found that team members became sufficiently specialized *and* unstructured. As a result, design meetings became a site for them to report on their independent progress toward the communal goal. In addition, lab access and computer assignments forced independent research outside the primary physical space of the project, which led to additional discoveries and project alterations. The point being that rules will always affect the outcome. The product of much of this independent research was improved use of our available tools and more accurate detailing of the simulated elements of our game. Yet the resultant shifts in our activity system also revealed a major flaw in our team's development practices: an emerging sense of isolation among the team members and a growing sense of disconnectedness to the object. When Robert connected his new knowledge of the development tools with Wilson's 3D imaging work, however, the activity—and the object—snapped back into focus. Robert's observation about the accurate design of the Peripatos was a connection between books on history and culture with the project's specially designed graphics. In this way, shifts in roles—

as when Robert's role shifted among design evaluation, content research, and dialogue creation—transformed the entire project's relationship to its extant tools, rules, and other roles. Subsequent examination of other transformations within this and other LGI projects bear this implication out: the critical connections among a project's tools, rules, and roles together constitute the nature of its activity and determine the possible outcomes for the object.

Object of activity changes according to mediated activity

The object of our original activity system was to make a culturally specific game that was not merely Greek looking, but that also simulated particular elements of ancient Greek life: politics, philosophy, music, and—where the look-and-feel of the game was concerned—architecture. By "Greek looking" we refer to the standard symbols that typically mark an image as being of ancient Greece: togas, laurel wreathes, Doric columns, and so on. In the course of this project, we discerned that the concept of "simulation" within the context of our activity could not easily be applied to political, philosophical, and musical elements of the game; rather, the "simulation" needed to touch all aspects of *Aristotle's Assassins*, at least to some degree. An historically accurate soundtrack, for example, made the game's historically inaccurate architecture seem anathema. Thus, the game's appearance evolved such that it now includes more historically and culturally accurate depictions of Aristotle's Peripatos, Lycium, and other Greek structures. In hindsight—and with the clarifying light of activity theory—we see the game's more accurate Peripatos as evidence of the critical connections amongst the LGI-USU team members, connections that ultimately shaped the object in profound but unexpected ways. The new description of the Peripatos became our exemplar for the ways in which even careful game designs can shift in seemingly insignificant ways and yet mediate the activity system such that new objects and outcomes are revealed and old objects and outcomes de-emphasized.[9]

Reflection is required by shifts in the activity system

After reflection, the activity system requires new descriptions. This new activity needs to include the kinds of research and observations that Robert was undertaking in our project. Instead of relying entirely on the execution of informed design choices made early in the activity, the activity is viewed as a constantly evolving project in which critical connections among tools, rules, and roles continually guide subsequent design choices. As a result, the design and design processes of educational game creation may be as educational as playing the final game itself—if not more so.

Project managers—a term which we expand to include teachers who use computer game design as an instructional tool—facilitate critical connections throughout the activity system, discovering that developers may move away from the implementation of preset design more and more as they become invested in the project and demonstrate ownership over their elements. The project manager's role

151

remains important insofar as she keeps the team cognizant of the evolving activity system, thus incorporating the various shifts back into the larger project.

CONCLUSIONS

We found that activity theory helped us to identify a large matrix of activities, motives, objectives, and subjects within the LGI-USU activity system, all of which had defining roles in the project's outcome. While there were many design meetings where the implementation of ideas altered the direction of the activity system, this chapter documents one in particular, namely, the discovery that our failure to accurately model the Peripatos at the beginning of the project undermined the veracity of seemingly more important elements of the game's simulated components. Other shifts include the results of our research on gender roles, class structures, and magic in ancient Greece. Each of these shifts led to significant redesigns, which again illustrates our main point: the student design of games and simulations is a highly educational process, and the steps they take throughout the design process can be helpfully interpreted by using activity theory as an analytical framework.

NOTES

[1] In this chapter, we have adopted the convention of referring to electronic games that require a computer to work—PC games, console games, handheld or mobile games, and arcade games—by the technology-specific term "computer games" rather than the sense-specific "video games" (cf. McAllister, 2004).

[2] Game engines control (among other things) how the physics of the game world work and how environmental objects look when the player's avatar moves around the screen.

[3] The callouts in the image refer to the most commonly used elements of the design tool. The toolbar calls up key features like saving, centering the image map, and accessing design options. The design options allow users to "paint" what the design tools calls "placeables": creatures, objects, landscape features, sounds, etc. The object tree is a list of all the areas in a particular mod: creatures, objects, conversations, etc. that have been previously painted into the image map. The image map is a visual display of the object tree. Users can rotate and zoom the image to orient the map in any way necessary. The view tools include the controls used to manipulate the image map.

[4] Game levels or "mods" developed in *Aurora* will run on both PC and Apple platforms, but the Aurora Toolset is restricted to Windows.

[5] The LGI-UA team included Judd Ruggill, Ken McAllister, David Menchaca, Jennifer deWinter, Bryan Pearce, James Johnson, Daniel Griffin, Jason Thompson, and Jeffrey Reed. The LGI-USU team included Ryan Moeller, Jason Cootey, Wilson Bateman, and Robert McConkie.

[6] Stealth learning is a contentious concept, but we use it here to describe learning that takes place without the learner's awareness. While the idea of making learning activities so engaging that students forget that they are being educated has ancient origins, the idea has experienced a resurgence of interest in recent decades with the use of popular culture as a teaching tool. Marc Prensky, citing research at MIT, has been one of the most prominent advocates of stealth learning within the context of instructional technology. Indeed, Prensky has situated stealth learning—a concept he borrows from Doug Crockford of LucasArts—as a cornerstone of his corporate training seminars: "Digital Game-Based Learning can certainly be [difficult] fun. But at its very best, *even the hard part goes away*, and it becomes *all* fun, a really good time from which, at the end, you have gotten better at something…" (18-19).

[7] *"Peripatos"* literally means "to walk around." In ancient Greece, the peripatos was a covered circular path in Athens where Aristotle was said to stroll with his students while teaching them.

[8] Ongoing building projects include *Aristotle's Assassins, Thirst* (a game about water politics between Palestine and Israel), the *Technology-Enhanced Language Revitalization* project (which is aimed at preserving languages at the brink of extinction), *Looter!* (an archaeological game based upon Cambodian grave robbing), and others.

[9] Such de-emphases are not always necessarily for the better. For example, in deciding not to use the stereotypical visual icons of ancient Greece, we let slip an educational opportunity to help student-players see these icons for what they are: suasory cues that have more to do with facilitating quick immersion into an environment than with historical accuracy.

REFERENCES/BIBLIOGRAPHY

Berkun, S. (2005). *The art of project management*. Sebastopol, CA: O'Reilly Media.

Gee, J. P. (2003) *What video games have to teach us about learning and literacy*. New York: Palgrave Macmillan.

Kafai, Y. B. (1995). *Minds in Play: Computer game design as a context for children's learning*. Hillsdale, NJ: Lawrence Erlbaum.

Kafai, Y. B. (1998). Video game designs by girls and boys: Variability and consistency of gender differences. In J. Cassell & H. Jenkins (Eds.) *From Barbie to Mortal Combat: Gender and computer games*. Cambridge: MIT Press.

Kaptelinin, V. (1996) Activity theory: Implications for human-computer interaction. In B. A. Nardi's (Ed.) *Context and consciousness: Activity theory and human-computer interaction*. Boston: MIT, 53-59.

Kirriemuir, J. (2002). The relevance of video games and gaming consoles to the higher and further education learning experience. *JISC*. Available at http://tecnologiaedu.us.es/bibliovir/pdf/301.pdf (last retrieved on 31 May 2006).

Leont'ev, A. N. (1978). In M. J. Hall's (Trans.) *Activity, consciousness, and personality*. Eaglewood Cliffs, New Jersey: Prentice-Hall.

Mwanza, D. (2001). Where theory meets practice: A case for an activity theory based methodology to guide computer system design. *Proceedings of INTERACT 2001: Eighth IFIP TC 13 Conference on Human Computer Interaction*, Tokyo, Japan.

McAllister, K. (2004). *Game work: Language, power, and computer game culture*, Tuscaloosa, AL: University of Alabama Press.

Nardi, B. A. (1996). Activity theory and human-computer interaction. In B. A. Nardi's (Ed.) *Context and consciousness: Activity theory and human-computer interaction*. Boston: MIT, 7-16.

Nardi, B. A. (1996). Studying context: A comparison of activity theory, situated action models, and distributed cognition. In B. A. Nardi's (Ed.) *Context and consciousness: Activity theory and cuman-computer interaction*. Boston: MIT, 35-52.

Papert, S. (1980). *Mindstorms*. New York: Basic Books, Inc.

Prensky, M. (2003). *Digital game-based learning*. New York: McGraw-Hill.

Puntambekar, S., & Kolodner, J. L. (2005). Toward implementing distributed scaffolding: Helping students learn from design. *Journal of Research in Science Teaching, 42*(2), 185-217.

Sanders, J. (2005). An activity theory perspective. *Work based learning in primary care,* 3:191–201.

Seif El-Nasr, M. and Smith, B. (2006). Learning through game modding. *ACM Computers in Entertainment, 4*(1).

Vygotsky, L. S. (1962). In E. Hanfmann & G. Vakar (Trans.) *Thought and language*. New York: John Wiley & Sons and MIT. (Original work published 1934).

Ryan M. Moeller
Learning Games Initiative,
Utah State University

Jason L. Cootey
Learning Games Initiative,
Utah State University

Ken S. McAllister
Learning Games Initiative,
University of Arizona

SECTION TWO: USE

With the increasing international interest of using games for educational purposes has come the empirical iteration of design, development and implementation in both formal and informal learning environments. Certainly we laud these efforts as being crucial to advancing our understanding of computer game use. The effort that began within the areas of science and engineering education has been expanded to incorporate learning across humanities and civics.

GAMES AS MEDIUMS FOR SOCIAL CHANGE AND LITERACY PRACTICES

The following three chapters describe situations in which gaming environments have been taken into innovative subject areas, and studied through a variety of complex, triangular means. The first offers insight into the Quest Atlantis project and the implementation of multi-participant environments to help teach children social awareness and responsibility. The subsequent chapter discusses literacy—its existence and practice within multi-player online games—and offers arguments of how real-world learning parallels the activities within these kind of make-believe environments. These chapters provide insight into how studying the teaching and learning that takes place naturally within simulated realms can inform the effective design of educational games. The lessons learned lead us to recommendations in how we can design proper support mechanisms for the learning that takes place within these realms.

SASHA BARAB, TYLER DODGE, HAKAN TUZUN,
KIRK JOB-SLUDER, CRAIG JACKSON, ANNA ARICI,
LAURA JOB-SLUDER, ROBERT CARTEAUX JR.,
JO GILBERTSON, CONAN HEISELT

THE QUEST ATLANTIS PROJECT: A SOCIALLY-RESPONSIVE PLAY SPACE FOR LEARNING[1]

INTRODUCTION

Over the last decade, video games have become one of the most significant forms of media for the enculturation of youth, especially males. According to a Kaiser Family Foundation study, over 80% of homes have video games (Roberts, Foehr, & Rideout, 2005) and, according to a Pew Report, all college students interviewed had played a video game and nearly half of them play multiplayer video games regularly, breaking the myth that these games are isolating or anti-social (Jones, 2003). While few would disagree with the statement that children, and many adults, are spending large amounts of time and money playing video games, many would argue against the educational usefulness of the interactions that occur in these spaces or the significance of these interactions on the positive development of the children who play them.

Rather than simply being spaces for mindless play, we view many of these games as quite sophisticated and as being imbued with rich narrative structures, ideologies, and embodied practices that constitute game play (Squire, 2006). The linguist James Gee (2003), in particular, has documented the discursive richness, depth of collaborative inquiry, complexity of game play, opportunities for consequentiality, rich perception-action cycles, exploration of situated identities, and the complex forms of learning and participation that can occur during game play. At one level, curriculum developers and instructional designers can only marvel at the diverse ways these games support complex learning, thinking, and social practices.

In contrast to much of the rhetoric, not all games are anti-social and an increasing number of girl friendly games are being produced every year. Examples of successful non-violent games that appeal to both genders include *The Sims, Animal Crossing, Yoshi's Island, Zelda, Kingdom of Hearts,* and many others. Moreover, even games like *Barbie Fashion Designer,* while ostensibly lacking educational significance, can for some users connect with the larger *Barbie* narrative, including such empowering elements as the *Career Barbie* line. More generally, rather than simply being transgressive spaces for mindless killing and other nefarious behaviors, games are quite sophisticated and diverse in terms of the

B. E. Shelton & D. Wiley (eds.), The Educational Design and Use of Simulation Computer Games, 159–186. © 2007 Sense Publishers. All rights reserved.

plotlines and interactive rule sets enlisted. Squire (2006) refers to games as *ideological worlds* that communicate particular value systems and ways of interacting, and he provides numerous examples of games that engage players in complex problem solving and insightful, if not educationally valuable, plotlines. The game developer Peter Molyneaux refers to the spaces he develops as *ethical playgrounds*, in which players engage in particular actions that affect the actual dynamics of the game for better or worse depending on the actions the player chooses to engage. For example, punching a bully to reclaim a little girl's teddy bear or stealing an expensive antidote to save a sick friend.

Game developers, through the narratives underlying the games they create and through the rich interactions these games support, have become among the most influential storytellers for children today (Herz, 1997). One question that emerges is whether these are the storytellers whom we want educating our children. And while there clearly exist a number of computer games that emphasize character-oriented plots, highlight collaborative game play, emphasize issues of friendship and social relationships, and employ colorful graphics and playful rule sets, it is rare to find a game that advocates an explicitly pro-social agenda, especially if it is not one that sells titles. Further, while they may be benign or even empowering, they rarely are grounded in users' real worlds, and are not usually *critical* in orientation (see Barab, Dodge, Thomas, and Tuzun, in press). Additionally, though games exist with educational potential, there remain too few examples of computer games that would satisfy teachers and parents, appeal to girls as well as boys, support academic learning, and engage users in real-world issues.

The use of video games as an educational medium continues to entail issues of deep concern, including discrimination against girls and the commercialization of schools—with many video games still being designed to cater to the interests of white males, incorporating white male avatars in protagonist roles, presenting sexualized representations of women and tokenized representations of minorities, and framing participation within violent themes (Kolko, 1999; McDonough, 1999). To be sure, software manufacturers face a heady challenge in pursuing equity: showing that video games' mythological potential is at the whims of commerce. Herz (1997) explains, "the people transmitting their stories to the next generation aren't priests or poets or medicine women. They're multinational corporations. And they are not trying to appease the gods. They are trying to appease the shareholders" (p. 170).

Herein lies the irony of the promise of video games. The space available to youths to express their agency, according to Jenkins (cited in Laurel, 2002), has been reduced from several square miles to often a mere computer screen, yet even that domain is appropriated by commerce. As Taylor (2002, p. 229) wrote, "branding has assumed such a prominent role in our cultural lives that it becomes difficult to imagine spaces not touched in some way by corporatized signs." As Berger (1972, p. 131) explained, "publicity as a system only makes a single proposal. It proposes to each of us that we transform ourselves, or our lives, by buying something more." The divide resulting from commerce may not be easily overcome, for many consumers brand association is the road to societal identification and inclusion. When commercial interests stake a claim in education, we must scrutinize the messages being communicated to children.

Central to our work in the Quest Atlantis Project (QA) has been designing a context for learning that sits at the intersection of education, entertainment, and social action. Designing to support social commitment and real-world action— what we call socially-responsive design (Barab, Thomas, Dodge, Carteaux, & Tuzun, 2005)—involves a range of issues, including gender representation. QA is an immersive context with over 3500 registered members from the USA, Australia, Denmark, Singapore, and China. The project is intended to engage children ages 9–12 in a form of dramatic play comprising both online and off-line learning activities, with a storyline inspiring a disposition towards social action. A core question underlying our work is whether we can reclaim the story medium in one of its contemporary forms—video games—to use in a socially-responsive way and at the same time avoid the problems currently associated with the use of this form.

A core challenge in our research has been to optimize the positive aspects of videogames and brand-identification in order to create empowering self-identification of students with a pro-social agenda, while at the same time fostering critical social engagement. Our perspective on design entails the assumption that the technology is only one aspect of the larger brand context through which the design bears meaning and potential. Central to our thinking is the understanding that QA is not simply a technological product, but rather it constitutes a socially-responsive brand that integrates technology as part of its identity. Given that member participation is situated in the context of a larger QA community, the "brand" of QA is one that is both individual and social. Here, we illuminate the complexity of features that we have used to establish this brand, demonstrating how we were able to develop a videogame brand that was useful even in the context of schools.

QUEST ATLANTIS AS A COMPLEX EDUCATIONAL GAME

The core elements of QA are 1) a 3D multi-user virtual environment (MUVE), 2) inquiry learning Quests and unit plans, 3) a storyline, presented through an introductory video as well as a novella and comic book, involving a mythical Council and a set of social commitments, and 4) a globally-distributed community of participants (Barab, Arici, & Jackson, 2005). QA was designed to foster inter-subjective experiences through structuring interactions, toward helping children to realize that there are issues in the world upon which they can take action (Barab, Dodge, Thomas, & Tuzun, in press). At the core of QA is the narrative about Atlantis, a world in trouble in the hands of misguided leaders. Participation in QA entails a personal and shared engagement with this narrative, as children contribute information and ideas based on real-world experience to the activists of Atlantis.

The narrative helps to establish continuity among the QA elements and helps to connect the fictional world of Atlantis with the real world, an act of interpretation performed by each individual child. Significantly, it is the narrative that provides the meta-structure of QA; the online technology is simply one of the ways in which

161

participants are immersed in the narrative. While some projects wrap a rich context around the use of technology in order to make the technology and content more agreeable to girls, we have prioritized the context, with the technological structures being simply one element of the larger implementation. In the gaming industry, this larger frame—the meta-game—is the umbrella structure that gives unity and meaning to the underlying participant structures.

QA provides structures and experiences whereby students with little background in community participation can be introduced to the practice of social commitments as well as the inquiry process, while sheltered within an digital game-based context. The mythical backstory of QA, crossing the boundary between the Atlantian world and local contexts, motivates students to develop answers to social issues beyond their typically available experience. To participate in QA, then, is to engage in dramatic play characterized by learning, caring, and sharing of experience. Much more than the technological structures, this context additionally entails a rich collection of commitments, norms, participants, and interactions. This chapter will illuminate the complexity and sophistication of current videogames at the same time demonstrating that this medium can be used towards academic and socio-responsive ends.

The QA virtual environment, storyline, associated structures, explicit social commitments, and social policies constitute what is referred to as a meta-game context, a genre of play in which an overarching structure lends form, cohesion, and meaning to a collection of nested activities, each with its own identifiable rules and challenges (Barab, Thomas, Dodge, Carteaux, & Tuzun, in press). This meta-game serves multiple functions, providing a motivating context to stimulate engagement (entertainment), drawing on content and processes associated with various traditional academic disciplines (education), and instilling values in member behaviors (social commitments).

Like traditional role-playing games, this meta-context immerses students in role/identity–construction, but in contrast to these familiar games, in QA members' game identities and activities are dependent on their ability to participate in the real world as well as in the game-like context. Similarly, we are explicit about the kinds of values that we promote as good "gameplay," in contrast to games like *The Sims* that have only implicit values. Members learn about the QA storyline (the "Legend") and the underlying social commitments through a variety of media, including a video, a novella, a comic book, movie-style posters, and trading cards, and through a range of activities, such as through completing Quests, talking with other QA community members, and reading other resources in which more of the backstory is revealed. These varied media, more than simply structures for delivering the experience, are part of its overall meaning and help to establish the engaging experience that constitutes what is QA.

Central to this legend is that the people of "Atlantis" face an impending disaster: despite advanced technological development, their world is slowly being destroyed through environmental, moral, and social decay. The Council, led by a female teenager proficient with computers and a male teenager concerned with the environment, consists of three males and three females who are trying to save

Atlantis. To do so the Council developed the OTAK, a 3D virtual environment that serves as a technological portal between Atlantis and other worlds. Through the OTAK, children from other planets can help the Council by engaging in Quests and sharing their experiences, wisdom, and hope. The Council hopes that today's youths with their adventurous optimism can contribute just the sort of knowledge that they seek. The slogan "Two Worlds, One Fate," appearing on the movie-style poster and in the novella, suggests that Earth and Atlantis have similar problems and similar destinies. While children know that Atlantis and the Council are not real, they nonetheless consistently engage the myth and storyline.

The Quest Atlantis community consists of both the virtual space and the face-to-face QA Centers. In order to participate in QA, children must be associated with a particular QA Center (i.e., participating elementary schools and after-school programs) and register online. Once registered, Questers may participate at a QA Center or from other locations with Internet access. As part of QA participation, each child is supplied a account that is connected to an avatar, with which she can respond to Quests (inquiry-based activities that include a task description, specific goals, and useful resources). An avatar is a virtual placeholder symbolizing one's identity and allowing interaction with the virtual space. Upon entering the virtual environment, referred to in the storyline as the OTAK (see Figure 1), Questers can travel to different worlds where they learn about the theme of that world, complete Quests, talk with other children and with mentors, and build their virtual persona through their homepage functions.

The 3-D space contains the different worlds created by the Council, and each world features several villages that present a series of challenges called Quests, which are designed to help restore the lost Atlantian knowledge. Each village reflects a theme (e.g., urban ecology, water quality, astronomy, weather) and houses a spectrum of Quests, ranging from simulation to application problems of varying levels of complexity. Consistent with national calls for inquiry-based mathematics and science learning, the Quests were designed in a manner that supports children (and mentors) learning the process of inquiry as well as domain-relevant content and concepts (AAAS, 1993; NCTM, 2001; NRC, 1999; Zucker & Shields, 1995). Further, using national standards generated by MCREL (online at http://www.mcrel.org/), we connected each of the 400+ Quests directly to one or more national standards and continue to work with districts to draw links to local academic standards. These features have proven central to attracting teachers and administrators. Each Quest is also targeted toward empowering children and their communities: while connected to specific academic standards, the Quests are rooted in our social commitments and are framed by the types of issues and interests that the children themselves have expressed. An important research question relates to how complex and "educational" these academic Quests can be while still engaging students.

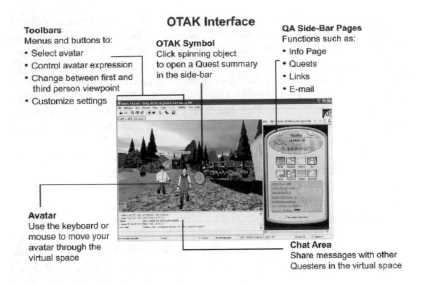

Toolbars
Menus and buttons to:
• Select avatar
• Control avatar expression
• Change between first and third person viewpoint
• Customize settings

OTAK Interface

OTAK Symbol
Click spinning object to open a Quest summary in the side-bar

QA Side-Bar Pages
Functions such as:
• Info Page
• Quests
• Links
• E-mail

Avatar
Use the keyboard or mouse to move your avatar through the virtual space

Chat Area
Share messages with other Questers in the virtual space

Figure 1. Screenshot from Quest Atlantis showing a virtual village on the left and a student homepage on the right

Completing Quests requires that children participate in academically meaningful activities, either in the real world (e.g., conducting environmental field studies, calculating rainfall) or through simulation (e.g., writing a story about travelling through various virtual biospheres, exploring a contaminated virtual environment and reflecting on lessons learned). Participants can select a number of these Quests based on their interests or as assigned by their teacher, if they are participating as part of a school project. Unit plans are two-week curricula composed of 5–8 Quests with a common focus or topic (e.g., water quality, environmental awareness). Submitted through an interface integrated with the client software, the children's work on Quests includes both content-area findings and personal reflections to foster retention, critical thinking, and meta-cognition. Both the content-based findings and the meta-cognitive reflections are assessed by teachers with expertise in the content area of the Quest. Through a Teacher Toolkit, teachers may create their own Quests, assign particular Quests for their students to complete, allow students to engage in Quests without overtly assigning them, or disallow specific Quests. Other functions include registering Questers, assigning reviewers to evaluate the children's responses, presenting points and customizable rewards to Questers, and monitoring their e-mail and chat. Through the Toolkit, teachers can facilitate the program and customize the experience in ways that suits the needs and interests of the particular class (Barab, Jackson, & Piekarsky, 2006).

THIS REPORTING

The focus of this reporting is to provide an overview of the QA context, describing these structures as an example of a game designed for academic learning at the same time illuminating the complexity that an academic game might take. As a context for learning, QA is not simply a technological innovation. We have referred to it as a "context of participation" in order to acknowledge the variety of resources and forms of participation that can take place as part of the QA experience. In this reporting, we examine the multiple forms of QA participation and discern the ways that these engage participants. As such, in this study we do not simply report differences with respect to a single form of participation, but instead report data related to the avenues of participation available to the QA participants. More specifically, we focus on a series of affordance trajectories that we believe games can leverage: learning and achievement, narrative engagement, identity development, collaborative participation, communication, and reflexivity affordance structures (see Table 1). By examining these multiple participant structures as opposed to just one or two of them, we develop a richer interpretation of participation in QA. The examination of these structures, taken collectively, will help to provide rich insight into multiple facets of the QA experience and, potentially, characterize a set of participant structures that others may wish to incorporate in their design work, especially if they are bringing together education, entertainment, and social commitments (Barab, Thomas, Dodge, Carteaux, & Tuzun, 2005).

Table 1. Quest Atlantis Affordances

Quest Atlantis Affordances	Elements
I. Learning & Achievement	Quests, Empathy
II. Narrative Engagement	Fixed Media, Media Interactions
III. Identity-Development	Avatar Choice, HomePages, Name Plaques, & Jobs
IV. Collaborative Participation	Collaborative Roles, Guilds
V. Communication	Chat, Email
VI. Reflexivity	Metacognition, Transactive Interactions

Participants from whom the data was derived consisted of individuals from the United States ($n = 2055$, inner-city = 128), Australia ($n = 924$), Singapore ($n = 60$), Demark ($n = 25$), China ($n = 50$), and Malaysia ($n = 28$). While some of the registration data make it difficult to determine registrants' core affiliation, there were approximately 2200 elementary school children in public schools aged 9–12, 300 children aged 9–12 in private schools, 150 children 9–14 year old children in after-school contexts, 450 undergraduate students, 50 teachers, and 10 staff in after-school contexts. In analyzing student participation, we have examined artifacts and various computerized records of children's communications, accomplishments, and choices in QA; we have also conducted dozens of interviews and multiple focus groups and have engaged in participant observation of dozens of classrooms as they used QA.

Below, we briefly overview these different data sources. At times, we statistically compared all 3279 registered Questers for whom we had data, but on some of the questions for which we conducted content analysis, the sample was simply too large to examine all their work. In these cases, we worked with a random sample of Questers and communicate the process of selection. In building qualitative interpretations, we used multiple raters and, where appropriate, inter-rater reliabilities were calculated. We used Likert-type questionnaires to help gauge the perspectives of 4th, 5th, and 6th grade students at one suburban school where we could directly interview students, and we also conducted some experimental studies, randomly assigning Questers to either the QA condition or a worksheet control condition to test the effectiveness of the QA context.

We developed pre–post assessment tests to examine learning gains and examined the number of Quests completed by children. Student responses in an experiment involving a personal narrative were also analyzed, with a .89 inter-rater reliability. To examine *narrative engagement affordances* within QA, we conducted focus groups to learn about their perspectives of QA fictional stories. The *identity development affordances* are represented primarily by quantitative data derived from the database logs with respect to each student's participation in the 3-D context. First, analysis involved examining the log files regarding avatar choices of both boys and girls. Second, Questers' customized homepages were analyzed. Third, participation through several structures in the virtual space was analyzed, including name plaques and applications for QA jobs.

Collaboration affordances involved examining chat logs to illuminate the various ways in which Questers collaborated with each other. Additionally, we examined Guild participation and the number of times both boys and girls broke allegiance with a Guild. *Communication affordances* included an examination of chat posts, QA emails sent, and telegrams sent. In addition to simply looking at overall quantitative differences, we also examined a subset of Questers to determine if they were more likely to engage in discourse with same-gender Questers. We also examined *reflexivity affordances,* focusing first on participants metacognitive reflections of individual Quests. Two raters, with an inter-rater reliability of .92, also examined the content-based reflections of a subset of students to discern gender differences in metacognition. From here, we looked at the participation of one particular Quester, showing how QA provided her an opportunity to reflect and transform her behaviors.

RESULTS

As of March 2004, 14 months after beginning the program, there were over 3300 registered Questers, including 1702 boys and 1609 girls. A number of registrants who serve as designers or researchers have been removed from any counts since they are not typical project participants. In terms of logins, individual girls have logged in on average 20.5 times ($\Sigma = 32, 960$) while boys have logged in on average 21.5 times each ($\Sigma = 36,643$). Unfortunately, it is not possible to tease out how many of these logins were voluntarily and how many were required in order for children to complete assigned work when participating as part of a class. Below we analyze differences between genders on the participation variables listed in Table 1 to characterize gender participation in QA. As described above, these data include both quantitative and qualitative data to create a rich overall picture of gender participation.

I. Learning and achievement affordances

Quests. The most visible learning and achievement structure of Quest Atlantis are the individual Quests and larger unit plans, representing collections of Quests focused on a common topic. Overall, there have been approximately 10,000 individual Quests completed with about 20% requiring revision by the teacher. Statistically significant learning gains have been documented for unit plans in the academic disciplines of science, social studies and language arts. For example, with respect to science learning, elementary students who participated in a three-Quest unit plan on plant and animal cells demonstrated significant learning over time (Pre$M$ = 10.6, Post$M$ = 47.1) ($t(79)$ = 38.62, p < .01), with respect to their conceptual understanding of cells. Similarly, students' learning of world history in the context of QA went from almost no appreciation for how this content related to their own life (Pre$M$ = 10.30) to a deep appreciation of its relevance to their life worlds, and students showed the ability to adopt multiple perspectives in the international arena (Post$M$ =47.45) $t(19)$=10.28, p < .01). As one example of the types of changes occurring between pretest and posttest, the following illustrates a sixth grader's movement from a relatively superficial description to one of much more depth.

> *Pretest Response:* The trade of illegal drugs is an important issue. Poor farming families know they can make money off of selling illegal substances. Drug usage is dangerous and this is an important issue.

> *Posttest Response:* In many countries, rainforest logging is a major issue. People from wealthy countries such as our own might protest it because it kills so much of our beautiful environment, but in a country where fine rainforest wood is a major industry and especially if the countries economy is weak, its not really fair to say they can't do it anymore. This is a very controversial issue, because we are basically weighing human life and animal life, two things that depend on each other.

While the pretest shows an attempt to respond with a factual issue, it lacks the depth and complexity of the posttest, which shows multiple perspectives, considers economic and societal issues, and weighs contradicting factors. No gender differences were found on either these or the science measures of learning.

Empathy Experiment. Student achievement can also be examined through specific Quests, where again, girls and boys both show the program to be effective. In an experiment comparing the QA context with a simple online worksheet, students were presented with a personal narrative and asked to respond to four open-ended questions. This narrative was presented to half the students as part of QA and to the others simply as a worksheet. Student responses were analyzed for content, with a

167

.89 inter-rater reliability. While student responses to several of the questions were similar for both conditions, when asked to engage in perspective taking, students in the QA condition offered character insights that were either deeper or better supported than did students in the worksheet condition ($t(14) = 2.62$, $p < .05$). Considering the developmental and epistemological roles of perspective taking (Batson, 1991; Hoffner, 1995; Ickes, 1997; Preston & de Waal, 2002), the QA program may bear important benefits.

Further, rather than being alienated by the videogame context, girls ($M = 137$ words) wrote significantly more than did boys ($M = 85$ words) ($t(18) = 2.55$, $p < .05$); considering that research has shown girls are made more anxious by computers than are boys (cf. Cooper & Weaver, 2003), this finding suggests that girls' use of technology within the QA context does not constrain their achievement. Moreover, the QA context seems to have positively benefited the boys, as they wrote more in the Quest condition than the worksheet condition ($ES = .74$), representing a medium-to-large effect size. Indeed, on the question concerning perspective taking, both boys and girls wrote significantly more in the QA condition (boys $M = 32.67$ words, girls $M = 38.20$) than the worksheet condition (boys $M = 15.88$ words, girls $M = 32.00$) ($t(18) = 2.17$, $p < .05$). Additionally, in terms of the question regarding perspective taking, girls (QA $M = 4.50$, Worksheet $M = 4.33$) overall offered character insights that were either deeper or better supported than boys (QA $M = 4.00$, Worksheet $M = 3.50$), regardless of condition ($t(18) = 2.55$, $p < .05$). Interestingly, while boys wrote less in the worksheet condition, boys in the QA condition wrote as much as girls wrote in the worksheet condition (see Figure 2). Considering that boys in general write less than girls do (Calvert, 2003), this suggests that QA can promote student achievement in a gender equitable manner.

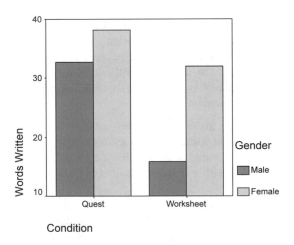

Figure 2. Condition by number of words written for boys and girls

II. Narrative engagement affordances

Fixed Media. While video games vary in the degree to which a narrative backstory is evident during gameplay, almost all games feature a narrative, which not only unifies players' activities within a common framework but also infuses their activities with an often rich and compelling storyline, replete with characters and settings, histories and possibilities. As mentioned before, the narrative backstory in QA is distributed across a range of fixed media, including not only an introductory video but movie-style posters, novels, printed and online trading cards, and a comic book as well. Indeed, the series of novels, involving the characters in Atlantis and children participating in QA on Earth, not only portray the history and current situation in the world of Atlantis but also communicates many of the norms of participating in the program. As one girl explained, the first novel made clear that "there is a reason for doing the quests." Because the novels represent the most robust narrative structure in the program, this discussion will focus on them to show how narrative can infuse children's participation—what seems to some to be just "playing a video game"—with interest, passion, and care.

Children's responses to the first QA novel were examined through a number of focus groups. Specifically, in an elementary school engaged in QA, one classroom that had read the first novel participated in four separate groups, and audio recordings from two of the groups were transcribed and analyzed qualitatively. As the focus groups revealed, the novel moves beyond being mere backstory to bring together the fiction of Atlantis, the Quest Atlantis program, and children's own lives. For example, many of the students mentioned that the book teaches about participating in QA, and beyond simply mentioning the connection between the story and the QA program, they expressed positively enjoying scenes when characters from either earth or the planet Atlantis discussed Atlantis and the Quest Atlantis program. The novel also connects with important aspects of children's lives. For example, because friendship is so central to their daily lives, the students expressed liking one of the Atlantian characters for his steadfastness: "he steps up for his friends." Similarly, many of the students recognized that the book addresses "life skills," a topic addressed weekly in their school, including "bravery, courage, and kindness."

Children's responses to a recurrent theme in the story—bullying—further demonstrate how the novel connects with children's own lives. In one scene, a clique of three girls verbally harasses another girl, and in a later scene, a boy bully physically taunts a weaker boy. Several students identified with the victims, explaining that "a long time ago, people were making fun of me," and "people made fun of my name...to make me mad." Similarly, several of the students found personal relevance in the girl bully and her infirmed father: one boy "related to [the girl] 'cause my mom had cancer but she survived," and another agreed, "I can probably relate 'cause my grandfather was in the hospital; he died." Moreover, these scenes brought the students to reflect on important issues in insightful ways. For example, some of the girls not only identified with the victim of the bullying but also appreciated that she responded without reciprocating the meanness.

169

Similarly, the scenes elicited critical self-reflection in some of the students: "sometimes you're mean to people that aren't in your little circle of friends." In these ways, buttressing activity in the virtual environment with a rich narrative served to enrich children's participation in the QA program.

Media Interactions. In addition to the more fixed media (introductory video, movie-style posters, novels, printed and online trading cards, a comic book), the narrative also is revealed through participants' interactions through media. Students exchange email with the principle characters in the Atlantis backstory, converse with them in the virtual space, post messages on the characters' Web-logs, and even create their own sites on the World Wide Web discussing QA and the legend of the world Atlantis. Through these media interactions, children relate to the characters with an easy sociability and sincere curiosity. For example, meeting Alim (the fictional girl at the center of the Atlantis narrative) inside the virtual space, a child asked her, "Do you ever get to do Quests? How often do u get on [log into] QA?" Similarly, in an email to the same character, one student wrote, "Hi, can you be my friend?" Indeed, Questers frequently include these characters in their list of friends in QA, alongside their classmates and other acquaintances. Further, children not only move easily between their own world and the narrative of Atlantis but also often connect with the narrative backstory in deeply personal ways. For example, through writing poetry, one student showed poignant and creative understanding of the Atlantis backstory, in which a cultural monument— the Arch of Wisdom—was destroyed. The poem concluded with the lines, "The grass shrank / The sun set / in the morning / and faucets ran dry / The world stopped spinning / when the Arch of Wisdom / shattered."

Children's interactions with the Atlantian characters through the characters' Web-logs represent an important form of engagement with the narrative because children can discuss topics that they consider important to both the characters and themselves. Moreover, these discussions typically demonstrate the socially responsive norms of the program—perhaps more so than most of the other media interactions. For example, responding to an article in which a character discussed mercury pollution on Atlantis, one boy wrote, "I'm sorry to hear that Lan. I wish I was there and could help. On Earth we have recycling. Recycling is when you get ride of stuff you used and then it gets reused." Seven weeks later, the same boy responded compassionately to a Web-log article about the 2004 tsunami. The Atlantian character had written, "I'm planning on giving some of the money I received for the Holidays for the relief efforts." In turn, the boy wrote to the character, "I hope your money gets to Asia in time. I also hope that all of the Questers in Asia are all alright. I also feel very sad for the people affected by the tsunami. I wish there was some way I could help." Similarly, another student responded to a Web-log article about street art, such as singing, reciting poetry, and making posters. Again moving easily between her own life and the narrative of Atlantis, the student wrote to the character, "Your writing is very interesting Alim. I think street art is a good way to express your feelings too! I feel so sorry that Atlantis is being destroyed!!!!!!!!!"

170

III. Identity-Development Affordances

There are multiple ways in which Questers can represent themselves in the virtual environment of QA. Through these different means, Questers can develop online personae (Turkle, 1995), but unlike most MUVES, these online personae are not simply fictional characters with little connection to real-world identities. In this section, we focus on four of these structures: choosing one's avatar, putting one's name on the QA wall, filling out one's homepage, and purchasing and building on the virtual land.

Avatar Choice. When Questers login to QA, they appear in the virtual environment as an avatar with attributes chosen by the Quester and persisting from one session to the next. Using the "avatar creator," Questers can choose a female or male avatar, customize hair and skin color, and select one of six clothing or body styles: adventure, punk, sport, summer, winter, and formal. Five of the clothing style choices are very similar between male and female avatars, but the "formal" type is an exception: male avatars have a tuxedo, and female avatars have a pink prom dress. We collected data from a single point in time showing the current avatar being used by each participant. After eliminating data regarding researchers and participants who had not yet used the avatar creator, we were left with 988 participants, including 507 females and 481 males—the Avatar Creator was a fairly recent introduction to QA, being only four months old when this paper was written. These were then sorted into categories based on chosen avatar style (see Table 2). The chi-square statistic of the difference between the avatar choices of female and male participants was strongly significant ($X^2 = 77$ ($df = 6$), $p < .01$).

Table 2. Count of avatar styles

	Avatar Style							
Gender	Adventure	Punk	Sport	Summer	Winter	Dress	Tuxedo	Σ
Female	75	63	64	38	63	193	11	507
Male	41	107	130	41	61	15	86	481
Σ	116	170	194	79	124	208	97	988

Among males, the "sport" style was the most popular, followed by "punk," whereas female participants chose the pink dress style far more often than any other. Also, overall, boys' self-representations show more variety than those of girls. Though most of the avatar choices are rather gender-neutral, girls seem to gravitate toward the very feminine dress style, and to a lesser degree the adventure style (which, with a cape and belt, may also be interpreted as a female costume). This pattern mirrors the problem in the commercial video game world of females being depicted in limited and stereotyped ways. By providing mostly gender-neutral clothing styles, we may be offering girls too few appealing choices for self-representation (Bruckman, 1998; Donath, 1998; Turkle, 1994). Further, when so many girls choose the same clothing style, their presence in the virtual space begins to appear homogenous. As one researcher put it, girls are "running into themselves all over." Discovering how this may effect girls' perception of themselves and of female involvement in QA will require further research.

Homepages. Each Quester also has a personal homepage that is displayed when another user clicks on the individual's avatar or clicks the sender's name of a QA email. The amount of information on one's page, including information about their likes, interests, talents, and possible future careers, is determined entirely by the individual. Girls ($M = 82$ characters) tended to write significantly more information on their personal homepages than did boys ($M = 55$) ($t(3340) = 6.50$, $p < .01$). This finding suggests that girls are more willing and invested in putting information on their homepages for others to read (or, another interpretation, are simply more likely to complete what they interpret as "assignments" even if the degree of completion is optional). Qualitative analysis also reveals that girls tend to present more information regarding hobbies and interests than do boys.

Name Plaques and Jobs. Another category of identity presentation involves leaving personal traces in the virtual environment that others can see regardless of whether the individual is currently logged on. First, once students complete more than two Quests, they can apply to the Council, describing how they have contributed to the Council's mission and, if approved, get their name posted on a plaque on a virtual wall. This activity produced equal interest, with 41 girls and 39 boys applying to have their names on the wall and indicating no significant differences between genders. On a related note, at the time of this writing, students can apply for QA helper positions, including greeter, tour guide, and chat monitor. These jobs had been active for only a month, but already, 50 girls and 69 boys had signed up, with no significant different among genders; as with placing one's name on the wall, this feature seems to be compelling to both boys and girls.

IV. Collaborative Participation Affordances

Collaborative Roles. An illuminating form of collaboration occurs when one child with more knowledge or experience helps another child in QA, through orienting, supporting, or assisting them. These scaffolding and apprenticeship activities have been observed throughout the duration of the project. Even when QA was in its formative stages, implemented only at an after-school youth club alongside other computer games, we witnessed children helping each other to a remarkable extent, for altruistic reasons, for the joy of collaboration, and for the cachet that expertise brought. For example, one child wanting to join others in the virtual space was helped by a friend: "You and him are chatting together. I wanna be there." He called for a staff member to figure out how—"I need help getting to..."—and his friend showed him, physically sharing the chair and appropriating the mouse.

As the program structures—and calls for support—grew more extensive, children helping each other became a cultural norm. As mentioned earlier, children with "jobs" in the virtual space submit reports on their experiences. In this report, a child demonstrates how his work as a greeter contributed substantially to the experiences of others, suggesting that his helping was its own reward:

> Then I greeted adejau0. He asked me to show him around the worlds, so I did. He told me I was a great friend. The next person I greeted was alexechr0. He asked me to tell him how to build. Now, thanks to me, he has a beautiful house in Qville. Then I greeted kirklau0. She said that it was a wonderful start to her time on Quest Atlantis. The last person I greeted was my friend zcorrKR, who is no longer doing Quest Atlantis. Because of that greeting, we became good friends.

Though sometimes these represent fairly simplistic collaborations, such as helping another navigate in the virtual environment, at other times they even rise to collaborative work on the academic Quests. This latter type of collaborative work began with children helping each other in parallel as they worked individually on the same Quest. Given the power of this type of collaborative work, this ability was eventually instantiated into a design affordance where Questers could submit collaborative work yet each be responsible for their own reflections on their individual contributions and experience. Whether in the physical space of the computer lab or the virtual space of the OTAK, children engage in scaffolding and apprenticeship activities that contribute significantly to the experiences of all participants and, indeed, to the ethos or cultural norms of the program.

Guilds. Another play structure of interest is Guilds: Questers can join a group in which they have a common mission and thus share percentages of points earned with fellow group members. Over the past year, the Guilds were active for only two months. However, in that period 112 boys and 91 girls signed up to join a Guild ($X^2(1) = 1.08, p > .05$ (again, no difference between genders). One aspect of these Guilds is that participants can break allegiance with one Guild and join a different one. While there are no significant differences in terms of the number of Questers who signed up for Guilds, there are significant differences in terms of "Guild disloyalty." Of the Questers who have signed up for a Guild, 63 boys have broken from one Guild to join another and only 24 girls have done so, indicating that boys are more than twice as likely to break their affiliation with a Guild ($X^2(1) = 12.75, p < .01$). One could treat this data as an example either of boys being more active or of a potential on their part to be disloyal. Clearly, member checking is necessary before any assertions can be advanced. In terms of Guild choices, girls were most likely to choose the Culture Guild with its focus on expressions of culture while boys chose the Ecology Guild with its focus on environmental issues.

V. Communication Affordances

The primary means of communication within QA is verbal discourse, usually typed on a keyboard and then read as text on another computer screen. Questers can communicate synchronously through chat and telegrams, and asynchronously through email and bulletin boards, all of which have their unique norms, and each of which engenders a different form of communication (Herring, 2004). Moreover, all of these forms of communication are used actively and extensively. Public chat consists of short messages sent by one participant to all other participants within "hearing range" of the sender, and in the first 15 months of the program, children typed almost 500,000 lines of chat. In general, girls tended to post almost twice as many chat messages as boys.

The QA email system supports longer messages consisting of multiple lines and quoting of previous messages, and supporting multiple recipients. No one outside the QA program can send or receive email within the system, and Questers cannot send emails to people outside of their local classroom or affiliation unless they first meet this person in the virtual space and add their username to their "Friends" list. In the first 15 months, children sent almost 1,500 emails with boys being almost twice as likely to send an email than girls. Telegrams are short private messages sent from one sender to typically a single recipient, and bulletin boards, like traditional online forums, support threaded conversations and entail topics initiated by both teachers and researchers. Girls tended to send more telegrams and make more posts than do boys.

Example of Chat.   Beginning with chat, we first look at three conversations from a randomly-selected day to illuminate the types of interactions that occurred and the extent that these are gendered. To reiterate, although the day was randomly selected, it is not necessarily representative of the chat in general. Still, this dialogue does provide a window into the types of chat interactions that occur. Identifying sender-recipient relationships for public chat is more difficult than identifying the relationships for mail or telegrams, as done below. Unlike mail or telegrams, chat messages do not have an explicit address that identifies the recipient. Therefore, we inferred these relationships by looking for topical cohesion between messages and explicit addressing by the participant to the sender (Panyametheekul & Herring, 2003). These relationships were processed by the software programs Ucinet and Krackplot (Borgatti, Everett, & Freeman, 1999) to build the network map shown in Figure 3.

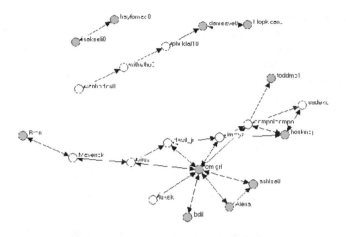

Figure 3. Network map showing sender–receiver chat relationships, with girls being represented as the darker nodes

In Figure 3, the conversational ties between after-school and late-night participants are displayed at the bottom of the figure. Two different types of conversations tended to dominate the discussion on this day. With respect to the first type, Emigrl (a U.S. girl) and Oompaloompa (an Australian boy) occupy central locations in the network due to the long period of time they spent online that day. As other participants dropped out of the space and new participants logged in, Emigrl and Oompaloompa were able to establish new conversational connections. Both male and female participants in QA can develop central positions within the QA social network by participating in the MUVE after school and actively engaging other participants in conversation. The cluster of nodes at the top of the diagram reflects the second type of conversation, in which an entire classroom logs in at the same time. Here, there are relatively limited chat connections among participants, usually because the teacher has an explicit goal for students in the virtual environment.

Example of Email. QA email postings tend to be longer in length and more substantive in content than the chat. The topics range from the building of friendships, to talking with the Council, to conversations among groups of Questers on a common topic. An example of students vying for social status among other classmates can be seen in the following thread. It is important to note, similar to other observations of the chat space, that neither the boy nor girl necessarily has more power than the other; instead the issue is socially-negotiated at the level of the interaction—not pre-determined by one's gender. In this interaction, one boy Quester, referring to the virtual hotel built by a girl classmate, stated,

175

Come one come all its Lisa's hotel and you wouldn't want to miss a spot in this totally awsome hotel. there is going to be a pool at least two floors at most I don't even know the answer to that question. If you guys and girls want a spot you better hurry.
P.S. You guys'll love it :)

Another boy student responded,

Dont go to Lisa's Hotel it stinks!!!!!

Defending her friend, another girl responded,

YOU HAVE TO GO THERE IT WILL BE AWSOME !!!!!!!!

Trying to get people to visit the hotel he and his friend built together, a boy responded to the thread,

My hotel rocks book a room in it now for freee you get whatever you want in it. Whatever you do dont go to Lisa's hotel.

Another boy, being a little more diplomatic, stated,

Mike is right you can book a room for nothing at my [our] hotel 2. But come 2 both hotels [referring to his and Lisa's].

Questers also use telegrams to communicate. Telegrams were usually abbreviated messages, a little longer than chat posts but shorter than emails. They also tended to be one-to-one in that the system requires them to be directed to a particular receiver. While power differences do emerge among Questers, in terms of email, telegrams, and even chat, power differences tended not to be defined along gendered lines. Nonetheless, girls did tend to use all of these communication structures significantly more than boys, as illuminated in the quantitative analyses below.

V. Reflexivity Structures

Metacognition. Another measure of student's success is the degree to which participants are able to think metacognitively about their work (Perfect & Schwartz, 2002). Within QA, students submit their work online on a response page which includes two parts: 1) the response to the Quest, and 2) a reflection on their response. The reflection is prompted and guided by the following three questions:

1. How does your response meet all the goals of the Quest?
2. What did you learn about the topic and yourself from doing this Quest?
3. Tell the Council how your response helps the mission of QA.

We designed a study to measure specifically the quality, depth, and qualitative trends of Questers' metacognitive responses to these reflection questions. Student reflection responses were gathered from 5 different Quests and were rated on a 5-point rubric with a .93 inter-rater agreement. The rubric was based on completeness, relevancy, number of reflections, and depth and complexity of reflection. A typical score of 1 would be minimally complete with only a single attempt to reflect. A score of 5 would address all 3 reflection questions at a level of metacognitive depth that is notable and that indicates that students are truly reflecting on how their work is connected to a deeper issue or broader context.

While both boys' and girls' reflection performance was found at the top and bottom of the rubric scale, girls ($M = 2.88$) scored significantly higher on measures of metacognition than did boys ($M = 1.90$) ($t(93) = 4.23$, $p < .05$). Girls' reflections typically demonstrated greater numbers and depth of metacognition. The difference between the two groups equates to an entire point on the rubric scale, which corresponds to one standard deviation. In addition, girls on average wrote longer, more detailed reflections, going beyond the minimum typically required for a Quest. Boys were more likely to leave the reflection section completely blank (10%, compared to girls at 5%).

In a review of the content of boys' and girls' reflections, qualitative differences between the two groups were evident. For example, in one Quest about societal problems, many boys' reflections focused on solving the problems. One boy's reflection on what he had learned (question 2) read,

> I learned that I hate smoking and I can make a good argument against it. Atlantis should have non-smoking laws too because smoking is harmful to everyone.

Certain social issues were too difficult to resolve, and in fact, many boys wrote that these things must be accepted. For example, one boy wrote the following answer to question 2:

> What I learned is that some things in life just can't be changed. With that I learned that some things can be changed, which reminds me of something; Don't cry over spilt milk.

Girls on the other hand spoke less of problem solving and more of relating to the individuals involved, and girls wrote that they share similar problems and that the girls in the story were fortunate in comparison to others. For example, one girl responded to question 2 as follows:

> When I did this Quest, I learned that Atlantians also had a lot of bummers too. I was sort of under the impression that Atlantians live in the perfect world. Now I know that the Atlantians are a lot like us. By doing quests I learn more and more that Atlantians are like us.

A girl who did mention solving problems did so within the context of talking about other people, not just solving the problem at hand. Her response to question 2 read,

> When I was writing this quest I learned how important it is to help others, how much my family did to help others, and it made me realize how many things you can do to lend a hand with things in the community.

In sum, the boys and girls not only showed significant quantitative differences in their metacognitive performance, they also show qualitatively different foci within their reflections.

Transactive Interactions.   Here, we present an extended case study of one student to show how, through participation in QA, she came to better understand her own behavior while at the same time transforming the Quest Atlantis context. Mary, an eleven-year-old child attending elementary school in a suburban Midwestern town, was considered somewhat of a "trouble maker" by the teacher and had consistently lower grades than her classmates. Still, she was outgoing and had two or three girlfriends who were considered popular in the class. Mary first came to our attention when another teacher reported that she was bullying a student in her class. More specifically, Mary had learned that she could get more QA points by finding someone else to sign up for her Guild and having them choose her as mentor. Below is an excerpt of the reported incident.

> Mary: sadie just please do what i say
> Sadie: but i just dont know
> Amy: PLEASE!!!!!!!!!!!!!!!!!!!!
> Mary: listen to what i am saying
> Mary: PLEASE JUST LISTEN TO ME
> Amy: PLEASE LISTEN TO HER!!!!!!!!!!!!!!!
> Sadie: i dont want to do it!!!!!!!!!!!!!!!
> Mary: WHY
> Sadie: im trying to work on a quest
> Mary: okay then bye
> Mary: letas go amee
> Sadie: r u leaving
> Sadie: fine bye
> Mary: yeah cuz ur not going to do it. if u do then for a mentor highlight my name

Following this incident, the mother of the bullied student, Sadie, called Mary at home and told her how inappropriate her behavior was, and Mary began to cry, claiming that she did not mean anything by her behavior.

The next day, the teacher pulled the class aside and told them that two students (Mary and Amy) were banned from QA because of their bullying behavior. In response to this incident, their class created a list of rules that later became known as I-BURST, an acronym representing particular forms of appropriate behavior. Though designed specifically for this class, the list was adopted by another classroom in the school, and a suggestion was even sent to the QA project team to implement the rules more widely. Following this suggestion, the I-BURST rules were posted in the 3D environment and began to establish a norm for behavior: for example, responding to some bad language, one student typed in the chat space, "QA is not supposed to be used for swearing.... Please review the I BURST chat rules."

Further, Mary herself was given the opportunity to rejoin QA. Told that she could serve "community service" hours to earn her way back, Mary became a "greeter" in the virtual space, helping to make others feel welcome, and sometimes serving as a "monitor," correcting them for using inappropriate language. After writing an apology, working as a greeter and monitor, and demonstrating a positive change in behavior, Mary became a role model in both the virtual world and her real-world classroom, where she was repeatedly referred to as the class leader in QA. For example, she was the first student in the class to earn enough points to purchase land, and she even built rooms for many of her friends and for an Australian girl who did not have enough funds to purchase land for herself. Mary also completed a number of academic Quests of her own volition. Demonstrating her pride in this transformation, when we visited her classroom, Mary told us how her house had evolved, and she proudly mentioned that her name was displayed on the wall. She discussed her contributions to her Guild and even printed out exciting chats and emails representing her online participation. Mary's transformation was plainly evident. Indeed, her teacher commented, "I even see changes in the classroom, where she is so much more helpful to other students," and, in an interview, Mary herself stated, "I think I have changed in that I am a lot more helpful both in QA and out. I really try to correct others when they don't use the rules." Significantly, these "rules" are the I-BURST rules that her own behavior stimulated and that she in fact helped to create.

We share this as an illustration of the transactions among the QA structures and individual members, with each affecting and being affected by the other. At other times, the impact was not so dramatic: for example, a Quester might simply post some text or greet another Quester. Still, because all participation—and even one's online identity—are reified into data, Questers can reflect on their participation and their individual trajectories in ways that allow them to evolve their online identity, shaping these personae and their participation in ways that align with that which they want to portray.

CONCLUSIONS

Given the fact that videogames engage users in rich (discursive, problem solving, inquiry, and collaborative) practices, that early videogame experience has been linked to greater comfort in using computers, that videogames represent one of the principal "storytellers" for children in the 21st century, that the content of these games is usually determined by commercial developers, and that videogames seems to be quite successfully engaging youth, we have suggested that it is a societal imperative to understand how to design games that engage all children. More generally, we know little about what a game would look like that would engage children in social commitments and academic content learning. At a minimum, we believe it involves fostering the same elements of motivation that game developers integrate into their designs and that have been discussed in the previous academic literature on motivation: challenge, curiosity, fantasy, control, and social interaction. However, we have also argued that it requires the design of a larger context of participation, one that involves going beyond the technological innovation itself to consider the larger context in which the innovation is situated and through which it takes on meaning. In our case, this involved developing a character-oriented narrative that included male and female protagonists, establishing structures that fostered friendship and social interaction, using bright, colorful visuals that contributed to immersion and engagement, adding interactive rule sets, and drawing on the complex set of motivational elements discussed above.

Overall, we have gathered much evidence that we have developed a socially-responsive game that is being successfully enlisted in the context of schools. Given our commitment to social responsivity, we were also interested in whether the designed space would prove motivating for both genders. We examined various structures of QA, and the data suggest that across the diversity of media, including those that rely on technology, girls and boys both engaged with QA. The identification of structures children found to be resonant, as well as their responses to these structures, suggest generalizations that may be useful to designers of virtual communities.

Both genders expressed enjoying fantasy settings: for girls, it was a fantastic natural scene, and for boys, a fantasy that harbors adventure, but the shared appreciation of other-worldly settings suggests the feasibility of designing virtual spaces inclusive of both genders. While the social, symbolic, and locally-customizable structures of the QA experience afforded many opportunities for gendered identification (e.g., avatar choices), performance (e.g., Quests), and interaction (e.g., email), we are heartened by the results found, ones that illuminate not simply gender differences but gender-specific benefits. For example, in some moments, contextualization in QA seems to have inspired more substantial engagement in academic tasks for boys than usual. In other moments, we see girls taking on substantial roles as community/communication leaders—across genders—in a complex, technological environment. This gender story reflects not the erasure of gender but, rather, a tempering of some conditions that often differentially support or limit the technological, social, and academic engagement of boys and girls. In fact, we saw numerous instances where girls were in positions of power, where they were the technological leaders of the class, and where they were considered the experts of the game.

While a more comprehensive ethnographic analysis is necessary to make substantial assertions, our analyses here lead us to believe that, in the context of QA, both boys and girls found legitimate avenues of participation, and, more importantly, neither gender appear to dominate the space. Instead, power seems to be based on the centrality of the individual to the community, with some structures favoring girls and others favoring boys, but with agency and voice being available to both. Issues of power are especially important in that they ultimately facilitate and legitimize use and ownership of particular structures. The more we are able to create technology-rich contexts of participation that help girls regard technology as supporting things that they value and spaces that they control, the greater opportunity we have of making technological spaces and participation become non-gendered.

We observed that the engagement of children lies in no small part to the resources, structures, and overall aesthetic that contributes to the QA context of participation. The network relies on various project resources—the movie-style posters, the novella and comic book, the trading cards and stickers, and other project resources—all of which portray girls and boys in positions of equal importance. Further, in developing these resources, we have worked to ensure that the storylines featuring Earth children and the Atlantis Council honor boys and girls equally. Coupled with these non-gendered or similarly gendered resources are a myriad of structures that appear to be compelling, although sometimes somewhat differently, to both boys and girls. Further, as highlighted in this manuscript, we have developed various participation structures, including those that support learning and achievement, identity development, narrative engagement, communication, collaborative participation, and reflexivity. With all that in place, we still monitor, participate in, and revise the community spaces, continually working to ensure that both genders may find equivalent agency and voice.

In reflecting on our development and those aspects highlighted in this chapter, we have highlighted six affordances that were central to our understanding of user participation. Specifically, these include tools, resources, and structures that afford learning and achievement, identity development, narrative engagement, communication, collaborative participation, and reflexivity (see figure 4). *Rather than representing individual elements, these affordances were considered transactive, collectively constituting the aesthetic and resultant ethos that is Quest Atlantis.* This aesthetic was strongly influenced by our particular commitments and assumptions, especially as they involve education and social responsivity. For example, rather than developing a backstory that involved killing fictitious creatures, the QA narrative centered on establishing empathy for the people of Atlantis, using this empathetic understanding to examine problems on Earth, and evolving one's character through sharing and reflecting on real-world accomplishments. For others interested in doing socially-responsive design work, we urge them to focus not simply on the technical structures and tools employed but also on the collective ethos that these resources are intended to engender.

We refer to this collective ethos and the various structures and affordances through which it is implemented as the *context of participation*. It is through this context of participation that meanings are made, and it is this larger context that is too often neglected in conversations by educators about technology. It is also important to note that these affordances, our particular aesthetics, and the emergent ethos, while influenced by us, also transacted with those who use the space. For example, we witnessed the emergence of norms, values, and even reified structures such as in the case of the I-BURST rules, all based on choices that participants made. While technical structures might be less impacted by users' actions than were formal or informal norms and rules, even those come to be impacted by user participation. In the gaming world, both sides of the spectrum exist, with some games having a very top-down structure that is pre-defined by the designers, and others having low levels of pre-designed space, with much of the game play being established by the players themselves.

Figure 4. Design structures affording user participation in the Quest Atlantis context

While much of a product's ethos emerges over time, one should not underestimate the role of aesthetics in informing the larger context of participation that is established. In other words, it is important to consider the packaging used to "market" the collective ethos of the space. Games that feature dark settings, incorporate violent themes, and objectify women, are likely to alienate girls from these early experiences with technology. Consider, for example, the success The Sims has had in engaging girls: we consider this in no small measure as due to its look and feel as well as its type of game play. To the extent that early experiences impact later life choices, as many have argued they do, we believe that educators have a responsibility to develop technological play spaces that welcome all children. This study highlights those features used in video games as offering a significant space for participation, at the same time demonstrating that it is possible to enlist this medium in academically and socially responsive ways. Our experience supports the value of the underlying goal of our work to bring together education, entertainment, and social commitment.

IMPLICATIONS

While few would deny that video games have captured the interests of today's children and adolescents, many would argue against the positive value of the interactions that occur in these games for the children who play them. In contrast, many current games researchers view video games as quite sophisticated, offering a play space for rich discourse, engaged problem solving, cooperative problem solving, collaborative inquiry, and opportunities for consequentiality and the exploration of situated identities (Gee, 2003; Steinkuehler, 2003; Squire, 2004). We have further suggested that video games are significant spaces that bear a rich potential in education, not only in teaching such content as history and geography or such skills as navigation or resource management, but also in accommodating and even fostering players' reflection on their game playing. When such reflection connects the gameplay with a player's real life, and when the reflection achieves such a pitch as to build upon itself, then it can achieve a critical or transformative effect, giving the player a new perspective on the game, on real life, and on the role of identity in bringing the two together.

Our work indicates that through the enlistment of a game-based context (i.e., a context entailing a narrative history, a setting with affordances and imperatives, and role-play identities that give rise to player participation), we were able to successfully engage players in critical reflection in terms of academic content and pro-social issues. Still, even in video games with such a rich backstory, the backstory serves to frame the gameplay; it need not be salient and perhaps should not relate to a player's real world to be commercially successful. Indeed, two compelling features of games are that they are transgressive and they are not real. Even among games with backstories analogously or metaphorically relevant to players' real lives, many players may not make the connection to their lives, so the potential of the game to support a player's reflection on its significance may not be realized.

Relevant and hence potentially transformative structures are not likely to figure centrally among the developers' concerns, so the employment of the structures to purposively occasion critical reflection are not likely to occur. For many players, a game must positively structure such reflection for the critical degree to be achieved. In our work, we have undertaken a design trajectory that conscientiously involves the development of an educational game with an explicit pro-social agenda. We have worked to develop the context of participation such that players are indeed compelled, if not required, to critically reflect on their participation and the world around them. In terms of next steps, we are currently integrating other methods used by game designers to engage players. For example, one current emphasis is on integrating extended trajectories of participation (affordance networks) in which the game play moves beyond the completion of linked Quests, and also involves *game-based missions*.

These game-based missions involve unfolding storylines in which plots are established, critical decision points are engaged, and opportunities to apply academic concepts to particular narratives are encountered. For example, developing a virtual park in which students interact with game characters, investigate various water quality problems, and use their emergent understandings of, for example, the process of eutrophication to analyze a water quality problem and propose a solution (Barab, Sadler, Heiselt, Hickey, & Zuiker, in press). Choices, such as suggesting the closing of the logging operation, might have initial environmental benefits, but also have negative consequences for the economic longevity of the park; thereby positioning the player in a storyline in which they are protagonist in determining how the story unfolds. The important point, in relation to this chapter, is the acknowledgement that digital video games provide an important experiential space for supporting meaningful learning, and that it might behove educators to understand and leverage this powerful medium. In this chapter we have demonstrated its utility for supporting academic learning in the context of schools, and for engaging players in significant issues upon which they are adopting and advocating pro-social stances.

NOTES

[1]   This research was supported in part by a CAREER Grant from the National Science Foundation, REC-9980081 and by the National Science Foundation Grant #0092831. Special thanks to Rebecca Scheckler for her constructive feedback on earlier drafts of this manuscript.

REFERENCES

American Association of University Women (AAUW) Educational Foundation, Commission on Technology, Gender, and Teacher Education. (2000). *Tech-savvy: Educating girls in the new computer age.* Washington, DC: AAUW. Retrieved from http://www.aauw.org/2000/techsavvy.html

Barab, S. A., Arici, A., Jackson, C. (2005). Eat your vegetables and do your homework: A design-based investigation of enjoyment and meaning in learning. *Educational Technology 65*(1), 15–21.

Barab, S. A., Dodge, T., Thomas, M, Jackson, C., & Tuzun, H. (in press). Our designs and the social agendas they carry. To appear in the *Journal of the Learning Sciences.*

Barab, S. A., Jackson, C., Piekarsky, E. (2006). Embedded professional development: Learning through enacting innovation. In C. Dede (Ed.), *Online professional development for teachers: Emerging models and methods* (pp. 155–174). Cambridge, MA: Harvard Education Press.

Barab, S. A., Sadler, T., Heiselt, C., Hickey, D., Zuiker, S. (in press). Relating narrative, inquiry, and inscriptions: A Framework for socio-scientific inquiry. To appear in the *Journal of Science Education and Technology.*

Barab, S. A., Thomas, M, Dodge, T., Carteaux, R., and Tuzun, H. (2005). Making learning fun: Quest Atlantis, a game without guns. *Educational Technology Research and Development 53*(1), 86–108.

Batson, C. D. (1991). *The altruism question: Toward a social-psychological answer.* Hillsdale, NJ: Lawrence Erlbaum Associates.

Berger, J. (1972). *Ways of seeing.* London: British Broadcasting Corporation/Penguin Books.

Borgatti, S. P., Everett, M. G, & Freeman, L. C. (1999). *UCINET 5.0 Version 1.00.* Natick: Analytic Technologies.

Bruckman, A. (1998). Community support for constructionist learning. *Computer Supported Cooperative Work 7*(1–2), 47–86.

Calvert, S. L. (2003). *Production features for intrinsically interesting learning environments.* Presented at IFIP Working Group 3.5 Conference: Young Children and Learning Technologies. University of Western Sydney. Retrieved from http://crpit.com/confpapers/CRPITV34Calvert.pdf

Cooper, J., & Weaver, K. D. (2003). *Gender and computers: Understanding the digital divide.* Mahwah, NJ: Lawrence Erlbaum Associates.

Donath, J. (1996/1998) Identity and deception in the virtual community. In M. A. Smith & P. Kollack (Eds.), *Communities in cyberspace: Perspectives on new forms of social organization* (pp. 29–59). London: Routledge.

Gee, J. P. (2003). *What video games have to teach us about learning.* New York: Palgrave.

Herring, S. C. (2004). Computer-mediated discourse analysis: An approach to researching online behavior. In S. A. Barab, R. Kling, and J. H. Gray (Eds.), *Designing for virtual communities in the service of learning* (pp. 338–376). New York: Cambridge University Press.

Herz, J. C. (1997). *Joystick nation: How videogames ate our quarters, won our hearts, and rewired our minds.* Boston: Little, Brown and Company.

Hoffner, C. (1995). Adolescents' coping with frightening mass media. *Communication Research 22*(3), 325–346.

Ickes, W. (Ed.). (1997). *Empathetic accuracy.* New York: Guilford Press.

Jones, S. (2003). *Let the games begin: Gaming technology and entertainment among college students.* Washington, D.C.: Pew Internet and American Life Project.

Kolko, B. (1999). Representing bodies in virtual space: The rhetoric of avatar design. *The Information Society 15*(3), 177–186.

Laurel, B. (2002, January). *Gender and technology: A case study in design research and ethics.* Presentation at Indiana University, Bloomington.

McDonough, J. P. (1999). Designer selves: Construction of technologically mediated identity within graphical, multiuser virtual environments. *Journal of the American Society for Information Science 50*(10), 855–869.

National Research Council (NRC). (1999). Designing mathematics or science curriculum programs: A guide for using mathematics and science education standards. Washington, DC. National Academy Press.

Panyametheekul, S., & Herring, S. C. (2003). Gender and turn allocation in a Thai chat room. *Journal of Computer Mediated Communication 9*(1). Retrieved from http://www.ascusc.org/jcmc/vol9/issue1/panya_herring.html

Perfect, T. J., & Schwartz, B. L. (2002). *Applied metacognition.* Cambridge University Press.

Preston, S. D., & de Waal, F. B. M. (2002). Empathy: Its ultimate and proximate bases. *Behavioral and Brain Sciences, 25*(1), 1–71.

Roberts, D. F., Foehr, U. G., & Rideout, V. (2005). *Generation M: Media in the lives of 8–18 Year-olds.* Menlo Park, Ca: Kaiser Family Foundation.

Squire, K. (2004). *Replaying history: Learning world history through playing Civilization III.* Unpublished doctoral dissertation, Indiana University.

Squire, K. (2006). From content to context: Videogames as designed experiences. *Educational Researcher 35*(8), 19–29.

Steinkuehler, C. A. (2003, March). *Videogaming as participation in a Discourse.* Paper presented at the American Association for Applied Linguistics Annual Conference, Arlington, VA.

Taylor, T. L. (2002). "Whose game is this anyway?": Negotiating corporate ownership in a virtual world. In F. Mäyrä (Ed.), *Computer Games and Digital Cultures Conference Proceedings* (pp. 227–242). Tampere, Finland: Tampere University Press. Retrieved from http://www.itu.dk/people/tltaylor/papers/Taylor-CGDC.pdf

Turkle, S. (1994). Constructions and reconstructions of self in virtual reality: Playing in the MUDs. *Mind, Culture, and Activity 1*(3), 158–167.

Turkle, S. (1995). *Life on the screen: Identity in the age of the Internet.* New York: Simon & Schuster.

Zucker, A. A., & Shields, P. M. (1995). *Evaluation of the National Science Foundation's Statewide Systemic Initiatives (SSI) Program: Second Year Report.* Menlo Park, CA: SRI International.

Sasha Barab
Learning Sciences
Indiana University

Tyler Dodge
Instructional Systems Technology
Indiana University

Hakan Tuzun
Instructional Technology
University of Turkey

Kirk Job-Sluder
Instructional Systems Technology
Indiana University

Craig Jackson
Quest Atlantis Project/Design Manager
Indiana University

Anna Arici
Cognitive Psychology & Educational Psychology
Indiana University

Laura Job Sluder
Instructional Systems Technology
Indiana University

Robert Carteaux Jr.
Instructional Systems Technology
Indiana University

Jo Gilbertson
Teacher Research Associate
Indiana University

Conan Heiselt
Instructional Systems Technology
Indiana University

CONSTANCE STEINKUEHLER

MASSIVELY MULTIPLAYER ONLINE GAMING AS A CONSTELLATION OF LITERACY PRACTICES[1]

Based on media coverage, one would think that the United States were in a modern day literacy crisis thanks particularly to new digital technologies such as videogames. Recent publications include books with titles such as "the collapse of literacy and the rise of violence in the electronic age" (Sanders, 1995)[1]. Survey experts report that videogames are now "the fourth most dominant medium, displacing print media" (Mandese, 2004). Meanwhile, news reports quote researchers as stating, "students will be doing more and more bad things if they are *playing games* and not doing other things like *reading aloud* [italics added]" (Wearden, 2001) [2]. This concern about videogames somehow replacing literacy activities is perhaps best summed up in a recent *New York Times* editorial by Solomon (2004), who states that electronic activities – videogames given as the quintessential example – are "torpid," "by and large invite inert reception, " and are one of the primary causes behind the "closing of the American book" (Weber, 2004). Yet, all the while, videogaming is only becoming more and more ubiquitous in contemporary American youth culture, with more than eight out of every ten kids in America having a videogame console in the home, and over half having two or more (Rideout, Roberts, & Foehr, 2005). Based on claims such as these, one might indeed feel cause for alarm.

There are two problems, however, with such arguments. The first is a lack of specificity about the "cause" of the purported problem. While videogames are often singled out as a (if not the) primary technological culprit of the supposed "literacy crisis," *which* games are being referred to is left chronically underspecified. Even when we ignore, for sake of argument, the fact that games are, by definition, a thoroughly *interactive medium* and are therefore taken up in dramatically different ways by different people, we are still left with the problem of their diversity in design. Games vary wildly in nature, including such diverse

---

[1] Reprinted with permission of the Executive Editor, Michael A. Peters. This article first appeared in eLearning, 4(3).

B. E. Shelton, D. A. Wiley (eds.), Educational Design & Use of Computer Simulation Games, 187–214.
© *2007 Sense Publishers. All rights reserved.*

forms as: arcade games (e.g., *PacMan*), first person shooters (e.g., *Deus Ex II*), sports games (e.g. *Madden*), adventure games (e.g. *Syberia*), the so-called "god games" (e.g. *Civilization III*), social simulation/doll-house games (e.g., *The Sims*), survival horror games (e.g., *Eternal Darkness*), real time strategy games (e.g., *Age of Empires*), massively multiplayer online games (e.g., *World of Warcraft*), role playing games (*Morrowind*), music/rhythm games (e.g., *Guitar Hero*), and puzzle games (e.g., *Bejeweled*). Precisely *which games* are such denouncements referring to? Without further specifying the "cause," it becomes a bit like talking about "reading" as a black-boxed variable (Reading what? With whom? In what context?).

The second problem with claims about videogames replacing literacy is another lack of specification: What definition of literacy is being used in claims that it is "at risk"? The term itself is a contested one, with (from a simplified view) at least two basic schools of reasoning defining it in markedly different ways. On the one hand, there is the fairly traditional definition of literacy used, for example, as the basis for determining national literacy rates: "an individual's ability to read, write, speak in English, compute and solve problems at levels of proficiency necessary to function on the job, in the family of the individual and in society" (National Institute for Literacy, n.d.). Although this definition does go beyond the mere ability to decode and encode alphabetic symbols, the primary emphasis remains on print-related activities in a singular national language. On the other hand and in contrast, there is the definition of literacy espoused in New Literacy Studies (e.g., Barton, 1994; Cazden 1988; Cook-Gumperz 1986; Gee, 1992, 1996, 1999, 2003; Gumperz, 1982; Heath, 1983; Knobel, 1999; Kress, 1985; Lankshear, 1997; Lankshear & Knobel, 2003; Street, 1984, 1993):

> …the increasing multiplicity and integration of significant modes of meaning-making, where the textual is also related to the visual, the audio, the spatial, the behavioral, and so on… particularly important in the mass media, multimedia, and in an electronic hypermedia. (New London Group, 1996, p. 64)

Here, strong emphasis is placed on the ability to both recognize *and produce* meanings in a given semiotic domain, with particular attention given to sense making in multimodal, multimedia spaces such as those enabled by digital technologies. If we are to claim that videogames are in competition with literacy in some way, we must specify not only *which videogames* but also and perhaps more crucially *which literacy* – the "mere literacy," as the New London Group (1996, p. 64) calls it, of decoding and encoding print (traditional definition) or the ability to make sense out of semiotic systems that include a diversity of communicative modes (contemporary definition)?

The claim that videogames are replacing literacy activities that is bantered about in the American mainstream press is based not only on unspecified definitions of both "games" and "literacy" but also on a surprisingly lack of research on what kids actually *do* when they game. In this chapter, I examine some of the practices that comprise gameplay in the context of one genre of videogames in particular –

massively multiplayer online games (MMOGs). Based on data culled from a two-year online cognitive ethnography of the MMOG *Lineage* (both I and II) (Steinkuehler 2005), I argue that *forms of videogame play such as those entailed in MMOGs are not replacing literacy activities but rather* are *literacy activities*. In order to make this argument, I survey some of the literacy practices that MMOGamers routinely participate in, both within the game's virtual world (e.g., social interaction, in-game letters and orally-delivered narratives) and beyond (e.g., asynchronous discussion on online game forums, the creation of fansites and fan fiction). Then, with this argument in place, I attempt to historicize this popular contempt toward electronic "pop culture" media such as videogames and suggest a potentially more productive (and accurate) framing of the literacy practices of today's generation of adolescents and young adults.

RESEARCH CONTEXT & METHODS

Massively multiplayer online games: The case of Lineage

Massively multiplayer online games (MMOGs) are highly graphical 2- or 3-D videogames played online, allowing individuals, through their self-created digital characters or "avatars," to interact not only with the gaming software – the designed environment of the game and the computer-controlled characters within it – but with *other players'* avatars as well. Conceptually, they are part of the rich tradition of alternative worlds that science fiction and fantasy literature provide us (e.g. Tolkien's *The Hobbit*, 1938); technically, they are the evolutionary next-step in a long line of social games that runs from paper-and-pencil fantasy games (e.g., Gygax & Arneson's *Dungeons & Dragons*, 1973) to main-frame text-based multi-user dungeons (e.g. Trubshaw & Bartle's *MUD*, 1978) through the first graphical massively multiplayer online environments (e.g., Kirmse & Kirmse's *Meridian 59*, 1996) to the now-common, high-end 3-D digital worlds of today (for a complete history, see Koster, 2002). The virtual worlds that today's MMOGamers routinely plug in and inhabit are persistent social and material worlds, loosely structured by open-ended (fantasy) narratives, where players are largely free to do as they please – slay ogres, siege castles, craft a pair of gaiters, barter goods in town, or tame dragon hatchlings. They are notorious for their peculiar combination of designed "escapist fantasy" yet emergent "social realism" (Kolbert, 2001): in a setting of wizards, elves, dwarfs, and knights, people save for homes, create basket indices of the trading market, build relationships of status and solidarity, and worry about crime.

Lineage, the MMOG context of this research, is now in its second incarnation. *Lineage I: The Blood Pledge* was first released in Korea in 1997. After three years of domination in the Korean gaming sphere, it expanded to America and currently boasts roughly 1.5 million global subscribers combined (both I and II) despite its steady decline in population since the 2004 release of its sequel (Woodcock, 2006). Its 3-D sequel, *Lineage II: The Chaotic Chronicle*, released in Korea in November of 2003 and expanded to America in April of 2004, currently claims over 1.2 million concurrent subscriptions globally (Woodcock, 2006). Within the game, members of all races (human, orc, elf, dark elf, dwarf) and classes (fighter, crafter, mage, etc.) join forces in the form of guilds to compete for castle control in server-wide sieges and battles. In both incarnations, the *Lineage* clan system is tightly coupled to both the guiding narrative of the game and the virtual world's economic system, resulting in a complex social space of affiliations and disaffiliations, constructed largely out of shared (or disparate) social and material practices.

Methods for research

Lineage constitutes a robust social and virtual-material world, one that warrants full investigation in its own right, much as a new country or culture in the tangible geographic world might. As an educational researcher, I am keenly interested in the intellectual substance of such virtual worlds: What do people learn through participation in such spaces? And how is it that such learning happens? How do the intellectual practices entailed in successful MMOG play align (or fail to align) with our educational standards? And how might the knowledge and skills leveraged in virtual worlds "pay off" in the purportedly "real" one? Toward answering those questions, I conducted a qualitative study of cognition and learning in MMOs (Steinkuehler, 2005). This study consisted of a two-year ethnography of the MMOG *Lineage* (first I, then II) conducted from a sociocultural perspective that views cognition as "a complex social phenomenon...distributed – stretched over, not divided among – mind, body, activity and culturally organized settings (which include other actors)" (Lave, 1988, p.1). The goal of this project was to explicate the kinds of social and intellectual activities in which gamers routinely participate, including individual and collaborative problem-solving, joint negotiation of meaning and values, and the coordination of people, (virtual) tools and artifacts, and multiple forms of text.

Cognitive ethnography (Hutchins, 1995) – the description of specific cultures in terms of cognitive practices, their basis, and their consequences – was chosen as the primary research methodology as a way to tease out what happens in the virtual setting of the game and how the people involved consider their own activities, the activities of others, and the contexts in which those activities take place (Steinkuehler, Black, & Clinton, 2005). This "thick description" (Geertz, 1973) included 24 months of participant observation in the game, several thousand lines of recorded and transcribed observations of naturally occurring game play, collections of game-related player communications (e.g., discussion board posts, chat room and instant message conversations, emails) and community documents (e.g., fan websites, community-authored game fictions, company- and community-written player manuals and guidebooks), and both unstructured and semi-structured interviews with multiple informants (a snowball sample of sixteen key informants throughout the course of the investigation). In this chapter, I analyze *Lineage* gameplay as a constellation of literacy practices, based on my two-year participant observation in the daily life of the game and critical reflection on the dataset in light of interviews and discussions with my informants.

THE LITERACY PRACTICES OF MMOGS

From the contemporary point of view

Let's begin with the New London Group (1996) definition – the notion that literacies (plural) crucially entail sense-making within a rich, multimodal semiotic system, situated in a community of practice that renders that system meaningful. Figure 1 shows the interface of the MMOG *Lineage II*, one of the primary virtual world contexts in which the ethnographic data described herein was collected. We might ask ourselves, how many adults (let alone tenured professors) can "read" such a space? Without prior experience in *Lineage II*, or at a minimum in some other MMOG design, few could make sense out of the seeming sundry assortment of images, bar graphs, texts, icons, and symbols. Yet, for gamers who have mastered this interface – a form of mastery that is prerequisite to any successful gameplay whatsoever, it is a completely transparent (albeit dense) semiotic system.

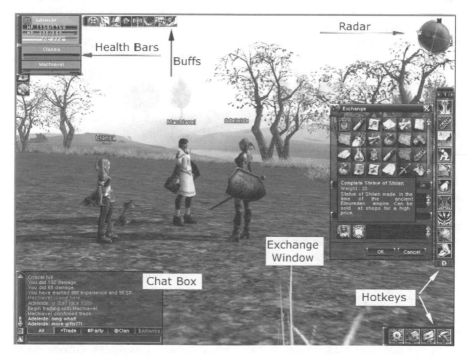

Figure 1. Interface of the MMOG Lineage II.

Bar graphs (top left corner) show the status of your avatar in terms of health points, mana points, and experience points, with your avatar's current level denoted by a number in the far top left. Below that is the status bar of all members of your current party, which allows you to monitor *their* overall health and adjust your own behaviors accordingly. To the immediate right of your avatar status window (top, mid-left of screen) are icons and symbols denoting magic spells cast upon your avatar, each of which has its own unique function and therefore changes what you can and cannot do. At the top right corner of the interface lies the radar, which displays your position in relation to the in-game cardinal directions and other members of your current party. In the bottom left corner is the chatbox containing multiple threads of conversation (denoted in different colors), each of which serves a different communicative function as determined by in-game community norms (Steinkuehler, 2006b). At the bottom of the chat window itself are buttons that denote the various "chat commands" used to engage in said chat channels, such as trade solicitations (on global channels), party chat, and alliance chat – each of which engages a different although overlapping group of other gamers, used for different purposes and in different contexts. On the bottom right of the interface are hotkeys that provide access to various management screens, each containing another complex set of symbols and text, that provide access to the game system settings, your avatar's current inventory, your character screen, elaborate maps of the virtual kingdom (and your current location within it), and even in-game threaded discussion boards. To the right side of the interface are action icons and symbols that, when clicked, enable your avatar to take various specific actions related to monsters you are hunting, other players in your party, or your own virtual self. In the main game window, on the right-hand side, is the exchange window that allows players to give or trade various items in their avatar's current inventory such as potions, raw materials, money, or supplies.

The particular scene portrayed in the main game window of Figure 1 is an instance of the *Lineage II* community ritual of gift giving. It was my "real life" birthday (Adeleide is my avatar) and therefore in-game friends were giving me celebratory symbolic tokens – gestures of good will, hard work, and camaraderie. Thus, despite the length of the above translation of the gaming interface, it still says very little about the actual sociocultural norms and the shared practices that tie them together into one coherent surface on which each gamer "writes" their own on-going narrative (Clinton, 2004; Robison, 2004), let alone the meaning of the avatars of other players that act on screen or how one comes to successfully inhabit the virtual kingdom of the game. The official strategy guide to *Lineage II* is a daunting 288 pages, yet most experienced gamers master these semiotic aspects within the first few hours of play.

Thus, if we take the contemporary definition of literacy as "sense-making" within a multimodal, socially situated space, then surely the most mundane versions of MMOGaming belie fluency and participation in a thoroughly *literate* space of icons, symbols, gestures, action, pictorial representations, and text. Gamers must continually "read and write" meaning within this complex semiotic domain as every successful move within the virtual environment requires participants to both recognize and produce meaning out of the overwhelming array of multimedia, multimodal resources that make up the game. Thus, there is a strong argument to be made, based on the New London Group (1996) definition, that playing an MMOG is itself a literacy activity, albeit one that the non-gaming but vocal public may find a bit too opaque to readily participate in and appreciate. Such a definition of literacy, however, for some may seem too liberal. It is worthwhile then, to interrogate MMOGaming as a literacy practice from the more restricted definition espoused by more traditional crowds.

From the traditional point of view

Let's start again, but this time with a more restricted definition of literacy as the "ability to read and write print text." Are videogames (MMOGs, in particular) in competition with text literacy? My goal here is to make the stronger argument that, even with a narrowed definition of what literacy is and means, MMOGs are indeed a constellation of literacy practices. When kids and adults play MMOGs, they read and write copious amounts of text. Figure 2 diagrams various forms of textual practices that make up online games. Despite its complexity, this diagram is actually based on those literacy practices found in *Lineage I*, an MMOG now considered fairly "retro" in its simplicity, and contains only a selected subset of the core literacy practices that constitute gameplay. At the center of the diagram are the text chat channels discussed previously through which players communicate with one another while in the virtual world (center square). Through these channels, participants engage in (inter)action using alphabetic and keyboard characters not only as *symbols* (e.g., to form morphemes such as those found in the "1334 speek" sentence "afk g2g too EF ot regen no poms." (for a complete analysis of this utterance, see Steinkuehler, 2006b) but also as *icons* (e.g., "@>~~~~" to represent a flower) and *indexes* (e.g., "*sniff*" to signal public pouting).

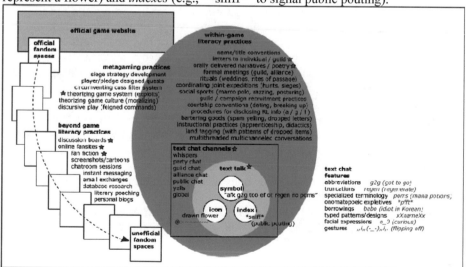

Figure 2. The constellation of literacy practices that constitute gameplay in the MMOG Lineage I. *Selected practices discussed within this article are starred.*

Each of the text chat channels themselves (whispers, party chat, guild chat, alliance chat, public chat, yells, global) has a defined function and social norms for use in different contexts. For example, the whispering channel is used for private conversation between two people whereas the public channel is used to communicate with others in your immediate virtual vicinity. Successful MMOGameplay requires mastery not only of each text chat channel individually but also the ability to "surf" across them such that the one can read and write text appropriate to each in each[3]. From the perspective of the individual, this means negotiating multiple threaded conversations across multiple chat channels, oftentimes while carrying on activities with one's avatar in the main game window. Out of these basic resources – the shared conventions of "Lineagese" and multiple chat channels for communication – participants engage in multiple forms of recognizable and coherent literacy practices within the game's virtual world (the center oval in Figure 2); for example: the titling of avatars (e.g. "[LoA]Princess to denote guild membership and rank), letter writing (discussed below), "orally" delivered narratives and poetry (also discussed below), formal conventions for holding meetings (e.g., introductions, agenda setting, discussion and debate, and collaborative decision-making), rituals (e.g., weddings, rites of passage, celebrations of individual and group successes), the coordination of joint expeditions (e.g., procedures for gathering supplies, coordinating targets, dividing up any riches obtained, and debriefing afterward in order to improve coordination the next time around), social sports (e.g., games of "marco polo" and "ritual insult," Goodwin, 1990), and instructional practices (e.g., apprenticeship, Steinkuehler, 2004), This is only to name a few. All such practices are accomplished through in-game actions and profuse amounts of reading and writing of in-game typed talk. Other literacy practices, however, go *beyond* the in-game virtual environment itself and spill out into world of the online fandom that surrounds it (the array of smaller boxes on the left of Figure 2). Online fandom is comprised of a vast array of beyond game literacy practices such as the development and maintenance of game-related fansites and blogs; discussion and debate of game-related issues on threaded discussion boards (Steinkuehler & Chmiel, 2006); the creation and distribution of fan fictions, fan art, annotated game screenshots and cartoons; and deliberation via game-specific chatrooms, instant messaging, in-character emails, and even voice over IP (VoIP) forums. Many important literacy practices, such as *metagaming (*described in greater depth below), actually span both the virtual in-game world and online fandom beyond it, shifting seamlessly from in-game conversation to online interactions in other forums and back again.

Thus, the "magic circle" (Huizinga, 1938) that purportedly bounds the game world from everyday life is, in practice, a fuzzy boundary: At the *macro level*, participating over time in MMOGs entails not only (inter)action in the game's virtual environment but also the production and consumption of online fandom content in the form of discussion boards, website contributions, creative endeavors such as writing stories, and the like. At the *micro level* of a given moment in an individual's gameplay, participation means movement among multiple "attentional spaces" (Lemke, n.d.), as shown in Figure 3. Thus, the literacy practices that comprise MMOGs are not isolated and autonomous but rather interrelated in complex and mutually defining ways.

Figure 3. Desktop during a typical moment in gameplay in which the virtual environment of the MMOG is only one window among several in which the individual reads and writes.

In what follows, I examine a selected subset of these literacy practices for closer examination, beginning first with in-game practices and then moving out beyond the game's virtual world into the fandom that surrounds it.

In-game text talk. As Turkle (1995) notes, the specialized linguistic practices that online gamers use to communicate appear to a non-gamer much like the "discourse of Dante scholars, 'a closed world of references, cross-references, and code'" (p.67). It is a sort of *hybrid writing*, "speech momentarily frozen into... ephemeral artifact" (p. 183). At first blush, the use of language within such digital worlds appears rather impoverished: Riddled with *abbreviations* (e.g., "g2g" for "got to go"), *truncations* (e.g., "regen" for "regenerate"), *typographical* (e.g., "ot" for "to") and *grammatical errors* (e.g., the adverbial form "too" in place of the prepositional form "to"), *syntactic erosions* (e.g., the omitted initial string "I have" from "[I have] g2g," Thrasher, 1974), and *specialized vocabulary* (e.g., "poms" for "potions of mana," a liquid potion that increases the rate at which one's "mana" or

195

magic power is restored after depletion from repeated spell use), typed utterances appear to be a meager substitute for everyday oral and written speech. However, its code-like appearance is misleading: Closer examination of such talk reveals that, in fact, Lineagese (and other MMOG variants) serves the same range and complexity of functions as language does offline (Steinkuehler, 2006b). It's simply forced to do so within the tight constraints of the given medium of communication (one small chat window, as shown in Figure 1, with a maximum turn of 58 characters allowed per turn) and the fact that communication typically occurs in tandem with ongoing activity (e.g., hunts, battles, trades) that require keyboard and mouse commands of their own.

The range of communicative activities one can accomplish through alphabetic and keyboard characters alone is rather remarkable, although for MMOGamers such facility with typed talk is simply par for the course. For example, one can dismiss another's argument without stating so outright (and therefore becoming accountable for the action) through the use of *onomatopoeic expletives* such as "*pfft*." One can convey *facial expressions* (e.g., "o_0" for curiosity or disbelief) and *bodily gestures* (e.g. ",,i,,(-_-),,i,," for making a rude gesture to someone using both middle fingers) with the use of only alphabetic characters and punctuation marks. And too, in such virtual spaces, distinctions among various national languages are, at times, blurred due to ready borrowings from one to another. For example, in *Lineage I*, which originated in Korea, English speakers readily borrow the romanized Korean word "babo," which translates as "idiot" or "stupid," and conjugate it into a variety of forms, such as "What you just did is total baboage." The use of such borrowings, within the game, tacitly signals a kind of social status: Korean players on American servers are generally seen as more "hardcore" than their western counterparts; thus, Korean borrowings integrated into English dialogue in social interactions displays status by implied affiliation with advanced players in the game.

At any given point during gameplay, an individual must negotiate not only the diversity of forms of typed communication described above but also multiple text chat channels, each with its own function and social norms for use. For example, consider the transcript shown of in-game chat in Figure 3 that transpired over roughly two minutes of game play[4].

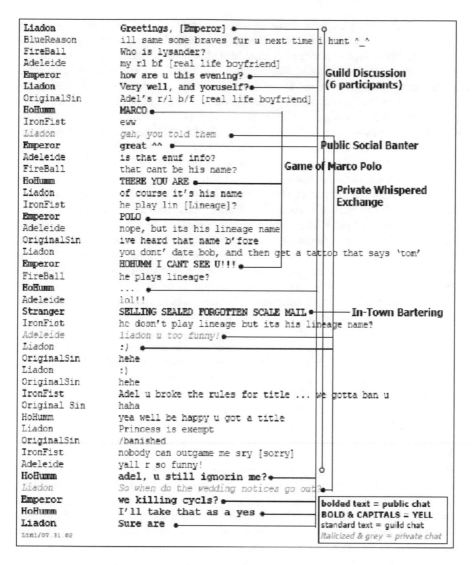

Liadon	Greetings, [Emperor]
BlueReason	ill same some braves fur u next time i hunt ^_^
FireBall	Who is lysander?
Adeleide	my rl bf [real life boyfriend]
Emperor	how are u this evening?
Liadon	Very well, and yoruself?
OriginalSin	Adel's r/l b/f [real life boyfriend]
HoHumm	MARCO
IronFist	eww
Liadon	*gah, you told them*
Emperor	great ^^
Adeleide	is that enuf info?
FireBall	that cant be his name?
HoHumm	THERE YOU ARE
Liadon	of course it's his name
IronFist	he play lin [Lineage]?
Emperor	POLO
Adeleide	nope, but its his lineage name
OriginalSin	ive heard that name b'fore
Liadon	you dont' date bob, and then get a tattoo that says 'tom'
Emperor	HOHUMM I CANT SEE U!!!
FireBall	he plays lineage?
HoHumm	...
Adeleide	lol!!
Stranger	SELLING SEALED FORGOTTEN SCALE MAIL
IronFist	he doesn't play lineage but its his lineage name?
Adeleide	*liadon u too funny!*
Liadon	:)
OriginalSin	hehe
Liadon	:)
OriginalSin	hehe
IronFist	Adel u broke the rules for title ... we gotta ban u
Original Sin	haha
HoHumm	yea well be happy u got a title
Liadon	Princess is exempt
OriginalSin	/banished
IronFist	nobody can outgame me sry [sorry]
Adeleide	yall r so funny!
HoHumm	adel, u still ignorin me?
Liadon	*So when do the wedding notices go out?*
Emperor	we killing cycls?
HoHumm	I'll take that as a yes
Liadon	Sure are
lin1/07.31.02	

Guild Discussion (6 participants)

Public Social Banter

Game of Marco Polo

Private Whispered Exchange

In-Town Bartering

bolded text = public chat
BOLD & CAPITALS = YELL
standard text = guild chat
italicized & grey = private chat

Figure 4.Transcript of roughly two minutes of multiple-threaded conversation during a typical evening in Lineage I.

Notice that, within the space of roughly two minutes of gameplay, there are at least five overlapping conversational activities happing at once. In the *public chat channel*, a group of guild members exchange greetings as they gather in the virtual town of Giran to engage in a joint hunting expedition in the nearby forests. In the *guild chat channel*, there is negotiation between the guild leader (Adeleide) and guild members about the addition of a new member to the group (the "real life" husband of the leader) and the subsequent self-designated titling of said leader as

"Lysanderv." This particular form of title (partner's name followed by "v" to represent a heart) is reserved within the guild for members who have gone through an in-game marriage ceremony. Adeleide and Lysander have not; therefore, the group conversation shifts from inquiry into the identity of the new guild member (Lysander) to comedic debate about the legitimacy of Adeleide's self-designated title. Note, toward the end of the guild conversation, the playful use of the feigned game command "/banished." Within the game world, individuals can accomplish various actions by issuing DOS-like commands ("/" followed by text). In this case, only the leader can "banish" another member from the guild; therefore, the use of this command is "feigned" and functions as a playful imitation of what the leader *would* do to someone who assumed a guild title without appropriate authorization (in this case, formal marriage), if it weren't for the fact that she herself broke the rule. In the *private whisper channel*, the author (Adeleide) and the general (Liadon) engage in personal banter. Meanwhile, in the *yell channel*, a game of "marco polo" transpires, followed by a stranger's announcement in Giran of equipment for sale. It is also worth noting what happens toward the end of the transcript when the author (Adeleide) fails to respond to a public statement from HoHumm. When her response is delayed due to the cognitive demands of keeping up with multiple simultaneous strands of typed interaction, Hohumm presumes *not* that she is unable to keep pace with the ongoing talk but rather that *she is ignoring him*. In the context of MMOGs, the ability to successfully negotiate multiple threaded conversations across multiple chat channels at once is *presumed* such that failure to do so successfully is interpreted not as lack of *ability* but lack of *intent*. Such constant conversation through this myriad of chat channels is not only necessary to navigate the virtual world's diverse challenges but is the very fodder from which individuals create and maintain relationships of status and solidarity and, in part, in-game community and cultural norms.

In-game written letters. In MMOGs such as *Lineage*, individuals also read and write letters to one another (or to entire guilds) as a way to communicate asynchronously within the game world. Such artifacts can serve a variety of functions, ranging from very formal (e.g. invitations to guild or alliance meetings, orders from leaders to their troops) to very informal (e.g., personal accounts for absences from the game, playful bantering among friends). Figure 5 shows two such letters, both of which fall on the more formal end of the spectrum. The two share common features one might find in contemporary business letters or other official correspondence, such as an opening greeting line, a closing signature, and a date (automatically added by game system). Both use rather antiquated language such as "assist to a meeting," "if you wish," "m'lady," and "granted the honor of acceptance." Letters, like turns of talk within the chat channels, allow only a set number of typed characters per page; therefore, both documents in Figure 5 also contain periodic abbreviations (i.e. "CST" for "central standard time" in the first, " wud gr8tly" for "would greatly" in the second). What is most curious about the two artifacts in Figure 5, however, is that both authors self-identified in interviews as "poor writers" – the first speaks English as a second language, the second works in technology and claims to be a "poor speller" – yet both display an observable mastery of the genre of in-game formal correspondence, including structural conventions, forms of address, and use of grammar and abbreviation (given spatial constraints).

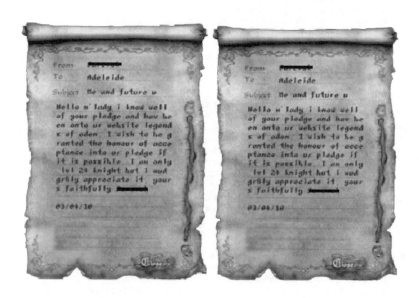

Figure 5. Two in-game letters written by two different authors in Lineage.

In-game "orally delivered" narratives. Another form of reading and writing that MMOGamers engage in when they play is the production and consumption of "orally delivered" narratives and poetry. In such performances, individuals adopt and adapt designed-in elements of the game narrative to craft their own "oral" story-telling performances. (Here, "orally delivered" simply means adapted for in-game speech, which must still be accomplished within the virtual environment as written text.) Figure 6 shows an example of such oral narration. Here, Liadon, a highly skilled gamer within *Lineage*, (an elf avatar over level 40) orally narrates the origins of fairies, small pixie-like butterflies that populate the Elven Forest within the game, to Adeliede (a very low-level or "newbie" elf). The episode occurs when the two characters are out hunting together in an area called the Elven Forest in order to give the less-experienced elf practice hunting with a bow.

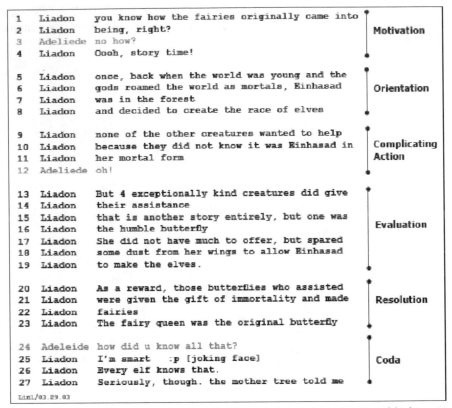

1	Liadon	you know how the fairies originally came into	
2	Liadon	being, right?	Motivation
3	Adeliede	no how?	
4	Liadon	Oooh, story time!	
5	Liadon	once, back when the world was young and the	
6	Liadon	gods roamed the world as mortals, Einhasad	Orientation
7	Liadon	was in the forest	
8	Liadon	and decided to create the race of elves	
9	Liadon	none of the other creatures wanted to help	
10	Liadon	because they did not know it was Einhasad in	Complicating
11	Liadon	her mortal form	Action
12	Adeliede	oh!	
13	Liadon	But 4 exceptionally kind creatures did give	
14	Liadon	their assistance	
15	Liadon	that is another story entirely, but one was	
16	Liadon	the humble butterfly	Evaluation
17	Liadon	She did not have much to offer, but spared	
18	Liadon	some dust from her wings to allow Einhasad	
19	Liadon	to make the elves.	
20	Liadon	As a reward, those butterflies who assisted	
21	Liadon	were given the gift of immortality and made	Resolution
22	Liadon	fairies	
23	Liadon	The fairy queen was the original butterfly	
24	Adeleide	how did u know all that?	
25	Liadon	I'm smart :p [joking face]	Coda
26	Liadon	Every elf knows that.	
27	Liadon	Seriously, though. the mother tree told me	

Lin1/03.29.03

Figure 6. Transcript of an in-game "orally delivered" narrative explaining the origin of the fairies in the Elven Forest. Stanza breaks and line numbers have been added for ease of reference.

First, Liadon sets up the motivation for telling the story by inquiring as to whether or not Adeleide knew about the origin of the fairies (lines 1-2). The topic is situationally relevant since the two are hunting together in the Elven Forest were such computer-generated fairies are quite prevalent, and the activity underway is one of apprenticeship (cf. Steinkuehler, 2004) in which Liadon, the master elf, engages Adeleide, the learner elf, in the joint activity of a normative elven hunting expedition in elven territory, thus rendering it safe to assume that the addressee is unfamiliar with the story – but should be, as it is part of the "shared history" of being an elf within the virtual world. In line 3, Adeleide indicates no knowledge of the tale, thereby prompting the "orally delivered" narrative ("Oooh, story time!" line 4). Liadon then goes on to produce a narrative that has all of the classical structural features (Labov, 1972, Labov & Waletzky, 1967): orientation (lines 5-8), complicating action (lines 9-11), evaluation (lines 13-19), resolution (lines 20-23), and coda (lines 25-27).

While the structural features of the "oral" narrative are not surprising, the way in which Liadon transforms the original game text into a situated performance is non-trivial. His story is based on a piece of narrative text built into the game (what "the mother tree told [him]" line 27), the first part of which is shown in Figure 7. Compared to the original text, Liadon's version is highly abbreviated with all non-elf related details removed and restructured in a way that reorients the evaluation (lines 13-19) toward elves and their origins' relationship to fairies rather than fairies and the full set of creatures the story is originally about. In this way, Liadon adapts the original narrative to the situated needs of the apprenticeship episode underway: the need to explain what fairies are and, tacitly, why one ought not hunt them as one would other creatures.

Figure 7. The original in-game source of Liadon's "orally delivered" narrative explaining the origin of the fairies in the Elven Forest.

In contrast to media claims, here gamers are going one step further than simply "reading aloud" (cf. Wearden, 2001); they are rewriting the story for situated oral performance, surely a literacy practice no less worthwhile than simply orating another author's text. Such performances within the virtual world are not uncommon, as gamers tend to place a high value on textually produced verbal interaction and, therefore, on story-telling, one of our most important forms of "making sense" (Bruner, 1986, 2003). As Cherney (1999) concludes in her study of

MUDs, the technological predecessors of MMOGs, "In all such systems, linguistic interactions have been primary: users exchange messages that cement the social bonds between them, messages that reflect *shared history and understandings* (or misunderstandings) about the always evolving local norms for these interactions [italics added]" (p. 22). Such authored and adapted narratives play an especially important role in in-game apprenticeship episodes, as this example illustrates, by enculturating newcomers into the game lore that constitutes the community's shared knowledge and history.

Metagaming practices. Metagaming is a common literacy practice for game communities of all forms in which participants theorize their own game, both within the virtual environment of the game world itself and also beyond it in the online fandom space (e.g. website, discussion forums, chatrooms, blogs, wikis, and sundry other online text) that envelops every successful title to date. In the context of MMOGs, such practices include, for example, strategy development for group or guild endeavors (e.g. the creation of research documents about a given location of interest and planning documents, based on such research, that provide a guide for future action), the development of game "exploits" (e.g. the construction, evaluation, and revision of mathematical models of game mechanics based on data collected in-game, such as what combination of player characteristics is most effective in specific collaborative problem-solving endeavors such as hunting a particular boss monster, Steinkuehler & Chmiel, 2006), and long deliberative discussions through which game communities actually theorize themselves, their own social network structures and functions, and what will and won't "count" for appropriate social engagement (e.g., moralizing on game discussion boards or within guild chat, or the development of and reflection on in-game norms for social interaction). Consider, for example, the in-game exchange from *Lineage II* shown in Figure 8, which occurred in the guild chat channel. After several hours of "solo" gameplay in which fellow guild members banter idly in the guild chat channel while pursuing their own solitary in-game activities, a conversation emerged in which guildmates develop a new "unit of measurement" by which efficiency within the game might be calculated.

In Lineage II, efficiency in experience points per hour (the mechanism by which you level your avatar and therefore gain more strength, better skills, etc.) is a highly valued and sought after goal. In order to maximize efficiency, many gamers actually time their rate of experience increase while hunting various territories in order to track of how well they are doing, on average, in different areas given their avatar's current level. Cruma Tower is a notoriously efficient hunting area within the virtual world of Lineage II; it is also, however, famous for grief play: gankers,

```
Zara       i dunno if it's just me but this lvl [level] seems so slooooow
Zara       i'm not at 63% [of current avatar level]
Adeleide   yea [level] 39 is really slow
Duncan     it only makes sense...19 was painful,it makes sense by
Duncan     L2 [Lineage II] logic that 39 would be 100x moreso
Zara       i'm lucky to get 6% [of a level] per hr
Adeleide   Cruma would give u 10% / hr but not much better
Duncan     Yea 10%/hr is what I expect from Cruma. It's become
Duncan     my marker for progress everywhere.
Adeleide   yea... cruma is evil that way
Duncan     I think we should make it a unit of measurement.
Duncan     1 cruma, 0.8 crumas
Zara       lol
Lin2/10.06.04
```

Figure 8. Transcript of Lineage II in-game conversation in which guildmates develop a new "unit of measurement" by which efficiency within the game might be calculated.

player-killers (PKers), trash talkers, kill-stealers (KSers), and sundry other unpleasant personae. Thus, few gamers care to stay there for very long periods at a time, despite how productive it is as an area for leveling one's character. In the exchange shown in Figure 8, one guild member initiates troubles-telling with a remark about how slow he is currently progressing. In response, guildmates first sympathize, then compare their current progress to hunting in Cruma Tower. What emerges is a new "unit of measurement" by which efficiency within the game might be measured in terms of "crumas" – the amount of leveling experience one would get, on average, per hour, within that not-so-pleasant area. The result is simultaneously entertaining and functional: if one knows how one's current hunting territory compares with the most efficient area in the game, then one can gauge whether or not the pleasure of hunting in the given non-Cruma area outweighs the decrease in economic use of time. Thus, through in situ reflection on in-game activity through the lens of shared regard for both productivity and pleasure, the guild community arrived at one theoretical construct (of many) by which to express the relative trade-offs the game design occasions between efficiency versus freedom of movement.

While the cruma unit "meme" (Blackmore, 1999; Lankshear & Knobel, 2003) largely remained a local practice, used within a single guild both in-game and within guild discussion forums and subsequent online conversations, other such metagaming practices have a much broader and extensive life of their own. Take, for example, the server-based practice of "farming the farmers" that emerged and took hold on the American *Lineage II* server Bartz (for a complete discussion, see Steinkuehler 2006a). In MMOG circles, it is now common knowledge that virtual, in-game money can be readily exchanged for real, out-of-game money (Castronova, 2001) through online trading sites (such as eBay), and that some people from Asian countries (and others) play on North American servers in order to work for real world pay from companies solely in the business of virtual currency trade (such as IGE). The practice in which individuals are hired by a virtual-currency selling company to spend long hours in-game collecting adena (the in-game currency of *Lineage*) has come to be called "Chinese adena farming." The practice continues to flourish, despite NCSoft's efforts to stop it (Russell, 2004) and despite intense negative response in the States, with a vast majority of the American *Lineage II* gamers resenting the effects that adena farming has had on their game (despite the fact that they are, indeed, one of the driving forces behind it).

Most relevant to our discussion, however, is the metagaming practice that so-called "Chinese adena farming" has occasioned American gamers to develop in response: a practice called "farming the farmers." Leisure players have forgone the usual between-guild competitions for castle control, the one game mechanic that made *Lineage* titles unique, and have instead joined forces in a sort of "us versus them" mentality to wage perpetual field war against all (perceived) Chinese adena farmers. The waging of this informal war is comprised of several key literacy practices, including the in- and out-of-game negotiation and coordination among various guilds to forgo all standard castle competition among them and instead join hands in scheduled "raids" against purported farmers in overtaken virtual territories of the game, the planning and execution of large in-game "extermination" campaigns called "Farm the Farmers Day" on all purported farmers within the virtual world itself, and finally (and perhaps more importantly) the documentation of such raids in the form of online debriefing discussions and commentary, websites, and fan videos. At last check, the fan videos, numbered chronologically, were up to "Farm the Farmers Day VI" and the practice has managed to jump games and spread virally to other MMOG titles (such as *World of Warcraft*). Figure 9 shows three screenshots from one such web-posted video from "Farm the Farmers Day II" (finalElf, n.d.) that documents one such collaborative expedition. In the left panel is the title screen of the fan video. The middle panel shows several "legitimate" gamers, including the video's creator (a renowned gamer named finalElf) clearing the Cruma Tower area (a particularly over-farmed virtual territory in the game), of Chinese adena farmers. In the right panel is final screen of the fan video, which reads: "Fuck the Farmers. And Fuck the lazy rich boys who pay them" (finalElf, n.d.).

Obviously, metagaming practices such as these are thoroughly caught up with both local (server) and global politics. But then, all literacy practices, even when defined narrowly as "the reading and writing of print text," are caught up with politics as such (Gee, 1996). They are also potentially quite transformative in terms of the context in which they are situated. Here, for example, the metagaming practice of "farming the farmers" has effectively transformed core game mechanics for which *Lineage* was once famous (between-clan sieges for castles in the virtual world) into Americans-versus-Chinese raids on said farmers by a community desperately trying to rid themselves of what they see as a "cancer" in the virtual world (Steinkuehler, 2006a). Gamer communities are necessarily in a perpetual state of development that crucially includes the development, maintenance, and transformation of thoroughly literate practices in order to maintain their fitness

Figure 9. Screenshots from the fan-generated digital in-game movie entitled Farm the Farmers Day II (finalElf, n.d.).

relative to the systems they co-evolve with (cf. Van Valen, 1973) – game designs and redesigns, economic realities, legal regulation, and even the emerging global technologies and practices that make up the broader online world, to name a few.

Official versus unofficial fandom. MMOGaming is participation in a domain of literacy, one with fuzzy boundaries that expand with continued play: what is at first confined to the game alone soon spills over into the virtual world beyond it (e.g., websites, chatrooms, email) and even life off-screen (e.g., telephone calls, face-to-face meetings). The online fandom that surrounds successful game titles are a rich yet nebulous sphere of multimodal multimedia including websites, blogs, threaded discussion boards, fan fictions, fan art, annotated game screenshots, cartoons, chatrooms, instant messaging, in-character emails, and even voice over IP (VoIP). A selected subset of the fandom terrain is "official" and linked to the corporate website (http://www.lineage2.com/), having met the company's purported standards of relevance (defined mostly in terms of exclusivity, as no multi-game sites are allowed), quality (they cannot contain incomplete webpages, outdated game information, or broken links), decency (no offensive material), originality (containing new information, not simply repeats of content from other sites), and compliance with the game's End User License Agreement (among other things, containing no references to trade of virtual items for real cash outside the game, despite the prevalence of the practice as discussed above). The primary fansites to make the company's cut are most commonly, in fact, vast database-backed research websites that function as unofficial – yet by far the most accurate – user manuals for the game. Such sites are instantiations of the community's "collective intelligence" (Levy, 1999): online repositories in which gamers publish what they know about the game and revise one another's findings on a range of topics as diverse as which monsters drop which items to which quests are and are not worthwhile to complete.

This official fandom, however, barely scratches the surface of game fandom entire, not only in terms of the volume of fan-authored content but also in terms of what gamers actually access and use as a regular part of their gameplay. As one informant aptly stated, "For the most part I enjoy finding my own information, it feels somehow rewarding because the majority of the information I come by is from interactive online communities, like fansites and forums." Unofficial fandom includes a wealth of resources that support not only social interaction among gamers but also research (e.g. to find what the most efficient and effective set of equipment for a given character might be) and development (e.g., inventing novel siege strategies) as well. Lineage fans (like all MMOG fans) take the resources provided them by the game itself, and building from it, create a rich culture of text, images, and ideas.

Fan websites. The fansite for the guild in which I personally participated is a case in point. Built originally by a member who works as a professional web designer in New York City, the LegendsOfAden (LoA) guild website is a collection of *player generated content*, created over a period of roughly three years of gaming together as one group (see Figure 10). Although our guild was lucky to have a professional designer among its membership who was willing to create the template for the website which members could then populate (averaging roughly 130 members throughout much of the guild's history), our site was considered fairly standard, no more elaborate than most guilds sustain. In truth, there is a "keeping up with the Joneses" attitude among guild leaders and their administration (guild members with officer rank of some form) such that novel online utilities and documents quickly become standard ones as guilds borrow and adapt useful ideas from one another in creating online out-of-game web content for their members.

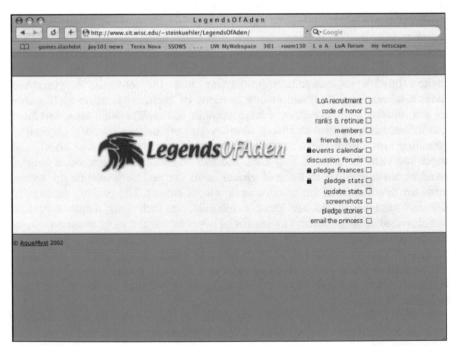

Figure 10. The LegendsOfAden guild website.

As a community shared document, the LoA guild website includes such diverse forms of writing as: formal statements about recruitment rules and the code of honor (social rules that guide members' behaviors); a list of the hierarchical ranks within the guild and their responsibilities; members pages, which include posed screenshots of each members' avatar and a brief write up on who they see themselves to be; password protected pages, accessible only to LoA members, that list the guild's friends and foes, a shared calendar that tracks various collaborative events within the community such as training days and sieges, the guild's pooled wealth from taxation and donations, and graphs of members' aggregated statistics in terms of character type and strength; online forms for gathering such information from individual members; links to public and private discussion forums (discussed below); annotated screenshots of significant in-game events which together function as a public scrapbook of guild triumphs and adventures (which, in turn, helps establish a sense of group affiliation both internally, among guild members, and externally, with the broader community of the game); collections of guild members' and guild friends' fan fiction (also discussed below); and links to in-character email accounts for reaching key leaders in the group.

Here, authorship is *thoroughly distributed* with multiple people "writing" the text that others, both members and nonmembers alike, then "read" as an instantiation of our guild identity. As Turkle (1995) notes, "Since [virtual worlds] are authored by their players, thousands of people in all, often hundreds as a time, are all logged on from different places; the solitary author is displaced and distributed" (p. 185).

Game discussion boards. Although *Lineage* has official discussion boards linked to their corporate website which are highly active, it is customary for guild and fan sites to have *unofficial* discussion boards of their own as well. Here, participants discuss a vast range of topics, from which skill path is best for a given class of avatar to in-game gossip about who-did-what-to-whom. Multiple genres of writing can be found within such forums, from argumentation to expository writing, from personal journal-like entries to game reviews, from historical essays (on topics such as the origin of the clan name) to journalistic accounts of important in-game events (such as the previous evening's war with another guild), from persuasive writing to jokes, stories, explanations, accounts, thank you letters, and even the occasional five paragraph essays at times. In fact, much of the content of the guild websites themselves begins here, within guild forums, as participants collaboratively propose, draft, revise, and polish text that later becomes official guild site content.

By providing spaces for social interaction and relationships beyond the workplace and home, such online discussion forums – much like the virtual worlds with which they are associated (Steinkuehler & Williams, 2006) – function as one novel form of a new "third place" (Oldenburg, 1999) for informal sociability much like the pubs, coffee shops, and other hangouts of old. However, unlike bricks and mortar ones, these are comprised thoroughly and nearly exclusively in terms of print text (in close second, digital images, and in more distant third, digital movie and sound). And as sites for literacy, they are non-trivial: As of July of 2005, the LegendsOfAden (LoA) forum linked to the website shown in Figure 10 contained nine separate sections (three LoA-members only sections that are password protected, six public sections where anyone can post) comprised of 298 separate topics discussion threads total across all sections for a grand total of 1600 written posts (and a full year of online text interaction has occurred since that time). Such reading and writing is part and parcel of what it means to participate in the MMOG guild community. Thus, when media experts report that gaming is displacing reading and writing text in the lives of contemporary adolescents, one questions the extent to which they have taken seriously what successful gaming entails, particularly the unofficial player-generated text content that gamers overwhelmingly consume and produce.

Fan fiction. Guild and fan websites also feature original creative work that players generate based on content designed into the virtual worlds they inhabit, such as art, poetry, and fiction. Like all interpretive communities, MMOGamers take up the symbolic, cultural materials offered them by media to collectively create the form and substance of their own cultural worlds (Squire & Steinkuehler, 2006; Taylor, 2002, in press). In this way, they are no different from the folk cultures of old, except that now the consumers have increasingly user-friendly tools at their disposal to work with, including online access to sociotechnical networks that enable their easy distribution, such as fan groups and guilds. As Jenkins (1998) points out,

> Historically, our culture evolved through a collective process of collaboration and elaboration. Folk tales, legends, myths and ballads were built up over time as people added elements that made them more meaningful to their own contexts. The Industrial Revolution resulted in the privatization of culture … Fans respond… by applying the traditional practices of a folk culture to mass culture, treating film or television as if it offered them raw materials for telling their own stories and resources for forging their own communities… (¶ 32)

Consider, for example, the fan fiction excerpt shown in Figure 11. The piece was featured on the official *Lineage* website in 2003 and was forwarded to the LoA guild website for distribution via the "LoA short stories" page. In it, the author writes about a pseudo-fictional adventure (partially based on an actual occurrence, partially based on the genre conventions of medieval fantasy stories) in which he and another character participated within the virtual world of *Lineage*. The story is written at a grade level appropriate to his age; however, what is most interesting here is the purpose for which he purportedly wrote it. The story is dedicated to the second main character appearing in its pages – a *Lineage* girl gamer roughly the same age as the author. In the email requesting its distribution via the LoA guild site, the author wrote, "I included a new story if you would like to read or post up, its awesome ^^ [raised eyebrows] even though I just used it to hit on this girl..."

208

Blinding Twilight
by
for

As dawn eclipsed the town of Aden, it seemed that its light would never reach the end of the grand city. Built under the tyrannical rule of Ken Rauhel and the corrupt mage Cerenis, it seemed almost impossible that such a beautiful city was grounded in their despotic ideals. I looked across the horizon and nudged at ███████, who had fallen asleep during last night's vigil

Figure 11. Excerpt of the fan fiction piece written by a Lineage I *gamer.*

It is difficult to imagine another context in contemporary American youth culture in which writing a short story might be viewed as a recognizable way to court girls. In the context of MMOGs, however, such writing is a central and highly valued practice. Here, adeptness with the pen, so to speak, carries a certain social status such that those who show exceptional skill in the creation of content oftentimes develop a rather large following. In MMOGs, such writing is *not* considered as ancillary to gaming but rather as a central part of participating. The following transcript (see Figure 12) is an excellent case in point.

```
SharpPaw      oh yeah! to celebrate me coming back to pledge &
SharpPaw      being rank ive decided to write another story!
SharpPaw      for site!
Adeleide      omg do it! we need more stories!

SharpPaw      ^^ o'course
SharpPaw      in fact ive planned it
SharpPaw      i got the PERFECT story idea the other day when
 .  .  .  .  .  .

SharpPaw      its called An Old Knight's Tale
SharpPaw      youll see it within the next 2-3months

Adeleide      wow! do u like to write in ur spare time?
SharpPaw      well na i like to play this in my spare time

LinI/03.01.04
```

Figure 12. Transcript of Lineage I in-game conversation in which a student discusses the short story he has recently decided to author over summer break.

209

In this in-game exchange, a beginning high school student who is on summer break discusses the short story he has recently decided to author in commemoration of rejoining the guild and being promoted in rank. When asked whether he likes to write in his spare time, he responds, somewhat baffled, "well na i like to play this in my spare time." In the context of MMOGs at least, school age kids are perfectly willing to engage in long, thoughtful writing projects – "2-3 months" planning, not including the initial work he did prior to this exchange – in their own spare time, not as isolated literary "assignments" but as part and parcel of what it means to game online.

DISCUSSION

Throughout this chapter, I have made the argument that, even when based on a restricted version of what it means to read and write, examination of what gamers actually do during play reveals that *gaming, at least in the context of MMOGs, is not replacing literacy practice but rather* is *a literacy practice*. If we compare what individuals do within these spaces to national reading, writing, and technology standards, it turns out that much of their activity can be seen as satisfying what we *say* we want our children to be doing. For example, as recommended by the National Council of Teachers of English (n.d.) standards, MMOGamers: "read a wide range of print and non-print texts" to build an understanding of texts and of themselves (Standard #1); use a wide range of strategies to "comprehend, interpret, evaluate, and appreciate texts," including "[drawing] on their prior experience, their interactions with other readers and writers" (Standard #3); use an equally wide range of strategies to author texts of their own (Standard #5); use their understanding of "language structure, language conventions… media techniques, figurative language, and genre to create, critique, and discuss print" (Standard #6); "gather, evaluate, and synthesize data from a variety of sources" in order to conduct research on issues of interest to them (Standard #7); and, perhaps most of all, "use spoken, written, and visual language to accomplish *their own purposes* [italics added]" (Standard #12). If we compare what such standards require to what MMOGs, in practice, exact from those who play, it turns out that videogames are not a threat to literacy in contemporary culture but rather one important (albeit novel) part of it.

If so, then what lies behind these claims of a "literacy crisis"? They are likely rooted in a long-standing fear of technology (Williams, 2006), an equally long-standing fear of youth culture (Jenkins, 1999), and a fear of *what* kids are reading and writing, not *whether* they are engaged in such practices per se. Games, like all new media before them, have roused deeply ambivalent feelings in American culture, often masking deeper societal tensions and problems (Wartella & Reeves, 1983, 1985; consider, for example, the media attention given to the gaming habits of the Columbine High School shooters), an attitude oftentimes rooted in societal guilt over the mistreatment of American youth, one that again casts them as the *source* of problems (in this case, violence and crime) rather than the *victims* of those oft-ignored risk factors associated with them (e.g. poverty, neglect, abuse).

Without taking a broader historical view, it is easy to recycle arguments made again and again in the past claiming that technology and/or popular culture are corrupting our youth, each time simply substituting in the latest "menace" (e.g. rock and roll, comic books, television, telephone, etc.) to all things cultural and good (typically, fine literature, the arts, and other expensive pastimes of the white, Christian, middle-class majority).

The third likely cause, a fear of *what* kids are reading and writing not *whether*, has a rich history as well but is perhaps a conversation, unlike the other two, worth resurrecting. In today's thoroughly networked, globalized, increasingly "flat" (Friedman, 2005) world, adolescents and adults are engaged with copious amounts of reading and writing as part of their everyday lifeworld; they just happen to be doing it in spaces and with content that may not be always sanctioned by adults. Perhaps it should be, though. There is much concern expressed about youth culture's seeming engrossment in "merely passive" consumption of corporate-owned and profit driven content. From that view, MMOs and other informal spaces look particularly promising, for it is through such virtual worlds that adolescents, through the very act of reading and writing, transform increasingly "corporate owned" culture into the "raw materials for telling [our] own stories and resources for forging [our] own communities" (Jenkins, 1998 ¶ 32).

ENDNOTES

[1] Violence in America is actually declining and has been for the past decade (Catalano, 2004), although this particular media misrepresentation is different from the one taken issue with here.

[2] Reading aloud? National statistics on the prevalence of this form of activity are lacking, but it is rather difficult not to imagine this as some form of nostalgia for a world as long gone as the days of Lord Alfred Tennyson.

[3] Evidence that each chat channel serves a designated social function is that, when communications meant for one (e.g. whispers) are incorrectly issued in another (e.g. public talk), individuals customarily signal the error with "w/c" which translates as "wrong channel" and reissue the text within the channel context for which it was meant.

[4] *All transcript excerpts are verbatim save changes for ease of reading, such as typographical corrections and supplementation of dietic references or truncations with appropriate, expanded referents [in square brackets]. Pseudonyms replace all avatars names save the author's.*

REFERENCES

Barton, D. (1994). *Literacy: An introduction to the ecology of written language*. Oxford: Blackwell.

Blackmore, S. (1999). *The meme machine*. New York: Oxford University Press.

Bruner, J. (1986). *Actual minds, possible worlds*. Cambridge MA: Harvard University Press.

Bruner, J. (2003). *Making stories: Law,literature, life*. Cambridge MA: Harvard University Press.

Castronova, E. (2001). Virtual worlds: A first-hand account of market and society on the cyberian frontier. CESifo Working Paper Series No. 618.

Catalano, S. M. (2004). *Criminal victimization, 2003*. (NCJ Publication No. 205455). Washington DC: Bureau of Justice Statistics.

Cazden C. (1988). *Classroom discourse: The language of teaching and learning*. Portsmouth, NH: Heinnemann.

Cherny, L. (1999). *Conversation and community: Discourse in a social MUD*. Stanford, CA: CSLI Publications.

Clinton, K. (2004). Being-in-digital-worlds as a new kind of resource for learning. Paper presented at 2004 meeting of American Educational Research Association, San Diego CA.

Cook-Gumperz, J. (Ed.) (1986). *The social construction of literacy*. Cambridge: Cambridge University Press.

finalElf (n.d.) Farm the Farmers Day II [digital in-game movie] Retrieved October 1, 2004 from http://lin2.warcry.com/

Friedman, T. L. (2005). *The world is flat: A brief history of the twenty-first century*. New York: Farrar, Straus, and Giroux.

Gee, J. P. (1992). *The social mind: Language, ideology, and social practice*. New York: Bergin & Garvey.

Gee, J. P. (1996). *Social linguistics and literacies: Ideology in discourses* (2nd Ed.). London: Routledge/Falmer.

Gee, J. P. (1999). *An introduction to discourse analysis: Theory and method*. New York: Routledge.

Gee, J. P. (2003). *What videogames have to teach us about learning and literacy*. New York: Palgrave Macmillan.

Geertz, C. (1973). *The interpretation of cultures*. New York: Basic Books.

Goodwin, M. H. (1990). *He-said-she-said: Talk as social organization among black children*. Bloomington: Indiana University Press.

Gumperz, J. J. (Ed.) (1982). *Language and social identity*. Cambridge: Cambridge University Press.

Gygax, G., & Arneson, D. (1973). *Dungeons and Dragons* (1st ed.). Lake Geneva, Wisconsin: TSR, Inc.

Heath, S. B. (1983). *Ways with words: Language, life, and work in communities and classrooms*. Cambridge: Cambridge University Press.

Huizinga, J. (1938). *Homo ludens: A Study in the Play-Elements in Culture* (R.F.C. Hull, trans.) Boston: Beacon.

Hutchins, E. (1995). *Cognition in the wild*. Cambridge, Massachusetts: MIT Press.

Jenkins, H., III. (1998) The poachers and the stormtroopers: Popular culture in the digital age. Paper presented at the University of Michigan.

Jenkins, H., III. (1999). Professor Jenkins goes to Washington. Harper's Magazine, *299*(1790), 19.

Kirmse, A. & Kirmse, C. (1996). Meridian 59. 3DO Company. Available at http://meridian 59.neardeathstudios.com/

Knobel, M. (1999). *Everyday literacies: Students, discourse, and social practice*. New York: Peter Lang.

Kolbert, E. (2001, May 28). Pimps and dragons: How an online world survived a social breakdown. *The New Yorker, 77*(13), 88.

Koster, R. (2002). Online world timeline. Retrieved Oct. 2, 2004, from http://www.legendmud.org/raph

Kress, G. (1985). *Linguistic processes in sociocultural practice.* Oxford: Oxford University Press.

Labov, W. (1972). *Language in the inner city: Studies in the Black English vernacular.* Philadelphia: University of Pennsylvania Press.

Labov, W. & Waletzky, J. (1967). Narrative analysis. In J. Helm (Ed.), *Essays on the verbal and visual arts* (pp. 12-44). Seattle: University of Washington Press.

Lankshear, C. (1997). *Changing literacies* (Changing education series). Buckingham UK: Open University Press.

Lankshear, C. & Knobel, M. (2003). *New literacies: Changing knowledge and classroom learning.* Buckingham: Open University Press.

Lave, J. (1988). *Cognition in practice: Mind, mathematics, and culture in everyday life.* Cambridge: Cambridge University Press.

Lemke, J. (n.d.). *Why study games? Notes toward a basic research agenda for education.* Unpublished manuscript.

Levy, P. (1999). Collective intelligence: Mankind's emerging world in cyberspace. (Robert Bononno, trans.). Cambridge MA: Perseus Books.

Mandese, J. (2004, April 5). Video games emerge as 'No. 4' medium, Media Daily News. Retrieved July 8, 2005 from http://publications.mediapost.com/index.cfm?fuseaction=Articles.showArticle &art_aid=4814

National Council of Teachers of English. (n.d.). Standards for the English language arts. Retrieved July 10, 2005 from http://www.ncte.org/about/over/standards/110846.htm

National Institute for Literacy. (n.d.). What is literacy? In Frequently Asked Questions. Retrieved July 9, 2005 from http://www.nifl.gov/nifl/faqs.html

New London Group. (1996). A pedagogy of multiliteracies: Designing social futures. *Harvard Educational Review, 66*(1), 60-92.

Oldenburg, R. (1997). The great good place: Cafés, coffee shops, community centers, beauty parlors, general stores, bars, hangouts, and how they get you through the day. New York: Marlowe & Company.

Rideout, V., Roberts, D. F., & Foehr, U. G. (2005). *Generation M· Media in the lives of 8-18 year-olds* (Publication No. 7250). Washington DC: The Henry J. Kaiser Family Foundation.

Robison, A. J. (2004). The "internal design grammar" of video games. Paper presented at the American Educational Research Association (AERA), San Diego CA.

Russell, M. (2004, October 11) Gaming the online games. *Newsweek International, 144*(16) 16, E32 2c.

Sanders, B. (1995). *A is for ox: The collapse of literacy and the rise of violence in an electronic age.* New York: Random House.

Solomon, A. (2004, July 10). *The closing of the American book.* New York Times, p A17.

Squire, K. D. & Steinkuehler, C. A. (2006). Generating CYBERCulture/s: The case of Star Wars Galaxies. In D. Gibbs & K. L. Krause (Eds.), *Cyberlines: Languages and cultures of the internet* (2nd ed.). Albert Park, Australia: James Nicholas Publishers.

Steinkuehler, C. A. (2004). Learning in massively multiplayer online games. In Y. B. Kafai, W. A. Sandoval, N. Enyedy, A. S. Nixon, & F. Herrera (Eds.), *Proceedings of the Sixth International Conference of the Learning Sciences* (pp. 521-528). Mahwah, NJ: Erlbaum.

Steinkuehler, C. (2005). *Cognition and learning in massively multiplayer online games: A critical approach.* University of Wisconsin-Madison, Madison, WI.

Steinkuehler, C. (2006a). The mangle of play. *Games & Culture, 1*(3), 1-14.

Steinkuehler, C. A. (2006b). Massively multiplayer online videogaming as participation in a discourse. *Mind, Culture, & Activity, 13*(1), 38-52.

Steinkuehler, C. & Chmiel, M. (2006). Fostering scientific habits of mind in the context of online play. In S.A. Barab, K.E. Hay, N.B. Songer, & D.T. Hickey (Eds.), *Proceedings of the International Conference of the Learning Sciences* (pp 723-729). Mahwah NJ: Erlbaum

Steinkuehler, C. & Williams, D. (2006). Where everybody knows your (screen) name: Online games as "third places." *Journal of Computer-Mediated Communication, 11*(4), article 1.

213

Steinkuehler, C., Black, R., & Clinton, K. (2005). Researching literacy as tool, place, and way of being. *Reading Research Quarterly, 40*(1), 7-12.

Street, B. (1984). *Literacy in theory and practice*. Cambridge: Cambridge University Press.

Street, B. (Ed.). (1993). *Cross-cultural approaches to literacy*. Cambridge: Cambridge University Press.

Taylor, T. L. (2002). Whose game is this anyway?: Negotiating corporate ownership in a virtual world. In F. Mäyrä (Ed.), *Computer Games and Digital Cultures Conference proceedings*, (227-242). Tampere: Tampere University Press.

Taylor, T. L. (in press). Pushing the borders: Player participation and game culture. In J. Karaganis & N. Jeremijenko (Eds.), *Network_Netplay: Structures of participation in digital culture*. Durham: Duke University Press.

Thrasher, R. H., Jr. (1974). *Shouldn't ignore these strings: A study of conversational deletion*. Unpublished doctoral dissertation, University of Michigan, Ann Arbor.

Tolkien, J. R. (1938). *The hobbit*. Boston: Houghton Mifflin.

Trubshaw, R., & Bartle, R. (1978). MUD1. Essex.

Turkle, S. (1995). *Life on the screen: Identity in the age of the internet*. New York: Touchstone.

Van Valen, L. (1973). A new evolutionary law. *Evolutionary Theory, 1*, 1-30.

Wartella, E., & Reeves, D. (1983). Recurring issues in research on children and media. *Educational Technology, 23*, 5-9.

Wartella, E., & Reeves, D. (1985). Historical trends in research on children and the media: 1900-1960. *Journal of Communication, 35*, 118-133.

Wearden, G. (2001, August 20). Researchers: Video games hurt brain development. CNET News. Retrieved July 6, 2005 from http://news.com.com/ Researchers+Video+games+hurt+ brain+development /2100-1040_3-271849.html

Weber, B. (2004, July 8). Fewer noses stuck in books in America, survey finds. New York Times. p. E1.

Williams, D. (2003). The video game lightning rod: Constructions of a new media technology, 1970-2000. *Information, Communication and Society, 6*(4), 523-550.

Williams, D. (2006). A (brief) social history of gaming. In P. Vorderer & J. Bryant (Eds.), *Video games: Motivations and consequences of use*. Mahwah, New Jersey: Erlbaum.

Woodcock, B. (2006). An analysis of MMOG subscription growth – version 18.0. Retrieved July 10, 2006 from http://www.mmogchart.com/

Constance Steinkuehler
Department of Curriculum & Instruction
University of Wisconsin-Madison

SUPPORTING THE IMPLEMENTATION AND USE OF SIMULATION COMPUTER GAMES

A variety of social, policy, and pedagogical issues must be considered if games are to successfully support learning. The final three chapters invite us to consider several issues related to the scalability of games as effective instructional artifacts, the ability of simulations to "unteach" faulty mental models, and ways in which technology can augment our experiences in the so-called real world.

The first chapter reminds us that there is a significant difference between the successful implementation of a game in a single classroom and an instructional technology that can be more broadly deployed while still supporting learning. If computer-based simulation games are ever to support learning at the degree of scale that will make their development sustainable, these issues must be understood and addressed. The following chapter describes how encouraging students to design and develop computer-based simulations can draw out fiendishly resilient misconceptions and provide a space in which students can confront these flawed models concretely and directly. The final chapter liberates computer-based simulation games from the monitor and transports them into the actual classroom, backyard, or city park, in what is called virtual reality gaming – an evolving pedagogy that leverages ideas of situated learning to help students experience "place" in new ways.

BRIAN C. NELSON, DIANE JASS KETELHUT, JODY CLARKE,
ED DIETERLE, CHRIS DEDE, BEN ERLANDSON

ROBUST DESIGN STRATEGIES FOR SCALING EDUCATIONAL INNOVATIONS

The River City Case Study

INTRODUCTION

Scaling up pedagogical approaches or curricular materials successful in specific conditions or contexts to a broader range of settings has proven very difficult in education (Dede, Honan, and Peters, 2005). For example, new teaching strategies that are successful with one practitioner rarely transfer even to other instructors in the same school, let alone to a broad range of practitioners. In general, the more complex the educational innovation and the wider the range of contexts, the more difficult it is to move a new practice from its original setting to other sites where its implementation could potentially prove valuable (Moore, 1999). To successfully transfer educational innovations, designers must resolve problems of magnitude (fostering the necessary conditions for change in large numbers of settings with average resources at considerable distances from one another) and variation (diverse and often unfavorable conditions across settings) (Wiske and Perkins, 2005).

Resolving the problem of variation when "scaling up" involves designing educational innovations to function effectively across a range of settings, some of which may be relatively inhospitable (Dede, 2004). In systemic reform situations, transfer of an innovation to another context can be made successfully by partnering with a particular school or district to create a setting that is conducive to the design. However, scalability into school sites that are not partners in innovation may necessitate developing interventions that are "ruggedized" to retain substantial efficacy. Such ruggedized innovations are especially necessary in settings where some conditions for educational success (e.g., a supportive administration, qualified and enthusiastic teachers, and a well maintained technology infrastructure) are absent or weak (Clarke & Dede, 2006). Under such circumstances, major aspects of an innovation's design may not be enacted as intended by its developers, even if the design includes professional development, connections to other innovations occurring within the school, and similar conventional supports.

B. E. Shelton, D. A. Wiley (eds.), Educational Design & Use of Computer Simulation Games, 209–231.

In this chapter, we describe our evolving strategy for scalability through design-based research on large-scale implementations of an educational multi-user virtual environment (MUVE) curriculum across a spectrum of contexts and conditions, such as public and private schools; urban, suburban, and rural neighborhoods; and schools with high and low socio-economic status (SES), minority, and English as a Second Language (ESL) learner populations. We describe elements our research has shown to be important conditions for success in implementing educational innovations and offer examples of robust design strategies we are undertaking to address these conditions as we scale *River City*, our MUVE-based curriculum for learning scientific inquiry and 21st century skills. This research is designed to explore whether robust-design can produce the educational equivalent of plant strains tailored to harsh conditions that are productive where the usual version of that plant would wither and die. The strategies we describe are generalizable to many other types of role-based learning-by-doing interventions, such as games and collaborative simulations.

THE RIVER CITY PROJECT

Designing for scalability — even into contexts in which "important, but not essential" conditions for success are weakened or lacking — requires enhancing the innovation's capacity to withstand adverse conditions. Such robust-design strategies are exemplified in our ongoing research into the use of the *River City* educational MUVE.

Educational MUVEs enable large numbers of learners to access virtual worlds, interact with digital objects (such as online microscopes and pictures), represent themselves through "avatars," communicate with other participants and with computer-based agents, and enact collaborative learning activities of various types (Nelson, Ketelhut, Clarke, Bowman, & Dede, 2005).

The *River City* MUVE is centered on skills of hypothesis formation and experimental design, as well as on content related to national standards (National Research Council, 1996) and assessments in biology and ecology. The *River City* virtual town is set in the late 1800's, and concentrated around a river that runs from the mountains downstream to a dump and a bog. Like most 19th century industrial towns, it contains various neighborhoods, industries, and institutions such as a hospital and a university (Figure 1).

In *River City*, students can interact with computer-based agents (residents of the city), digital objects (such as pictures and online microscopes), and the avatars of other students. In exploring, students also encounter various visual and auditory stimuli, such as the coughing of town residents and the buzzing of mosquitoes that provide tacit clues as to possible causes of illness. Content in the right-hand interface-window shifts based on what the student encounters or activates in the virtual environment, such as a dialogue with an agent or a virtual microscope that allows examination of water samples (Figure 2).

Figure 1: River City

The current site is Station_J

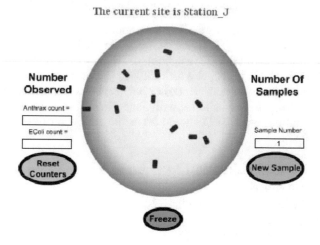

Figure 2: Virtual Microscope

Students work in small teams to develop and test hypotheses about why residents of *River City* are getting ill. Three different illnesses (water-borne, air-borne, and insect-borne) are integrated with historical, social and geographical content, allowing students to develop and practice the inquiry skills involved in disentangling multi-causal problems embedded within a complex environment (Ketelhut, Clarke, Dede, Nelson, Bowman, 2005). A sharing day at the end of the project allows students to compare their research with other teams of students in their class and to piece together some of the many potential hypotheses and causal relationships embedded in the virtual environment.

CONDITIONS FOR SUCCESS IN SCALING INNOVATIONS

Through our *River City* studies, we have identified a number of conditions for success likely to be attenuated in many contexts, and evolved the curriculum's design to retain considerable effectiveness under those circumstances (Clarke, Dede, Ketelhut, & Nelson, 2006; Clarke & Dede, 2006). In this chapter, we focus on three: teacher preparation (including teacher's knowledge of science and content-specific pedagogy, as well as fluency with learning technology), class size (affecting the degree of individualization and interaction possible), and learner engagement (illustrated by indices such as log files of participant behavior, student attendance at school, and teachers' perceptions of student motivation and classroom behavior).

In each of these areas, findings from our prior studies are now providing insights into how to "ruggedize" our current *River City* design when the implementation context is weak in terms of one or more of these conditions.

TEACHER PREPARATION: CONDITION FOR SUCCESS 1

As the professional demands on teachers increase, schools have turned to teacher professional development (TPD) as a way to help teachers meet these requirements. It is estimated that school districts spend approximately $200 million on TPD (Killeen, Monk, & Plecki, 2002). Yet, there are questions as to whether this money is well spent. Borko (2004) suggests that many of these TPD programs offer "fragmented, intellectually superficial" experiences. Research indicates that well-designed TPD should have the following nine characteristics (Maldonado, 2002):

- Prolonged contact;
- Choosing the correct model (e.g. expert training or individualized);
- Access to colleagues;
- Opportunities for continuing support beyond initial professional development;
- Constant evaluation and feedback;
- Content-specific curriculum;
- Inquiry-based;
- Collaborative;
- Development of learning communities.

In our previous *River City* implementations, we used these criteria to design several methods for preparing participating teachers. Initially, all of the professional development for teachers was online, not only to allow them to access it on their own schedule, but also because we were working across distance. This TPD fulfilled many of the 9 characteristics, but did not offer teachers access to colleagues and opportunities for collaboration. Perhaps as a result, some teachers ignored all or most of the professional development. Not surprisingly, these teachers then encountered problems in implementing *River City*. Many did not understand the purpose and process of the curricular intervention, lacked knowledge about the inquiry skills and standards-based scientific content the intervention helps students to learn, and missed pedagogical strategies for leading interpretive discussions in class about students' MUVE experiences and the data collected. As discouraging as this list of missing teacher capabilities may seem, in practice our curricular intervention worked fairly well even in these situations. The River City MUVE is designed for scalability, creating curricular interventions so compelling for students that with sufficient internal guidance, they have a fulfilling, self-directed learning experience—albeit with reduced educational outcomes—even with a confused teacher (Clarke, et al, 2006).

However, in an attempt to create strong classroom facilitators, we modified our TPD in order to help teachers remain motivated and not feel isolated. Instead of online individualized training, participating teachers were trained on *River City* directly by research staff, sometimes mediated by technology, but primarily face-to-face. This provided teachers with the missing elements of a collegial and collaborative environment, as observed in teacher surveys. One teacher who underwent both formats of professional development stated, "I thought that this year the PD was easier to follow, more to the point," while a new teacher felt that "the PD was very useful."

Robust design solutions

In response to attenuation of the teacher-preparation condition for success in our early studies, we are evolving the professional development portion of the intervention to increase its scalability. Three primary strategies we are employing involve a "train-the-trainers" approach, a highly individualized web-based training approach, and the use of a sophisticated web-based "Teacher Dashboard" (Clarke & Dede, 2006).

Train the trainers.
As indicated, in past implementations participating teachers were trained directly by research staff, and all of the research observations and just-in-time support for teachers were also provided directly by project personnel. However, this training strategy does not scale well when increasing the number of participating teachers while holding the number of research staff constant. In our current project, implementations simultaneously occur in multiple states and countries, making it impossible for project staff to be personally involved in all implementations.

213

Therefore, modifications to teacher training, just-in-time support, and in-class research data gathering have been made.

To create a more scalable system, we designed a "train-the-trainer" (T-t-T) method of professional development, where our team could train local people in each participating location in training the teachers, providing teachers just-in-time support, and gathering observational data for the research team on the progress of each implementation. This method had the advantage of putting a person intimately aware of local conditions in charge of teacher support. We felt that this method was superior to our previous method for two reasons: a local person would know how to access local school-based help that a teacher might need, and teachers would be more likely to ask for help from this person than they were from researchers. While the trainers might not be as well versed in *River City* as the project personnel were, they were all highly experienced in working with K-12 teachers. In addition, each of our trainers had another area of expertise: technology, science education, or professional development. Two of the trainers were education doctoral students and the other four were current or former teachers.

The purpose of the trainer professional development was to develop the trainers' understanding of the *River City* curriculum directly and to model for them our successful methods of teacher professional development. Therefore, trainers underwent 16 hours of professional development. The first 8 hours were spent learning professional development as a teacher. This allowed trainers to become familiar with the curriculum and how it is used in practice. The following 8 hours were spent scaffolding the trainers on how to support teachers technically and pedagogically as they work through the project.

A good example of this style of training took place in a Midwestern state, where 29 teachers participated in the *River City* project in spring 2006. Four local trainers underwent professional development under the guidance of members of our research team, supported by online training materials. These trainers underwent 16 hours of professional development, working face-to-face with project staff. The local trainers then offered 8 hours of professional development to up to 10 teachers each. Amongst themselves, these trainers chose to collaborate on the training, where three trainers would attend each teacher professional development training session of approximately 10-20 teachers. These trainers felt that multiple trainers would offer more one-on-one support during the professional development and questions would most likely be more fully answered. In addition, these trainers provided just-in-time support for teachers, and gathered observational data for the research team. Ongoing email communication and periodic phone conferences were held between trainers and project staff to allow staff to answer questions for trainers and for trainers to update staff on implementations. As was hoped, this worked very well and resulted in strong teacher-trainer and trainer-researcher relationships, as evidenced by the number of teachers and trainers who opted to spend multiple years working with River City.

IndividualizedtTraining. Unfortunately, the "train-the-trainers" teacher preparation approach needed to be modified in other implementations. The first challenge we encountered with this method was that its logistical feasibility required that a group of teachers in one geographical area express interest in implementing River City. That was not always the case. For example, we had one teacher participating in Australia. Clearly, having project staff fly to Australia to train a trainer to support one teacher was not feasible. Therefore, we created an in-depth individualized teacher professional development package (IPD) for situations such as this. When constructing the IPD, the research team drew on materials used in face-to-face PD (PowerPoint slides, anecdotal stories, best practices, and so on) and distilled them into a single, all-in-one-place printable guide. Coupled with the IPD guide is just-in-time support made possible through e-mail and Skype-based support. For both T-t-T and IPD the mechanisms for ongoing support are the same. Teachers contact support personal (either trainers or a member of the research staff) with technology-related and pedagogical questions. Although IPD is not as personal as face-to-face training, we have invested significant resources in to providing clear information and frequent opportunities for reflection, when teachers monitor their own understanding.

Although the Train-the-Trainer model is the gold standard in our scaling up model of TPD, IPD *is* far better than providing nothing. We designed our TPD to overcome the *fingertip effect*: the naïve belief that novices will automatically understand and take advantage of a tool's affordances to the same extent as an expert, just by receiving access to the tool. Instead, IPD is a low tech alternative to "front-end," pre-implementation TPD. In both models, teachers seeking help rely on the same media, which is summarized below.

The IPD outlines the trajectory of *River City* by supporting teachers as they prepare to complete their implementation activities. A variety of media were considered before electing to develop IPD as a printable document. The research team agreed that teachers needed to distribute materials between those on the screen and those on paper. Our professional development model requires teachers to move between a student laboratory notebook, the simulation interface, and information contained in PowerPoint slides.

This package was delivered to teachers who implemented solely or in very small groups and was supported in varying amounts with technologically mediated contact from one project researcher. Six teachers underwent this form of training in Spring 2006. Pilot results of the IPD led members of the research team to conclude that all teachers might benefit from having such a resource as a reference, and so the package was offered as an ancillary resource to anyone implementing River city regardless of how they were trained. However, while training and support seemed to work well for these teachers, the only observational data that we have from those classrooms are teachers' self-reports.

A second complication we discovered in our trainer based strategy for teacher professional development was that, in situations where the project staff was not local, finding trainers was often difficult. This problem occurred in two of our remote sites. In each of these sites, we were eventually able to find trainers, but not until after project staff themselves conducted on-site teacher professional development. Therefore, trainers-to-be were trained with the IPD. Project staff worked with the trainers -- mediated by phone, computer-based chat, and face-to-face -- to help them understand more about their roles and responsibilities. Trainers then went on to observe classrooms and provide ongoing support to teachers. Twenty-two teachers and 2 trainers were trained in this manner.

Teacher dashboard. As we scaled, we wanted to provide teachers with more control over the running of the River City project, so we created a simple-to-use infrastructure through which they could "drive" the implementation. The result is the "Teacher Dashboard," a web-based portal that provides teachers with all the tools and resources necessary to successfully implement the River City project (Figure 3). On the front end, teachers log into a web interface that has links to pages housing different features that allow them to (a) register students into the River City system, (b) assign students to teams, (c) set class and student access to River City worlds, and (d) access documents and resources for working with River City. On the back end, the Dashboard is linked to a relational database, enabling teachers to communicate with the database through simple web pages, and allowing the research team to easily record and store generated data. The Teacher Dashboard contains a number of components pertaining to areas such as teacher information, class management, chat monitor, and resources.

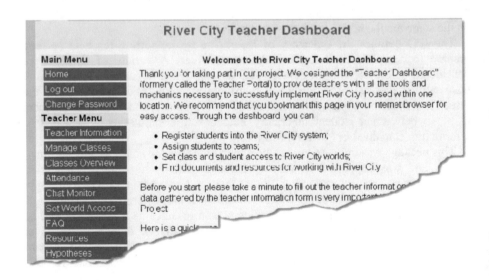

Figure 3: Teacher dashboard

Teacher Information:
In prior implementations, we provided teachers with a document template through which they could provide information about their class schedule and contact information. While we preferred to have the forms emailed back to us, we were able to accept hard copies from teachers and transcribe the data ourselves. As we scaled, we realized the importance of managing such information electronically. Therefore, we created an online form in the Teacher Dashboard that is linked to a central database accessible only to selected members of the research team. This allows us to maintain records of schools involved in the project and also to link school demographics to student data seamlessly. As a bonus, information collected in the database allowed the research team to send letters of appreciation to principals, acknowledging their teachers' and students' good work and thanking them for their participation in the project.

Class Management:
Through the Teacher Dashboard, teachers can directly create student accounts and passwords for the *River City* environment. In the past, this process was controlled through multiple exchanges of spreadsheets between teachers and the research team. In essence, teachers would send class lists with preferred student account logins; and we would create accounts, randomly assign students to teams and notify teachers. Teachers would then provide student demographic data in a second spreadsheet. Unfortunately, teachers often failed to check the final spreadsheets where student team and final student account IDs were identified. Now, through the Dashboard, participating teachers can set up classes and enter student information directly into the database through a web-based form. Since the Dashboard is linked to the database, if a user name is already taken, the teacher is aware of it immediately and can create an alternate. Teachers generate all this information; thus, they can easily look up student accounts and make changes.

When they create student accounts, teachers now also enter demographic data about their students and classes, as well as creating teams of three. A series of drop-down menus facilitates the entry of demographic data. This ensures that we have necessary demographic information and can link this seamlessly to other data. As mentioned above, teachers can maintain their class information, add additional students, and make changes to team assignments. For example, if a student moves suddenly or falls ill, and so cannot participate in the project, teachers can readjust teams and make "on-the-fly" modifications. Enabling local teachers to create and manage student accounts and teams makes the project easier to scale, as the teachers rely more on themselves and less on the research team. We no longer receive any frantic phone calls from teachers regarding questions about student logins or email complaints about team assignments. Perhaps more importantly to successful scaling, this has the advantage of putting the teacher in control of his or her class and implementation.

Chat Monitor:

One of the first questions teachers tend to ask us about the project is how we monitor student chat for improper language. Because students conduct team-based investigations in River City that include the use of text-based chat, teachers are concerned about the potential for swearing and inappropriate talk taking place at school. In fact, in many of the participating schools, instant messaging among students not allowed during the school day. Over the years we have tried various methods to monitor and help reduce inappropriate language use with the chat tool in River City. When we worked with a small number of classes, we had live "chat monitors" who scanned all utterances and could whisper to students when they used improper language. As the project grew, we created an automated system that output all chat to a dynamic webpage for review each evening by a member of the research team. Teachers were then notified if any of their students used inappropriate language. Again, this process was only manageable for a small number of classes and required that the research team understand what language was considered inappropriate in each location, something that is very context-dependent.

When we built the Teacher Dashboard, we wanted to place chat monitoring in the hands of teachers, not only because we knew that we could not keep up with slang of students, but also because this allowed teachers more control and less reliance on the research team. Therefore, we created a "swear monitor" that allowed teachers to input words they deemed improper into a monitor. An automated system would output chat containing these identified words on a webpage housed within the dashboard. This automated process was built on language parsing, but turned out to be too taxing for the database server. For example, words such as "hello" were tagged for containing "hell."

As we scaled and worked with hundreds of teachers and thousands of students, we knew we needed to create a system for monitoring student chat that would not be taxing to the central server. While it is useful for teachers to be aware of bad language, we realized how much more empowering it would be for teachers to have access to all student chat. While we encourage teachers to review student lab books and keep up with student progress via written work in the project, teachers have had little detailed knowledge about what each student is doing in the environment itself. Therefore, we have added a Chat Monitor feature to the Teacher Dashboard (Figure 4) that allows teachers to run reports on the "team chat" at the student, team, and/or class level on a nightly basis if they choose. Through this feature of the Teacher Dashboard, teachers are able to review the team chat of their students. The Chat Monitor enables teachers to monitor their students' progress (whether they are actually on task) and language (whether or not they are using bad language).

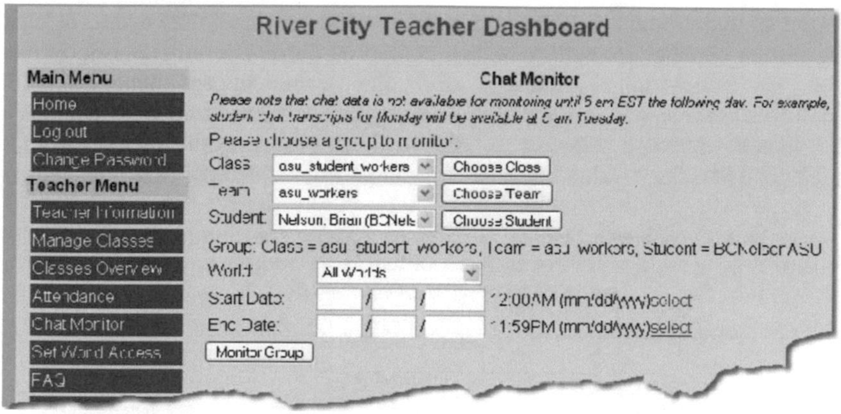

Figure 4: Chat monitor

Resources:

The resource section of the Teacher Dashboard contains links to all the materials and documents needed for the project in a single webpage. The content is organized to make documents easy to find and accessible for teachers. They can access videos, student and teacher lab books, day-by-day schedules, Frequently Asked Questions (FAQs), and other documents related to the project. Storing all resources in one place makes it easier for teachers to find and access what they need. It also makes them less reliant on the research team and trainers and more self-reliant.

TPD Implementation. We are still gathering teacher post-surveys from this current year, and so our comparative analysis on the different methods of TPD is just beginning. Of the 20 teachers (out of 53) who have returned surveys to date, 8 underwent TPD led by the River City research team, 11 were trained and supported by trainers, and 1 experienced the individualized TPD. In their post-implementation survey, these teachers were asked to respond on a scale of one to five (one being strongly disagree and five being strongly agree) to a list of statements regarding their professional development experiences:

- The Professional development helped me understand the *River City* curriculum and science content
- Professional development helped me understand how to use the *River City* program and technology
- I felt comfortable with the curriculum after the professional development
- The training materials were clear and easy to understand
- The training sessions were clear and easy to understand
- The *River City* professional development was a waste of time

219

In order to understand the effect of our different methods of TPD and to help in making design changes for next year, we compared the results of these questions for the researcher-trained teachers and the trainer-trained teachers (the individualized teacher was not included in this analysis since there was only one). Table 1 lists the average response to each of these 6 statements for each group. This table also lists the p-value for the t-test comparing the arrays.

Table 1: Professional Training method comparison: The average response to each post-survey item on professional development for teachers who were trained by River City researchers or by trainers (n=18).

	Trained by:		Probability that these values are different, based on t-test
	Researchers (n=8)	Trainers[1] (n=10)	
The Professional development helped me understand the River City curriculum and science content	4	4.3	0.83
Professional development helped me understand how to use the River City program and technology	4.6	4.3	0.34
I felt comfortable with the curriculum after the professional development	4.5	4.1	0.25
The training materials were clear and easy to understand	4	4.1	0.35
The training sessions were clear and easy to understand	4.6	4.1	0.13
The River City professional development was a waste of time	1.1	1.9	0.07

The first conclusion to be drawn from Table 1 is that overall the teachers found the professional development very useful. On average, all teachers, regardless of who trained them, agreed with the statements that the TPD helped them. And, based on a t-test, the first five statements showed no significant differences between the two different groups. However, there was a small difference between the groups on the response to "The *River City* professional development was a waste of time." The researcher-led group disagreed strongly with this statement on average (mean=1.1) while the trainer-led group also disagreed but less strongly on average (mean=1.9). The t-test between these two groups of responses shows a borderline significance (p<.07). While we intend to follow this as the remaining

---

[1] One teacher in the trainer group responded to all questions with a 5 including the reverse statements. As a result, that teacher's data was removed from the analysis.

surveys are analyzed to see if the trend continues, the difference is very small and still indicates that all teachers found the professional development very helpful.

The quantitative analysis indicated few differences between the groups, and the open-ended comments are similarly alike. Both groups felt that the TPD prepared them and helped them feel "comfortable" with the project. In addition, they both specifically mentioned that the hands-on piece was the most useful, "The time spent actively exploring the software in the context of the training was the most valuable time in my opinion."

Likewise, comments from both groups mentioned the need for more support on various teacher aspects (paperwork and control tools). While we tried to make the Teacher Dashboard user-friendly, there are a lot of technical pieces to cover. Further, we realized that 8 hours is simply not enough time to cover the *River City* curriculum, technology, and dashboard functionality. Therefore, we are revising our professional development and support materials to reflect what we have learned to date.

While we caution that these results are preliminary, we nonetheless offer the following thoughts about teacher professional development in the context of scaling up.

- Trainers can be trained to conduct TPD successfully in a minimal amount of time;
- In contrast to our initial hypothesis, teachers do not appear to prefer trainers to researchers;
- Initial stages of scaling up require flexibility and options in planning the professional development models;
- Hands-on activities are highly valued by teachers;
- Solo online professional development is not as effective as experiences that provide structure and personal contact;
- Continuing support beyond the professional development experience is helpful;
- Logistical tools such as our teacher dashboard can overwhelm teachers unless careful structure and training are provided.

CLASS SIZE: CONDITION FOR SUCCESS 2

Research has shown that low achieving students and students from low socioeconomic backgrounds perform better academically when in smaller sized classes (Akerhielm, 1995; Boozer & Rouse, 2001). Boozer and Rouse (2001) found class size to "account for anywhere from 18% to 47% of the difference in African-American and white test score gains between the 8th and 10th grades, and potentially all of the difference in Hispanic and white test score gains between the 8th and 10th grades." Reducing class size requires that schools have available classroom space, access to qualified teachers, and money to pay for increased salaries and resources. The state of California has spent over 8 billion dollars in an effort to reduce class size (Sack, 2002). Our ruggedized design takes into consideration the fact that reducing class size is a complex issue in education that not every school is able to address successfully. Therefore, robust designs that not only retain effectiveness with large class sizes, but that might help mitigate the deleterious effects of many students per teacher are important for scalability.

Robust design solutions

In school settings where students are unaccustomed to exploratory learning and student-centered curricula, or where large class sizes make individualized instruction difficult, absence of embedded guidance in computer-based learning environments can pose powerful barriers to success (Brush & Saye, 2000). In an attempt to ameliorate issues of large class size, we have created an Individualized Guidance System (IGS) embedded in the *River City* MUVE environment. The IGS assists students in making sense of the complexity of the virtual worlds and scaffolds each student's explorations (Figure 5).

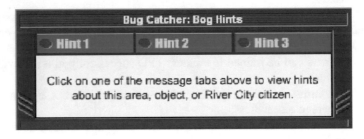

Figure 5: Individualized Guidance System (IGS)

Constructivist theorists believe students benefit from embedded guidance in exploratory learning environments that provides them with tools to build and test hypotheses (Jonassen, 1991; Lebow, 1993). To offer customized guidance, the *River City* IGS utilizes extensive data collected in real-time on each student's in-world activities. The guidance offered by the IGS consists of reflective prompts about the students' own learning in the world, with the content of the messages based on in-world events and basic event histories of each student.

To create the ruggedized IGS, all the items with which students can interact have been programmatically tagged with identification codes. Every time a student clicks on an object or "speaks" to a *River City* citizen, a record of the event is stored. The cumulative record of events results in a personalized history for each student. A guidance model, operated by an invisible software agent, is triggered after each student interaction event in the MUVE. A subset of events is associated with guidance scripts, and the guidance model uses these scripts to offer a specific selection of messages to each student. The scripts contain a set of rules for selecting guidance, based on a student's history of interactions with objects and citizens.

The following brief scenarios offer examples of the kind of guidance messages a student might receive, along with an explanation of how the guidance model individualizes guidance messages (Nelson, 2005).

Guidance example 1: Akiko enters *River City* for the first time. Through her avatar, she wanders around the town for several minutes to get her bearings. The first building she enters is the hospital. When she clicks on the admissions chart in the hospital, the Individualized Guidance System appears in the upper right-hand corner of the MUVE web pane with the title "Admissions Chart Guidance." Below this headline are three buttons, "Hint 1", "Hint 2", and "Hint 3". Clicking on the first hint button, a message appears in the guidance system window stating, "What kinds of symptoms do you see in the chart?" Clicking on the second hint button reveals the message "Where do most of the sick people live?" Clicking on the third button reveals the message "Is there anything about this hospital that is different than the ones you have seen?"

Guidance model methods: When Akiko clicks on the hospital admissions chart, she triggers a guidance event. The guidance model uses an identification tag associated with the event to add the fact that it was triggered to Akiko's personal history, and to look for any guidance scripts associated with the event. Finding that there is a script associated with the event, the model runs it. Because Akiko has not triggered this event before, and there are no relevant events recorded in her personal history, three default guidance message links are displayed.

Guidance Example 2: The next day, Akiko re-enters *River City* and explores the tenements, asking questions of a couple of residents. She then returns to the hospital. This time, when she clicks on the hospital admissions chart, a new set of messages is available. Clicking on hint button 1 reveals a message stating, "Welcome back, Akiko. I noticed that you have talked to some of sick tenement residents. How many people are sick from that area?" Clicking on button 2 reveals the message, "Last time you were in the hospital, you talked with the doctor. What does she have to say this time?" Clicking on the third link reveals the message "Have the symptoms of the patients changed since last time?"

Guidance model methods: The model agent records all tenement interactions and events to Akiko's personal history. It also checks for guidance scripts associated with the interactions, and shows messages as necessary. When Akiko returns to the hospital and clicks on the admissions chart, the agent records the event and runs the guidance script. The guidance script contains rules for three individualized messages. Akiko's previous visit to the tenement and her past interaction with the doctor causes two of individualized messages to appear. The third individualized message appears because the season in the virtual town has changed from fall to winter.

The IGS provides access to three individualized scaffolds per location, object, or citizen in *River City*. To accomplish this, each guidance script in the IGS contains three default messages and rules for the creation of three individualized messages. Consequently, each student has access to some combination of three individualized or default guidance messages for each interaction event or location in *River City*. The IGS does not automatically show specific guidance content, but instead displays "hint" buttons linked to guidance messages (Figure 5). To view guidance messages, students need to click on these hint buttons. In this way, we are able to monitor IGS usage levels and patterns.

Guidance system implementation

In a large-scale pilot implementation of the IGS conducted in 2005, we found a positive link with learning outcomes for students who accessed the individualized guidance system (Nelson, 2005). Students with access to a "high guidance" version of the system who viewed more guidance messages earned higher score gains on the science content test, on average, than those who viewed less hints. In addition, we found an interaction between gender and guidance use. Girls using the guidance system outperformed boys, on average, at each level of guidance message viewing (Figure 6).

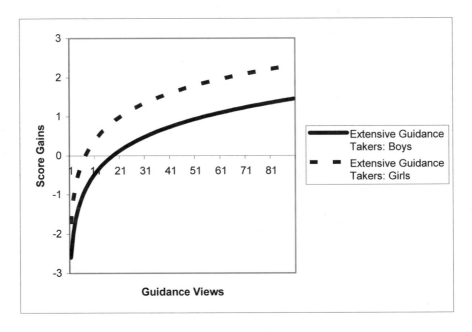

Figure 6: The fitted relationship between levels of guidance system use and content test score gains by students exposed to extensive levels of guidance who chose to "take up" the guidance at least one time in a MUVE-based curriculum, by gender (n=272).

While there is nothing our group can do to reduce the number of students present in the classes taking part in the *River City* project, through the design and deployment of individualized guidance within the virtual environment, we can alleviate some of the problems associated with learning in large classes. Based on our early positive results, we are now implementing the IGS on a wide scale, and will analyze the system to see if our initial findings are reconfirmed on a large scale.

While our robust design strategies aimed at improving teacher preparation and mitigating the negative effects of large class size are useful approaches to scaling, little can be accomplished if participating students are not engaged in the innovation. Consequently, design strategies aimed at increasing student engagement and motivation are important for successful implementation in multiple educational contexts.

Student autonomy and optimal level of challenge (sometimes referred to as competence) have been shown to be critical elements in students' motivation for and engagement in learning (de Charms, 1968; Malone & Lepper, 1987; Ryan & Deci, 2000; Lepper & Henderlong, 2000; Clarke, et al., 2006). In past implementations of our *River City* curriculum, we have designed elements based on these concepts to help boost and maintain student motivation (Dede, Nelson, Ketelhut, Clarke, and Bowman, 2004). For example, to increase girls' motivation and interest in science, we designed key figures in the MUVE curriculum to be female. We also have used historic tenements in *River City* to involve students of low socioeconomic status; they find a strong resemblance in living conditions and disease factors between their own housing and this historically accurate poor part of town.

Robust design solutions

As one example of ways our research team continues to ruggedize our design to cultivate and maintain student motivation, we have added the ability for a student's avatar to gain special "powers" that reward achievement of various curricular objectives with enhanced capabilities in the MUVE, each linked to academic content. In commercial multi-player games such as the popular "World of Warcraft", the attainment of special powers with greater capabilities is a major force in participant engagement (http://www.worldofwarcraft.com). In educational gaming environments, it is important to keep motivational elements such as the achievement of special powers closely associated with the learning goals of the curriculum, to enhance student engagement while avoiding distracting them with extraneous 'eye candy'.

Consequently, following a design-based research model, we have focused our efforts on a round of rapid prototyping of a *River City* powers system. This system consists of a back-end Powers Goal Achievement Monitoring Engine (P-GAME) and a powers mansion with hidden rooms containing access to extra curricular material.

To keep our P-GAME system centered on the learning goals of *River City*, we first analyzed the kind of curricular objectives we wanted students to achieve in order to earn special powers. In our research with the *River City* curriculum, two umbrella learning objectives are (1) forming and testing hypotheses about the causes of illness in the virtual city, and (2) developing scientific inquiry skills in a realistic, cooperative context. Within these broad objectives, there are a large number of procedural and knowledge-based tasks that students need to perform. These include:

- Clicking on in-world pictures, signs, and charts to gather data;
- Asking questions of *River City* residents (computer controlled agents);
- Using virtual inquiry tools such water sampling stations, bug catchers, fecal testers, and an environmental health meter;
- Interacting with team members via text-based chat and a shared online notepad;
- Seeking guidance from an individualized "Hints Machine"; and
- Using an interactive map to locate themselves in the environment and teleport to various locations.

Having identified the main curricular tasks within the overarching learning objectives, we set about designing a back-end system that would monitor the achievement of these tasks and assign powers upon their completion. This P-GAME system could keep track of the activities of all students in the MUVE and grant powers continuously to those who successfully achieved them.

With a socio-constructivist focus on collaborative knowledge building, students complete the *River City* curriculum in small teams of 3-4 members. Consequently, we wished to promote cooperative achievement of in-world curricular tasks by teams, rather than completion of all tasks by individual students. Therefore, in the design of the P-GAME system, we created the requirement that each member of a team of students complete some proportion of the tasks required to achieve powers in a given world. By dividing requirements among team members, we could encourage teams to "share the load" in terms of data gathering, and to communicate with each other as they worked through the curriculum.

With the P-GAME system, the research team had great flexibility over the assignment of curricular tasks. We could assign different sets of tasks in each world, on a team-by-team basis, and/or on a time-specific basis. In the year one pilot testing, we performed a blanket assignment of task menus for all teams, but varied the specific tasks in each of the four worlds in which powers were enabled. In future implementations, we could randomly assign varying sets of powers tasks, with the sets putting different levels of focus on specific types of team-based activity we wish to promote.

While the technical details of the operation of the P-GAME system are fairly arcane, Table 2 presents a basic description of how the system operates.

Table 2: P-GAME operation

Student actions	P-GAME action
Students log-in to a *River City* World	P-GAME records their entry and notes which other team members are present
A student performs an in-world action	P-GAME checks to see if the action is in the list of Powers tasks for that team. If so, it checks to see if that task has already been completed. If not, it records completion of the task by the student.
Students continue to perform in-world actions	P-GAME follows task-checking (see above). As each 'node' (collection of related tasks within a larger required task) is completed, P-GAME records the achievement of the larger task.
A student on a team completes the final task required for achievement of powers	P-GAME follows task-checking, notes that all tasks required for achievement of powers have been completed, and awards powers to the entire team.
Students who have achieved powers continue to perform in-world actions	P-GAME notes that this team has achieved powers and does not perform task-checking

Powers Mansion. In conjunction with the design and development of the P-GAME system, we designed a collection of powers that teams could achieve within the worlds. Our team spent a great deal of time analyzing the kinds of powers we wanted to award students. We used the model of commercial game design in which the achievement of powers is often tightly related to the narrative and context of a given game. For example, powers are a common feature of Massively Multi-Player Online Role-Playing Games (MMORPG). The most popular of these MMORPGs have players inhabiting virtual worlds with a fantasy theme and storyline. Players begin at a relatively low rank in the society of the game, and work their way up through completion of 'quests' (game-related collections of tasks). In the highly successful MMORPG "World of Warcraft", players complete quests to achieve powers and skills that directly enhance their ability to interact with the environment and continue through the storyline of the game.

To accomplish something similar in *River City*, we centered our powers narrative on a specific location inside the world: the powers mansion. This mansion (Figure 7) was designed as a somewhat spooky building that is initially closed to all students. When students who have not achieved powers visit the mansion in the October 1878 world, an undertaker greets them on the front porch, informing them that they may not yet enter the building. Along side of the mansion, all students see a graveyard with a collection of tombstones that grows with the passage of time.

Figure 7: Powers Mansion exterior

In each of the first four *River City* worlds (October, January, April, and July), achievement of powers opens up a new floor to explore inside the *River City* mansion. When a team of students achieves powers for a given world, they are automatically teleported to the front of the mansion, congratulated on gaining access to a new room in the house, and invited to enter. Inside each newly opened room in the mansion, students find a number of special tools or objects that allow them to gather additional information related to the events taking place in the city. For example, when students gain access to the first floor of the mansion, they enter a room that looks like a museum gallery (Figure 8). In the gallery, they see several objects along the wall. One of these is a special interactive map that allows students to check on the health of all residents of the city. A table features a stack of a child's marbles. When students click on the marbles, they see a *River City* resident's diary. This diary reveals the thoughts and feelings of a boy who lives in the town and also reveals more clues about what is happening to the residents.

It is important to note that, although achievement of powers provides access to additional information about the town, its residents, and the diseases affecting the area, it is not necessary to earn powers to form hypotheses and complete the curriculum. We designed the system of powers in an effort to motivate students across a spectrum of classroom settings, without 'punishing' those students who did not achieve powers.

Following our overall design-based research strategy, we will pilot the Powers System and database in fall 2006 and will continue to adjust the technical and curricular aspects of the system based on feedback from students, teachers, and technical support personnel. We are hopeful that by integrating a system shown to increase and maintain student motivation in the commercial gaming world, we can similarly boost engagement in our educational environment.

Figure 8: First Floor (October Powers)

CONCLUSION

We do not expect our current robust-design strategies to produce MUVE- based interventions that perform better than our previous treatments do under ideal conditions, since our previous treatments are designed for classrooms that have all the necessary conditions for success. The advantages of ruggedized interventions may well be weaknesses under better circumstances; for example, high levels of support for learner help and engagement that aid unengaged pupils with low prior preparation could well be intrusive overhead for better-prepared, already motivated students. This research is designed to explore whether robust-design can produce the educational equivalent of plant strains tailored to harsh conditions that are productive where the usual version of that plant would wither and die.

Also, the robust-design approach has intrinsic limits, as some essential conditions that affect the success of an educational innovation cannot be remediated through ruggedizing. As an illustration of an essential condition for success whose absence no design strategy can remediate, for *River City* implementations in some urban sites, student attendance rates at classes typically averaged about 50% prior to the intervention. Although attendance in science class improved during the implementation of the curriculum, an encouraging measure of its motivational effectiveness through robust-design, clearly the *River City* MUVE nonetheless had little value for those students who never experienced it due to their absence from school during its enactment. Further, in the shadow of high stakes testing and accountability measures mandated by the federal "No Child Left Behind legislation", persuading schools to complete a 20 class-period intervention is very difficult. Essential conditions for success such as student presence and district willingness to implement pose challenges beyond what can be overcome by the best robust-designs.

However, design-based researchers can still get some leverage on these essential factors. For example, the *River City* MUVE curriculum is engaging for students and teachers, uses standards-based content and skills linked to high stakes tests, and shows strong outcomes with sub-populations of concern to schools worried about making adequate yearly progress across all their types of students. These capabilities help surmount issues of student involvement and district interest, giving our intervention traction in settings with low student attendance and a focus on test-preparation.

REFERENCES

Akerhielm, K. (1995) Does class size matter? *Economics of Education Review, 14*, 3 (September), 229-241.

Boozer, M., & Rouse, C. (2001). Intraschool variation in class size: Patterns and implications, *Journal of Urban Economics, 50*, 1 (July), 163-189.

Borko, H. (2004). Professional development and teacher learning: Mapping the terrain. *Educational Researcher, 33*(8), 3-15.

Brush, T., & Saye, J. (2000). Implementation and evaluation of a student-centered learning unit: A case study. *Educational Technology Research & Development, 48*(3), 79-100.

deCharms, R. (1968). *Personal causation.* New York: Academic Press.

Clarke, J., Dede, C., Ketelhut, D., & Nelson, B. (2006). A design-based research strategy to promote scalability for educational innovations. *Educational Technology, 46*(3), 27-36.

Clarke, J. & Dede, C. (2006). Robust designs for scalability. Paper presented at the AECT Research Symposia, Bloomington, IN.

Dede, C. (2006). Scaling Up: Evolving innovations beyond ideal settings to challenging contexts of practice. In R.K. Sawyer (Ed.), *Cambridge handbook of the learning sciences*, pp. 551-566. Cambridge, England: Cambridge University Press.

Dede, C. (2004) *Design for defenestration: A strategy for scaling up promising research-based innovations.* Chicago, IL: NORC.

Dede, C., Honan, J., & Peters, L., Eds. (2005). *Scaling up success: Lessons learned from technology-based educational innovation.* New York: Jossey-Bass.

Dede, C., Nelson, B., Ketelhut, D., Clarke, J., & Bowman, C. (2004). Design-based research strategies for studying situated learning in a multi-user virtual environment. *Proceedings of the 2004 International Conference on Learning Sciences*, pp. 158-165. Mahweh, NJ: Lawrence Erlbaum.

Jonassen, D. H. (1991). Objectivism versus constructivism: Do we need a new philosophical paradigm? *Educational Technology Research & Development, 39*(3), 5-14.

Ketelhut, D., Clarke, J., Dede, C., Nelson, B., & Bowman, C. (2005). Inquiry teaching for depth and coverage via multi-user virtual environments. Paper presented at the National Association for Research in Science Teaching Conference, Dallas.

Killeen, K. M., Monk, D. H., & Plecki, M. L. (2002). School district spending on professional development: Insights available from national data (1992-1998). *Journal of Education Finance, 28*(1), 25-49

Perkins, D. (1992). *Smart schools.* New York: The Free Press.

Lebow, D. (1993). Constructivist values for instructional systems design: Five principles toward a new mindset. *Educational Technology Research & Development, 41*(3), 4-16.

Lepper, M., & Henderlong, J. (2000). Turning "play" into "work" and "work" into "play": 25 Years of research on intrinsic versus extrinsic motivation. In *Intrinsic and extrinsic motivation: The search for optimal motivation and performance* (pp. 257-307). San Diego, Calif.: Academic.

Maldonado, L. (2002). K-12 professional development: Effective professional development: Findings from research. College Entrance Examination Board. Available: http://apcentral.college board.com/repository/ap05_profdev_effectiv_41935.pdf [2006, July 1].

Malone, T. W., & Lepper, M. R. (1987). Making learning fun: A taxonomy of intrinsic motivations for learning. In R. E. Snow & M. J. Farr (Eds.), *Aptitude, learning, and instruction: III. Conative and affective process analyses* (pp. 223-253). Hillsdale, NJ: Erlbaum.

Moore, G.A. (1999). *Crossing the chasm* (Rev. ed.). New York: Harper Perennial.

National Research Council. (1996). *National science education standards: Observe, interact, change, learn.* Washington, DC: National Academy Press.

Nelson, B., Ketelhut, D. J., Clarke, J., Bowman, C., & Dede, C. (2005). Design-based research strategies for developing a scientific inquiry curriculum in a multi-user virtual environment. *Educational Technology, 45*(1), 21-27.

Nelson, B. (2005). *Investigating the impact of individualized, reflective guidance on student learning in an educational multi-user virtual environment.* Unpublished Dissertation, Harvard University.

Ryan, R. & Deci, E. (2000). Self-determination theory and the facilitation of intrinsic motivation, social development, and well-being. *American Psychologist, 55*, 1, 68-78.

Sack, J.L. (2002). Smaller classes under scrutiny. In *Calif. Schools. Education Week, 21*, Issue 24 (February 27).

Wiske, M.S., & Perkins, D. (2005). Dewey goes digital: Scaling up constructivist pedagogies and the promise of new technologies. In C. Dede, J. Honan, & L. Peters, Eds, *Scaling up success: Lessons learned from technology-based educational innovation.* New York: Jossey-Bass.

Brian C. Nelson
Arizona State University

Diane Jass Ketelhut
Temple University

Jody Clarke, Ed Dieterle, & Chris Dede
Harvard University

Ben Erlandson
Arizona State University

KENNETH E. HAY

BUILDING THE WRONG MODEL

Opportunities for Game Design [1]

INTRODUCTION

Even the most highly educated among us have and maintain profound misconceptions of the world. For example, as highlighted in the film A Private Universe (Schneps & Sadler, 1988), 21 of 23 Harvard graduates described profound misconceptions about the cause of the seasons. Studies conducted across age groups reveal that these misconceptions do not fade or disappear as students grow older; in many cases, they strengthen, become highly resilient to change and are unaffected by traditional instruction. This is because they are not simply incorrect information that can be replaced; rather they are rival models of the phenomenon that almost always include some "true" elements and in some way "work." Traditional classroom-based instruction is inadequate at confronting misconceptions because it seldom requires learners to confront the implications of their thinking. Understanding the implications of your thinking is a hallmark of learning the deep structure of a domain. A particularly powerful way to understand your thinking is to "enact" your thinking through the construction of a computational model which requires the integration of facts, concepts and relationships of a phenomenon. Further, a deep understanding of a particular domain requires you to reconcile the resulting model to the facts of the phenomenon. This chapter will present software and research findings on our Virtual Solar System (VSS) project and the use of a novel way of confronting misconceptions through the learners' construction of "wrong" 3D dynamic models in the domain of astronomy. These "wrong" models are not simply based on a lack on knowledge, but rather are models learners have that contain "true" elements and on some level "work." This chapter will then present the issues of developing the architectural and social affordances of a 3D environment that enables learners to create these types of "wrong" models and their implication for learning. Further, the chapter will bridge the world of school-based inquiry-based learning activities to the world of interactive computer games to explore how these insights can inform game design for serious learning. In particular, it will explore the MMORG World of Warcraft and the construction of characters through talent-builds, spells, and the purchase of gear as a type of model-building activity. Finally, the paper will engage a comparison between the WOW and VSS modeling activities as a possible way it exploit the learning potential of modeling building in game contexts.

B. . Shelton, D. A. Wiley (eds.), Educational Design & Use of Computer Simulation Games, 233–263.

VISION

...One group of students narrowed their investigation to ants. Unlike the hundreds of Ms. Perez-Drake's students over the years who simply drew pictures to memorize ant anatomy, these students used an animation simulator. With this tool, the students created a three-dimensional moving ant model. When they forgot to include all the limbs, their creation hobbled jerkily. This humorously reinforced basic facts about movement and structure...

(CEO Forum School Technology and Readiness Report, June 2000)

The CEO Forum's image of 3D modeling is both visionary and provocative, and it represents a strategy clearly aimed at prominent goals in standards-based reform efforts (i.e. AAAS, 1993 & NRC, 1996). It addresses the three key learning goals identified in the *Inquiry and the National Science Education Standards* (2000): 1) conceptual understandings in science; 2) abilities to perform scientific inquiry; and 3) understandings about inquiry. Students develop conceptual understandings of ants' physiology and biomechanics as they build, test, evaluate, and use models in inquiry, thereby deepening their understanding of the roles modeling plays in science. The most visionary and provocative aspect of the CEO Forum's image is that the isomorphic model is constructed in a 3D-computer environment – not the simple drawings of Ms. Perez-Drake's past students or the abstract formalisms of the scientist. The power of the 3D ant is that it can incorporate a variety of abstract formalisms of ant biomechanics to "drive" the model both in its constructive abilities formalize ones thinking and the demonstrative abilities to illustrate the implications of that thinking.

During the past 8 years we have developed powerful modeling-based pedagogies and tools for learner creation of isomorphic 3D models and visualizations in weather (Hay, 1999a), astronomy (Hay and Barab, 2001, Barab, Hay, Barnett, & Squire, 2001), and animal behavior (Hay, Crozier, & Barnett, 2000). These pedagogies and tools combine to create powerful learning environments that promote significant learning in the deep structure of a domain (i.e. Barab, et.al., 1998).

NEED

During the recent past, numerous studies [116 since 1988 according to Pfundt & Duit's (1998) bibliography] have reported difficulties in student understanding in many domains. The example used as a basis for argument within this chapter will be on basic astronomical phenomena (Wandersee, Mintzes, & Novak, 1990). A 1988 survey conducted by the Public Opinion Laboratory at Northern Illinois University determined that only 45% of US adults knew that the Earth orbited the Sun and that it took one year to complete the trip (Fraknoi, 1996). Zeilik et al. (1997) note that the most common student misconceptions were related to eclipses, speed of light, inverse square law for light, gravitation/Newton's third law, seasonal position of the sun at noon, moon's rotation, relative motion of sun/stars, and the reasons for seasons. Students use a variety of alternate conceptions to explain these phenomena (Baxter, 1989).

Introductory astronomy courses focus specifically on the physics' concepts of light, motion, and force. Research continues to document student misconceptions in understanding basic concepts about light (Bendall, Goldberg, & Galili, 1993; Fetherstonhaugh, & Treagus, 1992; Langley, Ronen, & Eylon, 1997), motion (Halloun, & Hestenes, 1985a, 1985b), and rotational motion and gravity (Berg, & Brouwer, 1991; Treagust, & Smith, 1989). Studies conducted across age groups reveal that alternate conceptions do not fade or disappear as students grow older; in many cases, they strengthen and become highly resilient to change. Alternative methods are needed to provide the opportunity to develop conceptions that are more consistent with a scientifically accepted view (Eylong & Linn, 1988; Smith, diSessa, & Roschelle, 1993).

Among the most relevant to National Science Standards are the misconceptions about the phases of the moon (i.e. Sadler, 1998). These include two prominent misconceptions: 1. Phases are caused by the Moon moving in and out of the Earth's shadow and 2. Phases are caused by its' own light source. Although the VSS project encompassed an entire undergraduate laboratory course, these misconceptions will be the focus of this chapter.

MODELING IN SCIENCE EDUCATION

Models provide powerful ways to represent understanding; they can be exploited by scientists and learners alike. Our approach to research is consistent with several researchers developing and studying modeling technologies and pedagogies in science education (Jackson, Stratford, Krajcik, & Soloway, 1994, Linn, diSessa, Pea, & Songer, 1994, Penner, Lehrer, & Schauble, 1998, White & Frederiksen, 1998, etc.). Two prominent approaches have emerged: simulation and model building. In simulations, models are pre-developed and serve as a surrogate for the real world. The *SimCity* series is a popular example; *ThinkerTools* (White & Frederiksen, 1998) is another that has been rigorously studied. In such simulation programs, students use models to conduct systematic inquiry much as they would in the real world. The advantages of simulation-based inquiry over real-world inquiry are that everyday pragmatics of time, distance, safety and the like can be overcome as students focus on collecting rich data sets for their inquiry. Additionally, simulations create opportunities to experiment with "what if" scenarios that are impossible in the real world.

A second rich history of research supports student model-building approaches (Feurzeig, 1988; Roberts & Barclay, 1988; Roth, 1992, Tinker, 1993 & Ogborn, 2000). Students construct their own models either through physical means (i.e. Penner, Lehrer, & Schauble, 1998), model-building toolkits (i.e. Jackson et. al., 1994), or meta-modeling languages (i.e. Resnick, 1996). The act of model building allows students to engage in a design process (Jackson et. al, 1994; Lehrer, Horvath, & Schauble, 1994), which begins with a set of tentatively accepted theories that evolve into coherent understandings as represented in their models (Roth, 1996; Sabelli, 1994). Model building has been shown to force students to "make explicit their own conceptions of phenomena" (Confrey & Doerr, 1994), validate their resultant model, and iterate the process to develop increasingly richer conceptions.

VIRTUAL REALITY IN LEARNING

Virtual reality (VR) refers to synthetic, computer-based, three-dimensional interactive worlds. Researchers have been exploring the unique features of VR environments and their interaction with student cognition and learning in diverse high-end, laboratory-based projects. VR has been used to explore Newton's Laws, electrostatics, and molecular structures in the ScienceSpace Project (Dede et al., 1999), to explore how the earth can be round when it looks flat in the Round Earth Project (Johnson, et. al., 1999), and to explore the ecology of Puget Sound in the Virtual Puget Sound Project (Windschitl & Winn, 2000). Each project explored scientific concepts where 3D models were important to conceptual development, and each used VR's ability to shrink or expand 3D distances to make them easy to manipulate. VR's capacity to "reify" unseen forces via 3D images was demonstrated in both electrostatic forces as well as wind and water current vectors. Salzman, Dede, and Loftin (1999) concluded that students' ability to move in three dimensions between egocentric and exocentric points of view was advantageous to learning the models. Each project integrated simulation models in science learning environments and implemented VR to more accurately present the phenomena to the student.

VR MODELING-BASED INQUIRY

The core innovation of the VSS project builds on a specific pedagogical strategy, Modeling-based Inquiry, and an isomorphic 3D modeling environment (Astronomicon) to support the process. Modeling-based Inquiry focuses on scientific methodologies involving phenomena that are difficult or impossible for scientists to study empirically. Scientists use computational models as both the source of their data and to bolster their conclusions. Modeling-based Inquiry puts the student in the position of scientist (see Table 1).

The Modeling-based Inquiry (Hay, 1999b) approach combines the instructional benefits of inquiry-based and constructionist approaches. Virtual reality technology offers a unique and powerful way for students to refine their understandings. VR creates a relatively seamless and accessible transition between understanding through students' own observations of the phenomena or accounts of the phenomena in secondary sources (textbook, websites, etc.) and their individual models. Further, because models are built with the inherent goal of

236

addressing questions, design is guided by the knowledge and understanding needed to address their questions. This stands in contrast to typical modeling pedagogies that rely on teachers constraining the unattainable goal of "realism." In the data collection phase of Modeling-based Inquiry projects, students use their model as a surrogate for the real phenomena. However, unlike simulation-based inquiry pedagogies, students themselves build the model and either understand its inner workings or are in the process of understanding them. This familiarity with their model allows students to warrant their tentative conclusions using explicit assumptions reflected in their model. They act and reason as scientists as they develop the capacity to assess the strengths and limitations of both their own as well as others' models. This chapter presents research comparing three different curricula based on a Modeling-based Inquiry approach (Conceptual Coherence Curriculum, Historical Recapitulation Curriculum, and the Alternative Theory Curriculum).

Table 1. Modeling Based Inquiry

1. *Begin with an inquiry question.*
2. *Plan the model & collect data.*
3. *Create a model of the phenomenon*
4. *Validate the model and revise if necessary.*
5. *Use the model as a source of data to address the original question.*
6. *Visualize data to explore relationships.*
7. *Develop a warranted conclusion.*
8. *Present conclusion to colleagues.*

VIRTUAL SOLAR SYSTEM PROJECT

The Virtual Solar System (VSS) Project (Hay & Barab, 1998) is an undergraduate education reform effort in the astronomy department at the University of Georgia (UGA). Learners create virtual 3D computational models of the solar system within a Modeling-based Inquiry pedagogical framework. In summer 1999, a partnership was formed with Cybernet, that allowed us to build on their initial larger research and development investment.

As a result, we built a scaffolded VR creation tool, *Astronomicon*. This is a model partnership that allows us to distribute the costs and risks associated with developing innovative core technologies. Astronomicon is the cornerstone of the Astronomy 1010 lab, which introduces students to Modeling-based Inquiry. From the outset of the course, students address questions through the construction of virtual solar system models. This following sections focus on a subset of this course involving questions related to light (phases) and planetary motion which is one of several topics covered in the larger project.

RATIONALE

We have found it useful to describe model-building environments at two levels: isomorphic and behavioral. Our environments are scaffolded to enable learners to easily create isomorphic models of the objects they are studying. In our Virtual Solar System project students easily create 3D photorealistic Earth or Jupiter representations, and in the Virtual Gorilla Project, students create a silver-back mountain gorilla just as readily.

These instantly accessible representations are isomorphic to their real world referent, but they do not have an underlying behavioral model that makes them "run." We have found that, due to the photo-realistic nature of the representations, novice model builders have stronger transfer between their models and the real world, as discussed below. The deeper conceptual work involves behavioral modeling, where the deep structure of the model is created. Learners need a range of behavioral modeling tools (BMT) as their conceptual understanding emerges and evolves.

1. Isomorphic Models

Analogies are a cornerstone of learning and discovery; the learning environments we have built are essentially analogy-building environments. The power of analogy in thinking is first evident before three years of age when children see pictures and scale models as representing the real object (DeLoache, 1989). At this stage, young children are strongly influenced by surface information in an analogy (Keil & Batterman, 1984; Kemler, 1983; Shepp, 1978; Smith & Kemler, 1977). This tendency interferes with the true goal and power of analogy to promote understanding that "focuses on shared systematic relational structure" (Gentner & Toupin, 1986, p. 283). Nonetheless, surface features seem to be critical for novices, while surface similarities play important roles for all learners. Initial understanding based on surface similarities and analogies can improve transfer. When analogies have a high correlation between surface similarity and structure similarity [what Gentner & Toupin (1986) labeled "high transparency"] transfer accuracy in analogies improves at all levels (Reed, 1985; Ross, 1986). Students begin to understand analogies based on surface similarities, providing the best transfer accuracy.

When viewing modeling as a specific form of analogy, similar research findings are reported. Penner et. al. (1997) found that when young students create physical models of an elbow (e.g., a Styrofoam ball instead of a hinge to model the elbow) they often focus on surface level features rather than the underlying function. Similarly, when initially creating planetary models in the VSS Project, students would first put a photorealistic texture onto generic white spheres to represent each planet. Next, they would enlarge or shrink the planets and the sun to sizes that "fit" with their understanding of the solar system (Hay & Barab, 2001). We found that, consistent with Sadler (1998), initial models are often highly inaccurate in terms of appropriate sizes and distances. We concur with Lehrer and Schauble (2000), however, that "similarity-based representations can give good initial purchase" to new modelers. When engaging novice model builders, the environment should, and indeed must, support their initial focus on surface similarities between reality and the model. The 3D photorealistic virtual models allow students to create isomorphic models as the basis for their scientific modeling. Isomorphic modeling helps learners to strengthen connections between models and phenomena under study.

Isomorphic modeling is beneficial in two ways. First, isomorphic modeling obviates the learner's need to attend to the surface features of a computational model. When learners constructed models within a generic VR construction tool (*CosmoWorld*), they tended to emphasize surface features (look, label, aesthetics, etc.) to the detriment of the underlying conceptual structure of the model (Hay & Barab, 2001). In our existing system it takes only a few clicks to create a photorealistic 3D planet, so attention quickly moves beyond surface features. Second, isomorphic modeling grounds subsequent behavioral modeling in a clear connection to the object being modeled. Thus, analogical transfer is improved.

Available modeling tools generally follow one of two paths. Tools such as *Logo, StarLogo, Boxer,* and *AgentSheet* exemplify "programming-based" modeling, while tools such as *Stella, Model-it,* and *Link-it* exemplify the "concept map-based" modeling. While essential in the development of modeling-based pedagogy, such environments have been criticized because they "do not help students connect their models to real-world concerns" (Forbus, Sherin, Carney, & Harris, 2000). In these environments it is difficult to see or understand the real world phenomenon being modeled. Low transparency, we hypothesize, initiates student thinking and modeling through the lens of generating programming code or connecting nodes and links instead of modeling a real world object. This approach can confound the underlying scientific concepts under study and result in little transferable knowledge. Programming per se is not necessarily inappropriate, but it is not where most novices will start thinking or where transfer will most likely take place. Some of these environments have incorporated the ability to use 2D graphical elements that look similar to the object in question (i.e. *StarLogo*[2]), some others have incorporated photorealistic backgrounds in which to conduct the modeling (i.e. *Model-it*[3]), and some do both (i.e. *Agentsheets*[4]). Nonetheless, these innovations are bound by the historic realities of what can be done on classroom level machines.

We have created and deployed 3D isomorphic modeling environments in three areas–weather, gorilla behavior, and astronomy–and tested them in studies (Hay, Marlino, & Holschuh, 2000, Hay, Crozier, & Barnett, 2000; & Hay & Barab, 2001). In each case, learners easily created photorealistic dynamic 3D models. We accomplished this by moving innovative 3D graphics hardware from high-end workstations during development and initial prototyping to the classroom-level machines prevalent in schools and universities today. We now have the technology to explore the cognitive and instructional benefits of isomorphic modeling in everyday settings, enabling greater access to the models and better transfer between individual student models and the real world.

2. Behavioral Models

Isomorphic modeling provides powerful mechanisms for model builders. However, the power and the goal of analogies and models lay in understanding the underlying "systematic relational structure" of what we refer to as the *behavioral model*. This aspect of the model defines attributes that enable the gorilla to walk or the Earth to orbit the Sun. They move learners developmentally from dependence on literal surface features to understanding analogies and models involving deeper, often underlying functional features. Put simply, deeper understanding evolves as the focus shifts from isomorphic to behavioral models.

Move from Isomorphic Models to Behavioral Models
The significance of isomorphic models is underscored by widely reported problems associated with students "getting stuck" or continuing to rely exclusively on surface features. For example, sustained focus on surface features interfered with students' conceptual understanding of physics problems (Chi, Feltovich, & Glaser, 1981, Larkin, 1983; Larkin et al., 1980). While we concur that many learners initially need to build models with surface features that approximate the real world (isomorphic models), they must move beyond surface features for complex learning to occur. However, this is a challenge for novice modelers. In building models of the elbow Lehrer and Schauble's (2000) found that at some point when students built a Styrofoam ball elbow, their focus on surface features created a conceptual dead-end that stymied further inquiry. Students needed to discard the Styrofoam models and start anew with different materials better suited to modeling functional features.

The flexible integration of our isomorphic and behavioral modeling environments precludes conceptual dead-ends by allowing learners to quickly create isomorphic models and transition to deeper issues. In our early work with the VSS Project, students would first put a photorealistic texture onto generic white spheres to represent each planet's surface appearance. However, later they found that white textures with latitude lines (a simply implemented change) were more valuable than the realistic textures for their inquiry into the seasons (Hay & Barab, 2001). This confirms Lehrer and Schauble's (2000) observation that as students gain skill and understanding, "the properties of resemblance that initially sustain them fall away." Representational systems are usually grounded in resemblance between the model and the world, but these representations typically "undergo fundamental transformations via inscriptions[5]" (Lehrer & Schauble, 2000).
Learners must evolve from their isomorphic models to models that reflect "higher-order relations" to guide ongoing inquiry. It is critical to differentiate the affordances of isomorphic modeling in model building from those in a simulation-

learning environment. In a model- building environment, the isomorphic properties create linkages between the real world and the model, keeping learners from becoming mired in a disconnected world of code or concept maps. Isomorphic modeling bridges reality and the underlying relationships represented in the model. In contrast, simulations emphasize "high fidelity" representations deemed fundamental to learning; an error in realism may lead learners to draw incorrect conclusions. In modeling environments, feature omission is acceptable and even expected, provided the features are not central to the current inquiry. "The focus is not on whether a particular model is right or wrong but the degree to which it is able to account for the phenomena as currently construed" (Penner, Lehrer, & Schauble, 1998).

The Cascade of Behavioral Models
The transformation of surface features into something useful to inquiry is the first necessary step but it is not sufficient in the evolution of models. Students should be involved in what Hestenes (1992) called the "modeling games" evident in the practices of scientists. These have variously been called "cascades of inscription" (Latour, 1990), "families of models" (Penner, et. al, 1997), and "a multiplicity of epistemic forms and games" (Collins & Ferguson, 1993). In an ideal cascade, the learner's activity should flow naturally from the surface features to the underlying behavioral model that represents the relational structures of the model. The key theoretical contribution of the proposed effort will be the refining and testing of different approaches to facilitate this transformation. Specifically, we pursue theoretical and technological insights that guide learners through the transformation from isomorphic to behavioral representations of scientific phenomena. The **first step** is to identify model elements that are unseen (i.e. forces in *Interactive Physics*) or unseeable (i.e. molecules in *ScienceSpace*). Unseen or unseeable elements are important not only because they represent much of the most interesting science, but also because they are difficult for learners and are linked to a wide range of scientific misconceptions (Pfundt & Duit, 1998). The key is that unseen or unseeable elements are grounded within isomorphic models - forces are applied to the molecules to make up "real" objects. The power of computational modeling is that these unseen or unseeable elements become reified (Winn, 2000) within the virtual environment, making them "visible" and subject to inquiry. Thus they become accessible and usable in students' models and influential in testing and refining their understanding. In our Virtual Solar System project, for example, learners visualize the orbital planes of the Earth and Moon – key elements in deepening their understanding of eclipses. In our atmospheric science project, learners used powerful 3D visualization tools to observe previously unseeable elements such as airflow in a global convection cell of the Walker Cell and the local convection cell of a thunderstorm cell.

The **second transformation** priority is ensuring that as isomorphic models evolve smoothly as increasingly complex models, understanding, and inquiry are

241

developed. Lehrer and Schauble (2000) discuss increasing complexity in cognitive terms: *representational systems, syntactic models,* and *hypothetical-deductive models.* Conversely, Hestenes (1996) characterizes increasing complexity in structural terms: *systemic, geometric, temporal,* and *interaction.* In our work with students building 3D solar system models, one particular case exemplifies this transformation. The student's goal was to create a moon orbiting earth. The software environment was a general purpose VRML modeling software designed for content developers. In his initial explorations, the student created an Earth and moon of an arbitrary size on a portion of the screen and found that he could grab the entire space as if it were a clear glass cube containing the Earth and moon. Almost accidentally, he found that, with quick click, drag, and release manipulations, he could grab and release the cube and the objects would continue to move — to spin somewhat like a top. The moment of inspiration was palpable and readily discerned. Because the cube was spinning at its center, the student began the quest to identify the center and place the earth at the center. He then asked the professor to demonstrate how to model the moon orbiting the earth. This started an important conversation around the strengths and weaknesses of the model. The experience started the student on the "cascades of inscriptions," or better yet the cascades of models, to a model that was considerably more mathematical. The learning environment must support a wide range of different types of underlying model building tool kits, starting with direct manipulations.

A **third step in transformation** is the exploration of rival models. It took thousands of years to move from a geocentric view of the solar system to a heliocentric one. In real world inquiry, this type of conceptual leap is difficult for learners — even when presented strong evidence contradicting the initial model (Chinn & Brewer, 1993). It is also problematic in modeling environments. Children generally struggle to generate competing models of a phenomenon (Grosslight, Unger, Jay, & Smith, 1991). The modeling environment must enable learners to easily create rival models in the same space. Whereas Penner, Leher, and Schauble's (1998) learners initially constructed non-isomorphic physical models using different "modeling materials," our modeling environment supports a multiplicity of modeling "epistemic forms and games" enabling "ruptures in understanding". Such ruptures require new tools for modeling, not simply incremental accumulation of new lines of code or nodes on a semantic/concept map.

Such 3D modeling tools can be used to test and validate alternative representations in the same environment. For example, two rival orbital models of earth can be put into the same solar system and tested; in doing so, learners naturally and authentically transform their understanding of planetary orbits from an intuitive explanation to an equation-based structure to a physics-based model. Specifically, students can create an Earth model, generate a hypothesized equation, and then insert a new model Earth and explore force and velocity vectors in an attempt to create a similar planetary orbit. The representation of multiple, but differently conceived, models could help learners transform their understanding of planetary motion. Modeling environments need to support "epistemic forms and games," but not by becoming a general purpose modeling language (e.g., Logo, StarLogo, Boxer, AgentSheets, etc.) or scaffolded construction kit (e.g., *Model-It, Stella*, etc.). The VSS software Astronomicon takes advantage of multiple modeling environments, enabling the co-existence of different "forms and games" that can be used to develop the underlying systematic relational structure underlying students' isomorphic models.

RESEARCH CONDITIONS

The finding presented here are apart of a larger research project looking at different versions of the 15-week lab using the same learning objectives, and same Modeling-based Inquiry approach; but with differing curricular themes, each with five modeling-based inquiry exercises and supporting technology features. For the purpose of this chapter we will focus on two of the three conditions, namely the Conceptual Coherence Condition (CC) and Alternative Theory Condition (AT), the Historic Recapitulation Condition (HR).

Conceptual Coherence Condition (CC)

The CC condition provides inquiry questions by following a "conceptual coherence" model. As typified in conventional curricular models and rooted in classical associationist models of learning, this condition starts with easier questions and modeling tasks and progresses to more difficult ones. An entire range of modeling tools is presented in a cafeteria style menu so that learners can select them according to the needs of the prescribed inquiry. Exercise 3: Phases occurred during weeks 7-9 of the semester and included inquiry questions about phases of the Moon, Venus, and Mars. The activity involved creating virtual models of the solar system with known facts about the planets and Sun's body characteristics and orbital characteristics. Students then used their model as a referent to study, observe, and collect data in the form of images and numeric data. One question also included creating a fictional Moon that was always in a Full Moon Phase.

Alternative Theory Condition (AT)

Sadler (1998) reports that students' progress through prototypical alternative conceptions of fundamental concepts in astronomy. He recommended instruction that follows from directed and explicit to alternative concepts to the scientifically accepted conception. The AT condition provided an ordered set of inquiry questions and modeling tools that support this path through alternative conceptions. The instructor dictated the type of modeling tools to be used with each question.

The curriculum was divided up into five modeling-based inquiry exercises. Exercise 4: Phases occurred during weeks 9-11 of the semester and included questions about Moon, Earth, superior planet and inferior planet phases. In the AT condition, three possible theories are supplied that answer the inquiry question. Two of these theories are based on empirically derived misconceptions of lunar phases found in the literature and one theory is the scientifically accepted one. This research focuses on the Modeling-based Inquiry question: What causes lunar phases? The three theories presented to the learners where:

1. Lunar phases are caused by the changing position of the Moon with respect to the Sun

2. Lunar phases are caused by a shadow from the Earth

3. Lunar phases are caused by its own light changing

Whereas the CC condition focused on the creation of a single model to answer a question, the AT condition focused on the creation of 3 alternative plausible models that may answer the question.

FINDINGS AND THE IMPLICATIONS FOR LEARNING GAME DESIGNS

The full set of findings are reported in Hay and Kim (2004); however, for the purposes of this chapter our pre/post tests findings showed that the AT condition was superior across all the implementations of all curricula through the two implementations of each curriculum. This establishes the powerful potential for explicitly building wrong models and comparing them to scientifically accepted models as a way of learning in 3D dynamic virtual environments. However, more importantly for game designers is the way in which the AT curriculum promoted learning, Here we will present the basic understandings, models, and images of phase that the students developed in these inquiries.

The phases of the Moon are caused by two basic notions: a point light source illuminates only half of a sphere and a changing viewing angle. In the solar system, the half of any sphere that faces the Sun is illuminated by the Sun. The *viewing angle* is formed by a light source (the Sun), a viewpoint (the Earth) and a viewing object (the Moon). As the Moon orbits the Earth in a 360-degree orbit, the viewing angle changes, which changes how much of the Moon's illuminated side we can see. In both conditions, students build models where they can see both the persistence of the half illuminated Moon and the changing angle. Below (See Figure 1) are the standard phases and how the students would see them in Astronomicon. The Phases are ordered in a standard way: Full Moon, Waning Gibbous, Waning Quarter, Waning Crescent, New Moon, Waxing Crescent, Waxing Quarter, and Waxing Gibbous.

Figure 1: Student Generated Data from the Three Different Phase Models

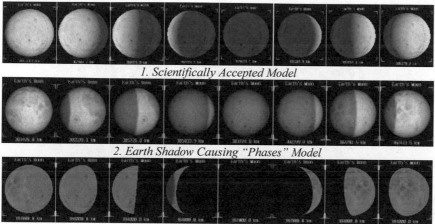

1. Scientifically Accepted Model

2. Earth Shadow Causing "Phases" Model

3. Moon's Own Light Source "Phases" Model

The CC students would build a model that would look like the Scientifically Accepted Model; as would the AT students when they built the model for Theory 1. AT students would also build separate models that would operationalize the moon moving in and out of the Earth's shadow on a monthly basis and create a Moon that has one light side and one dark side irrespective of a light source. The AT students must use the data they collect to prove that Theories 2 and 3 are incorrect. From the illustrations, the Earth's Shadow Model looks similar to the Scientifically Accepted Model; but on close inspection two major problems are revealed. First of all, on the waning phases, the light and dark sides are reversed from the correct model. Second, the shape of the dark side is convex instead of concave. This is due to the shape of the Earth and is most noticeable at the crescent phases. These are the key piece s of evidence necessary for students to reject Theory 2. The Moon's Own Light Source Theory 3 has some superficial visual differences, i.e. the light side is lighter and the dark side darker. The first piece of evidence is that there is always a different face of the Moon facing the Earth. One real Moon always faces the Earth. Another piece of evidence against this model becomes apparent when the student broadens the view of the waxing quarter phase (see Figure 2), where the Sun is revealed. The Sun appears in the top, left corner of the display.

Figure 2: Evidence that Theory 3 is Incorrect

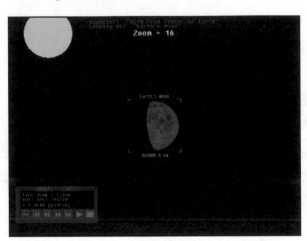

Students' understand that this visual indicates that it is daytime and that the Moon and Sun are tracking together throughout the day. This cannot happen in the real world; in fact, the moon should be in a New Moon phase if the theory was correct. With this theory, it is possible to have the Moon be in any conceivable phase at any time of day or night. Based on this evidence, students should reject Theory 3.

CHALLENGES OF CREATING MODELS OF MISCONCEPTIONS

This creation of the Alternative Theory unit created unique instructional and learning tool design challenges. Now there is nothing special about creating a "wrong" model with any open ended modeling tool from the most primitive programming language, to the most highly scaffolded modeling tool. Creating a wrong model can be accomplished by forgetting critical information, implementing incorrectly, adding erroneous information, etc. The challenge is designing a modeling tool that will enable students to create the *right* wrong model – i.e. models of *their* misconceptions. Furthermore, the construction of these wrong models has to be accomplished within a reasonable amount of instructional time. The use of programming languages requires a huge up front training cost and even then requires significant time to build each model and thus does not result in an appropriate learning/instructional ratio. Our goal was for each unit to be accomplished in 2-3 2½ hour class periods. This included all the steps in the modeling-based inquiry approach. The second learning tool design issue was that although misconceptions have correct elements, they are not completely coherent. These misconceptions often had some magical or bizarre elements, such as light bending or bouncing in an unexplained fashion. This led to certain misconceptions not be able to be modeled or at least modeled within the timeframe of the instructional unit. Modeling misconceptions often required new interface and modeling elements to the software. This lead to the final learning tool design issue. The modeling tool needed to provide an interface to both scientifically accepted modeling functionality and functionality based on misconceptions. This had to be done in ways that did not obscure the way learners understood the scientifically accepted models or make them harder to create.

On the level of the instructional unit, in the AT condition we created an overarching narrative for the students. They were a research director of an astronomical science center and they had 2-4 teams of scientists reporting to them different theories that would address the questions at hand (What causes phases of the moon?). The students would be presented with each theory and they had to create models that would represent each theory, validate the models (i.e. did the model have a full set of phases and was the period of the phases correct?), collect data from the model, and then accept one model and reject the others based on evidence.

GAME AND MODELS

With the back drop of this VSS research, we will now turn our attention to modeling within commercially available 3D virtual games. There is clearly a rising movement in education and training to seriously consider the potential of computerized dynamic 3D virtual games for the purposes of learning traditional content. The work of Gee (2003) demonstrates that there is powerful learning taking place within these environments and that the designers of these games employ principles that are consistent with currently learning theory. The rest of this chapter will look into the world of computer games and explore the potential of the games whose goals would more align with the goals of education. In particular, this chapter will look at the role of models and model-building within the computer game World of Warcraft (WOW), explore how gamers think and learn about models, and connect this back to the VSS research.

WORLD OF WARCRAFT

World of Warcraft (WOW) is the archetypal massively, multi-player, online role playing game (MMORPG). Blizzard, the company that produces WOW, recently broke all sales records with approximately 3.5 million copies release of the Burning Crusade extension in the first month of sales in early 2007. The worldwide subscription totals for WOW are now more that 8.5 million. Players sell their on-line charters for over $1000, in-world gold coins sell for real-world money, economists have analyzed the WOW economy and estimate it rivaling developed nations (Castronova, 2001). It has been estimated to take an average gamer over 750 hours to go from level 1 to level 70. Many, if not most, develop multiple characters as they explore WOW. This level of engagement blows away the traditional goal of a 40-100 hour gaming experience. The huge fan base has spawned enormous websites, forums, playing guides, talent calculators, gamer constructed mods, guild website, and general advice[6].

MODELS AND MODELING OF WORLD OF WARCRAFT

As the name implies World of Warcraft revolves around a basic interaction of killing an opponent. WOW's economy, social interactions, gear purchasing, score keeping, leveling, gathering resources, producing resources, consumable purchasing, resources allocation, logistics, character construction is focused and driven by the goal of killing just to kill, killing to loot, or killing to gain access to or control over a resource. However, what sets WOW apart from most other computer games is the diversity and importance of these other activities, that while driven by the need to kill to win, are only indirectly related to the actual killing an opponent and the relatively large part of the in-game time that is devoted to these activities[7].

The central hypothesis of this chapter is that the majority of these activities are focused on the construction of a model and shares significant overlap with the modeling based inquiry to warrant both analysis as a modeling activity and comparison. To use the language introduced earlier, WOW is both a simulation and model building environment[8]. It is a simulation of combat between opponents that establishes rules and representations of combat. The combat at the center of game's driving force is a simulation which, in simple terms, is the interaction between what are essentially two models: your character model and your opponent's model. WOW is also a model building environment because the other major driving force is the slow construction of your character through the initial one time selection of a race and class and then continual acquisition of armor, weapons, potions, enchantments, spells, abilities, and talents as you *level-up* from 1-70. Some acquisitions are consumable, can last as little as a minute, and must be replenished (i.e. potions); others are used for a long time period within a player determined level range (i.e. a level 48 weapon can be used when the player is at level 48 and can be used until she is level 52, perhaps to level 55); and still others are built upon throughout the leveling process and are relatively stable throughout the character's duration (i.e. spells, abilities, and talents). While this process is embedded within the game's overall narrative framework and the narrative framework of each race and class which provides different sets of affordances and constraints for a player this process is a model-building endeavor.

At a high level, the constructed character (i.e. the model) can be looked at as two models: an offensive model and defensive model. The offensive model delivers damage to your opponent by describing the type of damage and the magnitude of the damage. In WOW, there are several different types of damage (i.e. fire, nature, arcane, etc.) that is determined by the weapon or spell that is used. The magnitudes range from 1 to thousands of damage points. While most attacks with weapons are compared by their DPS (damage per seconds) ratings, all attacks have a speed, how often they can be used, and a damage magnitude range that is randomly determined. For example a 1-handed level 63 mace called the Spirit-Clad Mace has 41.2 DPS, 43-97 damage range, and 1.70 speed[9]; whereas, a level 63 wand called the Conjurer's Wand deals fire damage and has 91.8 DPS, 109-203 range, and 1.70 speed. Your class determines what types of attacks are available to your character and how many you can use at a time. The game play within a given fight is how you deploy the range of attacks based on the model you have created and the opponent that you are fighting. This most often will involve your character will employ several different attacks in combination to maximize your damage and killing your opponent as quickly as possible.

The defensive model determines how a particular attack is going to affect the health of your character. When you have no more health points, your character dies and you must resurrect it. Your defensive model includes random chances that you will dodge, block, parry or take an attack; then it will calculate the damage reduction[10] based on your armor to determine how much the damage is going to affect your health. There are spells and abilities that completely protect your model from any damage for a short time period and there are other spells that transfer damage to other players. As you level up, the amount of health increases. There are also special abilities and potions temporary increases your total heath or that heal and restore lost health points within a particular battle. The defensive model is the development of armor, spells, abilities, and potions that minimize the damage to your characters health. The game play is the deployment of the defensive model in a way that protects you from the current opponent before the fight and use spells and potions to heal. Sometimes the defensive model employs the use of stealth of the character or stuns to the opponent to reduce the times they can attack.

There is considerable interaction between the offensive model and the defensive model. For example, a paladin can put a "blessing" on that heals himself every time his/her weapon strikes an opponent and some gear carries add-on characteristics that increase strength, stamina, ability in dodge attacks, etc. Armor carries protection but can also increase damage potential of weapons used.

The overall game play in WOW is that you construct a character, comprised of an offensive model and a defensive model, and then using that model to fight other characters – other models. The challenge is to employ the model in ways that offensive model output (aka. Damage) can overcome the opponent's defensive model to maximize the reduction to their health. At the same time, you employ your defensive model to minimize your opponent's attacks to maintain or restore your health. While the game narrative invokes images of fighting anyone of over 6000 monsters (Hellboars, Swamp oozes, Berserkers, Shadowpriests, Basilick, and the like), other players' characters in duals, or other invading opponents in the overall Alliance or Horde narrative in PVP[11] mode; what is really happening is a competition of your model versus either another players' model or Blizzard's NPC model. Simply put, the WOW game is centrally about model building and model vs. model competition.

Figure 3. Human Paladin in WOW

COMPARE AND CONTRAST WOW MODELING AND VSS MODELING

The comparing and contrasting WOW modeling and VSS modeling will give us a way to see how the insights of both can be used to understanding the possibility of using gaming activity structures for educational purposes. For the sake of illustration and argumentation, this section of the chapter will primarily focus on the part of the WOW modeling building through the development of a character's *Talent Tree*. This is not the entire model that the gamer constructs, but provide a more condensed discussion that we believe is applicable to the entire modeling process in WOW.

Every class of characters has a unique Talent Tree and it is foundation of creating a character for play. The Talent Tree is comprised of three parts of tree competing talents. For example a Paladin (See Figure 3) has Holy (associated primarily with healing), Protection (associated with protecting himself and his team), and Retribution (associated increasing the damage of attacks). Beginning at level 10, the gamer is give 1 talent point every time she levels up, so there is a maximum total of 61 talent points a gamer can allocate. Building a Paladin this means the allocation of by 61 talent points into anyone of a total of 194 possible places (Holy=62, Protection=67, and Retribution=65). The focus of the WOW modeling building experience is on how gamers learn and understand their building of this Talent Tree component of their overall model.

Figure 4. Paladin Talent Tree and One Possible Build [12]

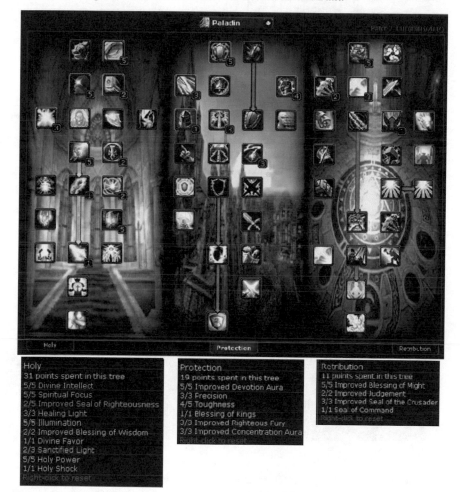

ISOMORPHIC MODELING

WOW has some properties of that were described as desirable for modeling-based inquiry. The first is isomorphic modeling. Clearly the modeling that is being undertaken in WOW has an isomorphic quality. You are modeling a character that looks differently has you build your character. The models are built within an understandable context or world with relatively straight forward consequences and implications. However, this is primarily through the addition of equipment (armor, shields, and weapons). When the focus is on the model building through the talent building process, there is almost no perceivable difference in your character. There are some notable exceptions with talents associated that include shape shifting (turning into a wolf, cat, bear, sea lion, etc) and talents associated with stealth. The talents associated with isomorphic aspects of the model are limited. In fact, there are some isomorphic elements in the environments that are counterproductive in the game play. For example, the visual perception of the model is often at odds with the underlying model. Often a novice player will compete against an opponent that appears to be weaker or similar to a previously vanquished opponent only to find out that they are easily defeated by them. Players learn quickly to use non-isomorphic references to assess an opponent model[13].

BEHAVIORAL MODELING

The behavioral modeling building in WOW is remarkably similar to the VSS modeling experience. Both have underlying formula that are somewhat opaque to the user, who only interacts with the formula via the manipulation of parameters. As you can see in Figure 4, the parameters of the core Offensive Model can be seen for a Paladin in the "Melee" and "Spell"[14] windows and the Defensive Model can be seen in the "Defenses" window. The Base Stats" window apply to some degree to both the models.

Figure 4. WOW Character Behavioral Model Parameter Display

Base Stats		Melee		Spell		Defenses	
Strength:	178	Weapon Skill	350	Bonus Damage:	127	Armor:	10489
Agility:	75	Damage:	158-241	Bonus Healing:	243	Defense:	345
Stamina:	331	Speed:	2.50	Hit Rating:	0	Dodge:	3.71%
Intellect:	315	Power:	543	Crit Chance:	7.99%	Parry:	5.00%
Spirit:	104	Hit Rating:	0	Penetration:	0	Block:	5.00%
Armor:	10489	Crit Chance:	5.68%	Mana Regen:	199	Resilience:	0

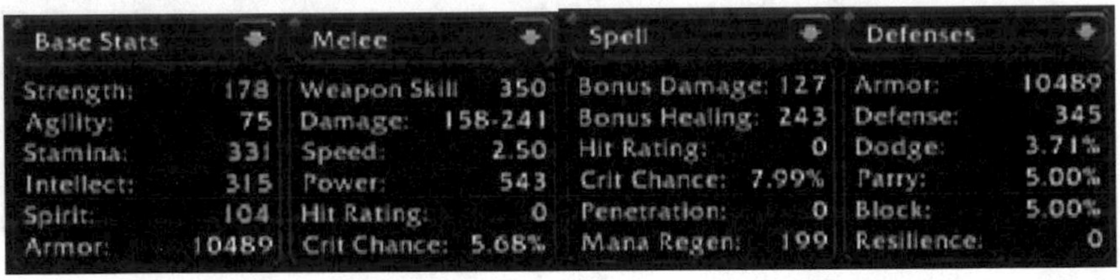

In the VSS software, Astronomicon (See Figure 5), learners manipulate the parameters of "Body Characteristics," "Thermal Characteristics" and "Orbital Characteristics."

Figure 5. Astronoimcon Behavioral Model Parameter Display

The most significant difference is that in Astronomicon the learners manipulate the parameters directly through typing in different values; whereas, in WOW players manipulate the parameters with acquiring gear, talents, abilities, potions, etc. that have particular values or collections of values. So the armor parameter is the accumulation of all the armor characteristics of each piece of armor plus the enhancements of armor through talents, temporary potion, and permanent enchantments. The down side of this form of parameter manipulation for learning is that it becomes much less fluid and dramatically impacts the ability to compare models. This will be taken up below.

TRANSITION BETWEEN ISOMORPHIC TO BEHAVIORAL MODELS

The interaction between and transition from isomorphic model to behavioral model is also similar. Both use an object oriented approach where the isomorphic character in WOW or the planet in Astronomicon can be opened up to see the behavioral model. This forms a seamless connection between isomorphic and behavioral models that can help eliminate students learning the models in inert and disconnected ways.

Cascade of Models

The final and the most important comparison and contrast is between the ways in which the Alternative Theory Curriculum and the Astronomicon software and the WOW game narrative and character building technology address the evolution of models for deeper understanding and learning. As described earlier, the first step is identification of model elements that are unseen or unseeable.

Transformation 1 – Identifying Unseen and Unseeable Model Elements
One of the significant parallels that support learning between VSS and WOW is the depiction of important model elements that are unseen or unseeable. In VSS, there are visualizations of light rays, orbital planes and paths, temperature, axis, and compasses. In WOW, there are visualizations that aid in understanding health, energy, mana, rage, breath, opponents that are attacking you or your partners, range of weapons or spells, etc. In both environments these visualizations are not removed and abstracted, but are grounded both within the concrete particulars of the isomorphic models and the abstract formalisms of the behavior model. Furthermore, they are vital in the overall narrative of the contexts. In VSS, they provide evidence and enable comparisons for the overall scientific inquiry. In WOW, the aid in understanding status and enacting strategies effectively.

Transformation 2 – Increasingly Complex Models
The ability to construct qualitatively different types of models that are useful within the context is one way that WOW and VSS differ dramatically. In the VSS, learners can construct models based on increasingly complex models. In modeling orbits for example, the Astronomicon can create circular orbits, elliptical orbits and physics-based orbits. The orbit modeling tools in VSS support learners in their transition from beginning understanding to more complex understanding of the orbit of a planet. The VSS modeling tools supporting the easy transition for one model to the next by the transferring of non-orbital elements and relevant parameters of the model from a learner's current model to the next more complex models. The WOW model build tool supports a single and somewhat arbitrary model build space. While there are many different combinations in which to build a paladin's talent tree, again placing 61 talent points in 194 possible places, at no time does the model fundamentally change. It is a single model.

Furthermore, an investigation of the various user websites and guides about the elements of the talent tree reveal dissatisfaction and a perceived arbitrary nature of the talents. In this example a guide author comments on one of the top talents in the Protection tree for a paladin:

Tier 8: Weapon Expertise (5/5),

Increases your skill with all melee weapons by 2/4/6/8/10%
I don't understand why paladins have this talent, much less have it in the
protection tree. Either I'm missing something or this is a joke, because
weapon skill does little enough for us when dpsing already, why bother
giving it to us tanking? Skip this.

(Geld's Revised Guide to the Paladin Class, 2007)

The author's comments highlight that this talent does not even seem to belong to
this talent tree and does not seem valuable. To be fair to WOW, the game play
relies on a single unified model and model build process. It maintains a rock,
paper, scissor[15] balance within the game play and unique value for each character
class for team play. The results on undercutting this would be everybody being the
same "best" character.

Transformation 3 – Exploration of Rival Models
The exploration of rival models is at the heart of the insights of the VSS research
and this section will explore the two environments across the four opportunities
that modeling offer learning: A. Iterative Trail and Error, B. Ability to See
Incomplete Models, C. Comparing Different Models, and D. Modeling
Misconceptions

A. Iterative Trail and Error
In WOW, the core learning through model building is through the competitive trial
and error in model versus model competition. The gamer learns through literally
thousands of battles what aspects of their model to employ under what conditions.
Death and resurrection, that cost the gamer both in terms of gold and time, is a
consent reminder of the limits to one's character model. The gamer is subtly
pushed by the game rules to challenge opponents that are higher level they their
characters because they are rewarded with more experience points that determine
level. The trail and error learning process can be somewhat obfuscated in WOW
because the gamer must employ the elements of the model within a battle. So, it is
not just a model versus model trial, but rather a gamer/model versus computer
model[16] trail. At the zone where gamers play to maximize their experience points,
the strategy that the gamer employs her model is just as important as the model that
she has constructed[17]. Failure results in lost of the time and in-game gold and
generates learning through new trails; the most important learning seems to take
place as when the gamer moves from a concern on her Health Bar and death to a
concern with the individual attacks and their effects on the model. The game
provides a moment-by-moment accounting of these attacks through a *Combat Log*
window that will generate 25-50 interactions (attacks, blocks, rejuvenation, spells,

255

etc.) in a 30 second battle. It is not atypical for a battle to go on for 5 minutes in some cases. The exploration of both the characters' Offensive model and Defensive model via the Combat Log can push gamers to understand the implications of the models and strategies. There are other 3-party *mods* and *IUs*[18] that compile these data for gamers so they can use to understanding how to employ their models.

In the VSS, iterative trail and error is a component of learning especially at the validation stage of model-based inquiry. Trial and error is driven by student expectations rather than a competition. The challenge of "how do I get the moon to move in and out of the Earth's shadow with the known validation criterion" (i.e. a full set of phases in 27.3 days) drives students as they build and refine. Building the VSS model and refining it is at the core of learning through iterative trail and error, whereas in WOW it is through the use of the built model where trail and error is partaken.

B. Ability to See Incomplete Models
In WOW, the building of a model is built almost exclusively through a developmental path of incrementally adding talents to the talent tree. In each aspect of the talent tree the gamer has 2-4 options that build with every 5 points added to that aspect. Sometimes talents are dramatic (i.e. acquiring a pet, porting to other areas, shield from damage) but for the most part they are very subtle increments to the model (i.e. Increase speed of movement by 4%, Increase damage caused by 1%). However, there is no way to build an incomplete model, only models that do not play a particular role as well as others. For example, a Paladin could have most of the talent points in Holy so that it can heal within a group. While another Paladin with talent points all in Retribution can also heal and defeat opponent much quicker, in a group with he would probably fail as a healer. New player always come on the chat lines and ask where they should put their talent points and almost always there a bombardment of responses: What do you want to do? The point is there is no incomplete model in WOW.

As you can see through the illustration of the CEO Forum's Ant model and through the discussion of the VSS project the ability construct an incomplete model provides for powerful opportunities for learning. It provides a means for learners to understand the implications of their thinking in a very direct and observable way. This is most apparent when the model is missing important information that the learner has not considered but is obvious when the model is running. The subtle and highly structured nature of the model building process of WOW prohibits this type of insight. In WOW all models are complete, they just represent different trade-offs in game play situations.

C. Comparing Different Models
How you specify your characters in WOW is significant to the game experience and the ability to participate in groups. Some guilds require applications that

demonstrate that you have spec'ed your character in a way that will help the guild in team events. Much thinking and talk goes around how you build your model. However, the rules of WOW support a relatively stable specification of your Talent Tree. While it is possible to reallocate your talents, it costs you gold. The more you reallocate the more it costs the character. It also interrupts your identity with your groups of friends that you engage team-based quests as a healer or protector for example. It is also possible to construct multiple different characters with different Talent Tree builds, however it is once again very difficult to do without a huge time investments. However, it is done by some people that both spend the money to reallocate one character and/or put in the time to create multiple characters. Most people don't. What most people do is to just the web-based fan sites and guides to discuss the trade-offs for creating different Talent Tree builds. There are Talent-Tree calculators and recommendations for each talent and for collective "builds" for different purposes.

The lesson from the VSS project is that the creation and comparison of models is vital for understanding. Comparing models enable learners to identify differences that add in deep understanding. For this learning to occur, the building of alternative models and the ability to compare them is vital. Furthermore, this must be done in a way that is relatively easy. This would be possible within the context of WOW interfaces and tools, but it is actively discouraged in service of the narrative and the promotion of character's relatively stable identity.

D. Modeling Misconceptions

There is no doubt that misconceptions abound within the models of WOW. WOW is a very complex and intellectually challenging world to understand and engage in successfully. The argument presented earlier on the difficulty of creating incomplete models can be extended to models based on misconceptions. WOW simply can not effectively build "wrong models," it only enables the construction of different types of "right models" that are based on trade-off and are more or less effective within certain roles or challenges within the game. The arguments also presented earlier on the difficult of comparing models obviously undermines the makes the power of creating multiple models (scientifically correct models with other models based on misconceptions). These structural impediments make the central finding of the VSS unattainable with the rules of the game structure although they are possible within the technology infrastructure. Gamers can not reap the benefits of understanding through learning acceptable models and unlearning less useful models.

CONCLUSION

What can we take away from this analysis of the Virtual Solar System project and World of Warcraft in terms of the potential for gaming technology and learning? My goals were to convince the reader that 3D dynamic models provide powerful potential of learning, that modeling-based pedagogies attuned to misconceptions were a powerful way to focus that potential, that likewise 3D games have a powerful potential for learning, that 3D games can be seen as modeling activities, and finally that although there are similarities with gaming modeling activities there are critical differences that must be designed to realize the potential. Hopefully those goals have been realized. As a means to conclude and look forward, how would we as a community take these research findings and realized them within a gaming environment?

The first and most obvious is the focus on contexts, narratives, and content that is not centered on killing opponents. The volume will provide many examples of this step. What I would like to focus on is the steps one would employ to construct gaming environments where building and comparing models would be promoted. I have identified 4 steps in doing so called the Keys in Architectural and Context Design for Educational Games.

1. Start with misconception, not just an error

The key insight of the misconception literature is that a misconception is not simply missing information, it is an alternative theory. Most every content has a number of important misconceptions that must and most often have been discovered. These misconceptions must be at the forefront of the design.

2. Identify the terrain of the misconception(s)

Once a misconception is identified the terrain of the misconception and the accepted conception must be studied and mapped out. Misconceptions that are most difficult to overcome are the once that make the most "sense" to learner and are most useful. Key element of these misconceptions must be understood so that leverage point can be found.

3. Develop interface architectures.

Develop modeling interfaces that enable the construction of misconceptions as well as accepted conceptions. This is a challenging step because the design must make the wrong models easy to build without making the accepted models more difficult to build.

4. Develop contexts

Developing game contexts (rules and goal structures) where learners find both the misconceptions and accepted conception useful and reasons for them to engage the comparisons. However, the context must favor the accepted conception and reveal the shortcomings of the misconceptions in a game relevant manner. The use of the accepted model must be the goal to winning the game.

The road to developing games that enable the learning academic content will be a long one that will, at least in the short term, be under funded. However, the key will be to identify the places where the potential is greater and that connects to what is known about learning. Hopefully, this chapter has identified one such rich potential for future development in a wide range of academic learning contents and support a rich future of games designed for learning.

FOR MORE INFORMATION

If you have any questions concerning the above, please do not hesitate to contact the author, Kenneth E. Hay: <kehay@indiana.edu>.

NOTES

[1] This research was supported by a grant from the National Science Foundation under the Directorate of Education and Human Resources, Division of Research, Evaluation and Communication's Research on Learning and Education Program (REC-0106968)

[2] For more information - http://education.mit.edu/starlogo/

[3] For more information - http://www.goknow.com/Products/Model-It/

[4] For more information - http://www.agentsheets.com/

[5] An inscription is scientist generated representation of a scientific phenomena (i.e. pictorial description, graphs, tables, etc.)

[6] The author is a gamer that is currently playing WOW primarily as a Human Paladin that is currently at level 61 and has just recently gone through the "Dark Portal" that is the gateway to the Burning Crusade. The game tells you how much time you have put into each character and my Paladin currently has 535 hours and 26 minutes. I have engaged WOW primarily as a means to understand the learning potential for these types of game after reading scholarship based on this one game. I have found that playing the game has been vital to my understanding of these issues and the exploration of the learning potential. Although I could explain WOW in much more detail in this chapter, it is my experience that these games must be lived and that while my reading of WOW-related articles prior to playing was informative, re-reading them after the WOW experience is extremely important. Therefore, I will focus my description on the models and modeling of WOW. It should also be noted that I make no claim to be an expert in WOW and my examples will be grounded in my experience as a human paladin and some reading about other characters.

[7] Estimate based on personal game playing is as much as 30-40% of the game play time are related to activities that are not directly related to killing.

[8] It is also a social space that is devoted to discussions of strategies and assembling teams (or raid parties).

[9] Time between attacks

[10] Damage-Reduction Percentage = armor / (armor + 85*level + 400)

[11] Player versus player

[12] Image created with the Talent Calculator at http://www.wowhead.com/

[13] Clicking on an opponent will display their level and a color-code scheme to indicator whether an opponent is within an a good range for potential competition or too low or too high. NPC with the label of "Elite" posess increased abilities beyond those indicators and a skull and cross-bones represents an opponent of much greater abilities.

[14] There is also a standard "Ranged" window for most characters. Paladin's do not have ranged abilities.

[15] This reference to a game structure where there is no superior character. Rock beats scissors, scissors beats paper, and paper beats rock. If rock beat both paper and scissors the game would not be interesting to play.

[16] For simplicity sake I will just use the example of gamer battling a non-player character (NPC) although he could be playing against another gamer/model.

[17] Playing an NPC much lower than you does not require a thoughtful strategy because your offensive model easily overpowers the NPC Defensive model and vice versa battling an NPC at a much higher level.

[18] Mods and IU are user-developed and shared programs that enhance the game experience.

REFERENCES

AAAS – The American Association for the Advancement of Science (1993). *Benchmarks for Science Literacy*. New York, Oxford University Press.

Barab, S. A., Hay, K. E. & Duffy, T. (1998). Grounded constructions and how technology can help. *Technology Trends*, 43(2), 15-23.

Barab, S. A., Hay, K. E., Barnett, M. G., & Squire, K. (2001). Constructing virtual worlds: Tracing the historical development of learner practices/understandings. *Cognition and Instruction, 19(1),* 47–94.

Baxter, J. (1989). Children's understanding of familiar astronomical events. *International Journal of Science Education*, 11, 502-513.

Bendall, S., Goldberg, F., & Galili, I. (1993). Prospective elementary teachers' prior knowledge about light. *Journal of Research in Science Teaching*, 30, 1169-1187.

Berg, T. & Brouwer, W. (1991). Teacher awareness of student alternate conceptions about rotational motion and gravity. *Journal of Research in Science Teaching,* 28(1), 3-18.

Castronova, E. (2001). Virtual worlds: A first-hand account of market and society on the cyberian frontier (CESifo Working Paper Series No. 618). Fullerton, CA: Center for Economic Studies and Institute for Economic Research, California State University. Retrieved November 16, 2006, from http://ssrn.com/abstract=294828

CEO Forum (June 2000) *School Technology and Readiness Report.*

Chi, M., Feltovich, P., & Glaser, R. (1981). Categorization and representation of physics problems by experts and novices. *Cognitive Science*, 5, 121-152

Chinn, C. A., & Brewer, W. F. (1993). The role of anomalous data in data acquisition: A theoretical framework and implications for science instruction. *Review of Educational Research,* 63(1), 1-50.

Collins, A. & Ferguson, W. (1993). Epistemic forms and epistemic games: Structures and strategies to guide inquiry. *Educational Psychologist*, 28(1), 25-42.

Conceptual Coherence and Alternative Theories Trials. Paper presented at the annual meeting of the American Educational Research Association, San Diego, CA.

Confrey, J. & Doerr, H. M. (1994). Student modelers. *Interactive Learning Environments* 4(3), 199-217.

Dede, C., Salzman, M., Loftin, B., and Sprague, D. (1999). Multisensory immersion as a modeling environment for learning complex scientific concepts. In W. Feurzeig and N. Roberts, (Eds.), *Computer modeling and simulation in science education*, 282-319. New York: Springer-Verlag.

DeLoache, J. S. (1989). The development of representation in young children. In H. W. Reese (Ed.), *Advances in child development and behavior*, 22, 1-39. New York: Academic Press.

Eylong B.S. & Linn, M. (1988). Learning and instruction: An examination of four research perspectives in science education. *Review of Educational Research,* 58(3), 251-303.

Fetherstonhaugh, T., & Treagust, D. F. (1992). Students' understanding of light and its properties: Teaching to engender conceptual change. *Science Education*, 76, 653-672

Feurzeig, W. (1988). Apprentice tools: Students as practitioners. In R.S. Nickerson & P.P Zodhiates (Eds.), *Technology in education: Looking toward 2020*. Hillsdale, NJ: Erlbaum.

Forbus, K. D., Sherin, B., Carney, K., & Harris, R. T. (2000). Explanations: The missing leg. Paper presented at the Workshop to Integrate Computer-based Modeling and Scientific Visualization into Teacher Education Programs held in Arlington, VA, 64-79.

Fraknoi, A. (1996). The state of astronomy education in the U.S. In J. Percy (Ed.), *Astronomy education: Current developments, future coordination,* 9-25. Astronomical Society of the Pacific: San Franciso, CA.

Gee, J. P. (2003). *What video games have to teach us about learning and literacy*. New York: Palgrave/St. Martin's.

Gentner, D. & Toupin, C. (1986) Systematicity and surface similarity in the development of analogy. *Cognitive Science* 10, 277-300.

Grosslight, L., Unger, C., Jay, E., & Smith, C. (1991) Understanding models and their use in science: Conceptions of middle and high school students and experts. *Journal of Research in Science Teaching,* 28, 799-822.

Halloun, I. & Hestenes, D. (1985a). The initial knowledge state of college physics students. *American Journal of Physics,* 53, 1043-1055.

Halloun, I. & Hestenes, D. (1985b). Common sense concepts about motion. *American Journal of Physics, 53,* 1056-1065.

Hay, K. E & Barab, S. A. (1998, April). Building worlds: Tools of virtual practice. Paper presented at the annual meeting of the American Educational Research Association, San Diego, CA.

Hay, K. E & Kim, B. (2004, April). Virtual reality modeling-based inquiry.

Hay, K. E. (1999a, April). The digital weather station: A study of learning with 5d visualization. Manuscript presented at the annual meeting of the American Educational Research Association, Montreal, Canada

Hay, K. E. (1999b). Computational Science Inquiry Cycle (CSIC): Students "doing" new science enabled by virtual reality. Paper presented at the annual meeting of the American Educational Research Association, Montreal, Canada

Hay, K. E., & Barab, S. A. (2001). Constructivism in practice: A comparison and contrast between apprenticeship and constructionist learning environments. *Journal of the Learning Sciences, 10(3),* 281–322

Hay, K. E., Marlino, M., & Holschuh, D.R. (2000). The virtual exploratorium: Foundational research and theory on the integration of 5-d modeling and visualization in undergraduate geoscience education. In Fishman, B. J. & O'Connor-Divelbiss, S. F. Proceedings of the *International Conference of the Learning Sciences: Facing the challenges of complex real-world settings.* 214-220

Hay, K.E, Crozier, J., & Barnett, M. (2000). The Virtual Gorilla Project. Paper presented at the annual meeting of the American Educational Research Association, New Orleans, LA.

Hestenes, D. (1996). Modeling methodology for physics teachers. *Proceedings of the International Conference on Undergraduate Physics Education,* College Park, MD.

Hestenes, D., Wells, M., & Swackhammer, G. (1992). Force concept inventory. *The Physics Teacher,* 30(3), 141-158.

Jackson, S. L., Stratford, S. J., Krajcik, J., & Soloway, E. (1994). Making dynamic modeling accessible to precollege science students. *Interactive Learning Environments*, 4(3), 233-257.

Johnson, A., Moher, T., Ohlsson, S., & Gillingham, M. (1999). The Round Earth Project. Collaborative VR for Conceptual Learning. *IEEE Computer Graphics and Applications*, 19(6), pp. 60-69.

Keil, F., & Batterman, N. A.(1984). A characteristic to designing shift in the development of word meaning. *Journal of Verbal Learning and Verbal Behavior*, 23, 221-236.

Kemler, D.G.(1983). Holistic and analytical modes in perceptual and cognitive development. In T. J. Tiche & B. E. Shepp (Eds.), *Perception, cognition and development: Interactional analysis.* Hillsdale, NJ: Erlbaum.

Langley, D., Ronen, M., & Eylon, B. (1997). Light propagation and visual patterns: Preinstruction learners' conceptions. *Journal of Research in Science Teaching, 34*(4), 399-424.

Larkin, J. (1983). The role of problem representation in physics. In D. Gentner and A. Stevens (Eds.), *Mental models* (pp. 75-98). Hillsdale, NJ: Erlbaum.

Larkin, J., McDermott, J., Simon, D., & Simon, H. (1980). Expert and novice performance in solving physics problems. *Science,* 208, 1335-1342.

Latour, B. (1987). *Science in action: How to follow scientists and engineers through society.* Milton Keynes, England: Open University Press.

Lehrer, R., & Schauble, L. (2000). Signatures of modeling. Paper for the Workshop to Integrate Computer-based Modeling and Scientific Visualization into Teacher Education Programs held in Arlington, VA, 1-28.

Lehrer, R., Horvath, J., & Schauble, L. (1994). Developing model-based reasoning. *Interactive Learning Environments, 4*(3), 219-231.

Linn, M. C., diSessa, A., Pea, R., & Songer, N. B. (1994). Can research on science learning and instruction inform standards for science education? *Journal of Science Education and Technology, 3,* 7-15.

National Research Council. (1996). *National Science Education Standards.* Washington, DC: National Academy of Sciences.

Ogborn, J. (2000). Modeling clay for thinking and learning. In W. Feurzeig & N. Roberts (Eds.) *Modeling and simulation in science and mathematics education.* 5-37. NY: Springer-Verlag.

Penner, D. E., Giles, N. D., Lehrer, R., & Schauble, L. (1997). Building functional models: Designing an elbow. *Journal of Research in Science Teaching,* 34, 125-143.

Penner, D. E., Lehrer, R., & Schauble, L. (1998). From physical models to biomechanics: A design-based modeling approach. *Journal of the Learning Sciences, 7*(3&4), 429-449.

Pfundt, H., & Duit, R. (1998). *Students' alternative frameworks and science education bibliography.*5th ed. Kiel Univ. (West Germany). Institut fuer die Paedagogik der Naturwissenschaften.

Reed, S. K. (1985). *A structure-mapping model for word problems.* Paper presented at the meeting of the Psychonomic Society, Boston.

Resnick, M. (2000). Decentralized modeling and decentralized thinking. In W. Feurzeig & N. Roberts (Eds.) *Modeling and simulation in science and mathematics education.* 114-137. NY: Springer-Verlag.

Roberts, N., & Barclay, T. (1988). Teaching model building to high schools students: Theory and reality. *Journal of Computers in Mathematics and Science Teaching,* Fall, 13-24.

Ross, B. H. (1986). This is like that: Object correspondence and remindings and the separation of similarly effect on the access and use of earlier problems. *Journal of Experimental Psychology: Learning, Memory, & Cognition, 13*(4), 629-639.

Roth, W. M. (1992). Bridging the gap between school and real life: Toward an integration of science, mathematics and technology in the context of authentic practice. *School Science and Mathematics, 92*(6), 307-317.

Roth, W.-M. (1996). Knowledge diffusion in a grade 4-5 classroom during a unit of civil engineering: An analysis of a classroom community in terms of its changing resources and practices. *Cognition and Instruction, 14,* 170-220.

Sabelli, N. (1994). On using technology for understanding science. *Interactive Learning Environments, 4*(3), 195-198.

Sadler, P. M. (1998). Psychometric models of student conceptions in science: Reconciling qualitative studies and distractor-driven assessment instruments. *Journal of Research in Science Teaching, 35*(3), 265-296.

Salzman, M., Dede, C., & Loftin, B. (1999). Virtual reality's frames of reference: A visualization technique for mastering abstract information spaces. *Proceedings of CHI '99*, pp. 489-495.

Schneps, M. H.& Sadler, P. M. (1988). *A private universe.* Santa Monica, CA: Pyramid Films

Shepp, D.E. (1978). From perceived similarity to dimensional structure: A new hypothesis about perceptual development. In E. Rosch & B.B. Lloyd (Eds.), *Cognition and categorization.* Hillsdale, NJ: Erlbaum.

Smith, J. P., diSessa, A. A. & Roschelle, J. (1993). Misconceptions reconceived: A constructivist analysis of knowledge in transition. *Journal of the Learning Sciences, 3*(2), 115-163.

Smith, L. B. & Kemler, D. G. (1977). Developmental trends in free classification: Evidence for a new conceptualization of perceptual development. *Journal of Experimental Child Psychology, 24,* 279-298.

Tinker, R. (1993) Modeling and theory building: Technology in support of student theorizing. In D. L. Gerguson (Eds.) *Advanced educational technologies for mathematics and science.* Berlin: Springer-Verlag.

Treagust, D. F. & Smith, C. L. (1989). Secondary students' understanding of gravity and the motion of planets. *School Science and Mathematics, 89*(5), 380-391

Wandersee, J. H., Mintzes, J. J., & Novak, J. D. (1990).Research on alternative conceptions in science. In D. L. Gabel (Ed.), *Handbook on Science Teaching and Learning* 177-210. New York: Macmillan Publishing Co.

White, B. Y. & Frederiksen, J. R. (1998). Inquiry, modeling and metacognition: Making science accessible to all learners. *Cognition and Instruction, 16*(1), 3-118.

Windschitl, M. & Winn, W. (2000). A virtual environment designed to help students understand science. *Proceedings of the International Conference of the Learning Sciences.* Ann Arbor, MI, 290-296.

Winn, W.D., & Jackson, R. (1999). Fourteen propositions about educational uses of virtual reality. *Educational Technology, 39*(4), 5-14.

Zeilik, M., Schau, C., Mattern, N., Hall, S., Teague, K. W., & Bisard, W. (1997). Conceptual astronomy: A novel model for teaching postsecondary science courses. *American Journal of Physics, 65*(10), 987-996.

AFFILIATIONS

Kenneth E. Hay
Associate Professor
Learning Sciences and Cognitive Sciences
School of Education
ED4022
Indiana University
W.W.Wright School of Education
201 N. Rose Ave.
Bloomington, IN 47405-1006
812-856-8555
812-856-8333 (fax)
kehay@indiana.edu

KURT D. SQUIRE, MINGFONG JAN, JAMES MATTHEWS[1], MARK
WAGLER[2], JOHN MARTIN, BEN DEVANE, CHRIS HOLDEN

WHEREVER YOU GO, THERE YOU ARE:
PLACE-BASED AUGMENTED REALITY GAMES FOR
LEARNING

"Fun is the original educational technology." – Chris Crawford

Games are among the oldest forms of experiential learning. Game-based learning
scenarios are a staple in the military; games have been used to represent,
communicate and explore the dynamics of complex situations with multiple
interacting variables. Today's videogames allow new kinds of interactions,
including real-time 3D and physics simulation. Learners can participate in complex
systems over distance and time, and express themselves through game tools (Casti,
1997; Squire, 2004). In recent years, the military has embraced gaming (Prensky,
2001). However, the lack of clear purpose, rationale, and theoretical framework for
educational games has hindered their uptake in other environments. (Gredler,
1996). Games may create "greater engagement," but they have, with few
exceptions, have rarely demonstrated long term learning gains.[1] Positivist research
paradigms have failed to detect changes because they have overlooked the
interdependences between gaming and other instructional strategies, the
importance of social interactions in the gaming experience, or unanticipated
learning outcomes (Squire, 2004). Better developed pedagogical models that can
be refined and tested through iterative research and design and more open and
flexible assessment models might push the field forward (Barab & Squire, 2004).
  With the rise of computer and video games research, there is renewed effort to
simultaneously build theories of learning through game play, while designing
learning interventions (Barab et al., 2005; Gee, 2003; Davidson, 2005; Klopfer &
Squire, in press; Squire, 2005, in press; Steinkuehler, 2006). A current wave of
educators wants to acknowledge the *new* learning experiences that games can
produce and understand how their consequences for how we think, act, play, and
learn (Shaffer, Squire, Halverson & Gee, 2005). For example, consider persistent
world games such as *World of Warcraft*, where millions of people from around the
world can become an international financier, gathering, crafting, and trading
materials, buying and selling goods in different markets to maximize profits
(Castronova, 2001; Steinkuehler, 2006). Whether these experiences are valuable in
and of themselves is an interesting question under debate; minimally, they put
implicit pressure back on educational technologists to reconsider the kinds of

B. E. Shelton, D. A. Wiley (eds.), Educational Design & Use of Computer Simulation Games,265–294.

experiences we make available through our designs as much "edutainment" seems primitive in comparison.

  Many game-based learning approaches are emerging, including open-ended sandbox environments for identity construction (Squire, in press), and epistemic games (Shaffer, 2005), and multi user virtual worlds such as *Quest Atlantis* and *Riverworld* that seek to build gamelike, problem-solving environments online (See Barab, 2006; Dede, Clarke, Ketelhut, Nelson, & Bowman, 2005). In MMO activities, players role play as scientists and concerned citizens, gathering and analyzing data, and forming causal models of scientific phenomena. Barab's *Quest Atlantis* goes further, seeking to create curricular systems that give learners embodied experiences within narrative worlds that result in participants knowledgably participating in society (Barab, Zuiker, Warren, Hickey, Ingram-Goble, Kwon, Kouper, & Herring, in press). These programs, occurring primarily through virtual interactions, are excellent examples of twenty-first century learning pedagogies that build on game principles.

  This research around emerging handheld technologies builds on this research, but uses ubiquitous digital technologies such as GPS devices and handheld computers to reintroduce learners to *place*. As Klopfer and Squire describe, handheld computers have (a) *portability* – ability to take computers off site (b) *socioability*-ease at exchanging data and collaborating face to face, (c) *context sensitivity*-ability for devices to "know where they are" in the world providing real and simulated data in real time, (d) *connectivity* – ability to be connected to other handhelds, devices, and networks via integrated 8.02 11 and digital broadband (over cellphone spectrums), and (e) *individuality* – ability to provide unique scaffolding that customized to the individual's path of investigation.

Furthermore, students come to school with handheld devices already in their pockets, creating new opportunities for integrating technology into the classroom. Regardless of whether we as educators choose to integrate them in our classrooms, they are coming, and already we hear stories of students using them to take pictures, communicate over the Internet, or look up information online. We believe that ubiquitous access to the computing and communication technologies will place implicit pressures for educators to move beyond information retrieval type pedagogies. What is the use in asking a student to memorize and "spit back" information when the answer can be looked up in a matter of seconds?

  This chapter describes recent work in developing a model of experiential learning around place-based augmented reality games. Using an engine developed by Eric Klopfer and colleagues at MIT, we have designed, developed, and researched the efficacy of three augmented reality games cutting across science, social studies, and language arts designed for students ages 10-16. Each game is designed to remediate players' experience of places in Madison, WI. *Mad City Murder* places the player in the center of a murder mystery that involves environmental toxins; in *Dow Day* players are journalists chronicling the riots occurring on the University Wisconsin-Madison campus on October, 1967; and *The Greenbush*, a game where players learn that the city of Madison has plans to "revitalize" an historic neighborhood the Greenbush and redesign its future.

Although these games deal with diverse subject matter, each one seeks to open layers of meaning behind the surface features of the environment, ranging from chemical and environmental to cultural and historical processes. Each game focuses on *designing solutions*; players are confronted with emotionally compelling challenges, meet virtual characters, unlock new capabilities, and *design* solutions to problems. These pedagogies attempt to draw from more established pedagogies (e.g. learning by design) while also capitalizing on game design techniques and mechanics that boost engagement and learning.[2] This chapter begins with a brief introduction to the theoretical orientation behind place-based augmented reality game learning environments, then outlines four sample games. We finish with a discussion of key principles for designing such environments.

THEORETICAL FRAMEWORK: VIDEOGAMES AS DESIGNED EXPERIENCE

We argue that video games (as artifacts) can be thought of as ideological worlds, worlds constructed with assumptions about the world instantiated by rule systems and representations. Within game studies, so called ludologists have focused on the nature of interacting rule systems while media scholars have examined game representations. Both are important to educators, hoping that students will build conceptual understandings through interactions with representations within rule-based systems. As educational game designers, we produce roles within these systems for players to inhabit so that through performance within the system, they develop understandings of academic content.

These systems of rules, roles, and representations stand in stark contrast to most academic subject areas that are organized around content (e.g. history, biology) or exams. As opposed to traditional classroom environments, where the learning model is one of transmitting content, game-based pedagogies hold a situated, interactionist view of learning where players enter with understandings, identities, and questions, and through interaction with the game system, develop along trajectories toward more expert performance. Thus, educational games are systems of potential interactions (more or less) carefully orchestrated to guide user's experience (and learning), with academic knowledge, skills, values, and identities developing as a result.

Game systems are in a very real sense co-constructed by their players; they are less linear content and more constructed as a world for players to *enter*, to *perform* in, to *inhabit*. As a result, players' experiences of them differ wildly, according to their backgrounds, personal interests, and critically, the paths they choose to traverse within them. Studies of *Civilization* players (c.f. Squire & Giovanetto, in press) reveal that some players enjoy using the game as a metaphor for thinking about history, whereas for others, the game is nothing more than a strategic game whose representations are largely irrelevant. Similarly, whereas some players enjoy the narrative-based missions of *Grand Theft Auto: San Andreas,* others use the game primarily as a vehicle for constructing chase scenes, customizing automobiles, or constructing their own narratives.[3] Gee describes this process of learning as one of developing "embodied empathy for a complex system", and suggests that it is one of the chief benefits game-based learning has to offer.

Thus, educational game scholars need to focus on players' *performances* within these worlds, in addition to the properties of them. Whereas we can examine a textbook or film and judge if the content is accurate, we cannot examine a game system and judge its accuracy or effectiveness without examining the emergent properties of the game as a system. As Juul (2004) points out, games are not activated without their players, part of which turns Juul toward a temporal or time-based theory of games. Building from a quotation by legendary game designer Sid Meier that games are primarily a series of interesting choices, Juul reminds us that it is the player – game interaction that must be studied. Squire (2003; 2005b) extends this notion to include the social contexts in which gaming is situated. Players' experiences of *Civilization*, *GTA*, or *World of Warcraft* are also situated in social environments (guilds, clans, classrooms) which give context to the meaning of performances.

Cognition as materially situated

Underlying this perspective on games is a situated view of knowledge and knowing, one that sees knowledge as arising in context *as a part of* the environment. Rooted in the interactionalist ontology of Dewey, knowledge is situated in that cognition is stretched across physical, social, and institutional contexts. Cognition is materially situated, as stretched across tools and physical resources. In the case of games, players have access to digital tools (charts, graphs, representations, another skills and tools that mediate their interaction with the environment) (c.f. Pea, 1993; Solomon, 1993). How this mediation occurs differs by genre; in strategy games players routinely use complex charts and graphs to monitor data within the simulation; in more action oriented games, players also use (and gain) tools to interact with the environment. Most commonly, they also develop *skills* (which could be as simple as infrared vision) that mediate data. Theoretically, this perspective acknowledges how these resources contribute to our understandings and in a very real sense also constitute those understandings (Barab, Cherkes, 1999).

Educators pursuing place-based pedagogies have sought to "reintroduce" physical and cultural spaces into learning as a means of situating learning in meaningful contexts (Grunewald, 2003; Orr, 1992). Physically, place-based approaches resituate us in our physical environs (field sites, communities, cities) that are frequently at the basis of academic disciplines (such as environmental science, history, or geography). Responding to student and academic critiques of education as removed from personal experience and social consequences (thus removing from participation in social life), place-based approaches seek to connect students to the history, culture, and social life of places, making learning consequential for its participants.

On the surface, games, as imaginative contexts may seem antithetical to such place-based approaches, but games (much like historical fiction or science fiction) can immerse learners in deeper experiences of a place than might be otherwise possible. First, games are a spatial medium, allowing learners to explore the physical properties of place perhaps more readily than with traditional narratives (Jenkins, 2002; Jenkins & Squire, 2001). Many games are contests of space – struggles over access to or control over space, meaning that educational game designers might benefit by identifying such "contests" over space within academic domains – which, as suggested in the following examples within this article – might include toxic spills, urban redevelopment, or political demonstrations.

Cognition as socially situated

We can also think of cognition as stretched across social interactions. Our cognition develops *through* and *for* social interaction (Lave, 1988). From this perspective, conceptual understandings are developed on the fly, often through social interactions such as formal and informal discussions, and other various social interactions. Through language we seek to develop shared understandings, often for the purposes of future action (Levinson, 1983; Dewey, 1938). Conversations serve to coordinate action, and through them, people develop feedback on ideas, allowing actions and understandings to be adjusted on the fly. Crucially from this perspective, the language, action, and conceptual understandings are mutually constitutive, so that we cannot think of one arising without being in relation to the other.

Cognition is also socially situated in the sensed that it is embedded within social institutions that shape our actions and activity (Leontev, 1978). The larger social purposes of an activity (such as an academic writing to build a tenure file) shape our actions and resulting activity (activity being coordinated actions and operations toward social purposes). The kinds of understandings that emerge are also dependent upon the broader socio-cultural constraints, such as how particular practices and forms (writing papers, the structure of academic papers) structure cognition. Within schools, this point is particularly salient as the overriding activity structures (earning grades, credits, and graduating from school) constrains what kinds of learning will occur – which is especially important for educators pursuing pedagogies with values that run counter to those within most school practices (Barab & Hay, 2001; Squire, MaKinster, Barnett, Luehmann & Barab, 2003). Games offer the potential to dramatically "reframe" activity within new activity systems that may put pressures back on the grammar of schooling.

AUGMENTED REALITY SIMULATION GAMES FOR LEARNING

Augmented reality (AR) simulation games are games played in the real world, in locations such as neighborhoods, historical sites, or watersheds, but using technologies to layer data over the real world. These data might include video, text, or images, which designers manipulate to create fictional characters, events, and indeed entire worlds. Designers can also tie specific information to time and space, so that when a player arrives at a particular location, like a statue, s/he can be presented information on the sculptor, the history of the statue, or even an historical picture of the landscape before the statue was constructed. Whereas some approaches use head-mounted displays to layer 3D images over the real world environment, this approach uses handheld technologies to provide relatively low-resolution information tied to specific place.

AR games go beyond purely providing information; they give students *experiences* such as conducting a virtual investigation. Games are organized around problem solving activities, activities where players must research and discern the value of information, reason from evidence, and construct new representations of their understandings. Using simulation technologies, AR games may also go beyond project-based learning by entering students' plans and creations in simulated worlds, allowing them to learn through the consequences of their work.

A primary benefit of games-based approaches is that they ask students to try on roles other than being students; games can allow learning to occur through the lens of a particular identity (such as being a environmental engineer, journalist or historian) (c.f. Gee, 2003; Shaffer, 2004; Squire, 2006). Gee (2004) developed the notion of a hybrid identity between the player and the avatar to describe the unique coupling between players and characters as games, arguing that the potential exists to use roles as opportunities for learners to develop productive identities within games. As an example Gee describes how he as a *Tomb Raider* player becomes "James Paul Gee-as-Lara Croft". One might imagine educational games designed so as to produce "James Paul Gee-as-biologist" or historian. AR gaming technologies seek to create this kind of hybrid identity by placing players in roles where academic content is used in the service of socially consequential action, such as redesigning a neighborhood.

MAD CITY MYSTERY: MYSTERY GAMES FOR ENVIRONMENTAL SCIENCE
EDUCATION

Ivan Illyich is dead.

Police claimed that he drowned while fishing by the south shore of Lake Mendota.

Between January and the time of his death, Ivan put on 25 pounds and started drinking heavily. His health condition had deteriorated considerably.

As one of his friends, your task is to investigate the case with two of your best friends. It is your duty to present a clear picture about the causes and effects of these to the public.

Mad City Mystery takes place on the University of Wisconsin-Madison campus near Lake Mendota. The game takes from 90 to three hours including (1) briefing, (2) game play, and (3) debriefing. After learning of Ivan's mysterious death, players interview virtual characters, gather quantitative data samples, and examine government documents to piece together a casual explanation. Players work in teams that may or may not compete with other teams, depending on the teacher's preferences.

The primary educational objective is to help students develop scientific investigation, inquiry skills, and argumentation skills. Game play requires them to: (1) Observe phenomena in their environment and tie them to underlying scientific processes; (2) Ask questions about the effects of human processes in the environment; (3) Engage in scientific argumentation (forming hypotheses, refining them based on evidence, and articulating rationale to develop theory; and (4) Develop conceptual understandings of geochemical water cycles, specifically, how chemicals move through the water system.

Determining the cause of Ivan's death is open-ended and involves multiple causal factors. The most probable solution is that Ivan's health was deteriorating from from a combination of alcoholism, depression, and exposure to TCE at the workplace (TCE is a common degreasing agent). Ivan's exposure to excessive PCBs, mercury, and farm pesticides via fish consumption led to his general deterioration as well. No *one* of these causes would have caused Ivan to suddenly drown. In combination, however, Ivan may have become weakened so that he could drown. As such, the pedagogical goal of the problem is to immerse students in cycles of hypothesis formation, theory generation, evidence gathering and thinking, rather than necessarily happening upon the "correct" answer.

The game play model was constructed to support argumentation through negotiating multiple solution *problems*, make overt ties to educational issues surrounding place, and connect to local concerns. (c.f. Church, 2001). In Wisconsin, heavy alcohol consumption is a known public concern that can lead to several secondary health issues, cutting across population demographics. Fishing is a primary source of food in many poorer Wisconsin communities, presenting questions about how environmental issues interact with social class (e.g. which communities are most affected by pollutants). The open-ended format also allowed us to present associated sub-problems – such as low birth weight of infants due to excessive exposure to Mercury in fish, adding to the social import and emotional impact of the game.

Players must weigh the various symptoms, toxins, pollution sources (fish, water, work environment) and provide a coherent argument Ivan's death. Students were instructed to inform officials of their degree of confidence in their evidence, rationale, and findings. Further, they were to alert officials about any other important discoveries. Each student might not only succeed at the main narrative, but also uncover other important health concerns – allowing players to each have unique responses depending on which side areas they chose to explore (like the baby's low birth weight).

271

Roles

Players take on one of three roles (medical doctor, environmental specialist, and government official), each of which has different abilities and varied access to information. For example, the Medical Doctor may diagnose Non-player characters (NPCs) and retrieve their medical history. Players must work together, however, as the medical history is of little use without an understanding of local toxins (provided in documents to the government official). These roles were mapped to play styles identified within popular games and past research, namely the government official (appealing to those affiliating with power, i.e. the warrior), the environmental scientists (appealing to those affiliating with nature, i.e. the hunter), and the medical doctor (appealing to those who desire to help people). These are all productive roles that require scientific training, and expose students to a range of roles that they may adopt with science. Students were free to choose the roles most interesting to them.

Challenges

Players' challenges (including sub-challenges that arise in the game) are presented through virtual interviews and the artifacts. These provide clues about Ivan's lifestyle, friends, family, job, watershed, weather, pollutants and the complex interactive systems interlaced through them. Players decode the function of these virtual interviews and artifacts to develop either hypotheses or counterhypotheses. New evidence, such as a medical record from Ivan's coworker, usually verifies or disapproves the hypotheses. Each piece of information is designed with different functions in mind, and players are rewarded but by having the mystery unveiled piece by piece. They also suggest "red herrings," tangential questions inviting further investigation.

Place-based learning

The site, Lake Mendota, was chosen for its cultural and emotional significance, as well as its potential for supporting scientific understandings. Central to both the city of Madison, Wisconsin and the University campus, the site is situated on an isthmus between Lake Monona and Lake Mendota, which are the subject of great local political, scientific, and cultural attention. As an urban watershed, these lakes gather runoff from over-fertilization and pesticide misuse in lawns and gardens. They are heavily fished, particularly by lower income groups as a major food source, which raises health. As with most Midwestern lakes, high levels of mercury are occasionally recorded in fish as a result of point-source mercury pollution. Finally, local industrial sites introduce further complexity, as they add the potential for chemical spills (such as TCE) and industrial waste (such as PCBs).

Resources

In the context of play, players encounter up to thirteen non-player characters. Consistent with the game-based project orientation, the NPCs were written to be as engaging as possible. In this interaction, Ivan's friend and coworker Bartleby tells the doctor and environmental scientist about their friendship and his fishing habits.

> Fishing really isn't my thing, but it turned out to be fun, mainly because I got to hang out with Ivan. I don't really like fish, so I always gave mine to Ivan. Man did he like fish! I bet that you could find fish in his refrigerator at anytime. His wife Eve really loved eating fish, especially catfish because they were so much juicier... Honestly, the past few weeks I have been feeling kind of dizzy and dull. I don't know what's up though. I have to admit that doctors kind of freak me out, so I haven't been to one. No offense Doc. I worked out everyday and am feeling much better now. Working out is great. Don't you think? I don't touch the booze, though. You might work out sometimes, too, I think.

In contrast, the Environmental Scientist reads,

> Like Ivan, I worked at Eraser for a few months as a temp. eRaser is a typewriter correction fluid producer in the northwest side of Sun Prairie, not far from Token Creek... because of budget cuts, they are hiring more temporary workers which has, or had us both a little stressed.

Here, the doctor learns that Bartleby showed symptoms (dizziness, dullness) similar to Ivan, but does not drink alcohol, suggesting that a chemical at eRaser (which is TCE) may cause interactions with alcohol consumption. The environmental scientist learns about the location of the plant, which happens to be upstream from Lake Mendota, placing them as a possible contaminator of the water source via TCE. The government official received similar information, but in addition received a document describing the health effects of PCBs. Figure 1 shows the placement and functional roles of the various NPCs in communicating the story.

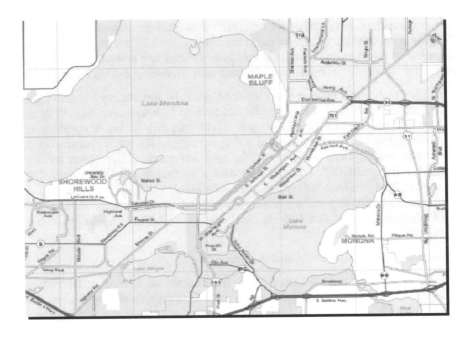

Figure 1: The Mad City Mystery Map and placement and functional roles of the various NPCs in communicating the story.

Collaboration and competition

In addition to receiving differentiated information and having differentiated tools, the game includes triggered events designed to support collaboration and reflection-in-action. Players must decide with whom they should speak, requiring them to anticipate, estimate, and debate the relative quality of information. Earlier studies of augmented reality environments (See Klopfer & Squire, in press) suggest that triggered actions promotes *inquiry* as opposed to "treasure hunt" activity. Thus, as players talk to NPCs new NPCs become available, causing them to reflect on what they know and do not know.

NPCs were also designed to introduce counter-theories or induce reflection. Late in the game, Willy Lowman, an insurance investigator appears, providing a counter-theory that Ivan's death was suicide:

> Let me tell you the truth. Ivan's death was an insurance fraud. This man could not live without a full-time job, and he had problems finding one. His addiction to alcohol made him sick, and he simply lost the will to live. He was a good husband, but he could not afford to raise his family. What would you do if you were Ivan? He set everything up to make it look like an

accident so that his wife could get insurance compensation from his death. I know that it is hard to swallow, but what evidence suggests otherwise?

The hope was that, confronted with a strong counter theory, students would draw on existing evidence and link together rationale to provide a counter example, launching them into a productive debriefing session. NPCs were designed and placed to propel action, build engagement, promote interaction, and scaffold thinking.

The following excerpt was typical for how the high school groups interacted during the game.

GOV: (Reviewing secret document he received) For TCE...symptoms of headache, dizziness, nausea, and unconsciousness...Bartleby said he was...(interrupted).

MD: So TCE. We never found anything about TCE though.

GOV: I think we did.

SCI: We did in the fishery talks.

MD: So it may not have been mercury. Could have been TCE!

The teams regularly went back and forth across the multiple resources available on the PDA. They regularly formed new hypotheses bringing in new evidence. Much of the game play involved the players trying to advance their case – in the hopes that they could develop a collective case that would convince the police officer to continue with the case (and perhaps beat their friends in the other groups).

Students presented their findings as a team to a police investigator (played by a facilitator) whom they had to convince to re-open the case (as well as pick up on any other important questions). Participants had mixed success reaching a confident final solution, but more importantly, each group took several variables into account and produced a sophisticated explanation that included al of the key data points. As a general pattern, we found that adult groups were able to synthesize data as they played and with a little time, develop a defensible, plausible solution. High school students were able to develop similar conclusions after 45 minutes of debriefing. Elementary and middle school students were only able to do so after significant scaffolding from adults.

In post interviews, an overarching comment from students was "Now I look at the lake differently." One commented, "We are using technology, thinking with complicated science content, what more could you want?" Another reported that he had heightened interest in the subject matter, "Before I never would have picked up a book on TCE, but now, I definitely would." Another said, "I would pay for something like this outside of school." Of course, the self-reported nature of this data makes these statements somewhat suspect, but they speak to their enthusiasm for the learning experience. A year after the implementation in this classroom, students made similar comments and asked when we would return to play another game with them.

DOW DAY: AR GAMES THAT SIMULATE HISTORICAL EVENTS

Dow Day is a model of an Augmented Reality game where students "experience" a specific historical event from a first person perspective. The game revolves around a series of anti-Dow Chemical protests that took place on the University of Wisconsin-Madison campus in October 1967. The protests were intended to raise awareness about Dow Chemical's production of napalm and stop the company from conducting student interviews on campus. Pame, players role-play as journalists who have been asked to investigate the root causes of the protests and report on why and how they turned violent.

The game itself, which takes approximately 1.5 hours to play, is part of a larger inquiry-based unit. During the unit students (1) read and analyze documents (newspaper articles, photographs, charts, graphs, and video clips) that provide an initial contextual understanding of the historical time period from both a local and national perspective, (2) develop one or more inquiry questions surrounding the protests, (3) travel to the University of Wisconsin-Madison campus to play at the actual location where the protests took place, (4) write a newspaper article based on the observations and interviews that they conducted during the protests, (5) develop an additional inquiry question based on their investigations, and (6) conduct further independent research in order to answer their inquiry question. The game and associated curriculum scaffolds the students' inquiry and progressively transitions from a highly structured analysis of primary documents provided by the teacher to a more open-ended inquiry that is based on students' individual interests.

This process is informed by Drake and Brown's (2003) model for developing students' historical thinking skills which breaks historical resources into three categories: first-order documents (an initial document used to begin the overall inquiry), second-order documents (documents which support or challenge the initial document and provide a broader context for the historical time period), and third-order documents (documents that students select on their own). In Dow Day, the first-order documents are those provided by the teacher before the game begins, the second-order documents are those obtained by students as they play the game, and the third-order documents are those that the students gather as part of their post-game research.

One of the primary design goals of *Dow Day* is to actively engage students by situating their inquiry around an authentic historical problem. Brush and Saye (2005), argue that "problem-based learning activities provide learners with opportunities to move beyond the memorization of discrete facts in order to critically examine complex problems." They acknowledge, however, that this "requires learners to remain *engaged* in the problem for an extensive period of time, and to *weigh competing perspectives*, or critically examine various points of view regarding the historical problem."

One reason that Augmented Reality games have the potential to create this level of engagement is that they structure student learning around compelling narratives and authentic historical problems. In *Dow Day* for example, players are tasked with writing a newspaper article that reports on the protests from their newspaper's perspective. In order to write their article, players must walk around the campus to conduct background research, observe the protest activities "first-hand", interview people and read primary documents (leaflets, letters, press releases) representing multiple perspectives, examine photographs, and watch video clips. All of these are activities that actual reporters engage in.

By taking on the role of local journalists while playing *Dow Day* students experience the curricular content differently than if they simply studied the same concepts as part of a traditional textbook-centered curriculum. Students' remarks in closing interviews suggested that AR games can create a hybrid identity as suggested by Gee, built around *academic* roles. One student commented that the game "was a good way to learn because it made me feel like a reporter." Another said that playing the game actually makes you feel "…as if you are walking around interviewing people."

The active, challenge-driven nature of game play – where players are driven by solving problems and acting through roles had an impact on students, with them remarking that the game experience differed from the way they usually studied history at school. One student said that the game "…presented facts, but in a more interesting way. It gave like a story or scenario that you could follow, so it kind of made it into a game. You got more engaged than just reading out of the textbook." Students also mentioned that it was a good a way to learn because it was "interactive", "gripping", "hands-on", and "active".

By situating the players' inquiry in the actual places where the historical events took place, students became active agents who were required to inhabit the same buildings, walk the same sidewalks, and talk to virtual characters representing the people who occupied the same place some 30 years earlier. Students mention this as one of the more engaging components of the game/curriculum experience. One player said, "It was kind of powerful to see the places and you can realize that you were standing there when in the same spot these people were doing all this." Another said that he felt that being in the actual place "…helped us get the point across…seeing what happened like you were actually living that event." This sense of "being there" is a critical component of historical thinking because it encourages students to reflect on how different people experienced the event and perhaps develop an empathetic understanding of the multiple perspectives surrounding the protests. It also suggests the importance of students emotional reactions to the learning environment, something often overlooked in mainstream education (although theorized to be important for learning), out of greater value placed on efficiency or expediency.

Playing the game where actual events took place also became part of the inquiry process itself. For example, players need to locate the Chancellor's office in order to obtain documents stating the University's official position. It is here that they can also run into and virtually interview Dean Kaufman, the Dean of Students, about his position on the protests. Part of their challenge became understanding how the physical location shaped the events. For example, after standing in the same hallway where the protestors attempted to prevent Dow Chemical from conducting interviews players better understood the role that the hallway's narrow design and limited number of exits played in facilitating the violence that eventually took place. In this way, the physical space actually becomes part of the curriculum and provides an additional layer of content for the students to analyze (Squire, Holland, & Jenkins, 2003).

AR games that foreground local place allow students to connect with, think about, and experience the places around them in new and unusual ways. Some of the students who played *Dow Day* were surprised by the fact that the protests took place so close to where they live. One player commented that, "It was intriguing, at least for me, because it happened here. I didn't know that anything like that happened in Wisconsin. Especially like downtown where I have actually been there in spots where it shows on the video, and I didn't know. It's like, something happened here years ago?"

In this case, as in many of our games, we find that an affordance of AR may be that it encourages students to connect academic content to lived experiences, particularly via place. The next game, the Greenbush picks up on these themes but immerses students in an even longer, more sustained inquiry experience through the process of game design.

THE GREENBUSH GAME: DESIGN AS CURRICULUM

The Greenbush Game, an investigation of a multiethnic neighborhood in Madison just south of the University of Wisconsin, seeks to engage *students* as researchers and designers of AR games. The research and design process formed a major component of the social studies and language arts curriculum, and is presented here as the unfolding of a game / design curriculum. In researching the community, players adopted the roles of historians, ethnographers, and neighborhood planners – which eventually became the roles for the players of the game. This research took 1 ½ years to complete, with students acting as game developers and designers, and the teacher acting as producer.

The project kicked off in February 2005 with a lecture by Columbia University psychiatrist Mindy Thompson Fullilove, author of *Root Shock: How Tearing Up City Neighborhoods Hurts America and What We Can Do About It*. Fullilove visited Madison to discuss the devastations of Urban Renewal and research about the Park Street corridor.[4] Dr. Fullilove met with twenty-five fourth graders, university students, and scholars to hear former Greenbush residents tell stories about their community: Italian and Jewish immigrants settling this neighborhood in the early 1900's, African-Americans migrants coming soon after; the harmonious mingling of ethnic groups; Ku Klux Klan marches descending on the community and Prohibition-era bootlegging; customs of daily life and humorous events; and the heartbreak residents felt when Urban Renewal gutted the community in early 1960's. Next the group toured the community, guided by former residents, noting the contrasts between bulldozed and rebuilt areas and those where older buildings still stand.

Perhaps not surprisingly, student engagement was high. To quote the teacher / designer, "The students were hooked--deeply moved by this event and eager to begin an in-depth study of the community." A student, Sophie, later wrote, "It's like the Greenbush has been cut up into pieces when it was urban renewed and put back together the wrong way." That spring, the teacher (Wagler) began the game design research process, starting with a fieldtrip to the Archives of the Wisconsin Historical Society to examine Urban Renewal documents—photos, descriptions, and appraisals of many of the condemned properties (See Figure 2).

Figure 2: Greenbush game materials.

Figure 2.1: Map of Greenbush game

Figure 2.2: A Greenbush Grocery

Figure 2.3 shows St. Joseph's church being demolished during urban renewal. Figure 2.4 shows a student's box art depiction of the Greenbush. In figure 2.5 a student presents her work before the city council.

Most of these students returned as 5th graders for the 2005-06 school year and began an intensive year-long inquiry project.[5] The class made regular fieldtrips to the Greenbush (a five-minute bus ride or a twenty-minute walk from their school). These walks helped students encounter the present day community, both redevelopments in the destroyed area which includes housing for new immigrants, buildings housing people with disabilities, and an Asian grocery) and areas outside of it that survived Urban Renewal. Students took extensive fieldnotes, and rewrote these notes for use in various presentations.

Next the students interviewed African-Americans who are former Greenbush residents. This trip, and earlier interviews with people with disabilities, confronted students with their major personal challenge—how to understand racism and discrimination, and indeed their own attitudes about race and disabilities. Past and present residents, community scholars, a neighborhood planner, and an alderman visited the classroom to discuss these issues, and students wrote reflections about their experiences. The students also read articles, documents copied from local archives, sections of books, and viewed photos and videos. Additionally, the class developed a survey, delivered it to over 1000 residences, and for two months analyzed the results received from 200 community residents. "I never really knew how much 25 fifth graders could accomplish. We did masses of research," Micah reflected. "This year, I pushed my achievements to the limit."

Figure 2.3. St. Joseph's Church

Besides the overarching goal of creating a game, students presented their research and their ideas with other media. Each student made cardboard models of historical Greenbush buildings, and the class displayed this "Box City" model on three different occasions. Next, each student chose a research question for a long-term investigation leading to an article in a journal of student inquiry. They wrote about immigration, Greenbush families, past and present groceries, a synagogue and a church, Urban Renewal, possible futures for the Greenbush, the history of Longfellow School, property values, survey results, and Sicilian traditions.

The teacher, several community and university partners organized a Greenbush Community Conference held May 2, 2006 at the Italian Workman's Club. Past and present residents, scholars, service providers, university students, city staff, and Randall 5th graders presented a wide range of talks, panels, exhibits, and videos.

281

On June 6, 2006, the Madison City Council unanimously adopted a resolution presented by the Randall classroom that established an annual Greenbush Day on March 21, asked City departments and commissions to restore historic Greenbush values, and committed the City to maintain the Greenbush as a mixed use, mixed income, and mixed ability community.

While the Randall students have moved on to middle school, some still meet weekly to complete *The Greenbush Game,* and the game was launched to the general public on Greenbush Day 2007. Accompanying the game is a Greenbush Cultural Tour web site being created with the Center for the Study of Upper Midwestern Cultures, which contains 100s of notes, photos, scanned historical documents, and video and audio clips that will be a resource for playing *The Greenbush Game.*

What students experienced while developing *The Greenbush Game* is similar to what students experienced in previous years on their cultural tours, but including the *development* of AR games intensified and complicated every element of their experience. The elements of an AR game—place, time, roles, challenge, game items—allowed for increasingly complex understanding by this group of students, and became tools for moving beyond collecting information about the Greenbush to repeatedly rethinking the community.

Place

Space is shown as a map in AR games which is the center of the interface (See Figure 2) and in many respects, is the frame of the entire experience. The students exploring the Greenbush gradually moved beyond map coordinates to a "sense of place," learning the meanings that transform a space into a cultural place. At first students saw people, buildings, landscapes, and traffic as they walked around, but repeated observations created a deepening pattern of community. Talking with people at businesses and community organizations helped students gain multiple perspectives and a feel for present-day social relationships. "A neighborhood isn't just a bunch of houses," Micah came to understand, "It's a place where people know each other." Eventually Greenbush became thick with meanings, a dynamic place in which all information adhered to all other information. Theorists note that players identify with roles in games; the designers of *The Greenbush Game* began to identify with the place itself. Giulia wrote, "I feel like I'm sort of a part of the Bush."

Designing the game forced students to wrestle with more questions about place: What were the boundaries of the old Greenbush? Is there a present-day Greenbush, or are there only smaller separate neighborhoods where once there was a community? What parts of the Greenbush should be represented in a game? And what path or paths through the community should players follow to maximize their enjoyment, learning, and safety?

Figure2.4

Figure 2.5

Time

Time provides a story for changes in place. In our AR game engine, time can be structured in three basic ways: setting the duration of the game; breaking the duration of the game into distinct time periods; and creating casual links between players' actions and game item availability. Randall students' sense of place became complicated as they toured the Greenbush with former residents and heard stories connected to buildings and streets that no longer exist. They developed multiple mental maps of the Greenbush, corresponding to the changes they saw in hardcopy maps. Students often recalled a former resident saying during an interview, "The Greenbush is dead," as if the Greenbush was more a time than a place. Noah wrote, "If I lived in the Greenbush and could go back in time, I would try protesting to the city one last time. Or maybe I would even do something heroic like running in front of a bulldozer or chaining myself to my house so they couldn't destroy my home."

While elementary students tend to imagine the future as a high-tech utopia, the Randall students usually imagined the future of the Greenbush in terms of connecting the past, present and future. In their open-space and building designs, stories, and reflections, students especially wanted to honor the community's values: A sense of community, ethnic diversity, gardening, tradition, and people knowing each other. Most revealing was students' decision to have game players simultaneously access past, present, and future as they walk through the present-day community, and to use different maps for the different roles accessing these time periods.

Roles in our AR games provide lenses or perspectives for encountering a place. Part of a game drama comes from making available information only to certain roles, with each role getting only pieces of the story. While designing *The Greenbush Game*, students brainstormed many roles such as real estate agent, storekeeper, community activist, University of Wisconsin planner, and an older, lifetime Greenbush resident. Sometimes they created biographies for these roles--specifying ethnicity, occupation, age, economic interest—and then attempted to balance these identities so that roles would represent the community.

Ultimately, their game roles emerged from their research identities, something noteworthy for those designing educational games. A common teaching practice was that the teacher asked students to transcend their roles as 4th and 5th graders (the roles of the traditional "school game") and to think like scientists, mathematicians, writers, and other roles reflecting academic practices. To research the Greenbush, they adopted the roles of historians, ethnographers, and neighborhood planners, identities that overlapped with the social studies standards. Importantly, their work within these roles had consequences, as the history, writing and mathematics that they were doing was not just going toward a game that people would play, but was about documenting the lives of real people that they developed empathy toward. Ultimately these were the roles students selected for the game.

Critically, students worked with professional historians, ethnographers, and planners, community volunteers engaged in the same disciplines, and developing some of the tools (e.g. surveys) and practicing some of the skills (e.g. interviewing) used in these professions. Rosa D. wrote, "Studying the Greenbush has made me a lot more interested in history—I found out I might want to be a historian when I grow up." Elena likewise noticed her development as an ethnographer, "The study of Greenbush gave me a new look on mine and other people's lives, like opening up an eye I never knew I had." For their long-term investigations, some of the students worked as neighborhood planners: Noah chose the question, "Can we create a good future for the Greenbush?," Ava helped develop a neighborhood survey, and Rosa K. and Giulia created a design for a community garden.

Constructing *the challenge* of the game, the overarching goal players collaboratively work toward was difficult. When students first brainstormed a challenge for *The Greenbush Game*, they alternated between the overly simple (e.g. a treasure hunt), the overly active (image the Greenbush as a massively multiplayer game), and the overly bizarre. Over time, they discovered the problems Greenbush residents faced--not only Urban Renewal, but also immigration, learning a new language, poverty, ethnic and racial and ability discrimination -- and the persistence, ingenuity, traditions, and humor residents used to face these problems. Greenbush now became a "contested place," Urban Renewal became the climactic battle between good and evil, and the City of Madison became the evil monster that game players would overcome. We had a game.

The class could have stopped there, as some students argued for, with a lively game played in the 1960's. Several issues emerged, all stemming from students feeling responsible to tell the real Greenbush story. First, if the story ended in the 1960's, the "good guys" would end up defeated, and by implication the present-day community would be dismissed as inferior to the earlier era. Second, there was a lot of information (stories, people, places) students wanted to incorporate that had little relevance to Urban Renewal. Also, students began to see two key similarities between the old and present Greenbush--both with poor residents suffering from discrimination, and both threatened by development. The class finally decided to play *The Greenbush Game* in the present, where players will recall an old challenge while meeting a current one. In the process of rethinking the game challenge, students moved from their personal perspectives to the larger perspective of the whole community. Along the way, students asked game players to encounter issues that were most problematic for themselves, especially stereotypes related to race, poverty, and disabilities.

Being a game designer was the most transformative experience for students, because it combined all roles, data, and skills into an active identity. Indeed, game design became the ultimate curriculum, and the class was often a production team, as students alternated between individual work and group discussions. Students designed more than a game—they helped to design much of their classroom activity, research agenda, and other presentations. Sometimes students made individual choices about what to research and present—which fieldtrip components to write reports on, which historical buildings to model, which questions to research, which resources to use. Collaboratively the class made other decisions—what to present at the community conference, what to include in the resolution to the Common Council, which questions to include in the community survey.

Discussing place and time, evaluating roles, choosing a challenge, and selecting items required students to not only learn and fluently use language, research, cultural analysis, and mathematical skills-- but also decide what things meant and how they connected. They had to confront personal perspectives and values as well as weigh what would be most fun and educative for audiences. Deciding how to make a building a model, or how to turn the Greenbush into a website changed not only how students thought about the Greenbush, but also how they thought about themselves (as learners and creators and citizens), their families, and their neighborhoods.

Their thinking changed not only in academic subjects but also in out-of-school contexts. In students' words:

Sam R.: "In studying the Greenbush I unlocked a depth of learning that I never before thought that I had in me."

Cole: "My neighborhood is more complicated than I thought it was."

Henry: "I know much more about racism than when we started."

Sam B.: "Studying the Greenbush has helped me get more active in my neighborhood."

Ava: "When I visit new places I wonder what their past is and if they ever had something happen like what happened in the Greenbush."

Elena (speech to the Madison Common Council): "I wonder if our planning for the future could increase the sense of community."

This model further suggests that games can result in trajectories where students participate in meaningful social activities and rethink their own lives.

PRINCIPLES OF DESIGNING AUGMENTED REALITY GAMES FOR LEARNING

After several years of working with teachers designing and implementing augmented reality games, we are beginning to develop best practices that serve as principles to guide our practice. Building on the work of Reigeluth (1999), we submit these findings as design principles, with the intent that designers, researchers, and educators might apply them as fit to their particular contexts.

Identifying contested spaces

When we work with teachers, instructional designers, and students (both kids and adults) one of the first things we encounter is the challenge of developing good ideas for games. A principle that we've developed is that *when developing ideas for augmented reality games, it is useful to identify places where there are conflicts over space and place.* Games are a deeply spatial medium, and we can understand the design of games as contests over space (Jenkins & Squire, 2002). Many designers start with an interest around a particular topic or place (such as environmental science or a local neighborhood). Identifying conflicts over space gives designers a hook into a particular place, providing opportunities for players to have agency within the game system, a way to take what may be an "interesting area" (like the Greenbush) and turning it into a game system that players can inhabit (agency is a key component of games, see Malone & Lepper, 1987; Murray, 1999).

In some cases – such as the Dow Day Game, the conflict jumps right out at the designer. In other cases, such as the Greenbush, there are any number of contests that one might identify, and the process of refining the core conflicts driving game play can be a complex process of weighing educational, social and political forces. In both cases, game play became driven in part by the very real contests over political control of space: Bascom Hill and the corridors of administrative buildings in Dow Day and blocks of land in the Greenbush neighborhood. In our current work, we *start* by identifying locations with conflicts, or reciprocally, but conflicts within locations that can drive moments in game play.

Across these examples, we can think of the conflicts and context as along a dimension from "realism" to "fantasy", with examples like the Greenbush being highly realistic, and examples like Mad City Mystery involving a fantasy (yet hypothetical) scenario. In examples such as Mad City Mystery, we identified more abstract conflicts over space (such as political discussions over the health of local lakes), and then added a fantasy context of a toxic spill moving through the environment. Eric Klopfer and colleagues at MIT have built similar games but around the spread of infectious diseases such as SARS through a community. These games map theoretically plausible fantasy contexts on top of existing places, with a goal of deepening participants' experience and knowledge of place. Participants frequently draw on their knowledge of "real life" space to influence their game play (and indeed seem to enjoy it), suggesting that designers need to be careful when designing games with a mix of fantasy and reality – particularly as educators may not want students walking away with erroneous beliefs about the subject at hand.

Other games might be more place agnostic, in that they are using *space* as an organizing metaphor for content (See Figure 3). Games such as *Pirates*, developed by Falk and colleagues (2001) are examples of such games that map a completely fantasy context on top of real world spaces. Such formats allow for the creative juxtaposition of fantasy and space (we have turned our schoolyard into a pirate alcove). Such games may be particularly entertaining as they creatively juxtapose the familiar and the fantastic. When designed creatively, allow educators to map academic learning objectives to game play. At the same time as educators we do need to consider the philosophy and hidden messages behind our curricula. Endogenous games, games that seek to highlight and expand the interesting and gamelike qualities of a subject matter and place may have greater potential for developing students' intrinsic motivations for learning.

Interactive storytelling

Some of these examples can be thought of as interactive stories, stories outlined by developers and inhabited by players. In the case of Mad City Mystery, Dow Day, and the Greenbush, the game play is constructing a story – which includes building causal claims. In these examples, the game play consists of cognitively relating events, weighing and reconciling different forms of evidence to gain a holistic picture of events, represented as oral cases presented to a police officer (Mad City Mystery), designs for a new city layout (Greenbush), or news stories (Dow Day). The story in each of these is spread across multiple sources and multiple media (including mathematical representations, text, video, and so on). Game events are open-ended supporting multiple entry ways into the narrative and multiple plausible responses, also creating discussion opportunities.

In these games, the game play itself consisted of arguing through pieces of evidence in order to develop a model (or theory) of what happened (Squire & Jan, 2006). Players encounter primary and secondary pieces of information, information that is associated with characters and places so that the narrative events, space, and relationships serve as a scaffolding for students encountering complex information. As such, they are a little like "interactive case-based reasoning" environments, where the player's primary role is to interpret and make sense of documents in order to build a case and engage in future action, such as writing a story within Dow Day. This model of game play seems particularly well suited to fields that depend heavily on argumentation, such as history and certain forms of science, leading to a design principle: Narrative can both scaffold players thinking by attaching information to narrative events, as well as forming the basis of game play as players seek to construct narratives of events.

Transforming game research roles into game play roles

Developing roles for players to inhabit games is a second challenge designers face, and as the Greenbush example suggests, when creating roles for AR games, designers might benefit by transforming the roles that designers played in researching the game (such as ethnographers, journalists, and historians) into game roles. This approach creates a certain parsimony between game design and game play as designers can track the practices they engage in conducting research and transform them into game play moments.

Within this approach, the roles also function as scaffolding for students researching / designing games. Across our studies, we have been constantly reminded of (and impressed by) the complexity of engaging students as game designers, particularly as designers of games that seek not just to entertain but to engage learners in academic practices. Assigning students roles in researching the game, which will then also serve as the roles for players to inhabit, provides them a framework for thinking through design. Students can journal their experiences, note exceptional stories, characters, media, and moments and use these as the bases for game interactions. There still are plenty of opportunities for students to be creative in constructing driving challenges, selecting materials, and especially in *sculpting player experience* through the careful placing of objects, timing of events, writing and editing of text, and arrangement of space. Together, these efforts work together to create "interactive experiences of place".

Using transformative objects to trigger memorable moments and transformative experiences

Henry Jenkins (2001) uses the term memorable moments to describe the logic by which games operate. Drawing on the work of Seldes (1957) Jenkins argues that aesthetically, games are less about telling formal stories, and more about setting up interactions that result in memorable moments for the player. A challenge for educators is how to create such memorable moments that are not only fun, but academically meaningful.

Building on the notion of designed experiences (Squire, 2006), Galarneua (2005) suggests that a key educational property of games could be their ability to provide *transformative experiences*, that is, experiences that transform or provide a new framework for understanding phenomena. As these examples suggest, games allow us to do much more than memorize facts; they allow us to lead investigations, travel back in time, or rethink the design of a neighborhood. Thus, from an instructional perspective, we might think of games as a pedagogy well suited to creating such deep transformations, such as learning to think like a physicist, science journalist, or historian (Shaffer, Squire, Halverson, & Gee 2005).

When trying to produce such memorable moments and transformative experiences, educators can use what we call transformative objects, objects that seek to pull the player into a new framework of thinking. In Mad City Murder, Willy Loman functions to have players coalesce their understanding of the game events and create a narrative describing the causal chain of events. As such, he seeks to take players' current thinking and transform it into a coherent view of events by triggering an emotional and cognitive reaction whereby they are compelled to develop a solution. In Dow Day, lead designer James Matthews used media and place to link players with the past by having players trigger videos of demonstrations occurring in the exact place where players stood, eliciting emotional reactions from them. We see such events – particularly using media to augment players experience of *place* as a key affordance of the medium. AR games seem ideally suited for giving players a depth and appreciation for place that is otherwise difficult to obtain.

Games as a context into inquiry

An objection that progressive educators might have to games is that they are "unrealistic" or do not engage students in "real life" activities. In describing

SQUIRE, ET AL.

instructional approaches based on situated cognition, Barab and Duffy (1999) distinguish between practice fields and communities of practice. Practice fields are instructional approaches where there is a moratorium on the consequences of action – approaches where the practices of the learning environment have little impact on the outside world, whereas communities of practice are those where learning is situated within a socially valued practice (See Lave & Wenger, 1991). Games might be considered a classic example of a "practice field", in that games are contexts marked off from the world (allowing what people have called a social moratorium, a chance to experiment with new ideas and roles without consequence). When we examine contemporary video game culture, a very different picture emerges. They create and maintain databases of information, digital tools, interface mods, and any number of other texts to augment their game play and within games culture. Within games culture, texts routinely have a life outside of their immediate use, and to quote Bing Gordon, an Electronic Arts executive addressing the Department of Education, the first thing one might do to transform a traditional curricula into a gamelike one is to require students to have their work graded by "real world" criteria rather than school ones (Gordon, 2005; Leander & Lovvorn, in press).

From these examples, we see potential for linking games-for learning into other inquiry activities, as well as modes of participation in social practice. In the case of Mad City Mystery, students commented that they had increased interest in science, and many developed good inquiry questions as a result of the game (Is the fish safe to eat? What is the impact of local industry and run-off on local health?). Because (good) games emotionally engage learners, developing increased motivation in the subject area (and potential ownership over inquiry), we might think of them as good precursors for inquiry-based learning units.

In the Greenbush example, this process was reversed. Students used the creation of a game as a context for research. That research resulted in students participating in social and political functions with real consequence, such as presenting their findings before the city council and attending and participating in local history events. Across these games, we see a model emerging where participation in activities with social consequence makes a strong capstone experience to a game-based curriculum unit. Mad City Mystery players might write letters to the newspaper expressing concerns about water quality. The key idea here is that we might think of games as structured environments for learning that prepare students for future, more structured activities. Our hope is that in the upcoming years, these games will be expanded upon and modified so that other educators might develop them in new directions, adding to our collective understanding of how game-based learning environments operate.

290

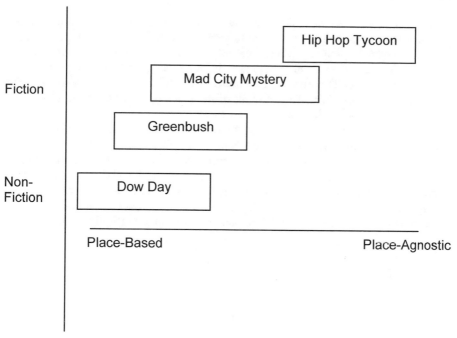

Figure 3.

Figure 3 describes our games along two axes: Fictional vs. Non-fictional games and Place-Based vs. Place-Agnostic games. Although all three games described here are non-fictional and place-based to some degree, we can usefully think of them along these continua. *Dow Day* (what we call an *event*-based game) literally could not be played in any other place than Bascom Hill. The *Greenbush* game (*neighborhood redesign* game) is similarly place dependent, although one could do urban renewal game for any number of cities that underwent similar processes in the 1960s. Mad City Mystery (an *environmental health mystery game*) is also built to be played on the shores of Lake Mendota, but realistically, the chemical and health issues describe here (Mercury, TCE, PCBs, fishing) are common to most lakes in the midwest United States.

Dow Day is almost entirely non-fictional. Players are literally retracing the steps of a particular day, and accessing almost entirely primary documents. Their role (a journalist) is an authentic one. There is some fictionalization in terms of some of the characters, as some of their interactions with characters has been fictionally created. Greenbush is almost entirely non-fiction as well in terms of content, although the context (the fact that it's the future and they are redesigning the neighborhood) is fictional. Mad City Mystery lays a fictional, but hypothetically plausible event over the environment. This game genre – which we call an environmental health mystery game -- has proven to be useful for us in terms of coming to a new location (such as Madison or Milwaukee) and creating authentic roles to inhabit and challenges for players to pursue.

In other games not described here, we employ even more fictional or more place-agnostic approaches. One of these games, Hip Hop Tycoon, places students in the role of entrepreneurs where they attempt to set up a hip hop store selling music, clothing, or musical equipment in their neighborhood. This game is playable in any neighborhood, and more fictional in terms of kids opening simulated stores. As such, we can think of the context, location, roles, challenge, and characters as being fictional to some degree.

An important implication of this framework is that educators need not be entirely *fictional* in order to achieve *fantasy*. In other words, if fantasy is a key element of games, we argue that educators can benefit by leveraging what is fantastical about particular academic domains (such as history or science). This approach – seeking what is intrinsically interesting about an area is critical to our design approach as it seeks to help players build identity trajectories into a domain, rather than use the game as a "trick" to push forward content (Squire, 2006).

REFERENCES

Barab, S. A., Zuiker, S., Warren, S., Hickey, D., Ingram-Goble, A., Kwon, E-J., Kouper, I., & Herring, S. C. (in press). Embodied curriculum: Relating formalisms to contexts. To appear in *Science Education.*

Barab, S. A. (2006). From Plato's Republic to Quest Atlantis: The role of the philosopher-King. Technology, Humanities, Education, and Narrative, 2(Winter), 22-53.;

Barab, S. A., & Hay, K. E. (2001). Doing science at the elbows of experts: Issues related to the science apprenticeship camp. *Journal of Research in Science Teaching, 38(1),* 70-102.

Barab, S. A., & Squire, K. (2004). Design-based research: Putting a stake in the ground. *The Journal of the Learning Sciences, 13(1),* 1-14.

Barab, S. A., Cherkes-Julkowski, M., Swenson, R., Garrett. S., Shaw, R. E., & Young, M. (1999). Principles of self-organization: Ecologizing the learner-facilitator system. *The Journal of The Learning Sciences, 8(3&4),* 349-390.

Barab, S., A., & Duffy, T. M. (1999). From practice fields to communities of practice. In D. Jonassen & S. Land (Eds.), *Theoretical foundations of learning environments.* (pp. 25-55). Mahwah, NJ: Erlbaum.

Barab, S., Thomas, M., Dodge, T., Carteaux, R., & Tuzun, H. (2005). Making learning fun: Quest Atlantis, a game without guns. *Educational Technology Research and Development, 53(1),* 86-107.;

Brush, T. A. & Saye, J. W. (2005). The effects of multimedia-supported problem-based Inquiry on student engagement, empathy, and assumptions about history. Manuscript under submission.

Casti, J. L. (1997). *Would-be worlds: How simulation is changing the frontiers of science.* New York: Wiley.

Castronova, E. (2001), Virtual worlds: A first-hand account of market and society on the cyberian frontier, CESifo Working Paper No. 618, December.

Church, D. (2001). *Abdicating authorship. Presentation made at the annual meeting of the Game Developer's Conference,* San Jose, CA. March.

Cordova, D. I., & Lepper, M. R. (1996). Intrinsic motivation and the process of learning: Beneficial effects of contextualization, personalization, and choice. *Journal of Educational Psychology, 88,.* 715-730.

Davidson, D. (2005). Plotting the story and interactivity in *Prince of Persia: The Sands of Time.* Paper presented at the Media in Transition 4: The Work of Stories: Cambridge, MA. Available online http://waxebb.com/writings/plotting.html

Dede, C., Clarke, J. Ketelhut. D. J., Nelson, B. & Bowman, C. (2005). Students' motivation and learning of science in a multi-user virtual environment. Presentation made at the annual meeting of the American Educational Research Association, San Diego, CA. Last retrieved May 9, 2006 from http://muve.gse.harvard.edu/rivercityproject/documents/motivation_muves_aera_2005.pdf

Dewey, J. (1938/1997). *Experience and education.* New York: Simon and Schuster.

Drake, F. & Brown, S. (2003). A Systematic Approach to Improve Students' HistoricalThinking. *The History Teacher, 36(4).* Accessed from: http://www.historycooperative.org/ journals/ht/36.4/drake.html

Falk, J., Ljungstrand, P., Bjork, S., & Hannson R. (2001). Pirates: Proximity-triggered interaction in a multi-player game. *Extended abstracts of computer-human interaction (CHI), ACM Press:* pp. 119-120.

Galarneau, L. (2005). Authentic learning experiences through play: Games, simulations and the construction of knowledge. Paper presented at the DiGRA, Vancouver, Canada.

Gee, J. P. (2003). *What video games have to teach us about learning and literacy.* New York: Palgrave

Gee, J. P. (2004). *Situated language and learning: A Critique of traditional schooling.* London: Routledge.

Gee, J.P. (2004). Video games: Embodied empathy for complex systems, Paper presented at E3, Los Angeles, CA.

Gordon, B. (2005). Presentation made to the STAR Schools Program recipients, Redwood Shores, CA, fall, 2005.

Gredler, M.E. (1996). Educational games and simulations: A technology in search of a research paradigm. In Jonassen, D.H. (Ed.), *Handbook of research for educational communications and technology,* pp. 521-539. New York: MacMillan.

Gruenewald, D. (2003). The best of both worlds: A critical pedagogy of place. *Educational Researcher, 32 (4),* (pp. 3–12).

Jenkins, H. (2002). Game design as narrative architecture. In Pat Harrington and Noah Frup-Waldrop (Eds.) *First Person.* Cambridge: MIT Press. Retrieved November 27, 2005 from http://web.mit.edu/cms/People/henry3/games&narrative.html

Jenkins, H. & Squire, K.D. (2002). The art of contested spaces. In L. King, (Ed.) Game on!. (pp. 64-75) London: Barbican Press.

Juul, J. (2004). Introduction to game time. In P. Harrington and N. Frup-Waldrop (Eds.), *First person* (pp.131-142), Cambridge, MA: MIT Press.

Klopfer, E. & Squire, K. (in press). Developing a platform for augmented reality platform for environmental simulations. *Educational Technology Research & Development.*

Klopfer, E., & Squire, K. (in press). Environmental detectives - The development of an augmented reality platform for environmental simulations. *Educational Technology Research and Development.*

Lave, J. (1988). *Cognition in practice: Mind, mathematics, and culture in everyday life.* Cambridge, England: Cambridge

Lave, J., & Wenger, E. (1991). *Situated learning.* New York: Cambridge University Press.

Leander, K.M. & Lovvvorn, J.F. (2006). Literacy networks: Following the circulation of texts, bodies, and objects in the schooling and online gaming of one youth. *Cognition & Instruction, 24(3),* pp. 291-340.

Leont'ev, A. (1978). *Activity, consciousness, and personality.* Englewood Cliffs, NJ: Prentice-Hall.

Levinson, S. C. (1983). *Pragmatics.* Cambridge, England: Cambridge University Press.

Malone, T. W., & Lepper, M. R. (1987). Making learning fun: A taxonomy of intrinsic motivations for learning. In R. E. Snow & M. J. Farr (Eds.), *Aptitude, learning, and instruction: Vol. 3. Conative and affective process analysis* (pp. 223-253). Hillsdale, NJ: Erlbaum.

Murray, Janet H. (1999). Hamlet on the Holodeck. The future of narrative in the cyberspace. Cambridge, MA: The MIT Press.

Orr, D. W. (1992). *Ecological literacy: Education and the transition to a postmodern world.* Albany: State University of New York Press.

Pea, R. D. (1993). Practices of distributed intelligence and designs for education. In G. Salomon (Ed.). *Distributed cognitions.* New York: Cambridge University Press, pp. 47-87.

Prensky, M. (2001). *Digital game based learning.* New York, McGraw-Hill.442

Reigeluth, C.M. (ed.) (1999). Instructional-design theories and models: A new paradigm of instructional theory, Volume II. Mahwah: Lawrence Erlbaum Associates, Publishers.

Seldes, G. (1957). *The seven lively arts.* New York: Sagmore Press.

Shaffer, D. W. (2004). Pedagogical praxis: The professions as models for post-industrial education. *Teachers College Record, 106(7).*

Shaffer, D. W. (2005). Epistemic games. *Innovate 1 (6).* http://www.innovateonline.info/index.php?view=article&id=79 (accessed July 27, 2005).

Shaffer, D. W., Squire, K., Halverson, R., & Gee, J. P. (2005). Video games and the future of learning (WCER Working Paper No. 2005-4). Retrieved October 20, 2005, from http://www.wcer.wisc.edu/publications/workingPapers/Working_Paper_No_2005_4.pdf

Shaffer, David. W.; Squire, Kurt D.; Halverson, R.; Gee, J. P. (2005). Video games and the future of learning. *Phi Delta Kappan,. 87(2)*. Retrieved October 27, 2005, from Humanities & Social Sciences Index

Salomon, G., Ed. (1993). *Distributed cognitions: Psychological and educational considerations*. Cambridge: Cambridge University Press.

Squire K.D. & Jan, M. (2007). Mad City Mystery: Developing scientific argumentation skills with a place-based augmented reality game on handheld computers. *Journal of Science Education and Technology, 16(1)* 5-29.

Squire, K. (2003). Video games in education. *International Journal of Intelligent Simulations and Gaming, 2(1):* 49-62.

Squire, K. (2004). Sid Meier's Civilization III. *Simulations and Gaming, 35(1)*.

Squire, K. (2005). Replaying history: Learning world history through playing Civilization III. Doctoral Thesis. University of Indiana. USA. Last retrieved 30th May 2006 at: URL: http://www.website.education.wisc.edu/kdsquire/REPLAYING_HISTORY.doc

Squire, K. (in press). Game cultures, school cultures. . *Innovate 1 (6)*.

Squire, K. D. (2006). From content to context: Videogames as designed experience. *Educational Researcher, Vol. 35, No. 8*, 19-29.

Squire, K., & Giovanetto, L. (in press). The higher education of gaming. *eLearning*.

Squire, K., Jenkins, H., Holland, W., Miller, H., O'Driscoll, A., Tan, K. P., et al. (2003). Design principles of next-generation digital gaming for education. *Educational Technology, 43(5)*, 17.

Squire, K., MaKinster, J., Barnett, M., Luehmann, A., & Barab, S. A. (2003). Designed curriculum and local culture: Acknowledging the primacy of classroom culture. *Science Education, 87*(4), 468-489.

Squire, K. (in press). Game cultures, school cultures. *Innovate*.

Steinkuehler, C. A. (2006). Why game (culture) studies now? *Games and Culture, 1*(1), 1-6.

Kurt D. Squire
Curriculum & Instruction, University of Wisconsin-Madison, and
Academic ADL Colab, Madison WI

Mingfong Jan
Curriculum & Instruction, University of Wisconsin-Madison, and
Academic ADL Colab, Madison WI

James Matthews
1 Academic ADL Colab and Middleton City Schools

Mark Wagler
2 Academic ADL Colab and Madison City Schools

John Martin
Curriculum & Instruction, University of Wisconsin-Madison, and
Academic ADL Colab, Madison WI

Ben Devane
Curriculum & Instruction, University of Wisconsin Madison, and
Academic ADL Colab, Madison WI

Chris Holden
Curriculum & Instruction, University of Wisconsin-Madison, and
Academic ADL Colab, Madison WI

Correspondence about this article should be addressed to Kurt Squire, Curriculum & Instruction, 544B TEB, 225 N. Mills St. Madison WI 53706 kdsquire@wisc.edu.

NOTES

[1] For a notable exception, see Cordova & Lepper (1996).

[2] From our perspective, intellectual (and ideally emotional) engagement is a necessary precursor to learning. In traditional classrooms, one might talk about someone memorizing information in a somewhat unengaged manner. However, if the goal of education in the 21st century is to produce deep conceptual understands, help students acquire specialized language, facilitate their ability to participate meaningful in professional (discourse) communities, and take on identities as productive participants in these communities, then real personal, intellectual, and emotional engagement is essential.

[3] Indeed, the loose construction of games poses a challenge to educators as the interpretations that we draw from these systems are personal and dependent upon previous experiences. Elsewhere, we have argued that fostering interactions between different communities of players may be a useful strategy for helping players overcome shortcomings in their own experiences.

[4] See http://csumc.wisc.edu/cmct/ParkStreetCT/index.htm. For more information

[5] In many respects, this project built on Wagler's previous work conducting year-long investigations and tours with his students of Dane County, Wisconsin Hmong communities, and Park Street. See Teachers of Local Culture < http://csumc.wisc.edu:16080/wtlc/> for more information.

Printed in the United States
By Bookmasters